For a Song and a Hundred Songs

A POET'S JOURNEY THROUGH
A CHINESE PRISON

LIAO YIWU

Translated from the Chinese by Wenguang Huang

New Harvest
Houghton Mifflin Harcourt
BOSTON   NEW YORK
2013

Foreword by Herta Müller reprinted by kind agreement of Carl Hanser Verlag

For information about permission to reproduce selections from this book,
write to Permissions, Houghton Mifflin Harcourt Publishing Company,
215 Park Avenue South, New York, New York 10003.

www.hmhbooks.com

Library of Congress Cataloging-in-Publication Data
Liao, Yiwu, date.
For a song and one hundred songs : a poet's journey through a Chinese prison / Liao Yiwu ;
translated from the Chinese by Wen Huang.
p. cm.
ISBN 978-0-547-89263-4
1. Liao, Yiwu, date. 2. Prisoners — China — Biography. I. Title.
HV9817.5.L5313 2013
365'.6092 — dc23
[B]
2012019558

Book design by Brian Moore

Printed in the United States of America
DOC 10 9 8 7 6 5 4 3 2 1

For my father and sister Fei Fei

Contents

Part III. The Detention Center

Part IV. The Prison

Foreword

HERTA MÜLLER

"WHAT A POWERFUL STAGE, the screen of the mountains as a back-drop: theater, writing and real life, impossible to separate — but then why did it hurt?" asks Liao Yiwu in *For a Song and a Hundred Songs*. And the act of writing he calls "obsessing like an obnoxiously buzzing fly, you have to watch out for flat hands."

"Why does it hurt" and "you have to watch out for flat hands" — with language of the utmost concision Liao Yiwu manages to express both how writing can overcome the experience of prison so painfully lodged in his head, as well as the police state's threat to send him back to prison for writing about his time there.

The circumstances surrounding the emergence of *For a Song and a Hundred Songs* call to mind the publication of *Doctor Zhivago* some fifty years ago. Boris Pasternak was determined to see his novel published by Giangiacomo Feltrinelli in Italy, and soon communications with the publisher began to sound like a thriller, with Feltrinelli warning Pasternak not to trust any courier who couldn't produce the matching half of a torn bill. Then Pasternak smuggled out a message on cigarette paper that the Italian should disregard any letters not written in French. And all these clandestine maneuvers came about because the Central Committee of the Communist Party of the Soviet Union did everything it could to stop the book from appearing. Soviet delegations called on the Italian Communist Party to help prevent its appearance. Pasternak himself was forced to sign letters disallowing the publication. And the president of the Soviet Writer's Association, Alexei Surkov, personally visited Feltrinelli in Milan in an attempt to thwart the publication by presenting falsified statements from Pasternak; Feltrinelli described his visitor as a "hyena dripping with syrup." But Pasternak held his ground: he wanted the book published, no matter the cost.

Similarly, the Chinese Communist Party tried everything it could to stop Liao Yiwu's book. The pressure on the writer became enormous. He had to promise the officials that he no longer wanted his book published in Germany. And though his German publisher, Fischer Verlag, knew there was nothing he desired more, the house had to postpone the book's publication — half against the author's will — to protect him from being arrested, even when Liao communicated that he was committed to having the book published and was willing to go to prison if need be. Fortunately it didn't come to that.

In Liao Yiwu's case the Chinese government's intervention was a disastrous failure. But often enough the government succeeds. A series of twelve photos by a well-known German photographer was planned to be part of a German-Chinese group exhibition; after the Chinese censor intervened, only two of the photos remained. And that interference was accepted by the curators as well as the German artist.

During Pasternak's day such obstruction required intrigue, secret service plots, and pressure applied by various delegations. Today German business leaders are simply blinded by their financial statements, to the point where they're willing to look the other way when it comes to human rights violations. Even some German writers are blinded by Chinese flattery. During a visit to Peking, Juli Zeh voiced sympathy for the notion that in order to prevent a civil war in China thumbscrews had to be applied, potential rabble-rousers persecuted and imprisoned, the press censored, and Internet communication restricted. And she wonders who will dare to stand up and demand "Bring democracy, and bring it now."

Just like Pasternak, Liao Yiwu had to endure much before his book was published: constant surveillance and house searches with the repeated confiscation of his manuscript. But he persisted in starting over each time, and we have his integrity and moral responsibility to thank that he did not stop until he had finished writing.

It isn't only the odyssey surrounding this publication that brings Pasternak to mind, it's also the content of the writing. *For a Song and a Hundred Songs* opens our eyes. As in his previous book, *The Corpse*

Walker, we see beneath the glitzy foil of the nouveau riche power-hungry empire. A regime that administers its prisons and camps according to the model of the gulag is not a modern state but a Maoist relic disguised in the suit of an economic miracle. The people themselves are the ones who pay, with disenfranchisement and repression.

The facts are one thing, but this is also a book of tremendous literary force. The author's linguistic prowess renders it disturbingly cold and invitingly warm, angry and charismatic at once. Inside the cell, time passes second by second. Sadism alternates unpredictably with compassion. One and the same person is now a monster, now a heap of misery. Every form of behavior is as absurdly normal as the prison itself. "Deaths from inmate beatings at the investigation center were as commonplace as rice for staple food," writes Liao.

The brutality of the thieves and murderers is not downplayed; it is undemonized, precisely through accurate description. Within the system of the state prison, violence inevitably acquires legitimacy: the rationale for the dehumanization of prisoners, according to Liao, is the Chinese state itself, its practice of "employing prisoners to manage fellow prisoners." Liao Yiwu's literary art is such that the sarcasm found in his sentences is always shown to be the other side of pain. Testimonial passages alternate with poetic ones, and the resulting mix not only bores into the brain, it presses against the stomach. Liao Yiwu's language has a physical impact because it has physically suffered. Like the author, his language has swallowed disenfranchisement and torture, it roars and whispers all at once and finally frees itself.

Even while they're still alive, the inmates condemned to death are known in the cell as "Dead Chang" or "Dark Skin." The latter was a murderer. When his wife betrayed him with others, he literally butchered her with a knife. Because executions do take place, Liao writes petitions of pardon for many fellow prisoners, and then, before their deaths, a final letter to family members or a last testament. And when one of them is taken out of the cell to be executed, the book says simply, "He went on his journey." This is put so kindly it gives you the shivers. But then you go on to read how during the night before the execution, the inmate was taken to a separate cell where the prison doctor drew his blood. That, too, is taken by the state.

Paper and pencil are allowed in the cell only two hours a month, during which time ten letters have to be written. As a result, Liao was unable to record a single conversation. So the dialogue is re-created, reconstructed from memory. Nonetheless, the word-clashes display a full range of emotions: anger, sadism, concern, deprivation, abandonment, and loneliness.

His images of the landscape are just as affecting: "The crescent moon had reddened even more, I lay down in this wound, the stars as green-headed flies swallowed the endless nighttime twilight." Or: "The streetlights cast a meager glow, it was like on the moon, the high-rises dissolved in the vault of the sky, one after the other, the small alleyways were unfathomably deep, mean thoughts seemed to have reached their end, projected by dream lamps."

And of himself, Liao writes: "You were born with the soul of an assassin/But at the time of action,/You are at a loss, doing nothing."

The poem "Massacre," which Liao wrote about the June 4 massacre, proved fateful. A lament for the dead, a torrent of images:

> In the name of mothers, throttle children!
> In the name of children, sodomize fathers!
> In the name of wives, murder husbands!
> In the name of urbanites, blow up cities!

And the soldiers "wipe their army-regulation boots with the skirts of dead maidens."

And over and over, like a refrain:

> Open fire! Blast away! Fire! It feels good! Feels so good!

This epitaph is written, or rather screamed, in a panic-stricken imperative, in the commanding tone of powerlessness; the force of this upended command is to keep the army from killing.

And after the bloodbath, Liao writes, resigned:

> The slaughter takes place in three worlds.
> On the wings of birds.
> In the stomachs of fish.

Carry it out in the fine dust
In countless living organisms.

The book contains countless ghastly occurrences described in a glittering vortex of language. This is an author from whom nothing escapes. Apart from that this book is a wonderful feat of memory. But such a phenomenal recall can come only from close observation during the experience. From listening to Oskar Pastor's reports on the labor camp, I am familiar with how memory works at the "absolute zero of existence," how events are recorded unconsciously but all the more precisely. This is exactly the way it was with Liao: his perception was always working — sometimes with intent, sometimes without. At the "absolute zero of existence" the head clicks away, storing the seconds. A snapshot instinct, which operates independently and even against one's self. The broken nerves create a compulsion for observation. The disgustingly close quarters for people who have been crammed into camps and prisons becomes even more excruciating through obsessive fixation. The compulsion to observe wrenches every detail into the personal, sapping whatever needed strength is left.

Still, this compulsion to observe is a blessing, because it preserves one's humanity, sparing the observer behind his back, probably even saving his life. Because if you are observing you're already halfway outside, even if you're completely inside. Where neglect and a vegetative existence are the order of the day, such observation is the only possible mental and spiritual occupation. Perception is a torment and the torment of perception is a blessing.

In this book, torment and grace are constant companions, and very familiar with each other's ways, because the impetus for both is self-observation. Liao's prison book is a mental staging that recollects experience into memory, a monologue in conversation with everything that transpired. But this recall is also a relapse, as the experience gets amplified after the fact, and while it now exists in abstract form, it remains forever stuck inside the head as phantom pain and lingering fear. They cannot be gotten rid of, either at home or abroad. They never go away, but they do come back.

"Old sleek-headed friend" is what the Nobel peace laureate Liu

Xiabo calls Liao Yiwu. The two belong together. Each in his own way has opened our eyes to today's China. But Xiaobo is sitting in prison for his brilliant Charter 08, an intelligent catalog of suggestions for reform for a democratic China — which is what constitutes his "crime." The Communists' vanity, the Eternal Party's fear of losing power is so boundless that Liu Xiabo's hope for change won him a prison sentence of eleven years. That the regime's mania for self-preservation is not only a total loss of face but also an implicit declaration of bankruptcy doesn't seem to bother the iron comrades, who guard their autocracy with dogged, blind determination. This is also the only way to explain the cruel zigzag of events with which they previously drove off Ai Weiwei. One false accusation after the next is concocted to invent the needed "crime" — but nothing holds up because the accusations contradict themselves — a despotic stack of cards. The verdict against Liao Yiwu isn't even legitimate under Chinese law. A further example of state tyranny.

I am happy that Liao Yiwu managed to come here to Germany, to this foreign place, instead of landing in prison. For him it is a bitter happiness, far more so than we can comprehend. But a bitter happiness such as that is inherently worth more than smooth luck — it invariably costs too much, but it spares even more. Bitter happiness is not something that carries us away, it has to be dragged along. It reigns over us with all its "other worldly tenderness."

Home is the place where you are born and live.

Or where you are born, live a long time, then leave and keep going back to and from.

For people saved from persecution, home is the place where you are born, live a long time, flee and can never return to.

You say: to hell with it. But that doesn't work. This home is the most intimate enemy you have. You've left behind everyone you love, and they are still as exposed as you are: if they aren't in prison already they have to "watch out for flat hands."

Liao Yiwu will not be allowed back home in the near future. But bitter happiness is cunning, it intentionally mistakes homesickness for the absence of homesickness. And it is an excellent master of the subjunctive. It says very bluntly: you really never wanted to be the way you would have had to be if you'd been allowed to stay home. This particular subjunctive is not used to express a wish: it is a conclusion. It drives away all melancholy, knowing full well it will come back without going away. But then the master subjunctive comes back, too.

We speak of home — I think the bitter happiness is the home of the subjunctive. In exile you experience that every day with this-worldly wrath and "other worldly tenderness."

Dear Yiwu, to bitter happiness the slick happiness will also come. Actually, it's already here today.*

—HERTA MÜLLER
AUGUST 17, 2011

---

* This speech was delivered on the occasion of the publication of *For a Song and a Hundred Songs* in Berlin. The quotations that appear here are rendered from the German translation of the novel; the precise language may vary in the English edition.

Preface

I have written this book three times, thanks to the relentless obstructions of the Chinese security police.

I first started scribbling it on the backs of envelopes and on scraps of paper that my family smuggled into the prison where I was serving a four year sentence from 1990 to 1994 for writing and distributing a poem that condemned the infamous, bloody government crackdown on the 1989 student protest movement in Tiananmen Square.

Even after my release in 1994, the police continued to monitor and harass me. On October 10, 1995, police raided my apartment in Chengdu, Sichuan Province, confiscating the handwritten manuscript of *For a Song and a Hundred Songs*. As a punishment for what they called "attacking the government's penitentiary system" with my writings, I was placed under house arrest for twenty days.

I started on my book again from scratch. It took me three years to finish a new version, which was seized in 2001, along with my other unpublished literary works. This time, the police also absconded with my computer.

Writers like to wax poetic and brag about their works in an attempt to secure a berth in the history of literature. Unfortunately, I no longer possess many physical products of my years of toil. Instead, I have become an author who writes for the pleasure of the police. Most of my past memories — the manuscripts that I have painstakingly created about my life, and my poems — are now locked away at the Public Security Bureau. This time, the police also took my laptop computer, a gift from my younger sister.

Chinese police officers have amazing memories. A director of a local public security branch could memorize many of my poems and imbue them with more complicated ideas than I had originally intended. So in a sense, my writing found a way to the minds and lips of at least one eager audience.

Indeed, the police proved to have an insatiable need for more of my work. So after each successive raid, I dug more holes like a rat, and I hid my manuscripts in deeper and deeper crevices across the city, in the homes of family and friends. My furtive efforts to conceal my work called to mind those of the Nobelist Aleksandr Solzhenitsyn, whose handwritten manuscript of *The Gulag Archipelago* had famously faced similar threats from the KGB. The only way to preserve his writings was to get them published.

In early 2011, after this book was finally smuggled out of China and scheduled to be published in Taiwan and Germany, I again met resistance from the Chinese authorities. My police minders, who were occasionally stationed outside my apartment during the height of the Arab Spring, invited me out for "tea." In a nearby teahouse, they asked me to sign an agreement canceling publication. "Your memoir tarnishes the reputation of our country and harms our national interest," said a police officer who had read the confiscated manuscript.

"Why can't you write books about harmless romances, and we can get them published here and make you rich?" the officer added in a matter-of-fact way.

When I politely declined, the officer issued me a warning: If I disobeyed, they would either prosecute me or have me "disappear for quite a while," just as they had done with other writers and artists such as Ai Weiwei and Ran Yunfei.

I never signed the agreement and opted, instead, to leave my homeland of China. With the help of intrepid friends, I crossed into Vietnam and safely landed in Germany, just in time to promote the release of this chronicle of my life, which was twenty years in the making.

In China, the government continues to erase and distort the collective memory of the country to suit its all-encompassing political agenda. However, an individual's memory, with its psychic encoding and indelible scars of oppression, can never be erased.

Part I

THE WANDERING POET

1988–1990

Fei Fei

IN 1988, WHEN THE ERA of automobiles dawned in China, my older sister, Fei Fei, died in a freak car accident. She was thirty-seven years old.

It was the first time I had experienced the death of someone close to me. My grandpa had passed away earlier that year, but he had lived in a remote village and had never been part of my life. Mourning for him seemed merely a family obligation. But Fei Fei was my beloved sister; we were two melons from the same vine and her death affected me profoundly.

I have composed many heartbreaking essays and poems about her death, deliberately avoiding the bloody and gruesome details of her final moments. Describing her death as a formless abstraction was more tolerable in my state of ravenous grief and possibly even less repugnant to the gentle, refined spirit of the deceased. But, between truth and eternity, I chose to focus on another dimension. In the mystical world traversed by many romantic artists, Fei Fei's spirit merged with nature where it could soar, transformed. If Fei Fei had been looking down, though, she would have been embarrassed by the decorous phrases I heaped upon her. She was an angelic being, I wrote, "bathed in rays of static light."

When I first began secretly jotting down ideas about this memoir at the Sichuan Provincial No. 3 Prison in 1993, I constantly returned to memories of Fei Fei — she was my first imaginary reader. Over the subsequent years, when the prospect of getting this book published was nil, writing for Fei Fei became my sole motivation to continue.

As the oldest child, Fei Fei toiled all her life. Her job since she was a little girl was to wash the family clothes by hand, kneading them against the ridges of a washboard. Incredibly, the hard work seemed to lift her spirits — she would burst into old movie tunes, singing lyrics I retained for many years. At night, she liked to regale me and my other siblings with horror stories that conjured up dead bodies reanimating themselves in the morgue, or a grisly murder inside the city's ancient bell tower. Often my sister's stories would send us under a quilt with only our ears exposed to hear more.

In 1966, on the eve of the Cultural Revolution, Fei Fei left home to take up a job at a logging firm in the faraway Pingwu County in northwest Sichuan. Before long, the whole country was engulfed in turmoil. Our family similarly fell apart under the attacks of the Red Guards. Our father, the son of a former landlord, taught Chinese literature at a high school in Yanting, a small city in northeast Sichuan. For this, he was labeled a counterrevolutionary. To protect us, our parents divorced and we were placed in the sole custody of our mother, who packed our meager belongings and hurried us south to the capital city of Chengdu. There, we took shelter with our aunt.

I had turned eight that year, and life was hard without my father. Soon after our arrival in Chengdu, my aunt's neighbors reported on our supposed infractions. Accusing my mother of being the wife of an escaped landlord and living in the city without a permit, the authorities expelled us. Once again we had to pack and leave, and this time found another home in a nearby suburb. We had no money to buy food. One day, a relative gave my mother a coupon that was good for a piece of two-meter-long cloth. My mother intended to sell the coupon on the black market in exchange for some food for the family, but she got caught by the Public Security Bureau. In those days, it was a serious offense to sell government-issued coupons. They detained her and then denounced her along with other criminals on the stage of the Sichuan Opera House in front of thousands of people. Somehow, I was sheltered from the news initially, so I was devastated when many of my classmates informed me that they had seen the authorities parading my mother around the opera stage.

In Pingwu, Fei Fei was spared the family's hardships and political troubles. In fact, she later said those years in Pingwu were the happiest of her life. By fabricating a more politically suitable family history, she was even able to join a singing troupe responsible for propagating the thoughts of Chairman Mao and won rave reviews for her portrayal of an underground Communist Party member masquerading as the proprietress of a teashop in the Beijing opera *Shajiabang*. My inventive sister soon became a minor celebrity. Even now, my mother keeps an old picture of a tall, slender Fei Fei in her teashop owner's costume, posing on stage against a backdrop of snowcapped mountains.

Fei Fei's fans in Pingwu could easily have filled an auditorium. Not surprisingly, she had many suitors and her love life was filled with drama. One handsome young fellow relentlessly pursued Fei Fei. After she rejected his affections, he committed suicide by swallowing several boxes of matches. In later years, Fei Fei fell deeply in love with a military officer. The army, however, disapproved of their union after finding out that our father was a "counterrevolutionary." The relationship ended.

Three years later, Fei Fei married a former colleague, relocated, and gave birth to two girls. Though her own family demanded her full attention, she always found time to take care of her siblings and to help our parents. My older brother had been sent to work in the countryside after high school, and during breaks, he would travel hundreds of miles to stay with her. My younger sister and I also visited her often. She shared her food rations with us and bought us clothes with her savings.

During the lunar New Year's celebrations in 1988, Fei Fei and I sat around the charcoal stove, chatting and catching up until dawn. Life wasn't too easy for her. She was planning a business trip to Pingwu to purchase some lumber on behalf of a company in Chengdu. With commission made from the deal, she intended to take Mom and Dad to Jiangxi Province, where they had first met.

"It's been so long since I had a vacation," Fei Fei reflected.

A week later, I saw her off at the Chengdu train station. Passengers swarmed the check-in gate. Fei Fei took her bag from me, slung it over her shoulder. Before she was swept away by the wave of humans, she yelled back, "I'm going now! Bye!"

That was our final farewell. Each time I think about it, my throat feels like it is filled with stones.

As planned, Fei Fei traveled to Pingwu with a friend. She had taken the winding mountain path countless times, but on this occasion the minibus, with seven passengers on board, spun out of control. Careening down a ridge, it teetered perilously on the edge of a cliff with its front wheel jutting into the air. In the violent descent, Fei Fei was flung out of the bus. Her body flew through the air until it was impaled on a sharp tree limb that cut through her waist. When they reached her, she was soaked in blood. The driver was able to get the bus back onto the road, and as he sped to the hospital Fei Fei's friend kept her awake by softly calling her name while urging the driver to go faster. She never reached the hospital. The moment before she died, Fei Fei pressed her lips to her friend's ear, apparently trying to murmur something. Then she was gone.

I've always wondered: Did Fei Fei's soul take the minibus to Jiangxi in search of the village where she was conceived?

Our parents met in Jiangxi in 1948. They never talked about how they met, but over the years we managed to piece together a rough sketch from our maternal grandmother of how their life began.

My mother's younger brother owned an itinerant Beijing opera troupe that performed in the provinces along the Yangtze River. They drifted into a small town in Jiangxi's Panyang Lake region. Known for his quick temper, my uncle offended a local landlord, who, along with some hired thugs, beat him to death. My grandma hurried to the little town with my mother to bury my uncle. As the two women burned paper money in front of the new grave and bid farewell to the departed, a young teacher happened to pass by. He was touring the scenic area on his spring break. From their common accents, my future mother made my future father's acquaintance. It was fate.

Before her death, my grandma entrusted my mother to the care of the young man. They were married and had four children; Fei Fei was the eldest and I the third. It was not, however, a tranquil domestic life. As far as I could remember, my parent's marriage was marked by turbulence, and they spent much of the ensuing years bickering and squabbling. My mother would say, "We never thought about whether we loved each other or not. We had to survive and raise a family."

There were no pictures from the early years of our family life. Only one group picture survived of my maternal grandmother, my father, my older brother, and Fei Fei. We treated it like an excavated artifact. And when Fei Fei came of age, she filled the void by taking many rich and colorful pictures in those drab and monotonous years of the Cultural Revolution. She had a waist-high stack of photo albums filled with black-and-white snapshots chronicling every important milestone in the family.

From that accidental encounter of my mother and my teacher-father on a hilltop in Jiangxi, our family was born and expanded into different parts of the country. Four decades later, Fei Fei was the first one to return to that cemetery.

I received the news of Fei Fei's death by telegram in Fuling, a city in the mountains of eastern Sichuan Province where I was poet in residence at a municipal institute there. Tucking the telegram into my breast pocket, I left my tearful wife, A Xia. For the next two nights I traveled, first by boat, then by train, to my sister's home in Mianyang nearly a thousand kilometers away. As the train approached Mianyang, I began to realize how much I dreaded seeing her body in the morgue after days of seeing her in my mind's eye as I remembered her.

When I reached her home, the house had already been cleaned out. Stacks of black mourning sheets lay piled up in a corner. Outside, on the balcony, scraps of half-burned paper wreaths danced up and down in the evening wind. Relatives stood around stoically like pieces of old furniture in the living room. An urn stood on a table at the center of the room.

"What took you so long?" my younger sister, Xiao Fei, snarled.

"We waited three days for you," said my brother-in-law. "With the weather so warm, we had to act fast."

I reached into my pocket to get the telegram and checked the date. Somehow, it had sat for two days before being transmitted. Tears flooded down my cheeks. By missing the funeral, I had been spared the sight of my sister's corpse. The realization hit me like thunder — Fei Fei's spirit must have intervened. I put on a black armband and retreated to the balcony. At dusk, claps of thunder echoed around us. The earth vibrated like a stage on the verge of collapsing. I left my sister's home and pushed my way through the thick curtain of pouring rain, wandering aimlessly. Streetlights blinked like the eyes of ghosts. Cars swam in the water like sea animals. The vendors' makeshift shelters were flimsy and bent with the wind. I waded in the water and kept going, too afraid to stop; afraid that I would be drowned in sadness.

I sought out a poet friend. We sat at a nearby restaurant, drenched from the rain and drinking. In an attempt to distract my attention from the family tragedy, the friend brought up the perennial topic of literature. Very soon, we bantered loudly about the future of avant-garde poetry in China. The argument helped my appetite, but the mouth that did the talking and eating seemed to belong to someone else. A stern voice inside me said it was time to grieve, but the beautiful, serene night after a heavy rain eclipsed it. I rejected grief, preferring instead the image of Fei Fei smiling at me radiantly with her perfect white teeth and dimpled cheeks. How could my sister, this gentle breeze, have been mangled by the violence of a car accident?

The stare of a young woman seated nearby seared my cheeks. I craved a healthy body glowing with animalistic desire; the burning heat of desires could certainly dry my wet skin. I needed to bury my head in her breasts and hide myself inside that familiar childhood shelter to escape the illusions that Fei Fei's death had shattered.

Half an hour later, I followed her to her door. The stranger turned out to be a newlywed, and her husband was away on a business trip. Silently, we kissed each other in the darkness before fumbling our way to the bed. In her house, we quickly turned into two hungry wolves, as if trying to tear out each other's intestines and lungs. She moaned with pleasure, and at the height of her passion, bit me like a piece of bamboo shoot, leaving bruises on my neck and back. My mourning outfit lay strewn on the floor. The trees rustled outside, their shadows flickered on the window. It sounded to me as though Fei Fei was sighing in disappointment and anger. I had stained the memories of my sister.

In the decade after Fei Fei's death, guilt over that sexual escapade in the immediate aftermath of her funeral has haunted me, but when I was with my poet friends, I fell back into my old ways.

It was a period of time when the old had given way and a new era was still waiting to be defined. Under Mao, ordinary citizens were subject to detention and jail sentences for premarital sex or adulteries. With the death of Mao, old puritanical moral values were gradually evaporating, especially in the world of literature. Young poets not only contended for the recognition of their genre-defying works, but also competed over the number of women with whom they had slept. A well-known society for avant-garde poets was practically a smoke-filled sex club, where group orgies and swinging were common.

I never fully joined this epicurean poetry society, but I led the similar life of a well-dressed hypocrite, a poet who portrayed himself as a positive role model but all the while breathed in women like I was breathing air, seeking shelter and warmth in random sex. I had turned into a ghost. As we are well aware in Chinese culture, ghosts possess no heart and never need to repent.

The Poet as a Young Man

IN 1985, AFTER SETTLING down in the city of Fuling with my wife, A Xia, I stayed away from the sex-obsessed avant-garde poets and focused instead on my writing. My literary ambition ballooned.

Unlike other poets of my generation, I never had the opportunity to receive a formal and solid education, even though my father, who lived to the age of eighty, had been a teacher of Chinese literature and nurtured thousands of students in his teaching career, which spanned four decades. I entered the world in the middle of a terrible famine, which claimed the lives of thirty million people nationwide between 1959 and 1962. My father would tell me how, at the age of one, my little body became swollen from malnutrition. I didn't even have enough strength to cry. An herbal doctor in Niushikou near Chengdu recommended that my parents hold me over a wok filled with boiling herbal water every morning and every evening. The steam eventually drained yellow liquid, drop by drop, from my body. Thanks to the doctor, I survived.

Hunger followed me during my entire childhood, stunting my growth and hampering my cognitive development. I was a slow child, but my father never gave up on me and attempted to nourish both my body and my mind. At the age of three, when I was still experiencing problems talking and walking, my father began teaching me to read Chinese characters. A year later, he force-fed me ancient Chinese poems. Every day, I was supposed to memorize simple poems and essays written by what he called the ancient literary masters. The writings meant nothing to me and I simply chanted along, like a novice monk learning the scriptures. Oftentimes I forgot what my father had taught me even before he left the room, but my father was patient. He never resorted to spanking, a common practice in old Confucian thought. Instead, he lifted my tiny body up and made me stand on the family's octagonal dining table. If I failed to memorize a certain poem, he would not let me come down. I was a meek little boy, too scared to jump down, to beg for mercy, or to protest by crying.

My only salvation was to close my eyes and chant the poems and essays again and again until they were firmly committed to my memory. Thus, in two years, I could fluently recite many well-known poems and articles, even though I could not grasp their meanings. I used to hate my father, and in the world of my imagination I murdered him numerous times. As I grew older, my feelings toward him changed. The seeds that my father had planted began to blossom. The meanings and beauty of each poem and essay that I had memorized began to reveal themselves.

During the Cultural Revolution, I constantly played truant from school and drifted intermittently between the cities of Yanting and Chengdu. I would snatch free rides by chasing and jumping aboard trains, fabricating travel documents, trekking for days on circuitous mountain paths, and lodging in the huts of my poor relatives in the rural areas. After high school, I continued to travel around the country, first working as a cook, then as a truck driver on the Sichuan-Tibet Highway. It was during that period that I started to take an intense interest in contemporary poetry. In my spare time, I read previously banned Western poets, from Keats to Baudelaire, and began to compose my own poems to publish in literary magazines. Throughout the 1980s, I contributed to national magazines and underground publications many contemporary Western-style poems considered by the government to be "spiritual pollution." Contrary to the criticism, the writings produced in me an intense feeling of euphoria.

The summer of 1988 was unbearable. If one left a window open in the morning, the indoor temperature could go up to 104 degrees. In a state of high anxiety, I composed my poems compulsively, without much food or sleep. Still, my body remained resilient and strong.

I walked around in a pair of shorts all day or, oftentimes, stark naked. Occasionally, I squatted on a wooden bench like an ape, with a wet towel dangling over my shoulder. My face lay hidden in thick, unkempt hair and unbridled tufts of beard. Sweat trickled down my forehead and cheeks, leaving dirty imprints like furrows in a field. It was in such a delirium that I finished my long poem, *The Master Craftsman*, with more than three thousand stanzas, and went on to compose *Bastard* and *Idol*, each of which contained five hundred stanzas. Between writing those mammoth poems, I also churned out several poetic essays. Words poured out of me in buckets. When I wrote, I strictly observed the grand principles of abstinence; my pen bolted ahead on the paper. The pecker in my pants was eager to jump out to work, too, but I resisted. When every nook and cranny of my life had been filled with poetry, I left the stacks and stacks of disjointed, illegible manuscripts to my endlessly patient wife, who had a day job as a secretary with the local municipal government. In the evenings, I lingered around her like a foreman, urging her to manually copy every word without stopping. A Xia quietly endured, often in tears, a lonely widow using her artful penmanship to fill the void created by my neglect.

As fatigue set in, the weather also cooled down. I began cooking up excuses, some blatantly flimsy, for "business trips." I felt an irrepressible itch to travel. I was influenced by the American Beat writers like Jack Kerouac and fantasized about aimless wandering. The midnight boat sirens on the Yangtze pierced through the darkness, like the sonorous lowing of a hungry bull. I was entranced and would stand at the window, obsessively gazing at the boats gliding on the water.

One day in the fall of 1988, A Xia slipped and broke her leg. I hurried her to the hospital and waited anxiously outside for the doctor to finish. When I saw her again, she wore a heavy cast. I carried her home on the back of my bicycle, cleaned the house, picked up groceries, and prepared her a meal. While she was dozing off in bed, I slipped out and ran all the way down to the pier to buy a boat ticket, and then clawed my way back up the hill like an Olympic runner.

Around dinnertime, I told my wife that I was setting off on a business trip that night. I lied and said it had been arranged a long time earlier.

A Xia seized my arm, begging me to stay and look after her.

"I'm going to be late," I replied. I hardened my heart and extricated myself from her grasp. The boat siren sounded in the distance. A Xia burst into sobs. "Don't do this to me, please." I glanced at my watch while wiping her tears with a handkerchief.

As I shut the door behind me, I could feel her helpless look on my back. I bolted down the stairs with no idea where I was headed. "I'll figure it out once I'm on the road," I assured myself, using a phrase that was common among my wandering friends. We often set off with a vague goal for our travels, hoping to find new literary and sexual targets that would stimulate our interest on the way. Writing poetry at home was a type of action, but when the mind burned out, wandering was the tonic that could return the psyche to a state of restful intro-spection. I was on the road for two months.

I found it difficult to remain entirely introspective, however, and quickly returned to my old philandering ways. In March 1989, soon after A Xia recovered from her broken leg, I left her again and enrolled in a writing program at Wuhan University in the neighboring Hubei Province. One month into the program, I had a scandalous affair with a graduate student who was engaged to be married. The affair landed me in a hospital with serious stab wounds inflicted by the woman's fiancé. Not long after, I was expelled.

Barely recovered from my injuries, I turned restless and traveled with a friend to Beijing to attend the First Contemporary Poetry Awards ceremony, presided over by Bei Dao, a leading member of China's avant-garde poetry movement. The city was in a state of agitation. Hu Yaobang was dead. The grief from the death of China's former Communist Party secretary, who had been purged for his liberal views, seemed to have consumed the city. A deluge of flowers, bouquets, and wreaths covered Tiananmen Square. Thousands of people were coming out to mourn the popular leader. My friend and I roamed the streets, hungrily devouring everything we saw. We could feel that a revolution was imminent. Didn't Mao tell us that "a single spark can ignite a prairie fire"?

As the protest was gaining momentum in Tiananmen Square, I became distracted by what was happening at the award ceremony. When I learned that none of my works had won any prizes, I made a fool of myself by accusing Bei Dao of hijacking the award process and marginalizing other contemporary poets.

Disillusioned because my poetry had failed to vanquish the capital, I left the center of the political storm and went south, traversing half the country. Thus, I missed the most important political event in China in half a century. A week later, I returned to Fuling, bitter and cynical.

The River Town

IN EARLY MAY OF 1989, friends from Chengdu, Beijing, Guangzhou, and Wuhan wrote to me, raving about the booming protest movement in their cities. I stayed oblivious to the political turbulence outside, however, and resumed my rigorous writing routine.

On May 16, student leaders in Beijing started a hunger strike in Tiananmen Square after the government refused to recognize the patriotic nature of their movement. Their actions galvanized the whole nation. University students in other cities responded by staging similar hunger strikes. One hundred singers in Hong Kong launched a musical marathon to raise money and awareness for the protesters. All types of open letters, pamphlets, and petitions seeking signatures filled my mailbox. I tossed them out with contempt. As the country was whipped into a frenzy, I took pride in my own coolheadedness.

My indifference was short-lived. Late one night I heard fireworks crackling outside. I pushed open the window. The sound of the Communist anthem "The Internationale" wafted through the air, like the soft harmonious chorus of a children's choir. I could tell it was coming from Fuling Teachers' College on the other side of the Wu River. Unlike a rousing party anthem, though, the singing became more distinct, and the song, with its slow, gentle motion, reverberated in the air like a requiem, filled with tears and prayers. "I didn't know you could turn this motivational hymn of the proletariat into a song of mourning," I remember thinking.

Racing upstairs to the top of the building, I joined a small crowd of colleagues at the Municipal Art Agency who had gathered on the rooftop, straining their heads to look south. The Chinese lyrics grew distinct:

> The blood which fills my chest has boiled over,
> We must struggle for truth!

Another barrage of fireworks followed. I could see lines of torches snaking around and crossing the Wu River to our side of the town.

Before long, demonstrators marched into town. Building lights switched on as people in every street descended into their doorways to see the commotion. Looking down from the top of the Municipal Art Agency, we watched the crowd pour into the neighborhoods carved into the mountain slope. The crowd was propelled as if on a conveyor belt — a medley of human-size peas, corn, and wheat tumbling along in color and song. The sights and sounds of the revolution drew me out of my seclusion. I, too, turned into a pea, bouncing down the stairs and rolling out onto the street. Soon I was swept up in the tide of grain and blown into the small city square.

There were islands of people who stopped to discuss loudly what was happening. Some residents spontaneously stepped up, giving stirring speeches, urging the government to do something, anything, to stop corrupt cadres. I tried to battle my way into the whirlpool but the crowd spat me out. In the end, I climbed up to the top of the Workers' Club building, from where I had a view of the whole square. Wiping away my perspiration, I looked down. Student demonstrators had finally arrived, carrying big banners made from white bedsheets. On each banner, written in big characters, were slogans such as "Down with Government Corruption," "Patriotism Is Not a Crime," and "Support the Students in Beijing." Their leaders marched at the front with white-and-red headbands like those worn by Hokkaido fishermen in Japanese movies. Onlookers conscientiously moved to the side to make a path for the protesters. Soon, the whirlpools in the square merged into a giant, powerful maelstrom.

Students and residents became indistinguishable. I couldn't believe what I was witnessing: Thousands of fists rose in the air again and again. The thunderous slogan-shouting droned on for almost an hour before the students regrouped and marched out of the square toward the city's largest sports stadium. As more people joined, the student line swelled from a garter snake into a massive python coursing forward.

As the python's body thickened, its progress slowed. A student organizer raised his handheld megaphone to urge nonstudents to stay out of the march and to keep the revolutionary ranks free of impure elements. Before he finished his sentence, the raucous crowd jostled him aside. People chatted and hooted; they wrapped their arms around each other's shoulders, pausing occasionally to raise their arms or fists to punctuate a slogan.

The party continued until dawn. When people were tired they simply retreated to the side of the street and squatted down in circles. Neighbors, colleagues, and strangers mixed together. Strangers offered each other cigarettes.

I tried to keep sleep at bay but failed. Reluctantly I went home. The crescent moon turned red. The stars were eating away the night sky like swarms of green flies. An elderly man near me remarked that it had been the most memorable night in the history of Fuling.

By the time I awoke the next day, it was already noon. A Xia reported that the students had taken over the municipal government building. I marveled, "Do you think it's a coup?"

Without even washing my face, I ran out in my flip-flops. Nothing unusual was happening in the street — pedestrians bustled about on sidewalks sheltered by the tiled eaves of apartment blocks or businesses. A couple of stray dogs strutted about, swaggering nonchalantly in the path of honking cars that raced down the slope. Traces of the previous night's revolution were still visible — scraps of paper, pamphlets, and rags rustling in the breeze.

The wrought-iron gate of the administrative building, sixteen feet high, remained shut. I had heard that the students were preparing to hold a demonstration inside the compound. A small side entrance stood guarded by a group of headband-wearing students, who only left a narrow gap between them for anyone to pass. I was told that only those with student IDs were allowed to enter. Outside the fenced government compound, the vegetable market was bustling as usual. A small group of peasant vendors left their vehicles and bags, and clustered around the fence. A young boy stood on a stranger's shoulders like a circus monkey and clutched at the fence, cheering and screaming. A student guard pushed him off with a broom. I elbowed my way through to the front and greeted a guard. "Excuse me, I need to see my wife," I lied. "She works in there."

He didn't even raise his head to look at me. "Your wife is gone for the day."

I stuck my head in through the crack. "But my mistress is still in there," I persisted.

I heard snickers from the crowd. "Another smart-ass trying to get in," one person said.

"The government building is empty," another person quipped. "All the officials fled last night."

The news did not surprise me. In Beijing, conservatives and reformists within the senior Communist leadership were fighting over a solution to end the protest movement in the capital. Because it was hard to discern which faction would gain the upper hand, many local leaders had chosen to wait patiently on the sidelines until clear political signals had emerged. The party secretary of Sichuan Province, at the height of the student protests in Chengdu, escaped the city with a large contingent of his cronies. A newspaper had recently carried a picture of him ostensibly "conducting social investigations" on the deck of a boat on the Yangtze River.

In Fuling, with a population of one million, the mayor had disappeared, leaving a retired deputy director to hold the fort. I was there when he addressed the students in front of the administrative building the next day. The shrewd deputy stood in front of us like a turtle with his neck sticking out, but ready at any instant to retreat inside his shell. Sweat dripped from his forehead. A female student led the crowd in several rounds of vigorous slogan shouting: "Down with government corruption!" and "Learn from the students in Beijing!" The crowd roared its approval, whipping itself into a frenzy. The retired deputy was all smiles and shouted out his message between the slogans:

"My dear students, respected patriotic students, spirited, dynamic, and energetic students! I just want you to know that we share your goals. The government welcomes you to come in and engage in a heart-to-heart talk with us. As you know, the Chinese word for nation consists of two characters — one means 'country' and the other 'family.' The two are interconnected. The stability of a country benefits families. Dear students, you are the same age as my granddaughter. I see you as my own children. If you have financial hardships or run into problems in your studies, I'll try to resolve them on the spot. For questions to which I cannot provide an immediate answer, I'll bring them up with a higher authority."

At one point during his talk, the official even shed patriotic tears and patted the shoulders of a female student leader standing next to him. The spectacled student flinched and pushed his hand away. "What are you trying to do?" she said sharply.

Before the old coot could pull back his hand and regain his composure, other students began to fire questions at him.

STUDENTS: Do you think we should fight against corruption and corrupt officials should be punished?
OFFICIAL: Yes, absolutely.
STUDENTS: Do you think we should bring down Premier Li Peng?
OFFICIAL: No, I mean, I will pass on your demands to senior leaders at the provincial government.
STUDENTS: We are asking you. Don't you think we should bring down Premier Li Peng?
OFFICIAL: Yes, ten thousand yeses.

That retired deputy kept nodding his head, like a rooster pecking at a pile of rice. His obsequious reaction confounded the student leaders, who were at a loss for what to do next. They raised their voices and started another round of slogan-shouting. The retired deputy took the cue and applauded vigorously.

"My dear patriotic students! I'm so touched by your enthusiasm today. Please have faith in our party, the greatest political party in the world. We are not afraid to correct our mistakes. And please take care of your health, because we need you to take over our socialist revolution in the near future. I know many of you haven't had a chance to eat or sleep for two days. Quiet, please. The cooks have prepared lunch for all of you. If you show them your student ID card, you'll be able to get a bun and a bowl of soup for free. Once you've filled your stomach, you can all go home and figure out what to do in the next phase of our revolution, *Okay?*"

At the end of his speech, the old rascal instinctively applauded at his own brilliance and looked surprised when he realized that there was no response from the audience. He grabbed the microphone and shouted with bravado, "Please follow me!" and, with that, he elbowed his way through the crowd and strutted toward the cafeteria.

Free food was indisputably alluring. The students paused for a few seconds and then followed him. Seeing that they could not reverse the situation, the dejected student leaders followed along. Thus, gratis buns and vegetable soup derailed the surging student movement in the mountain town of Fuling. Meanwhile, the old rascal plunged into the kitchen, grabbed a bun, and slithered out the back door like an eel.

Germaine Greer, a feminist Australian writer, once said, "Revolution is a festival for the oppressed." Fuling, on the brink of a revolution, was no exception. Collection booths for student hunger strikers in Beijing appeared on every street corner. There was no shortage of generous donors. I saw an elderly woman who made a living collecting garbage totter up to a booth furtively. She brought out from her pocket a package wrapped in a stained handkerchief and revealed a wad of rumpled Chinese dollar bills. She was about to insert the notes into the collection box when a female student stopped her and refused to take her money. As the two argued, a small crowd gathered, laughing and hooting. Humiliated, the old woman sat on the ground and sobbed loudly. "Do you think the money from a beggar like me is dirty?" Everyone present was deeply moved.

Over the next few weeks, the sleepy river town stirred. The spirit of the revolution had taken hold. Regional media joined the foray, and the TV station conducted live interviews and repeatedly broadcast the impassioned faces of protesters and their impromptu speeches. This same footage was later used as evidence by police against those whom the government labeled as "hooligans and violent criminals."

For about a week, the party apparatus was paralyzed and the officials temporarily absent. It seemed that without the leadership of the party, people could truly be the masters of their country, rather than the other way around. On the street, strangers greeted each other warmly. Volunteers stepped up to keep order. As in other major cities, the pickpockets and burglars in Fuling declared a moratorium on their activities. Ironically, the moratorium notices were posted on the walls next to the big posters that exposed the corruption of senior party officials and the secret funds they had deposited in banks overseas.

The events in Beijing dominated every conversation in town. At the art agency's residential complex, people visited each other daily. Rather than watch TV in their own homes, my colleagues preferred to do it communally at their neighbors'. At my apartment, visitors dropped by unannounced at all times, regardless of what my wife and I were doing or how we felt. When someone knocked on my door around midnight, I felt obligated to host him as a grand gesture of solidarity.

For the next two weeks, we experienced a confusing lull in the action. The students continued to camp out in Tiananmen Square and there was no response from the authorities. Fatigue and boredom set in. I gave up on my newspapers and turned off the TV. Like a corpse, I slept day and night. A Xia was the only one who moved about in this tomb for the living. In the evenings, when I opened the windows for fresh air, I could hear, above the noise of the world, the murmuring conversations between the clouds and the mountains.

The whole world felt like a colossal grave for an idea that had died after a premature birth. I stared catatonically into the distance and was hit by an unfamiliar sense of emptiness, a serene surface that masked the turmoil inside me. Before then, I had always despised everything associated with politics — political parties, rallies and campaigns — but at the same time, I was frightened of being left behind or somehow forgotten.

Home turned into a solitary battlefield. One night in mid-May A Xia went to bed early but I remained awake. Stepping out of the bedroom barefoot, I quietly circled between my study and the living room. I turned on the TV and stood stark naked watching the news. Martial law had been declared, and troops were about to enter the capital and expel the students from Tiananmen Square. Reporters captured scenes of soldiers and residents celebrating peacefully on the outskirts of Beijing. At the same time, Tiananmen Square was littered with papers, bottles, and food containers. Zhao Ziyang, the then reform-minded party general secretary and a supporter of the student protesters, braved the rainy weather and appeared in Tiananmen Square. Choked with emotion, he advised the students through a bullhorn, "You are still young. You have a bright future before you. We are old and it doesn't matter what happens to us." He sounded so helpless.

Nobody knew that it was Zhao Ziyang's last public appearance before he was put under house arrest by the hardliners. I flipped to another channel and saw the same saddened face of Zhao Ziyang. I pressed the button again. Now the sad and helpless face morphed into the face of an agitated woman, a student leader who raised her fist in the air, calling on those innocent lambs to continue their war against the jackals.

"If she were the premier of China, she would be more ruthless than Li Peng," I thought. "What an evil troublemaker!"

I switched the TV off and murmured to myself, "It doesn't matter if the revolution succeeds or not, I wouldn't benefit either way." I dug out a half-finished poem and began writing. The night was long. The bloodthirsty moon sported a wolf's beard. I could hear the echoes of heaven's howling.

Revolutionary Fever

MICHAEL DAY, WITH HIS dirty shirt and black handmade cotton shoes, looked like an international beggar. He called out my name in his unmistakable booming voice as he disembarked from the river ferry on June 1, 1989. I had met this remarkable Canadian through a mutual friend, the Nobel Prize laureate Liu Xiaobo. Day worked at the China International Publishing Group and Liu had given him a copy of my underground poetry journal. Day liked my poems and wrote me a letter. In 1988, he visited me in Fuling during the Chinese New Year. I had developed a strong interest in the artistic Canadian because of Chairman Mao's famous essay composed in 1939 in memory of Norman Bethune, a Canadian doctor and Communist sympathizer who had traveled to China and died while volunteering at an army hospital serving Mao's army of irregulars. Since then, we Chinese saw Canadians as altruistic Samaritans who seemed to enjoy other countries more than their own. When it came to Michael Day, his love for China was heartwarming. He had joined a group of Chinese poets and marched in Tiananmen Square, shouting slogans in Chinese with his booming voice. Once martial law was in full force, Day had boarded a train and cursed his way south.

By the time I saw Day, he was a loaded gun. He had just come from

Beijing, where he had participated in the protest movement in Tiananmen Square. As he strode powerfully up the street, I, the host, trailed behind. At my house, before I had a chance to take a breath, Day bombarded me with exciting updates on the situation in Beijing.

"Can you stop for a minute?" I said, wiping sweat from my face. "Have some cold water first. You should probably take a shower. You smell terrible."

Day sniffed at his shirt and then bent down to rummage through his bag. He wasn't searching for clean clothes. Instead, he brought out a small shortwave radio. Picking a seat near the window, he pulled the antenna out and put the headset over his ears, like a telegraph operator in an old Chinese spy movie. Every now and then, Day would hunch over my desk to jot down notes.

"I'm listening to the BBC's live coverage of the events in Tiananmen Square," said Day in a delighted voice. "It's quite clear over here."

He listened to the English broadcast intently while translating, occasionally. I could feel the tension in the room, which seemed like an ammunition warehouse, ready to explode at any moment. For the next few days, all our conversations centered on Beijing and the student demonstrations. I tried to change the subject, querying him about his life in Canada, the status of the manuscripts that I had asked him to smuggle out of China, the progress of his graduate thesis, and his last girlfriend. Day responded absentmindedly in monosyllables and then immediately brought the conversation back to its main theme. "Many of the world's best-known China scholars are in Beijing, including my professor," he exclaimed. "They all wanted to witness the greatest transformation in human history."

Day's enthusiasm became infectious. My eyes reddened like his from sleep deprivation. We argued, waving our fists at each other. Our skirmishes carried over to the lunch table, where we talked all afternoon, beer bottles and empty plates scattered around.

"The troops are entering the city from different directions. They have been ordered to take over Tiananmen Square at all costs. The movement will be over," said Michael Day. "The students don't believe the troops will open fire on them. At most, they anticipate a few rounds of rubber bullets. We need to offer our support."

"Stop, Michael!" I shouted at him. "Don't bark at me like a bulldog.

I'm not the kind of poet that you think I am. I have never taken an interest in mass movements or foreign imports such as democracy, freedom, human rights, and love. If destruction is inevitable, let it be."

"Do you hope to see blood flowing in Tiananmen Square?"

"So what if I do? What can dog farts like you and I do?" I shouted, my face tilting upward, as if I were drowning in blood. "In this life, nobody cares if I live or die, except my mother and . . ."—I meant to say my sister Fei Fei, but her name stuck in my throat.

At noon on June 3, thick clouds hung low in the sky, choking the city of Fuling like frying pan smoke. Michael Day and I sat shirtless around the lunch table, bickering over the latest development in Beijing. A Xia, who was caught in the crossfire, had finally had enough with our obsession with the student movement, which she was afraid could get us into trouble. She threw down her chopsticks, screamed at the top of her lungs, and stormed into the bedroom. Embarrassed and outraged at her outburst in front of my friend, I kicked the bedroom door open and slapped her. A Xia fought back, yelling and crying. I wrestled her down to the bed. Michael Day stood by the lunch table, looking lost. The shortwave radio continued to blast its live broadcast.

Fortunately, a friend of mine stopped by and offered Michael Day temporary shelter at his place. After our guest left, the apartment fell into silence. Time ticked by, slowly. No sound came out of the bedroom. Worrying that something might have happened to A Xia, I peeked through a tiny window in the door. It was dark inside.

"A Xia," I called her name softly.

She didn't respond. Like a tamed leopard, I stuck my head in. "A Xia!"

Knowing that pushing A Xia would only fuel her anger, I slipped out. Sitting on the steps to the entryway, I examined my hands, mumbling to myself, "Damn, what's wrong with me? I never meant to hurt you. My hands are faster than my brain."

Back in our apartment, I sat stiffly on the wicker chair. After what seemed like a century of sound and fury, things had suddenly quieted down. Lying down on the couch, I could taste the saliva in my mouth and hear my own heartbeat and the ticking of the watch on my wrist. Darkness descended. I pushed open the window. The Yangtze and Wu Rivers joined together outside the city, emitting loud copulating noises. Stars appeared in the sky as the rusty sunset left striped imprints on the rooftops. A pale crescent moon hung in the middle of it all, and the wind blew like a ghost dangling from a noose, his tongue sticking out and breathing cold air. I picked up my pen and wrote:

> *You were born with the soul of an assassin*
> *But at the time of action,*
> *You are at a loss, doing nothing.*
> *You have no sword to draw,*
> *Your body a rusted sheath,*
> *Your hands shaking,*
> *Your bones rotten,*
> *Your nearsighted eyes cannot do the shooting.*
> *You are useless, so useless, trying to dodge bullets with a paper shield*
> *made from justice, morality, conscience, and responsibilities.*
> *When the masses were running, scared,*
> *It was your turn to step out.*
> *What's the point of stepping out?*
> *The bloody outcome is already predetermined.*

At dusk, I emerged from the study. I rolled up my sleeves to prepare supper. There were urgent knocks on the door. Michael Day stepped in, looking dejected. A Xia stepped out of the bedroom, pushed me aside, and took over the cooking.

The last supper commenced. Silently, the three of us bowed our heads, eating. Nobody wanted to be the first to touch the vegetable plate in the middle of the table. A porcelain soupspoon slipped from Day's hands and smashed into pieces on the floor. As I rose to pick up a new one, I noticed Day's childlike eyes moving nervously between A Xia and me.

At the end of dinner, rather than plaster his ear to his radio, Day sat awkwardly on his chair. Like a fish out of water, he struggled to open his mouth several times but nothing came out of it. "If you don't have anything else to do, why don't you go to bed?" I said, feigning a yawn.

An hour later, when I was lying in bed, I heard a soft knock on the bedroom door. Then, another one. The door trembled with the sound.

I got up and scurried to my study. Day stood on the balcony, half naked in his striped underwear, his hands gesticulating.

"They've opened fire!" he screamed.

"Where?" I stuck my head out, scanning the city.

"The soldiers, those bastards," he mumbled, his hand pointing randomly in the distance.

I pricked my ears — the sound of firecrackers came from the southeastern part of the city, like peas popping in a hot frying pan. I uttered a sigh of relief. "It's a funeral."

Day looked puzzled.

"In Chinese culture, the moment a person's soul departs his body, his relatives light firecrackers to inform the king of the underworld that a new ghost is on its way," I explained.

"That's not a good omen," Day grumbled. "The troops are approaching Beijing. The BBC reported that many soldiers have refused to follow orders. They have abandoned their tanks and fled. There are several dead tanks parked inside the People's University. Sporadic gunfire has been reported."

"A few dead tanks doesn't mean that the troops won't enter Beijing," I said.

"I pray for a big thunderstorm or an earthquake to befall Beijing. I pray that all the soldiers wake up to the call of their conscience. I know this is wishful thinking — oh, well," Day said. "I know you and many people are not willing to get involved. No matter how much blood is shed, you just don't care what will happen to your country and your compatriots."

"Do you think you love China more than I do?"

"Perhaps," Day persisted. "Unlike you, I have at least participated in demonstrations on the streets of Beijing. I led a group in chanting anticorruption slogans, and we distributed pamphlets. People on the street applauded us. I do think people are different this time. Those students, vendors, ordinary residents were so passionate and altruistic . . ."

"This is a collective delusion," I interjected.

"It's a type of great religious belief, but without a god or set of dogmas," Day went on, his eyes growing moist. "In China's long history, these people might be insignificant and their roles fleeting, but they helped change history. None of them desired to seize political power, nor do they want to profit from the chaos. Do you possess this type of pure passion?"

"No, I don't." His remarks began to incense me. "I don't need a Canadian to tell me how to be a patriot."

Day was shaking and his arms were crossed, clutching his bare shoulders. Following a long pause, he continued, "I don't love this country because of the government that lies at its center. But I love my friends. Maybe, the stinking warmth of China fits me better."

Massacre

At about nine o'clock on the evening of June 3, Michael Day heard on the BBC that tanks and government troops were advancing toward the center of Beijing. "People have flooded onto the streets and set up barricades along routes into Tiananmen Square," said the Canadian poet, who stood by the window and pressed his ear against his shortwave radio. "The troops are trying to break through and have opened fire indiscriminately at students and citizens. Many have been killed or injured."

"Those bastards," I mumbled and turned on the TV. The two anchors, the best at the China Central Television Station, took turns reading an announcement in a solemn and mournful tone—the Party would resolutely crack down on the counterrevolutionary riot in Tiananmen Square. Troops would take over the square soon and residents were advised to stay home. Then, a line of subtitles appeared— the mayor of Beijing had ordered a curfew. There was no mention of casualties.

Too agitated to hear what would happen next, I went back to bed, leaving Day alone with the radio. I lay down, but couldn't sleep. I rose and lay down again. An hour later, I gradually dozed off. In my dream, I stepped into the TV and onto the China Central Television Station broadcast set, kicked out the two anchors, and took their places. I shouted loudly, "Kill the Chinese premier to appease national anger!" A Xia's scream jerked me back to reality. She unballed my fist — I had been grabbing and squeezing her tightly, leaving a big bruise on her arm.

I got up, apologized to her absentmindedly, and stepped into the living room. My teeth clattered, and my knees shook. I ripped the cover off my tape recorder, hit the recording button, and announced clearly and unequivocally in my native tongue: "I protest."

Michael Day walked over, joining me with a voice from the other end of the world, "I protest."

The bloody crackdown in Beijing was a turning point in history and also in my own life. For once in my life, I decided to head down a heroic path, one on which I advanced with great fear, scampering at times like a rat with no place to hide.

We faced the direction of the Forbidden City. I roared out whatever came to my mind and wherever my mind took me. I felt as if my voice had been amplified through a hundred loudspeakers:

> And another sort of massacre takes place at utopia's core
> The prime minister catches cold, the people must cough; martial law
> > declared
> again and again.
> The toothless machinery of the state rolls towards those who have the
> > courage to
> resist the sickness.
> Unarmed thugs fall by the thousands; iron-clad professional killers
> > swim in a sea of
> blood, set tires beneath tightly closed windows, wipe their army-
> > regulation boots
> with the skirts of dead maidens. They're incapable of trembling.
> These heartless robots are incapable of trembling!
> Their electronic brains possess only one program: an official
> > document full of holes.
> "In the name of the Fatherland, slaughter the constitution!
> Replace the constitution, slaughter righteousness!

In the name of mothers, throttle children!
In the name of children, sodomize fathers!
In the name of wives, murder husbands!
In the name of urbanites, blow up cities!
Open fire! Fire!
Upon the elderly!
Upon the children!
Open fire on women!
On students. Workers. Teachers.
Open fire on peddlers!
Open fire! Blast away!"

. . .

In this historically unprecedented massacre only the spawn of dogs
can survive.

At the end, I picked the song "Let the World Be Filled with Love" as background music without realizing that the tape had been a gift from Fei Fei from her last trip to Chengdu. She had enjoyed the song so much that she'd bought two copies at a bookstore the previous Chinese New Year.

"Let me gently hold your hands," the children sang softly.

At six in the morning on June 4, I finished the audio production of "Massacre." I made three copies of the tape and wrote on the back of each cover "The era of protests." Day, my fellow artist-protestor, stuffed them in his huge vagabond's backpack. We jokingly decided that these were "sparks of fire." Then he left Fuling, carrying the sparks to Chongqing, Chengdu, Guangzhou, Shanghai, Nanjing, and Beijing, and finally he found his shelter in Xian. Wherever he visited, Day set up secret meetings with local underground poets, collecting their work and engaging in discourse on the future of China's literary movement. Public security officers tirelessly tailed him.

What made this otherwise laid-back Canadian nervous was Beijing, where fully armed soldiers controlled the train stations, universities, hotels, and key streets, checking the IDs of passengers and pedestrians at random. If any luggage appeared suspicious, they would stab it in with a bayonet before asking any questions. Day, a seasoned Chinatraveler, knew how to handle the situation with ease. He would voluntarily open his backpack before he was even questioned, spread his belongings on the ground, and then he was all smiles when answering their queries. As a result, the guards never checked it thoroughly.

One of the first things Day did was to set up a meeting with the literary critic Tang Xiaodu inside the Temple of Heaven. When they met, they each held a copy of the *People's Daily* in their right hand, and when passing each other they exchanged their illicit "goods" and quickly put them in their pockets, obviously a technique they had learned from Chinese spy movies.

Many years have passed and I still remember the many arguments that my Canadian-Chinese compatriot and I had in that period, when he returned to my apartment. Between the two of us, Michael Day was more diligent, getting up early every morning, reading and writing, or taking a stroll outside. Then, he would fidget around in my living room, listening to music from the boom box. He turned the volume up and the operas of Mozart pierced my eardrums. Perhaps rudely, I let him know that I couldn't bear operas. Even today, I still can't appreciate their beauty. Sometimes, if music was not enough to occupy him, he would chant a poem for me. He opened his mouth wide like a vampire, ready to swallow me.

Despite the oppressive political environment in China, Day nursed a wish to stay in China as long as he could. He reassured me before he left. "I'm not just in China to study Chinese poets and their works. I want to witness and experience the suppression, the resistance and the transformation inside this gigantic prison. You have to learn to survive and live well. Promise me, my friend."

Before Day left Fuling, he issued a black curse by giving me a black T-shirt. On the front was a picture called "Megadeth"—the name of a heavy metal band. I wore the shirt for many years and couldn't bear to part with it.

The public nightmare continued. In the first week after the massacre in Beijing, the government imposed a news blackout. Ordinary citizens had no idea that many students and residents in Beijing had been killed by government troops. Some turned to shortwave radios and learned about the truth from the BBC and the Voice of America, which quoted witnesses as saying that the number of fatalities could reach as high as several thousand. Inflamed by the bloody retaliation, students in other cities continued with their antigovernment demonstrations. One of the most memorable protests outside Beijing took place in a city in Hubei Province. Upon hearing news of the massacre in Beijing, hundreds of students from the city's only college draped themselves in white mourning outfits and wrapped long strips of white linen around their heads, their tails swinging and dragging on the ground.

The feet of the publicly grieving students shuffled in total silence through the city's streets under the bright sun — there were no slogans shouted, no banners, and no wreaths. Even the clouds followed them as though they were joining the parade of mourners. Onlookers held their breath, watching silently. The police who had been brought in to arrest parade organizers were spellbound. They stood motionless, looking lost and profoundly moved. They awoke from their reverie only when their commander rushed over. "Dammit. What has gotten into you? Why are you just standing here and doing nothing?" he rebuked them loudly.

In mid-June, all the TV channels broadcast the names of student leaders who were wanted by the government. In Fuling, local newspapers and TV stations urged those who had played a key role in the city's protest to turn themselves in to the Public Security Bureau. Everywhere I went — the train station, the pier, or shopping centers — I could not escape the ubiquitous government notices about the "crackdown on the counterrevolutionary riots." Patrolling soldiers in helmets and boots thudded around like robots. The harsh political conditions seemed to have affected nature as well. The scorching sun poured down on the city like bowls of hot chili pepper sauce.

At the end of June, I traveled to Chongqing with my friend Li Yawei, a rugged-looking poet who wore a trademark red headband, which helped to contain the long unkempt hair that draped his shoulders. From behind, he resembled a foul sorcerer. He used to visit me often, and we called him the Hippie Poet. Broke and penniless, Hippie Poet nurtured a dream of achieving nirvana through his words. In his younger days, he prided himself on his working-class demeanor and lifestyle — conversing with people while picking at his foul-smelling toes and, on most nights, going to bed cold and hungry. After I began chanting poetry for an audience, he joined in at any opportunity. "We should compose a series of short poems to commemorate the tragic event in Beijing," he suggested. "We can pay the beggars on the street to chant and sing the poems to Sichuan opera tunes."

In Chongqing, Hippie Poet took me to see his friend Liu Taiheng — a pair of huge glasses overwhelmed his small face, where the dominant feature was his big mouth. Big Glasses lived in a dorm converted from an abandoned surgery center at the Third Military Medical University. He greeted us while vigorously scratching his lower back. A chain-smoker, Big Glasses looked shriveled like a dry stick, as if all the fat had been drained and squeezed out of him. By contrast, his wife, Xiao Min, had the face and body of a model.

I heaved a sigh of relief. "I'm glad we are finally at your place." There were many checkpoints on the way there. It was like passing through endless rows of military camps.

Hippie Poet eyed the pretty hostess and joked, "If your wife donned a police uniform, all the counterrevolutionaries would surrender themselves to her."

"Watch your mouth," Big Glasses said listlessly. Xiao Min walked in, carrying two bowls of steamy minced-meat noodles. "More to come," she said, all smiles.

A curtain divided the room in two — on the left was the "master bedroom." Some space on the right served as a living room, which Big Glasses used as his study, music room, and guest bedroom for visiting poets from around the country. After dinner, Big Glasses took us to a movie theater. A show had just ended and we jostled our way through a huge crowd that was pouring down the stairs. Big Glasses pulled a red armband out of his pocket: "I have a part-time gig here as a security guard. I'll get us some liquor money."

While waiting for the next show, we lingered inside a dancehall adjacent to the theater. In the dim light, couples wrapped their arms around each other and swung to the melancholy melody like armless zombies. The dancers' intimate moves bothered an old guard, who shouted like a movie director who was coaching his actors on a set:

"Hey, everyone, move faster! No necking or petting!" When the crowd ignored him, the exasperated guard walked to the dance floor, tapping dancers on their shoulders, yelling, "Keep your hands off her! The police will be here shortly."

He was right. A few minutes later, a group of police officers appeared. The disc jockey immediately switched to a fast waltz and dancers quickly adjusted their moves to the tempo of the music. A few couples who were too slow to switch were escorted out.

When the movie finally started, Big Glasses went to work on his campaign to "collect" liquor money. As the theater's security guard, he inspected all the box seats by pulling back the curtains on each to ensure that none of the patrons were engaged in heavy necking or actual lovemaking. Behind the curtain in one box, he detected something — a young woman was sitting on her boyfriend's lap. Both sets of eyes were focused on the movie, as if they were totally immersed in the story. But Big Glasses could hear the two panting and moaning. Like a detective, he crouched down behind the couple and waited quietly for a few minutes before flipping on his flashlight. A beam of glaring light focused first on the man's big feet and then gradually traveled up his leg and then stopped on his crotch — he was still inside her.

The man freed one hand, fumbled in his pocket and handed over twelve yuan.

Big Glasses stood there, unmoved.

Another round of groping in the pocket produced another thirteen yuan.

Big Glasses flicked the flashlight off and the three of us left. Outside the theater entrance, Big Glasses ripped off the armband and stuck it in his pocket. Without wasting any time, we dashed over to a roadside restaurant.

"The money stinks but the liquor tastes delicious," Big Glasses said, savoring his first sip.

"What you did just now was quite risky, man. Sooner or later, you'll get caught," I warned him.

Big Glasses shrugged it off. "The government is in the middle of an antipornography campaign. Police not only detain people who watch X-rated videos and confiscate pornographic magazines, they also raid hotels and private homes to nab those who engage in illicit sex. Midnight movie theaters have become perfect venues for young singles or prostitutes. So, a little blackmailing is nothing."

"To a kindhearted revolutionary," Hippie Poet said, raising his cup. "Cheers."

As we were drinking, police sirens could be heard outside. I counted thirteen police cars. "Are they arresting anyone?" I asked.

"Oh, no, relax. It's just their routine patrol," said the owner, bringing food to the table and shaking his head helplessly. "They come around three or four times a night to prevent more counterrevolutionary riots."

Big Glasses turned to the owner. "Sir, I assume you must have made donations to student protesters."

"Those donations were so wasted," the owner said with visible anger. "I read government news reports that those student leaders embezzled all the donations and divided the money among themselves. What's the point of starting an uprising? Nobody can beat the Communist Party. Look at the lives that have been lost . . ."

"How could you believe what is said in the newspapers?" I was about to argue with him when Big Glasses kicked me under the table and said to the owner, "Sir, what if I tell you that I was a member of the student leadership?"

The owner's face colored. "Please keep drinking. I will shut up," he said awkwardly and quickly left us alone.

"Don't get too upset about other people's comments," Hippie Poet said to me. "After all, we are poets and we shouldn't have anything to do with the revolution."

Hippie Poet might be right, I thought. The massacre in the capital had nothing to do with any of us. Beijing and Sichuan were far apart geographically. Time and space could easily wash out the stains of blood. I was terrified on the night of the tragedy but at least I was able to scream out my fear. I also labored under the illusion that I was the only poet in the country who dared engage in such reckless action.

I bade farewell to my friends in Chongqing and continued my journey to Chengdu, my hometown. It was my first trip home since the student protest movement. My mother was relieved to see that I was safe. Grabbing my left wrist, she dragged me through two side streets and into a hair salon on a main thoroughfare. Without hearing me out, she said, panting, "Shave it all off."

I instinctively covered my head with both hands, trying to back away.

"Look at this long wild hair! What do you need it for?" she scolded loudly. "You look like an ape. Strangers will think you are older than I am."

Before I had time to react, she helped the barber pin me down on a chair. Then, with the buzzing of a clipper, a wide swath of hair disappeared from the top of my head.

A few minutes later, I became a shaved gourd, a popular nickname for bald people. I stared at myself in the mirror with self-pity, but my mother clasped her hands with joy. "Good. That's really good. Now you looked exactly like when you were little. We used to call you a sullen little piggy."

"He looks like a monk," the barber teased.

"But I have a wife," I declared. "I look more like a prisoner."

"Stop it," my mother intervened, still frightened by the potential prospect of my arrest. "It's not funny."

"Okay then, my head looks like a light bulb!"

"That's true," my mother chuckled. Everyone was happy.

I stayed at home for a few days, shutting myself off from the outside world. Insomnia tormented me. Late one night, after tossing and turning in bed for hours, I began chanting my poems. The next morning, my mother came into my room. She touched my forehead with her cold hand and inquired with an expression full of concerns, "You don't seem to have a fever."

"Mom, leave me alone, I want to sleep."

"How did you scream yourself to sleep? Tell me, what did you do last night? Sounded like you were a little crazy."

"I was reading poetry."

"What a damn liar!" My mother then smiled slyly. "I know what's going on. You must have a hard time with that wife of yours in Fuling. You have brought your misery home and are just venting it."

"I guess."

"You should record that too. Why don't you take my tape recorder, close the door and scream your heart out," she advised. "It's better to cover your head with the quilt. In that way, no matter how loud you scream, our neighbors won't hear you."

The next afternoon, my younger sister came home and recounted the story of meeting a man made lunatic by his son's death at Tiananmen Square:

The son of a middle school teacher in Chengdu had attended a prestigious university in Beijing and was killed on the night of June 3 as a "counterrevolutionary thug" by the troops who stormed Beijing. His father fainted when he heard the news. A letter arrived with a big red government stamp — if he wished to collect his son's ashes, he should bring three hundred yuan to the local civil affairs department. The old man set off for the government office and walked through the streets like a zombie, oblivious to crossing signs or the noise from honking horns and pedestrians yelling obscenities at him.

A few days later, a student who escaped from the violence in Beijing visited Sichuan and handed the young man's father a shirt, which he had pulled from the son's body. A name, address, and telephone number were written on the sleeve, and "Long Live Democracy" was written in blood across the front. It was apparent that the son had prepared for the possibility that he might not survive the onslaught.

The father spread the shirt on his lap and sat there quietly all day. At dusk he stood up, digging out all of his son's clothes from the wardrobe and writing "Long Live Democracy" over each item. After he finished, he scribbled the slogan on sheets and quilts, on the walls and floors, and then on his own wrinkled face.

The father then wrapped a piece of red scarf around his neck and stepped out onto the street. He began seizing passersby, trying to write "Long Live Democracy" on their clothes. Most people ran away; some threw rocks and bricks at him. My younger sister happened to be carrying her six-month-old baby and couldn't dodge the old man. So she waited while he wrote "Long Live Democracy" on her right arm.

In the sweltering summer, the city felt like a giant grave shrouded in silence. Without knowing that a noose was tightening around my neck, I moved around within this urban sepulcher with audio cassettes of "Massacre" hidden in my pocket. A friend of mine worked as a disc jockey for a dance club. I visited this club, slinking in like a young wolf before the dancing started and dashing past the dimly lit dance floor like a hardened criminal. I went onto the stage and sat next to the drummer for hours until the last lingering dancers abandoned the floor at the end of the final song.

When I finally had the whole floor to myself, my eyes closed and my poetry spewed out. My voice echoed in the big empty hall. The ceiling lights flickered like the starlit firmament. The DJ flung his arms and beat on the drums to drown out my chanting, but again and again, my howling triumphed over the deafening noises of the drums. "You are drunk and crazy," the exhausted DJ complained, collapsing to the floor. The stink of wine and sweat hung in the air. My head twitched and shook. I was afraid my brain would burst. We were intoxicated even though we had not touched a drop of liquor . . .

My ravings had a purpose, though, as a translation into timely art. Big Glasses soon introduced me to Zeng Lei, a language lab technician at the Third Military Medical University. A former soldier, the technician had fought in the China-Vietnam War in 1979. He was a man with a strong sense of justice and an appreciation of art. He agreed to violate the university rules and record me chanting my poems. Thus, the studio at the language lab became a key "crime scene" in the government's later investigations. Under the language lab's spotlight, I flung my arms into the air and filled the void with my voice. My shadow bobbed up and down on the wall, connected to me like a long tail. Carried away by emotion, I struck my face with my fist.

When I took a break from my poem chanting, I continued to wander aimlessly, like a stray dog. Longquanyi was a mountain town famous for its fruits. Tourists came from afar to pick and buy fresh peaches in August. The peach market stretched for two kilometers. Along both sides of the main road, vendors stood behind big piles of peaches under tarpaulins while bare-shouldered peasants carried even more fruit in baskets suspended from shoulder poles, peddling them to the crowd under the scorching sun. The sound of bargaining rose and fell. I bent over to pick some peaches from a basket. All of a sudden, a tan-colored hand poked in the basket from behind, snatched a big peach and disappeared. Startled and outraged, the vendor sprang to his feet and ran after the thief, in this case, a woman in tattered clothing.

The peach thief had not gotten more than a hundred yards before the crowd blocked her path and the vendor overpowered her, twisting her left arm behind her back. The woman started to fall but still managed to stuff the rest of the peach into her mouth. She choked on the big juicy fruit. "Fuck you!" the vendor cursed and slapped her. A small crowd pressed around. Several men turned the thief over and pried open her mouth, scooping out the pureed peach and the core. It was midday, and the hot sun was so scalding that the asphalt on the road had begun to blister and melt. The onlookers, some jeering or cheering the plight of the thief, had to keep moving, shifting their feet nonstop so their shoes didn't get stuck to the pavement.

Encouraged by the crowd, several men seized the thief's pigtail and dragged her body around. After a few steps, her trousers slipped off and her bare bottom touched the burning asphalt. She cried out in pain and wriggled around like a fish on a hot pier. Her exposed behind turned her torturers into animals — several pairs of hands fondled her and pulled at her pubic hair. The woman's screams sounded like music to the unruly crowd. Someone shouted, "She's wet!" Someone else disagreed. They hedged a bet and a third person was elected to be the judge — he poked a finger into the woman's vagina and then said in disgust, "She is not wet. She just peed." The crowd burst into laughter and gradually dispersed. The drama ended.

The brutal farce had lasted about half an hour, with the participation of two hundred cast members, including fruit vendors, peasants, shoppers, high school students, workers, office clerks, and college students. Some of the same people might have taken to the street to protest against government corruption and supported the prodemocracy movement in Beijing, or might have confronted the government troops by setting up roadblocks. A few months before, we were under the collective illusion that the Chinese people were brave and fearless, yet to witness the malice of this small-town mob showed that these same protestors were also capable of cruelly violating their fellow citizens.

When I was alone in the hotel, I was gripped by the urge to correspond with friends. I wrote letter after letter, adopting the tone of someone who might soon leave this world. While invoking the foulest images to condemn the government, I also declared repeatedly that I wanted to run away. I vowed to earn some money, bribe a coastal fisherman, and glide across the sea. Each time I saw old friends and acquaintances, I would play the "Massacre" tape and gauge the reaction to my reading. I never intended to be a hero, but in a country where insanity ruled, I had to take a stand. "Massacre" was my art and my art was my protest.

A Xia

WINTER APPROACHED. I RETURNED to Fuling and found that A Xia was acting somewhat furtively. She seemed to be in a hurry all the time — quietly slipping into bed after dinner without sitting down with me in front of the TV to watch the evening news. Sometimes she would come home late, claiming that she had spent time with a certain girlfriend of hers. Initially, I didn't think it unusual because I had never doubted A Xia's love and devotion for me. Then I began to wonder. In A Xia's many remarkable pen-and-ink drawings of that period, I noticed that every line and every dot exuded bewildering passion. The sun and the moon were indistinguishable and humans were lost in a vast and confusing universe. She portrayed disfigured women with bare breasts; who were in despair. In one drawing, she linked the sun and moon together like a beautifully designed handcuff.

I could feel that she was drifting further away from me.

A Xia and I had met in the winter of 1983, when I was invited to speak at a government-sponsored young writers' conference in Chengdu. She was eighteen and had just started her job at the municipal government in Fuling, but her aspiration was to become a poet or an artist. By then, her poems and oil paintings had already won many local awards. I was impressed with her talent and raw literary ambition. After the conference, we kept up our correspondence. A Xia sent me her new poems and sketches, and I shared with her my latest writings. Six months later, I started to receive flirtatious, yet coy notes, accompanied by pictures of her in parks or along the Yangtze River. In response, I bought a giant stuffed dog—my Chinese zodiac sign —and shipped it to her.

In early 1984, after I had taken a weeklong visit to Fuling, we started dating, but none of our parents approved of the long-distance romance. A Xia's mother burned the stuffed dog and forbade her daughter from writing to me. My mother refused to see A Xia when she came to Chengdu because she thought A Xia would pull me away from my home and my family. The strong family objections, however, further strengthened our resolve. In the winter of 1984, A Xia and I eloped.

Our first challenge was to obtain a residency permit for my new wife to move to Chengdu. The government had promulgated a strict family register system to control the movement of people. A person seeking to move from a rural to an urban area or from one city to another was made to apply for a permit through the local government. Without any connections, it was an impossible task. So I decided to take up residence in Fuling—it was easy to transfer one's residency permit from a major city to a smaller one.

Upon hearing my decision, my mother, who had spent years securing permits for my siblings and me in Chengdu after her divorce from my father, was outraged. She locked up our family registration card in a drawer. I smashed the lock with a hammer, seized the card, and made the transfer at the local Public Security Bureau.

In Fuling, my reputation as a nationally known poet soon gained me a position at the local art agency. Thus, in 1985, we settled down in the city where the Wu and Yangtze Rivers merged. Despite my occasional wanderings, I spent five relatively peaceful and productive years there.

Beneath the serene surface of our family life, however, a crisis was lurking.

One night, after I had sat numbly through all the programs on TV, my wife was still out. I looked at my watch. The hands pointed to eleven thirty. I paced up and down in the room and decided to take a quick jog outside. I walked slowly first and then broke into a trot.

The small lanes were deep and dark. As I was running, an ominous thought started to form in my head and expand. I remembered that she had carefully put on her makeup before stepping out and repeatedly asked if I was going to visit my mother soon.

Distractedly, I ran uphill on a small mountain street, the wind rushing in my big ears. I suddenly felt like I was wobbling inside the mouth of a monster, my limbs weakening and my body melting in its thick saliva. As I stopped, panting, I heard brisk footsteps on my right side. I turned around abruptly and saw A Xia standing in the shadows with another man. My mind went blank, as if my head had been severed from the rest of my body. I struggled for a few moments and then muttered through my teeth, "Hello, is that you, A Xia?"

Stunned by my voice, A Xia almost fell to the ground. She steadied herself against a tree that was blown in the wind. The man in the dark shadow bounded away like a wounded deer. I chased after him. The street under my feet stretched out like a tightened bow and I shot forward like an arrow. I seemed to have broken free from gravity, flying through space and dangling on the stars. Sweat flooded my forehead, back, and shoulders. Soon my opponent was within my grasp, so I clenched my teeth, leapt forward, and seized him by the waist.

We wrestled on the ground, both panting like two running locomotives. I raised my leg, trying to kick him off the narrow mountain path, but missed and faltered, almost tumbling down myself. The flickering city lights down in the valley were beckoning us. My rival held on to me to keep from falling. Outraged, I seized him by the throat while he reached down and attacked my balls. I winced with pain and resorted to my secret weapon — my "iron" skull banged hard against his, knocking him out. I then pounced on him and punched him relentlessly on the head.

"Have mercy on me," a moaning came out of that battered head. My victim was swallowing a mouthful of blood.

"How many times did you fuck her?" I sounded like a gangster.

"Three times . . . no, no. I mean I've only seen her three times, nothing physical. Each time we met, we simply talked . . . talked about you."

"Where the fuck do you work?"

"I . . . I'm the director at a government agency. A Xia is just afraid.

She is lonely and scared because the Public Security Bureau is investigating you."

"So, you are taking advantage of her fear."

"A Xia loves you but she doesn't think she could stop you from getting involved in politically risky activities. She said you never listened. She cried a lot."

"So you comforted her with sex," I said with a cynical laugh.

"No, no, I'm serious. There is nothing going on between us."

"I assume it is because you haven't found a place to commit the crime yet!" I roared. "I'm going to kill you tonight."

I grabbed him by the collar and dragged him to the edge of the cliff, where I allowed him to take one last look at the sleeping city below. "I'm going to put you on a fast track home!" I laughed uproariously, while kneeing him hard in the chest. My rival involuntarily bent over, vomiting blood. Instead of fighting back, he clutched my leg, sobbing, "Don't do anything silly, Little Liao."

Blood surged through my head as if someone was pounding on its top. Instead of appeasing me, my rival's begging further triggered my beastly thirst for blood.

Suddenly, hard white lights flashed at us, dazzling my eyes. "Stop it, you murderer!" an old man's voice bellowed. "Tie him up and send him to the detention center."

Several more police officers overpowered me, twisting my arms behind my back. My rival looked baffled; his body, which lay soft as a noodle next to me, stiffened. Getting up on his knees in front of me, he slapped his own face repeatedly. "My young brother! I deserve your beating. I shouldn't have mistreated our parents. Your beating is a wake-up call."

His outburst surprised the patrolling policemen. My handler loosened his hold on my arm while the actor continued his performance. "Brother, let's talk it out at home, okay? Even if you break my neck, we are still one family. I promise that I'll apologize to our parents. I agree to give them five hundred yuan this month as financial support."

He wiped the blood from his face and spoke with convincing emotion and sincerity. The older policeman softened his tone and pointed his finger at me. "Young man, you can't beat your brother like that. You could kill him. If your elder brother makes a mistake and mistreats your parents, you should seek help from the party branch at his work unit."

I wanted to throw up, I felt so emasculated. Without a word, I scrambled to my feet, turned around, and left. That bastard was still acting. "My young brother is a nice person but has a quick temper. Please forgive us. Thank you so much for your help."

The wind stopped and the night became eerily quiet. I staggered along the bow-shaped road. I paused for a moment on the side of the road. Facing me was a powerful stage — the screen of the mountains as a backdrop theater, writing and real life, impossible to separate. But then, why did it hurt so much? For years, I considered myself a talented and self-taught entertainer, but I could never have imagined that I would be unwittingly cast in an ugly love triangle. I laughed and howled, making up new soliloquies as I moved along. I had no idea what had spewed out of my mouth. The emotion from seeing A Xia with another man compounded the turmoil I had been feeling since the student movement was crushed.

In the following weeks, I mentioned a possible divorce to A Xia several times. She said "no" just once and thereafter steadfastly maintained her silence. In a chaotic and disintegrating world, A Xia had been my last refuge. Unfortunately, that precious sanctuary was stained. The A Xia of my poems became a myth.

Our life went on uneventfully, but our love was approaching its end. She would come home from work, cook, clean, and then sit in front of the TV, knitting. Every now and then, she would raise her head and smile at me. She seemed to be saying, "Don't go out and make trouble."

Maybe she was the old A Xia, who never changed. It was the world that had changed.

Requiem

ON THE EVE OF Chinese New Year in 1990, my friends Hippie Poet, Big Glasses, and his wife, Xiao Min, traveled to Fuling to spend the holiday with me and A Xia. Over dinner, we drank as if there were no tomorrow. Between drinking games, Hippie Poet uttered his usual complaint: "I've been a vagabond for years. It's time I found a wife. My biggest wish is to find a wealthy widow who provides food and accommodation. She doesn't have to write poetry for me. I can do it."

"I've heard this millions of times," I said. "I think you are getting old now and starting to live on your memories."

Big Glasses was more sympathetic. "After New Year's, when Yiwu, the technician, and I are shooting our poetic film to protest the government's crackdown in Beijing, , we might get funding from overseas. We've lined up several beautiful actresses, so I'll definitely fix you up with one. Have you finished all the poems for the film?" Big Glasses asked me. "You'd better come up with something new with a different style."

"I'm afraid I can't. I haven't written any poems for half a year now," I answered. "The political situation is bad and I'm not in the right mood."

"After June 4, nobody is in a good mood," Hippie Poet said. "I sometimes feel that being a poet is quite pathetic."

"The good old days are gone," Big Glasses said. "I miss old Hu," referring to former party secretary Hu Yaobang. "His liberal policies in the mid-1980s led to a renaissance in poetry. We were able to experiment with all sorts of poetic languages and forms, but now, the bloody suppression in Beijing has set back history by at least a decade."

The sobering conversation, coupled with the alcohol, drowned our spirit. Having spent the whole evening cooking, A Xia retreated to the bedroom, followed by Big Glasses' wife. All that was left were three men. The mood darkened even further.

"This could be the theme for our film." Big Glasses tapped on the table. "We live such a ghastly life. Every day, we pretend that nothing has happened, but deep down, fear is sapping our vitality and courage. Now that we have bowed our heads and surrendered once, we'll do it again. Look at the gray sky — the sun looks like it has been smeared with shit. It's depressing. I think we are counting on the film to recover our lost soul."

Firecrackers exploded outside. We all swarmed to the balcony to watch the spectacular scene on New Year's Eve — the city lit up, with spectacular flames shooting across the night sky. For ordinary people, lighting fireworks was not only a ritual to send off the old and welcome the new, but also a type of therapy — helping to ease long-suppressed frustration.

"It lasts so long this year." Hippie Poet checked his watch. "More than half an hour."

Big Glasses didn't find the fireworks soothing and entertaining. "If we add up all the money wasted on fireworks, we would have enough to buy the whole city."

"Such a miser!" we snarled at Big Glasses in unison as we went back in, but his remarks led to our discussion about funding for the film.

"We need money for lots of things," Big Glasses said. "We have to pay for props, research materials, and crew members. I'm going to personally donate three hundred yuan as seed money."

"I'm going to contribute seven hundred yuan," I said, following Big Glasses' example. "Between the two of us, we have one thousand. I have a friend who is filthy rich. I'm sure he'll give us some."

"Big Beard," Big Glasses addressed me by my nickname. "It's up to you now. Break a leg."

"We are doing it together," I answered, faking a humble smile.

I didn't go home for the Chinese New Year's celebration. My mother nagged about my absence. "Without my second son being here, I don't feel like preparing the dishes." She must have conveyed her grumbles and displeasure to me by telepathy. A week after the New Year, when A Xia and I seemed to have exhausted all possible conversation topics, I thought of my moody mother. She had been opposed to my relations with A Xia at the beginning. The night before I left for Fuling, my mother had stood in front of the armoire in my room, grabbing me and snarling like a mother wolf. I struggled free from her grip and walked out. The powerful force of love for A Xia had pulled me away from my mother who for many years continued to harbor grudges against her daughter-in-law.

After June 4, my mother, who never cared about politics, had become concerned about me and shown up in Fuling. The minute she disembarked from the boat, she railed against the steep stone stairs that would take her to my apartment. "Yiwu, you are such a bastard," she grumbled, panting as she climbed the stairs. "You are such an idiot. How did you end up in such a shabby town?"

In my charming apartment overlooking the mountain town, my obstinate mother managed to stay for only one day before she began whining and insisted on leaving. She was so eager that she was willing to take a midnight boat. I saw her off at the pier. Worrying about her safety, I decided at the last minute to escort her all the way to Chéngdu. During the trip, she warned me: "Now that you have left your old mama, you'll be in trouble sooner or later."

I could sense that trouble was waiting for me ahead, and over the next six months, I started to prepare for my escape. At work, I applied for an exit permit for a trip to Shenzhen, a city on the border with Hong Kong, and contacted a friend of mine there to plan an escape route. I even dreamed of bribing some coastal fishermen, asking them to ferry me across the water to Hong Kong. None of these plans went anywhere. I never acted on them and fell back on the naive belief that I could somehow survive unscathed. However, when my boss issued a ban on my business travel and the local Public Security Bureau denied me the Shenzhen travel permit, I knew that I was officially on the surveillance list. Almost certainly, news of my poem "Massacre" had gotten out.

Amid the endless cold rain, I huddled up inside my Fuling nest and gazed around me at the furnishings with nostalgia — the carpet, the couch, a floor lamp, a gigantic curtain with blue stars, and handmade posters on the wall. A Xia and I had lived there for five years. Friends had come to treat our place like a motel, a bar, and an artists' salon. They slouched on the couch and chairs, sipping liquor, chanting poetry, and listening to music. Over the years, we had gradually built this snug refuge, which, to my dismay, would likely be ruined. Everyone and everything dear to me would be taken away.

I sat there on the floor with my tape recorder and popped in Mozart's *Requiem* and listened to it again and again. The rain outside thrashed the window. A Xia lay in our bed behind me, her face hidden in the half-light. I hunched over, scribbling on a stack of paper, the characters stretching out like earthworms. I wrote continuously. Each time my hand hesitated, my thoughts ran ahead. I was leaving my will to the world. Mozart's melodies scratched my face like cold fingers.

Listen, the calling seems so far, yet close. It lurks around you. It hides in your body. Are you following the calling? The fire, the sky-shooting flames, the pamphlets, the angry scream, the scream of shock and the scream of tragedy. The tanks crawled into the forbidden city like mosquitoes. The nation's skin is covered with unbearable itchy bites. Where else can you go? Sleep, sleep, you cannot jump through rows and rows of fire, neither can you swim across pools of blood. Sleep, sleep, my dear, the calling can be so sweet. The Han Chinese, whose voice is murmuring? Who is responding to the death of the Han Chinese? Boots, bullets and the rusty taste of blood. The guns are aiming at you. . . . The murderers, the ghosts under the knives. Hot blood burned the stones, the moss turned so lush and shiny. The sun is a rock dripping with blood, Changing, peace morphs into war and war into peace. Under the blood-dripping sun, the tall buildings sleep. The streets sleep. The schools sleep, the air sleeps. Daughters sleep. The army camps sleep. And you, the idol of everlasting sleep, the utopia that is eternal as the sun and moon, sleep, one rooftop after another, one person leaning against another, the curtain of the end slowly rises, listen, the calling is so close, close. One silver naked body floats to the surface to answer the calling . . . the sounds of the falling heads of

millions of people. The sunset scatters down like flying snowflakes,
Children, sleep and rest in peace . . .

The music stopped, the notes hung in midair. When the rooster crowed to herald the arrival of another day, I completed the poem, calling it "Anhunqu," or "Requiem." It would be the basis for the upcoming film.

Exhausted, I went to bed. A Xia sat up, with her hair draped over her shoulders, and got ready to wash and go to work. In the afternoon, I stacked up the manuscript neatly on her dressing table and paced up and down the room, waiting for her to come home. That was the last poem that A Xia copied for me.

I couldn't remember who had said that love was like a wineglass that could easily break into pieces if it slipped from one's hand. When that happened, one was more than likely to bend over and pick up the broken pieces under the illusion that the glass was still intact and as enthralling as before, even though the shards of glass had already cut into one's flesh. As time went by, A Xia and I reconciled. Soon after, she became pregnant. The news excited me, but also plunged me into deep emotional turmoil. It was around the same time that my friends decided to start shooting the film in Chongqing. I knew that the film project would be a risky move.

"Why do I cut off my own roots and abandon my family?" I murmured, overtaken by remorse. "It's going to happen regardless. Better to do it earlier than later."

I went ahead with the plan and prepared myself for the inevitable. First, I photocopied many of my manuscripts. I hid one set at a friend's house and packed a few originals in my suitcase — unfortunately, following my arrest, my friend destroyed them out of fear, and police confiscated the originals that I had carried. While A Xia was at work, I sorted out all my letters, keeping a few that might carry historical or sentimental value. I burned the rest. Over a month's time, I shuffled in and out of the municipal government building dozens of times trying to obtain a national identification card and a travel permit to Shenzhen. The authorities used all sorts of excuses to defer acting on my application. I felt like a helpless mouse under the paw of a cunning cat.

In February 1990, Big Glasses, an experienced con artist, mailed me a fake invitation on the letterhead of the "Mountain City Film and TV Center." I was supposed to show it to my boss and request some time off, but he denied my leave on grounds that I would soon be assigned the task of editing the *Fuling Almanac*. I took my case to the local cultural bureau, but the director, a sly veteran bureaucrat, snared me in a new trap. He granted approval but secretly notified the Public Security Bureau. Unaware of his duplicity, I crept out of my den on the evening of March 1 and rushed headlong into their clutches.

Throughout that period, I kept A Xia in the dark about the film. I simply told her that I would be on another business trip. The night before I left, she clung to me like a nervous cat. I leaned over to hear the baby's kicking inside A Xia's stomach. My baby girl and I were physically close, yet she felt so distant. "The boat has already set sail," I thought. "Nothing can tie me down."

I pulled the bed lamp toward me and out of habit, picked up a book to read before going to sleep. The book was Milan Kundera's *The Unbearable Lightness of Being*. I flipped the pages and stopped at a chapter that described in detail the nonviolent resistance staged by citizens in Czechoslovakia following the Soviet invasion during the Prague Spring in 1968. Young women, in defiance of the curfew, walked on the street wearing miniskirts, flaunting their thighs and breasts or openly kissing their lovers in front of the well-disciplined Soviet invaders, who turned around helplessly at the provocative gestures. The Kundera-style humor, though from a foreign land, resonated with me. "Romantic," I mumbled, and I thought of my country's own match: the young man who stopped the advance of a column of tanks in Beijing who was equally heroic and romantic.

The next evening I left A Xia. Wearing navy blue pajamas, she stood at the stairway with her usual somber look. I noticed that the heightened color of pregnancy had started to appear prominently on both of her cheeks. "Take care," she said while stuffing some money into my pocket. Stiffly, I put the money back in her hand and scrambled down the stairs without the courage to look back.

In my suitcase, I carried an abundance of soon-to-be criminal evidence—handwritten manuscripts and audio recordings of "Massacre" and "Requiem." Except for a fake journalist's pass, I had no other identification cards or papers. When I embarked on the boat, darkness shrouded the river. The mountain town gradually disappeared behind me, like a gigantic ship carrying A Xia and our unborn child away.

As I departed, I quietly recited three lines from an old poem I had written:

> *No place to rest*
> *The body vanishes*
> *The soul continues to march forward.*

The next morning, I appeared on the doorstep of Big Glasses' apartment inside the Third Military Medical Academy in Chongqing. A gaggle of friends, all chain-smoking night owls, made a special effort to rise early and greet me. Without unpacking or washing, I sat down with the group for two hours and energetically discussed the different approaches to the treatment of the film. "With so many excellent brains here, we are going to do a great job," Big Glasses bragged.

By dusk, a long and complicated shooting script had been born. It would be a silent film, without dialogue, quite avant-garde and filled with loaded images. The opening shot was a close-up of wolf paws in the camera lens that morphed into human feet. Then the camera cut to a flight of stairs; it panned across a wide stretch of land, sea, and the sky. A leg poked out from the eye of a horse; the striped shadows of skyscrapers were transformed into steep cliffs.

"This is so bizarre," said a friend who had been hired to edit the script. "We have to revise."

A look of surprise flashed across the technician's face. "Revision? If we do, we are going to drag on for a year. Who is paying for this? Plus, I have to travel to Beijing in two weeks and do an educational film on military defense."

"Why don't we ask Ba Tie, the screenwriter, to do the revision?" Hippie Poet proposed. "We are so used to writing goddamn abstract poems."

Like a purebred dog with big, fat ears, the screenwriter "sniffed" at each page. "I will try and preserve your original intent," he promised.

Seeing that it was late, Big Glasses recommended that we eat first and celebrate our initial success at a nearby restaurant. However, the technician did not want to waste time; he pulled me from my chair and had me follow him. "It's time we get down to business and do the prerecording of the poems first," the technician said, his face looking stern. His years of military training had given him a soldier's bearing.

It was pitch dark inside the language lab building. We felt our way along, our footsteps echoing in the cavernous corridor, multiplying the auditory effect as if an invisible platoon were climbing the stairs.

"The place reeks of antiseptic," I said, panting. "I can't breathe."

"Two nights ago, a student, whose girlfriend had dumped him, went up to the top floor and jumped," the technician answered indifferently. "His body plunged to the bottom and exploded like a bomb, his blood and brain splashed everywhere. After the body was removed, the building cleaners scraped the floor with two big buckets of antiseptic."

"That's not a good omen," I muttered.

"We are doing a film called *Requiem* to appease the souls of the dead, including this unfortunate lover," offered the technician.

The recording room resembled a fishbowl. I could see the exaggerated movements of the technician's mouth through the glass — he was apparently yelling instructions at me but I couldn't hear a word. When I accidentally brushed the microphone, it gave out a loud piercing sound. I put my mouth close to the microphone and tested the sound. "I feel like I'm standing inside a vacuum." The technician's hands moved around on a panel of buttons, his head shaking vigorously and his body casting a shadow on the wall, like a silent gigantic wing.

"Flying, flying for millions of years," I tried again.

After several rounds of testing, we formally began. The technician tried to control me like a stern director. I closed my eyes and began chanting. I felt as though I were being tossed about in the turbulent sea, trying to hold on. Touching the edge of a desk, I imagined it to be the deck of a ship. I screamed to the roaring water.

"That was powerful. How did you manage to squeeze those animalistic sounds out of your body?" the technician asked at the end of the recording session. "It gave me cold sweats."

"My ass," I responded in total dejection, like a prisoner who indulged in a wild fantasy of escape and woke up to find that he was still incarcerated. "I had barely gotten into the mood before it was already over."

"Are you sure you have a human's throat and lungs?" the technician marveled. "That voice of yours, so damn loud!"

We returned to Big Glasses' apartment, where our friends were still drinking and talking. "Our hero is back," the crowd teased me. "Too bad we don't have a beautiful woman to pamper you."

"Speaking of women, Yiwu and I should go audition female cast members," Big Glasses said.

"Why don't we visit a couple more universities nearby," I added. "I'm sure we can get someone we like. But we need to agree on some rules — no one is allowed to lust after the actress during the shooting. What we are doing is serious and important."

"Dammit! I haven't touched a woman for half a year now," Hippie Poet said. "My dick is shrinking."

Early the next morning, we began working on the film in earnest. The technician went to scout for locations while Hippie Poet and I shopped around for tapes, makeup materials, and props. At noontime, the sky suddenly darkened. When we returned to Big Glasses' apartment, a power outage had left the building in total darkness. A gust of wind engulfed us, and we shuddered with cold. A bleating voice came from the end of the corridor: "What is going on here? Why are there so many people? Are you staging a peasant revolt or something?"

We paused, somewhat stunned. "Is that you, Chen Dong?" The tall and willowy figure swaggered toward us, shaking hands like a military commander greeting his subordinates. Chen Dong, a poet whom I had met in the early 1980s, was known for his brash and opportunistic personality. Two minutes into our conversation, he began his routine — bragging about his latest "achievement" in art and his prowess in bed. "I did some pencil sketches of this big girl last month and she fell head over heels in love with me," he said. "To tell you the truth, I have started to develop a strong interest in women on the plump side."

While listening to Chen Dong's blabbering, I quietly sorted through my purchases. "What are these for?" Chen Dong asked.

"We are making a movie," Hippie Poet stammered.

"What kind of movie?"

I interrupted them. "If you want to come with us, I'll tell you on the road. I have to go out for some more errands."

Baffled, Chen followed me. We dropped what I had purchased at Big Glasses' apartment and left again. Amid the loud traffic noise on the street, I ran through the plan and the script with him.

Chen Dong looked excited. "It should be easy, but the script is no damn good. You should get more inside shots, more people in action, more close-ups, more historical and international footage. Think explosion of the first atomic bomb, Chairman Mao greeting Red Guards in Tiananmen Square during the Cultural Revolution, Ayatollah Khomeini and Colonel Gaddafi delivering their fiery speeches . . . They seem unrelated or chaotic, but once we cobble them together in the editing room, they will start to make sense."

"Thanks for your suggestion, but we have already hired a director," I said. "He is a painter at the Sichuan Arts Academy. He'll also do set design. I like his artistic taste."

"Liao Yiwu, you are not much of a friend. How could you let this opportunity pass me by?" Chen Dong was furious.

"You are a painter and a poet, not a director. You don't even know how to operate a film camera."

"Why do I need to operate a film camera?" Chen Dong argued. "The technician can do the shooting and I can watch and direct him. Together, we can do a great job. Just think about it, we are a group of China's best avant-garde poets. If we can't manage a stupid film like this, who can?"

"What if I don't offer you the job?"

"I'm going to follow you wherever you go. When the shooting starts, I'm going to plant myself squarely in front of the camera so nobody can work," Chen Dong answered.

"You are desperate to be famous, aren't you?"

"Well, this is a big historical event. If we want to make history, we have to do it together." He was persistent.

"Don't be too optimistic," I said.

Then Chen Dong straightened his back, faced the passing traffic, and officially declared in his usual dramatic fashion, "With my participation, the film will become a history-changing event."

Chen Dong proved to be as good as his word, and he didn't disappoint as a director. No sooner had we sat down to work than he took out the *Requiem* manuscript to check every line against the audio recording. In places where he didn't understand the text, he would underline it with a red pen and ask me to explain. Then he listened and scrawled down his ideas for each scene. Three hours later, he wrapped up the editing, stretched his back, and then issued his first order as a director: "I think we are ready to roll."

Chen Dong distributed his instructions and ideas to everyone for input. No one was shy, and we offered additions and modifications. The technician voiced a concern: "We are short of actresses."

"Let's do the audition tonight," Hippie Poet volunteered in earnest. "We can easily find a bunch of pretty ones at college dance parties."

At lunch, I snuck into the post office, where I tried to make a long-distance call to a friend in Shenzhen but couldn't get through. So I sent a telegram, which said, "Yiwu is seriously ill and will arrive in Shenzhen on March 20 for treatment." I wrote two letters as well; one to A Xia and the other to my friend Zhong Zhong, a disabled writer and entrepreneur. After I sent them, the police intercepted both letters, and the prosecution later used them as evidence that I had attempted to escape China. In my letter to A Xia, I mentioned that "this damned motherland of mine has no place for me." This sentence was cited in my indictment.

The day went by fast. At night, we hurried over to the Sichuan Foreign Languages Institute to scout for female cast members.

Security guards stood outside the student activity center, where a weekend dance party was under way. Pretending to be young faculty members, we tried to get in without a pass, but failed. Fortunately, a group of young women who happened to be friendly with the bouncers came to our rescue. They escorted us in.

Like a panel of beauty pageant judges, we were impressed by the variety and versatility of the candidates. Director Chen Dong jumped into the fray, waltzing around with a voluptuous young woman while Hippie Poet went with a student on the petite side.

"I don't care about their weight," Big Glasses commented. "They can come in all sizes. As long as they have curvy figures and their faces have personalities."

"We need to cast those who are smart and cultured," the technician insisted, his face expressionless.

Committed to democratic principles, we decided that every crew member should be given the right to choose according to his own aesthetic standard. As a result, we gathered a large group of young women who were eager to audition for our film.

The technician stood near a building entrance and held the camera like a bazooka, targeting each young woman as if she were prey for the beast. Hippie Poet, who had just started warming up to a girl, was assigned to carry the floodlight. The rest of us served as production assistants, pulling electric cords, holding props, and carrying bags for our auditioning actresses. The director stood next to the camera like a dandy, bossing everyone around. Every now and then, he would push the technician's head away from the camera, bow his head and press his squinting eye close to the viewfinder while issuing instructions: "Hey, try to swing your body a little bit . . . cover your chest with that red silk scarf . . . walk toward the camera, slowly; don't act like you are rushing to work. Relax . . . Okay, next."

"My neck hurts," the technician groused. "Why don't you hold the camera?"

"No, no," the director refused. "I need to oversee the audition."

"Is that what a director does?" Hippie Poet said, sweating under the heat of the light. "I can be a director, too."

The colorfully dressed young women sang, posed, and cat-walked for the camera, like goldfish in a bowl. The audition carried on uninterrupted until midnight, but we still had not chosen anyone. The crew members became desperate, but Chen Dong remained calm. Like a master of bridge, he revealed his trump card. "I have invited two beautiful professional actresses to come for a meeting tomorrow morning."

"In other words, all our efforts today are for nothing," I pouted.

"It gives us something to compare them to." Chen Dong eyed me nonchalantly. "Without comparison, you wouldn't be able to appreciate it."

We all ended up crashing at the language lab with the technician for the night. At two o'clock in the morning, we heard a loud rumbling outside. "It's the sound of a spring thunder!" the director shouted. "We have just heard the first spring thunder of the year."

"It just thundered six times," the technician counted and then patted his forehead. "It's good. Like the saying goes, six and six, everything will be smooth."

The spring drizzle pattered softly against the window. The city of Chongqing was plagued with the worst acid rain problems in the country. The dirty sky reminded one of a stained diaper. Citizens' faces darkened like the gloomy weather. For two days, we shot inside without a clear focus. Even the director lost track of what we were doing. At lunch one day, he popped an unexpected question. "Yiwu, what the heck is *Requiem* about?"

"What do you mean?"

The director flung his arm to draw a big imaginary circle in the air and then poked his index finger into the heart of the circle. "There has to be a core — something to pull everything together."

"If you don't know where the core is, how did you manage to shoot in the past two days?"

"I know, everything moved ahead in a blur," the director said. "But now, I'm asking you a serious question. Is this piece written about the protest movement of June 4?"

"For myself," I answered bitterly. "There is a sharp knife poking at my heart. I had to take it out through writing. You can call this poetic therapy, if you want."

"I don't know what you are talking about," he said.

"Neither do I. Who can completely understand his or her own writing? The beginning of the poem is intended to appease the souls of those who were killed on the early morning of June 4 in Beijing," I explained. "Then, the theme changes to appease the spirits of those who died unjustly from both ancient and modern eras."

"Have you shared your thoughts with anyone else?"

"No, not really," I answered truthfully.

"Okay, there is no need. Since we are so muddleheaded, we'll just follow our creative instincts and see where it leads us."

Over the next few days, the project continued with new energy and great fanfare. Since nobody was willing to lend us a car, we had to cancel several of our shoots outside the studio. A shortage of funds also forced me to lay off three of the professional actresses. Even so, there were still a large number of idlers lingering around — thanks to Big Glasses, who had invited several poetry-loving young college students to the set. They were treated to free meals and drinks.

One night, we had to sneak into a factory affiliated with the military to shoot a scene. Fearing that a large contingent would attract attention, the technician ordered Big Glasses and me to avoid the entrance and get in by climbing over a back wall. Before my turn came, I ran over to a corner to relieve myself. Little did I know that a security camera had filmed me in the act. The absurd footage also was used against me in court.

On the first day of acting, I was blindfolded and led to the movie set by the technician. As soon as he let go of me, my body began to swing. My passion spilled forth, melting under the floodlights. The chandelier floated toward me, its five light bulbs clustered like a flower. I threw myself into the lights, the imaginary sun, and the flames jumping around me. I screamed but couldn't hear anything. I felt trapped in a cage like a canary bird, my eyes moving up and down the beams of light like a flittering insect. My thoughts tightened and broke, gushing forth with sparks as I chanted and roared.

"You are going too far," the technician reminded me several times.

"Let him do whatever he wants," the director would say. "Go ahead and go wherever your mind leads you. If you are spewing dog shit, we'll just shoot dog shit."

"What?!"

"Don't worry, keep going," the director shouted and then turned to the cameraman. "Do a close-up of those trembling hands, the twitching lips, and the foams at the corner of the mouth. He is totally out of it."

In another strange scene, the footage started with a thin paper wall. A hand poked a hole and tore the paper wall into pieces. Inside lay a stiff corpse (me) on a stretcher, tightly bound by strips of white cloth. This was the brainchild of Big Glasses and Hippie Poet, who, under the director's order, wrapped me up from head to toe. "Bear with us. The shoot will be done in ten minutes," the technician said sympathetically.

"I can't breathe and I'm going to die," I tried to yell, but with white linen covering my mouth I could only yelp like a puppy. The director ignored my pleas.

"We should do this scene inside a morgue. I'm going to see if I could steal the keys to the morgue at the Third Military Medical University," the technician beamed with inspiration.

"Excellent idea," the director said enthusiastically. I was still lying inside layers of cloth, sweating like a pig. By the time they unwrapped me, I was almost dehydrated. Ironically, the experience would turn out to be good training for prison life.

Fortunately, the technician did not get the morgue key the next day but suggested that we use the medical school's anatomy/dissecting room. "They have just opened up a body there and haven't had time to wash the platform yet. It will be perfect to put Yiwu on the platform."

I was very relieved when the shoot was over. Since the technician and the director had taken charge of editing and other postproduction tasks, I had planned to relax and recoup, but my mind was still deeply immersed in the scenes. I used the downtime to book a train ticket to Beijing so I could bring the footage to my friends there, who had promised to smuggle it out to Japan and find a distributor for me. I would then figure out a way to escape from Beijing. At the post office, I wrote A Xia another quick letter. Now that my family ties had been severed, I was prepared to live in midair from that point on.

The night before my Beijing trip, Big Glasses went shopping for food and liquor and cooked a large send-off meal for me. To enliven the atmosphere, Hippie Poet picked up a young married woman at Shapingba Street to keep us company. We filled our stomach with food before starting on the wine. The music played in the background. In the middle of our conversation, Big Glasses' wife, Xiao Min, handed me a photo album, asking me to pick a picture of her and Big Glasses, and bring it with me. I pulled one out and stuck it in my portable album, which also contained pictures that I had taken of A Xia. Her pregnancy was becoming increasingly obvious, but her looks remained that of an innocent young girl's.

Big Glasses and his wife danced to the melody under the dim light. I invited the young married woman to join me but my body was stiff as a shoulder pole and the woman felt like a bucket of water dangling from it. I was soon exhausted but pressed on with high spirits. After I stepped on her feet a couple more times, the woman stared at me in anger and then whispered to my ear in feigned tenderness, "You dance like a blacksmith."

The tunes became slower and softer, like one yawn after another. The married woman struggled to extricate herself from my arms, but I remained committed and kept my posture. In the end, she seemed to give up. She slipped her fingers under my collar and played with my neck. Was she seducing me or was she simply helpless? As I was trying to figure it out, she suddenly took advantage of my brief distractedness and slipped from my grip. She writhed away like a snake and landed her butt on Hippie Poet's knee, glancing at me in triumph. Hippie Poet, the stinky wanderer, felt greatly flattered by the woman's sudden interest and held her on his lap like a delicate dish. Jealousy overtook me.

I closed my eyes and began crooning "The Red Plums Are in Full Bloom," and at the end, where I couldn't keep up with the high notes, I howled my way through, turning a love song into the squealing of a desperate pig at a slaughterhouse. The exertion made me breathless but everyone applauded politely. I excused myself from the crowd and rushed to the bathroom to vomit. I had drunk way too much. Drinking weakened my will, and a love song easily sank me into a depression.

The party lasted until midnight, when Big Glasses decided to play the complete sound track of the *Requiem* film. We had included an audio smorgasbord of masterpieces of Chinese flute, Mozart's *Requiem Mass in D Minor*, yoga music, and recordings of the American poet Ezra Pound reading his poems. The married woman soon lost interest and suggested a game of mahjongg, but Big Glasses ignored her and, on the spur of the moment, offered to tell my fortune. I turned him down. "No, no, I never face the truth of my future."

But Big Glasses insisted. "You can break your rule for me," he pleaded and tossed six coins into the air, asking me to pick them up one by one. Based on the number of heads (yang) and tails (ying), he checked against the *I Ching*, the ancient "Book of Changes," and found a matching paragraph that described someone falling into a deep well, a portent of danger. My mind was too drenched with wine to take it seriously. I simply laughed if off. I rolled out my sleeping bag on the floor while Big Glasses and his wife, who had offered their bed to Hippie Poet and his new girlfriend, slept on the couch. Soon after the lights were out, Hippie Poet's bed rocked as if a locomotive was roaring past the house. I took a deep breath and tried to count myself to sleep — one, two, three . . . Exhaustion soon set in. Then, I was reawakened by another round of squeaking noises coming from the bed. Blood rose to my head. I rolled over, arching my body toward the window, the top of my head pressing against the wall.

Suddenly, footsteps sounded in the corridor. I instinctively sprang to my feet, jumped over Big Glasses and his wife, and stood nervously by the door, awake and alert. Someone tapped on the door.

Outside stood the director and the technician, like two undercover agents. Without allowing me to go back in and get dressed, they dragged me away in the early dawn. Several minutes later, the three of us were sitting inside the language lab of the Third Military Medical University. In the solemn spirit of mourning a tragic part of history, the technician played the *Requiem* film that he and the director had just edited. "Any place that you think we should change? Tell me now before it's too late," the director said.

"I really like it," I answered honestly, having sobered up quickly upon seeing the stark images and hearing the wails. The technician uttered a sigh of relief while the director slumped in his chair. Moving around briskly like a leopard, the technician rolled up the tape, and inserted it into a box. "Take this with you to Beijing."

It was cold outside. The director briefly waved his arm to say good-bye, before he disappeared. The technician whispered in my ear, "Good-bye, Yiwu. I'll always remember this moment."

As darkness receded, I rushed back to Big Glasses' apartment, where all the noises of mating had quieted down. I fell into a deep slumber. When I woke up, Big Glasses' wife, Xiao Min, looked down at me, smiling. She tucked some money and the train ticket into my hands. I leapt from the floor, grabbed my bag, and was ready to dash out. Hippie Poet was curled up on the corner of the bed like a pathetic beggar. "Take care," he mumbled while I clutched both hands in front of my chest in a gesture of farewell.

I stood on the crowded number 17 bus, dozing off. The passengers were looking out the back window at two police cars following the bus. Tired and distracted, I was oblivious. It never registered that the police cars outside were for me. Passengers emptied out at the terminal. I was the last one to get off. I planned to change to the number 1 bus, which would take me to the train station. Before jumping across a puddle of water, I looked at my watch — there were still forty minutes to spare before the train departed.

A misty drizzle began to fall.

Part II

THE INVESTIGATION CENTER

March 1990–June 1990

The Arrest

"LIAO YIWU!"

I vaguely heard someone calling my name as I was approaching the number 1 bus stop. Abruptly I stopped walking. Through the misty rain, I saw the hills of Chongqing, firm and voluptuous like a woman's breasts.

"Liao Yiwu!"

The words became more distinct. Three shadowy figures floated toward me. As they moved closer, the shadows turned into plainclothes policemen in raincoats. I immediately turned around, only to find another man standing behind me. A pair of handcuffs dangled from inside one of his sleeves.

I focused my eyes and thought of running away. One man grabbed my wrist and slapped the handcuffs on me but failed to get the pushpin lock to work. While he was banging away at it with his fist, I jerked my hand upward, frantically trying to push him away. Another hand came around me from behind, clamping down on my neck and choking me. My body felt like it was being covered with steel animal traps. Dizziness overcame me.

It took almost no time for the police to subdue me. They dragged me along in the mud like an eel and tossed me in the backseat of a midsize jeep. Two stereotypically muscular and grim-looking handlers sat with me, one on each side. The doors slammed shut. The two other policemen who had captured me were waving their fists outside and swearing at me through the window — one wiping blood from his nose and the other sucking on his broken index finger. Apparently, my resistance had injured and angered them. A curious crowd thronged around the car.

"How dare you resist arrest?" the big man sitting on my left screamed while twisting the sharp steel of the handcuffs into my wrist. By then, I was completely inured to pain.

A heavyset cop sitting in the front seat shouted excitedly into his radio, "Headquarters, Number One is captured! We are delivering him to Song Mountain." I realized that they were taking me to the notorious investigation center on Song Mountain Road in Chongqing's Shapingba district. The long row of police cars sped forward, lights flashing and sirens piercing the air. As always in times of stress, my mind flew quickly to literature, and my arrest reminded me of a scene from an old propaganda novel, *Red Rock,* about the underground Communist movement in the 1940s. In the story, a Kuomintang agent in Chongqing lured an underground Communist to a rendezvous. When the Communist arrived, agents tackled him from all sides. Unlike me, the Communist was fearless. He adjusted his handcuffed hands and calmly climbed into the police car. Compared to the fictional heroic martyr, I had behaved like a badly beaten dog.

The police car climbed up a hill. I took a quick glance outside and saw the entrance to the Sichuan Foreign Languages Institute where we had held the audition for my *Requiem* film. A cemetery for Communist martyrs sat not far away. Soon, we passed Zhajidong, a notorious prison where the Kuomintang had executed many Communists before their defeat in 1949. The prison had been turned into a museum to showcase the Kuomintang's brutality. The horrors of history may have been featured in that nearby museum, but the new investigation center, where I was heading, was built for those accused of crimes against the *new* China.

"Damn!" I shuddered. "My life is over."

The police car drove slowly on a narrow road that curved around a hill. Soon I could hear the pine forest moaning in the wind. The windscreen wipers swung back and forth vigorously as the spring drizzle turned into a heavy rain. We were approaching our destination — the Chongqing Municipal Public Security Bureau Investigation Center, otherwise known as the Song Mountain Investigation Center.* The reality started to sink in.

The car pulled up at the gate. I got out and held my handcuffed hands out before me. Two video cameras were thrust in my face to record my arrival. I raised my head and adjusted my posture, unconsciously knitting my eyebrows in a frown, like an entertainer annoyed that his performance had been interrupted. The police holding the cameras were not amused. One slapped me hard on the head and kicked me in the butt. "Get that look off your face." Despite the burning pain in my behind, I stood at attention and shouted, "Yes, sir!" I repeated it three times, but the officers kept yelling "Louder!" After the forth time, even though they were still dissatisfied, they switched off the camera. Then, I was shoved into an old-fashioned courtyard house, which looked improbably like a wealthy landlord's mansion in old prerevolutionary movies.

The agents shuffled around with papers in their hands, as if registering a patient at a hospital. The rain stopped briefly but then came down again with even more force. Water crawled over my face, gathering around my chin and dripping to the ground. I moved around, trying to shake off the rainwater, but a guard standing under the eaves pointed his rifle at me and ordered, "Stand still!"

A tall, elderly police officer heard the yelling and came out. He motioned to the guard to put his gun down. Like a robot, the guard saluted and left quietly. The officer beckoned for me to take shelter under the eaves. When I approached him, he examined my chafing handcuffed wrists and whispered, "Hang in there." I was surprised at the humane comment. Later I found out he was the head of the investigation center. Everyone called him "Director."

---

* In China, an investigation center, also known as "custody and repatriation center," is run by the Public Security Bureau and the Civil Affairs Department to detain and investigate those who have violated administrative rules or regulations (homeless people, thieves, or migrants without city permits) or those investigated by the court. In the 1990s, the law stipulated that a person should not be held for more than forty-five days, but authorities seldom followed the rules.

Fifteen minutes later, two officers led me into the backyard through an arched doorway with peeling paint. We entered a run-down building and traversed a long, dark corridor until we came to a stairway. The officer in front of me turned around and told me to stop. Then he walked over to show my permit to a guard, who nodded and urged me to step up. I remembered the lesson I learned at the front gate and shouted at the top of my lungs, "Sir, can I come in?"

"You bastard, how dare you shout over here?" the guard snarled and pointed his gun at me.

"Hey, shut up and say it again," the escorting officer reprimanded me but blocked the guard so he couldn't hit me. The officer said with an ingratiating smile, "Sorry, he's a newcomer and doesn't know the rules here."

Like a puppy learning to follow instructions, I repeated "May I come in?" a dozen times until the guard was satisfied with my tone and allowed me to go up to the second floor where the officer took off my handcuffs. He told me to sign and pressed my inked fingers on a stack of papers for an official copy of my prints.

After the officer left, I stood in the corridor, bewildered. Before I had time to take stock of the situation, though, five men with shaved heads in blue uniforms pounced on me from all sides. They took away my bag, my leather shoes, and my socks. As I found out later, they were Red Hairs — convicted criminals who had served out their sentences in prison and were assigned to work as assistants to public security officers. Like thuggish automatons, the Red Hairs pinned me down on the floor and tied my hands behind my back. One of them pulled at my ears while the other sat on my back with a buzzer in his hand. He tilted my head to the side and started shaving. The buzzer bulldozed a clean path on the top of my head before swiping up and down on the sides. My long, black fuzzy hair slid down my face and fell, defeated, to the floor. The job was thorough. It felt as if every single piece of my prestige and dignity had been shorn away with my hair.

After the haircut, the Red Hairs removed my clothes. First they went over every inch of my shirt and trousers to make sure nothing was hidden in the seams. Next, they turned to my body, carefully examining my mouth, my armpits and the bottom of my feet. Reflexively, I held my hands around my waist to pull up my trousers, forgetting that I was completely naked. Then, one Red Hair ordered me to crouch down like a dog with my bare bottom in the air. He poked my anus diligently with a pair of chopsticks, sending stinging sensations through my entire body. Finally, the Red Hair slapped my butt cheeks and said with an air of indifference, "Okay, all done."

That was the first time my naked body had been on full display in front of strangers. The whole process had lasted about seven or eight minutes, but it felt endless. My body trembled from both the cold wind and the utter humiliation. At the end of the strip search, one Red Hair motioned for me to sit down. I curled up in a fetal position, with my head between my knees. I was back in my mother's womb. I closed my eyes, desperately hoping that my violated body could shrink and disappear. I imagined that a young woman forced into prostitution might feel the same way on her first night with a customer.

I wanted to tell the Red Hairs that I used to be a poet, a celebrated one with a cult following, but the mere thought of it rendered me even more vulnerable. I broke down, tears streaming down my cheeks. For years afterward, I regretted that initial moment of weakness.

The check-in routine finally came to an end. My jacket, shirt, trousers, belt, and shoes had been confiscated. I held my long underwear in my hands and walked barefoot after a "Good Uncle," a civilian contract worker. We turned right at a corner. Cell 2 was a dozen steps down. We reached the door — an electric wrought-iron fence. Fresh detainees with assigned numbers, I soon learned, were referred to as "new inventory," and those who were prepared for their exit were "ready to ship."

"Cell 2, receive new inventory! Number 0-9-9!" the Good Uncle yelled, dragging out each syllable. This is how I started my new life with a new identity.

The electric fence slid open. In front of me sat two rows of cellmates with their legs crossed and their heads held high. Their shaved heads glittering under the light accentuated their sinister looks. In unison, they thundered, "Thief. Kill, kill, kill."

My scalp tingled and I nearly wet my underwear. My legs weakened and I dropped on my knees like a dog. A cellmate standing by the door waved a big iron lock at me, pretending he was going to smite my head with it. I crawled forward as fast as I could along a narrow aisle about twenty feet long and one foot wide, and stopped at a corner next to a big toilet bucket. I squatted down, my hands clutching my head. The hard concrete floor was smooth and shiny. I had never expected such a grand welcome ceremony.

A loud voice sounded from behind. "Come over here, thief."

I turned around perplexed and tried to dispel the misunderstanding. "I'm not a thief. I've never stolen anything." Everyone hooted. I found out later that all inmates at the investigation center were called "thief."

The chief of the cell clapped his hands three times and the laughter stopped abruptly. The chief's real name was Er Lukou. He was a notorious robber in Chongqing but he looked more like a scholar with his fair skin and soft hands. He had been in and out of the detention center and was well known to the officer in charge, who'd appointed him to monitor other inmates and enforce rules.

"Let the new thief order a dish," he commanded.

An inmate handed me a piece of paper that resembled a makeshift menu. I examined the items and was utterly confused. Fortunately, the bell in the corridor suddenly went off. I had a temporary reprieve. Later I would find out what the chief meant by "order a dish."

At the bell, everyone stood up. The chief remained seated but slowly lifted one foot. At this signal, a bunch of inmates clustered around him, taking his slippers off and helping him change into regular shoes. Then all the inmates lined up in front of the entrance. Each person had a fixed spot in the line based on his status in the cell. Soon, noises and heavy footsteps rang out in the corridor. The door opened and we marched out.

More than one hundred and fifty detainees from six cells converged, like dregs sinking to the bottom of a sewage pipe. Shoved and pushed from all sides, I surged forward in the human flow, around a corner and then was poured into a rectangular courtyard. Electrical wires lay plastered over the steep brick walls. Two watchtowers equipped with searchlights and machine guns perched on opposite corners.

At the piercing sound of a whistle, the inmates quickly formed six rows. A guard was posted on each end. They glanced up and down to make sure the row was straight. The whole group marched in place like revolutionary soldiers ready to leave for the battlefield — instead of holding weapons, each carried two bowls in his left hand and chop-sticks in his right. Our brisk footsteps crunched loudly in unison.

A few minutes later, the whistle blew again. The courtyard went silent. A baton-wielding officer appeared. With his hands crossed be-hind his back, he strolled up and down the human corridors and then made a gesture with his arm. Without a word spoken, the even-num-bered rows automatically turned around to face the odd numbered ones. As if according to a silent cue, the inmates squatted simultane-ously, placing the bowls in front of their feet.

Two muscular Red Hairs emerged from the kitchen with buckets of rice. They scurried back and forth along the rows, scooping rice into each bowl. The task was finished in no time. The second course was a dark, watery vegetable soup. The Red Hairs ladled it out fast. If an inmate was lucky, he might get a big lump of vegetable leaves. Luck was not on my side on that first day. I saw only two pitiful pieces of vegetable leaves floating on top of the thin black gruel in my bowl.

It also happened to be the day when meat dishes were served, but inmates had to buy it with their own allowance money. First, an of-ficer scooped up a few morsels of pork to check if they were properly cooked. Then he ordered the chiefs from each cell to hand over a list of those who had ordered meat and collect their vouchers. When a person's name was called, he would move up to receive his treat. At the end of the roll call, an officer stuck his head out from a second-floor window, asking the cook to allocate one for me. I looked up in surprise and saw that it was the director. I moved up to the front. The cook handed me half a bowl of stir-fried green peppers with a few slices of fatty pork. The special order from the director catapulted my status from the very bottom to the top. I later realized that those who could afford meat were considered first-class citizens in the cell.

After the food was distributed, the officer blew his whistle again. Inmates tackled their food like ravenous wolves, turning their faces upward and pouring the dark soup down their throats. Some ditched their chopsticks and used their hands to stuff lumps of hot rice into their mouths. When the hot food burned their tongues, they would open their mouths wide to inhale and blow on the food to cool it. The greedy eating scene stunned me. I held my bowl and observed what was happening around me. In a flash, the inmate next to me poked his dirty hands into my bowl. Before I had time to react, four slices of fatty pork had disappeared in his mouth. His sunken cheeks bulged, a blue vein protruding under his chin. Grease trickled out of the corner of his mouth.

Nothing, though, escaped the officer's sharp eyes. He strode over and grabbed the thief by the collar. The poor, cadaverous inmate dangled in midair for a few seconds before plopping down on the ground. "You bastard!" the officer shouted and slapped the thief repeatedly across the face. The inmate's body swung violently back and forth with each slap. Tidbits of pork flew out of his mouth and some landed in my bowl. Soon, his mouth was covered with blood and saliva. Even so, he was still chewing vigorously, trying to swallow what he had stolen.

The infuriated officer stepped on the reprehensible inmate's bowls until they were crushed out of shape. Then he blew his whistle abruptly, declaring that lunch was over. By then, most had devoured what had been delivered to them. A few slow eaters crammed chunks of rice into their mouths, stretching their necks like crowing roosters to help swallow. Before most of us could even begin to digest, dish-washing was next on the agenda. A line formed in front of the sinks.

An inmate who was thin as a monkey sprinted over to the waste-bucket, where the kitchen staff had just dumped some hogwash. His hands fumbled around inside and dug out a handful of slop, which he stuffed in his mouth. Soon, his face was smeared with the thin brownish substance. The officer came up behind him and smacked him with a stick. The hungry monkey jumped up and wiggled his way into the crowd like a worm. While the officer was trying to stop him, another inmate stepped forward and dove into the waste bucket with both hands. The officer shook his head in disgust. He covered his nose and walked out. My stomach was churning. I clenched my teeth to suppress waves of nausea and glanced at the sky to distract myself. The clouds were dissipating and the sun stepped out hesitantly.

Lunch break was over. Once again, I was swept up in the torrent of inmates and sloshed back to my cell. My cellmates' hostility had evaporated. Seeing that I was under the special care of the director, the chief abandoned his plan to rough me up. Instead, he had me sit next to a fellow in his seventies who also had special connections. The chief and his six assistants sat opposite me, neatly dressed, almost like respectable gentlemen. A narrow path in the middle of the room divided them from the rest of the crowd. After we were all seated, the chief and his cabinet members began their postmeal snacks. The rest of us watched while they munched on meat, slurped soup made from pickled vegetables mixed in hot water, and ate a few slices of fruits they had hoarded. Then the chief ordered me to come closer to him. With the solemn look of a judge, he asked my name, age, place of birth, level of education, and the alleged counterrevolutionary activities I had perpetrated. Once I had satisfied his curiosity, he asked an assistant to issue me a printed copy of *Guidelines for Detainees* and demanded that I commit the whole text to memory in two days. With that, he declared the proceedings adjourned. I looked around, stunned: I had been offered a task that at least involved reading, and been spared, at least for now, the full traditional initiation ceremony.

Accomplices

As I languished at the investigation center, the police closed in on my friends and supposed accomplices Big Glasses and Hippie Poet.

Soon after I left Big Glasses' apartment the morning of my arrest, he had gotten up and dragged Hippie Poet along to his job at the movie theater. The two of them, hungover and chain-smoking cigarettes, crossed the street and approached the theater. Several well-dressed undercover agents were waiting for them at the top of the stairs. The police politely shook hands and exchanged pleasantries with my friends, but quickly stunned them by suggesting they be escorted to the police car.

Meanwhile, Big Glasses' wife, Xiao Min, had dropped by the apartment on a short break from work at a nearby department store. Dismayed at the apartment's disarray from the previous night, she opened the door to air out the smoke and rolled up her sleeves to give the place a thorough cleaning. Unexpectedly, a friend showed up at the door. Xiao Min invited him in and they had barely sat down when they heard a loud commotion outside the building.

Sensing that something was wrong, Xiao Min reacted quickly. She scooped up a pile of audio and video tapes from a rack under their hi-fi set, including an audio recording of "Massacre," and stuffed them into the friend's pockets and bag. She and the friend left the apartment. The police were already approaching along the narrow corridor. Xiao Min and the friend nervously turned sideways to make way. Fortunately, the police didn't recognize them. Moments later, they broke into Big Glasses' apartment and ransacked the place.

Like a lucky fish that had escaped the fishermen's net, Xiao Min ran to the post office, where she sent a telegram to alert A Xia about my arrest with a coded message saying "Yiwu is dying of an illness."

Upon receiving the telegram, my wife knew that I was in political trouble. She ran over to an old friend, seeking his advice, but he was equally unsure of what to do. A Xia decided to act on her own. Before police arrived at our apartment, she burned the letters that could have been used as evidence against me and secretly transferred a small bag of my manuscripts, including the original *Requiem* draft, to another friend's house. Within hours, police detained A Xia and confiscated the rest of my writings and personal possessions including books, paintings, a camera, tape recorders, and all of my remaining cash. The night after police raided my apartment, looters arrived.

A Xia was detained for forty days. Upon coming home after her release, she faced a bare room, and did not know if the police or robbers had emptied it.

On the day of my arrest, Xiao Min also raced over to the language lab at the Military Medical University, where we had shot *Requiem*, and ran up the stairs to the fifth floor looking for Chen Dong and the technician, who had stayed lodged in a studio. Chen Dong was bending over a sink in the bathroom brushing his teeth. "Something terrible has happened," Xiao Min informed him, but she had barely finished speaking when undercover agents began banging on the door. She darted into the ladies' room across the hall and witnessed the arrest of Chen Dong and the technician through a crack in the door.

After they were taken away, Xiao Min watched from an upstairs window. My two friends stood in front of the police car, each carrying a stack of *Requiem* videotapes, which the police had found at the lab. Chen Dong had his long hair down like a woman, toothpaste foam still in the corners of his mouth.

Long after the police had gone, Xiao Min remained paralyzed with fear. She sat in front of the empty language lab building, her knees shaking. She couldn't figure out how the police had managed to find out where everyone was. None of our friends knew that she was three months pregnant at the time. Fortunately, in one fleeting moment, God's invisible hand had shielded her and the unborn baby from danger.

While Xiao Min was fortunate and evaded capture, the police arrested my friend Zhong a week later. It was late at night and he was home writing a novel. When he stepped out for a quick bathroom break—most houses did not have indoor plumbing—he noticed shadows moving outside his yard. "What the hell are you doing there?" he barked. Suddenly, beams of flash lights shot at him and Zhong soon felt a gun pressed against his waist. A squad of ten armed officers had been sent to apprehend a writer who was a victim of polio. Inside Zhong's house, police turned everything upside down. His valuable and exquisitely packaged books were trampled and littered on the floor. The head of the police squad even barged into Zhong's bedroom and tried to take his wife's lingerie. She told him off, calling him a pig.

Most of the crackdown on my friends took place in Chongqing, but the authorities also spread their tentacles to other cities in Sichuan, detaining and questioning those who were either my friends or who had distributed my "Massacre" tape. Understandably, the breadth of the investigation caused jitters among writers and poets around the country.

Shi Guanghua, a contemporary poet, was a widely revered figure in China's literary community. His open support of my poems also aroused police suspicion. Before undercover agents came to get him, Shi was attending a public poetry critique hosted by *Star* magazine in Leshan Mountain, not far from the place where the famed giant statue of Buddha sits. More than two hundred aspiring poets filled a hotel conference room to hear his lectures. The students were eager and the sessions intense. Each day, lively discussions continued late into the night. Little did the impassioned crowd know, however, that plainclothes policemen loitered in the hallway, waiting to snatch Shi without arousing any notice. Finally, an opportunity came. When Shi sauntered out of the room for some fresh air, they swooped. The poet, known for his eloquence and quick wit, was rendered speechless. He got into a brief scuffle and lost his slippers as he was dragged away.

The hotel's reception hall sat almost empty. A clerk lay dozing off to the soothing sound of the Yangtze River nearby. Nobody was aware that the star of the seminar had been abducted. He walked down the stairs barefoot, his hair unkempt and his face smeared with dirt. The police placed a newspaper over his handcuffs to cover them.

As the agents wiped their sweaty brows and smiled triumphantly at each other, an unexpected interloper headed their way. An eminent poetry critic, who had returned from an evening of drinking with friends, greeted Shi. Intoxicated, the poetry critic slurred, "Ah, you still have guests at this late hour!"

Shi didn't answer, and his steely looking captors pressed his head down. The critic was startled. As he turned sideways against the wall to let Shi and his "guests" pass, Shi suddenly raised his elbow, hitting the critic on the chest. The newspapers covering Shi's hands flew off and the glittering handcuffs were on full display.

Thinking that his friend was being kidnapped, the critic awoke from his drunkenness and started yelling for help. All of a sudden, doors flung open and people poured out into the corridor as fast as the vomit from a drunkard's mouth. The police found themselves surrounded by an angry crowd. A poet who worked for the army had a gun, and made it clear he was ready to use it on the agents.

The two sides pushed and shoved, and the confrontation escalated. When an official with the Sichuan Writers' Association showed up to mediate, the undercover agent flashed the arrest warrant falsely claiming that Shi had been implicated in a case involving the distribution of pornography. A teenage girl at the conference, however, was outraged at the false charge, so she seized her hero's leg and wouldn't let go. The drama continued for nearly an hour, until after midnight. In the end, after relentless efforts by the seminar organizers, the crowd grudgingly cleared a path and allowed the police to leave with Shi. They swarmed around him like he was a movie star, trying to shake his hand and bid him farewell. Shi was detained for a month for interrogation by police in his district. Fortunately, he was released after investigators found no evidence that he was directly involved in my case.

In the eyes of the police, every poet that had befriended me in the past was a suspect, even though none was what people would call a "dissident" or "democracy fighter." Even now, I don't know how many people were rounded up for questioning and how many of their manuscripts and books were taken. With their broad, senseless apprehension of poets and writers along with their countless volumes of work, the Public Security Bureau destroyed a vibrant underground literary community in Sichuan.

The "Menu"

AT THE INVESTIGATION CENTER, I gradually figured out the rigid hierarchical system. In many ways, it was modern slavery. A path in the middle of the room divided the upper- and underclasses. In the upper-class section, the chief was the king. Beneath him were his cabinet members, who were either the chief's friends or tough street thugs who passed in and out of jail. They possessed considerable clout and unscrupulously exploited and abused the underclass. The chief appointed two enforcers who carried out his orders and conducted initiation ceremonies. He also had a "housekeeper" who kept the underclass in line, making sure that people he supervised could satisfy the whims of the chief and the upper class.

While all inmates at the investigation center addressed each other as "thieves," those in the lower ranks were "slave thieves," who serviced and conducted all the menial jobs for the upper class. There were many different kinds of "slave thieves."

For example, every morning, "towel thieves" would fetch warm water and toothbrushes for the upper class and get clean towels ready for them. Following each meal, they washed dishes and chopsticks for the upper class, storing them in a separate place for reasons of hygiene.

"Entertainment thieves," also known as prison pop stars, were feminine, good-looking young men who would sing, dance and perform comedy skits for the upper class. When necessary, they would sleep with their leaders to satisfy their sexual needs.

"Hot water thieves" supplied cups of hot drinking water to the upper class several times a day and provided massages every night.

"Laundry thieves" washed clothes for the upper class and crushed fleas in their bedding.

"Floor thieves" swept the floor multiple times a day and took care of the upper class's shoes, making sure they were polished and placed in their proper place when their owners needed to step out.

"Toilet thieves" emptied the toilet bucket into an outside latrine twice a day. In addition, they had to stand, two at time, in front of the toilet bucket to form a human screen, giving privacy to the chief and his friends when they relieved themselves. When someone had problems sitting on the bucket, the toilet thieves would hoist the person over the bucket and let him use their shoulders.

Between these opposing classes sat the middle class, or idlers. In my cell, the middle class consisted of an elderly man and me because the two of us had been singled out by public security officers for protection. The elderly man was a wealthy antiques dealer and had been accused of selling ancient artifacts to foreigners. He was said to have deep connections with several top officials at the Public Security Bureau. Both of us were spared the initiation ceremony and enjoyed the same status as the enforcers and housekeepers. We could bring our meals back to the cell and eat at our own pace. However, as part of the bargain, we had to stay neutral in any disputes.

In my cell, which was no bigger than two hundred and twenty square feet for eighteen men, the rulers had created an exact replica of the state bureaucracy outside. The leaders' powers were clearly delineated. Leaders and cellmates alike carefully observed the rules and moved cautiously within the hierarchy. If someone accidentally strayed from the path, he risked losing everything. Those in power enjoyed unlimited privileges; the hierarchy even governed the usage of toilet paper, much as in outside society: The chief could use scented napkins to wipe his butt, but slave thieves had to resort to using wrapping paper or old newspapers.

When the chief was in a chatty mood, he would compare our cell to the political system in the country. "Considering how well I manage our cell, ruling the country would be no problem for me," he boasted. "It's more or less the same." When I expressed my skepticism, he balled up his right fist, rubbing it against the palm of his left hand. "You think I only know how to rule with this iron fist? I'm more than that. Let me give you an example. The senior leaders of our cell are like members of the Politburo and the Central Military Commission. People beneath us are the commoners of this nation. The senior leaders can eat what they want and do whatever they like. If we want to maintain the status quo, we need to prevent any internal division. We'll crack down on anyone who tries to stage an uprising. On the other hand, we can't be too harsh. We need to let people beneath us feel that we are like their parents."

"I think you are mistaken," I said. "Chairman Mao used to say that people are the parents of the party, not the other way around."

"That's goddamned nonsense! If a thief here wishes to have a nice, filling meal, it's up to me to decide. Do you see this cigarette in my hand? I can give it away as an incentive to anyone I want. By the way, the rewards system involves lots of strategies. Should I reward my slave with a whole cigarette, half of it, or just the cigarette butt? My thinking is to give away the cigarette butt first. Then, if the slave accomplishes a good deed, reward him with another cigarette butt. You have to start with something small. Otherwise, it's hard to manage people's expectations. Remember, you should always give people hope, something better to look forward to."

"You have built your theory of governing around a cigarette butt. That's pretty deep," I said sarcastically. "I think you should be the premier of China."

"Too bad I wasn't born into the family of a senior party official. Otherwise, things would have been different." The chief sighed.

At nap time on the first day, the enforcer allocated me a spot on the floor and handed me an old comforter that had so many holes it resembled a fisherman's net. The senior leadership retreated to the side, waiting for the slave thieves to make their beds for them. The slaves pulled the dazzling white sheets out, carefully searching for specks of dirt. When the leaders lay down, the enforcers and the housekeeper rolled out their bedding in the corner opposite the door. When it was my turn, I stretched out in my spot fully clothed, covering my head with the fishnet comforter. Suddenly, someone kicked my bottom. I poked my head out.

"Sleep with your clothes off," the chief towered over me and yelled.

"I . . . I'm not used to sleeping naked," I stammered, protesting mildly.

"That's the rule," the chief's number two explained.

"You stinky intellectual," the chief said derisively. "All the thieves have to go naked. You are no exception."

I was at a loss for what to do.

"Hey, hurry up. If you refuse an order, you can go get all sweaty with those folks," the chief threatened, indicating the underclass. From a glance, I saw that the seven senior leaders' bedding took up two-fifths of the cell. The middle class enjoyed comparatively spacious spots. Ten slave thieves were packed closely in two rows. Two people shared a quilt, their heads at opposite ends and their backs against each other, one inmate's rear end close up against the back of his mate's knees. Even so, the enforcers still complained that the thieves were not squeezed in tightly enough, and used a carpenter's tape measure to make sure each inmate stayed within his allotted space. Occasionally, if a person strayed over the border, he would get kicked in the head.

I began to remove my coat and undershirt.

"What about your trousers?" the chief asked.

"I don't have any underwear on," I lied.

The chief insisted on checking but I held my trousers and wouldn't let him. Exasperated by my refusal, he tossed me a booklet. "Read this menu," he said. "If you disobey me, you'll have to order a dish from the menu and we'll cook it for you."

The handwritten booklet was called *Song Mountain's One Hundred and Eight Rare Herbs.* I perused a couple of pages and mumbled with confusion, "How do you manage to get these delicacies in prison? It's not possible." I could hear snickering among the slave thieves. The chief was about to explode with anger when the door clanked open. "Liao Yiwu," a voice called from the outside — an officer came to summon me for interrogation.

Unfortunately, the authorities confiscated the "menu" during a prison inspection. The following "menu items" are based on what I remember, and I hope that someday, when the history of the prison system is written, other people will add to this testimony.

SONG MOUNTAIN'S ONE HUNDRED AND EIGHT RARE DELICACIES

◇◇◇◇◇◇◇◇◇◇◇◇

Homemade Dishes

PIG ELBOWS BRAISED IN HERBS
Also known as "getting off to a flying Red start." The enforcer jabs the inmate's back with an elbow repeatedly until it is covered with bruises. The dish is typically served during a newbie's initiation ceremony.

SAUTÉED BEAR PAW WITH TOFU
The enforcer slaps the inmate's chest repeatedly with open hands.

TOFU FRIED ON BOTH SIDES
Two enforcers punch the inmate on the chest and back. The sustained blows sometimes cause the inmate to go into shock. While I was at Song Mountain, several people died from this torture.

THROAT LOZENGES
The enforcer strikes the inmate's Adam's apple with the side of his hand. The victim can't swallow for days, or in serious cases loses his voice for weeks.

STEWED PIG'S NOSE
The enforcer squeezes the inmate's lips between chopsticks until they swell up.

BARBECUED PIG'S CHIN
The enforcer delivers a blow to the unsuspecting inmate's chin from below, crushing his teeth together.

STEWED OX NOSE

The enforcer rams two fingers up the inmate's nose until it bleeds.

FRESHLY GROUND TOFU WITH CHERRIES (LARGE PORTION)

The enforcer jabs the inmate's scalp with a chopstick, raising pearl-size purple bumps. Then, he rubs the bruises until they are bloody. A few days later, when the ring of bruises becomes infected, the enforcer squeezes out the pus. After the bruises heal, a permanent ring of red bumps remains on the victim's head.

FRESHLY GROUND TOFU (SMALL PORTION)

The enforcer pokes the inmate's gums until they bleed. A few days after the torture, the victim's teeth loosen and sometimes fall out. In addition to losing the ability to chew, the torture causes chronic pain and bleeding.

GRILLED BACKBONE

The enforcer dips a cotton ball in oil and rubs it on the inmate's backbone. Placing the cotton ball at the base of the spine, he sets it on fire, sending sparks climbing all the way up to the base of the inmate's neck.

SAW-CUT PORK

The enforcer soaks a thick rope in oil, ties it around the inmate's calf, and pulls it back and forth until it cuts the flesh like a saw.

SHISH KEBAB IN PEPPERCORN SAUCE

The enforcer wedges oil-soaked cotton balls between the inmate's toes and sets them on fire.

PIG TROTTER SOUP

The enforcer uses a thin stick to prod an inmate's ankle like he's stirring a pig's foot in a big soup pot.

BOILED SOFT-SHELL TURTLE

The enforcer forces the inmate to dip his butt in a bucket of hot water.

SICHUAN-STYLE SMOKED DUCK

The enforcer burns the inmate's pubic hair, pulls back his foreskin and blackens the head of the penis with fire.

GRILLED PORK CHOPS

Ten inmates stand facing each other in two rows. The victim walks in between them while they repeatedly punch him in the ribs.

DRAINED KIMCHI

The inmate is forced to extract human feces from the toilet bucket.

TWICE-COOKED PORK ON AN IRON PLATTER

The enforcer stabs the inmate's back with bamboo sticks and spreads salt on the puncture wounds. He covers the wounded areas with adhesive bandages. Once the bleeding stops, the bandages are ripped off, leaving the flesh on the inmate's back looking like cooked meat.

MAPO TOFU

The enforcer sticks a dozen peppercorns in the inmate's anus and stops him from pulling them out, even if he complains of swelling and pain.

TURTLE SHELL AND PORK SKIN SOUP

The enforcer smacks the inmate's knee caps until they are bruised and swollen like turtle shells. Walking is impossible.

NOODLES IN A CLEAR BROTH

Strings of toilet papers are soaked in a bowl of urine, and the inmate is forced to eat the toilet paper and drink the urine.

House Specialties

TWO MANDARIN DUCKS PLAYING IN WATER

Two inmates are forced to play with each other's genitals. The person who ejaculates first is declared a loser and punished.

FLOWERS DANGLING FROM CHILDREN'S MOUTHS

The enforcer inserts a chopstick or a blade of grass into a person's anus, and forces the victim to bend over and try to take it out with his lips.

AN ESTRANGED COUPLE

Two inmates are roped together back to back. At the enforcer's order, they are forced to grab each other's penis with their hands and pull it without seeing it.

FALLING ON A DOG'S BACK DURING AN EARTHQUAKE

The inmate is told to crouch under the ventilation window. An enforcer climbs up and hangs from the window bars. Then, he lets go, falling on top of the victim. I know of several inmates who died from their injuries, or suffered severe damage to their vertebrae, from this "dish."

RIDING A MOTORCYCLE

The inmate bends his knees and raises his arms, as if he is riding a motorcycle. He must remain motionless for at least half an hour or face more punishment.

SITTING AT A TEAHOUSE

The inmate sits on a chair with his legs crossed. When the chair is taken away, he must continue "sitting," and smile even if his legs tremble.

HUNGRY DOGS SNATCHING FOOD

The enforcer places a peanut or a pea on the floor. The inmate must dash forward like a dog and pick up the bait with his mouth, without using his hands. Many inmates ended up with facial bruises, bloody noses, and broken teeth.

FREE-RANGE DOG JUMPING AT TREATS

The inmate lies on the floor until being ordered to jump up for food tossed in the air.

WATCHING GOLDFISH IN A BOWL

The enforcer plunges the inmate's head into the toilet bucket.

FLYING AN AIRPLANE

Four inmates toss the victim in the air and let him land without catching him. This often led to head and back injuries.

INTERROGATING THE WIFE

The enforcer places an inmate's fingers in between four chopsticks and squeezes. This is a re-creation of a scene from the movie by the same name.

MONKS STRIKING THE BELL

Two inmates hold a toilet bucket aloft while four others hoist the victim horizontally in the air and thrust his head against the bucket. The sound his head makes was the chief's favorite sound. Every time the punishment was imposed someone usually passed out.

NAKED SCULPTURE

The inmate stands stark naked on top of the toilet bucket and strikes different poses ordered by the chief.

SONG MOUNTAIN RABBIT WRAPPED
WITH SILKY STRINGS

In one variation, the enforcer ties string tightly around the inmate's arms or legs, cutting off circulation until the victim experiences pricking pain, burning, and shivering cold and numb limbs. If the enforcer lets the torture go on too long, it causes permanent damage. In another version of the punishment, the enforcer wraps the inmate's penis with string, causing urinary infections, incontinence, or impotence.

THE TURTLE'S HEAD

The enforcer inserts a peppercorn into an inmate's foreskin and then ties it up.

DROWNING THE PIG

The enforcer force-feeds an inmate cold water until he vomits.

HUMAN SPITTOON

The chief spits or flicks cigarette ashes into a kneeling inmate's open mouth.

Interrogations

FIVE HOURS AFTER MY arrival, I was summoned for interrogation. Still reeling from my introduction to the cell, I stepped outside and glided through the corridor in a daze. Near the staircase, I recognized the plainclothes policemen who had arrested me. One of them patted me on the shoulder. "You look drunk. They certainly wasted no time wining and dining you," he said sarcastically. "Congratulations! You seem to be doing well in there."

"You should count yourself lucky to have run into compassionate people like us," said another agent. "You resisted arrest. For this alone, you deserve a couple of dishes from the Song Mountain menu. They haven't served you any because we specifically told the chief not to do it yet. So behave yourself and cooperate. If you talk, you can leave here early. It will make everyone's job easier."

I nodded and followed them obediently. We descended the stairs and scrabbled around in the dimly lit corridor. Unlike the second floor, where the big detention cells were located, all the rooms on the first floor were small interrogation offices. The chief interrogator couldn't decide which one to take. He opened door after door, and each time, blinding sunlight poured out toward me like cascades of water. We paced up and down and eventually took a room at the end of the corridor. When I walked in, a stink of mold assaulted my nostrils. Several long, narrow skylights hovered above us like elusive passages to heaven.

I leaned against a wall solemnly. An assistant politely asked me to sit down. When I asked for a chair, the stern-faced interrogator simply pointed at the floor. I had no alternative but to squat. Soon, my legs tired and I slumped to the floor.

I was asked to provide my name, age, and place of birth before the interrogator read the list of accusations against me — slandering Communist leaders in my writings, attacking the party's decision to crack down on the rioters in Tiananmen Square in my film, and collaborating with foreign spies to undermine the rule of the party. Each time my eyes drifted, my interrogator yelled, "Look up at me!" When I failed to answer a question, he glared. I could tell he was trying to project an air of importance. Unfortunately for him, he was thin as a monkey and nearsighted as a mouse. He had to rely on his big desk and electric baton to maintain the grandiose illusion that he was part of the dictatorship of the proletariat. I patiently answered questions relating to every accusation, but the interrogator claimed I was lying. I protested with silence.

Between questions, I looked up at the skylights and put my head between my knees. The monkey lost his cool and towered over me, yelling and swearing. Then, as we were approaching the end of the session, his tone suddenly softened. "Liao Yiwu, let's make a gentleman's agreement." He moved closer to me and I could see the sweat on his face. "If you spill the beans about why you made the film *Requiem* and who was behind it, I promise that I'll have you released tomorrow."

"Really?" I said, feigning the desperate look of a collaborator. "All right! I'm going to put in overtime working on my confession. But, before I do that, can you help me get a refund for my train ticket to Beijing? Can you also send a telegram to my friend Old Ma in Beijing telling him that I have decided to postpone my trip for two days?"

"No problem. I'll ask my staff to take care of it," the interrogator answered happily. With a sly look, he asked, "By the way, who is Old Ma?"

"He is the son of our senior leader Ma Bufang," I responded with a tone of reverence.

"Ma Bufang? That name sounds familiar . . . Why are you meeting him in Beijing?"

"He works for a newspaper called *Chinese Culture*. He's very well-connected," I said, continuing to pretend innocence. "I want to see if he will use his connections to broadcast my film *Requiem* on national TV."

It suddenly dawned on the monkey that I was playing a joke on him. Ma Bufang was a well-known Chinese warlord at the beginning of the twentieth century.

"You *liar!*" The monkey banged his fist on the desk and stood up. "Liao Yiwu, we represent the people. We are not to be screwed around with. You'll be sorry if you do. Be honest and 'fess up everything to the party, including your relations with Michael Day and that Taiwanese rock singer Hou Dejian. Tell us what they intended to do when they joined the students in Tiananmen Square in the last days of the counterrevolutionary riot."

While Michael Day was my friend, I did not even know Hou Dejian. I liked his folk songs and had seen him on television, but that was the extent of our relationship. Knowing it was futile to explain, though, I simply acted surprised and stared at the interrogator in silence. In fact, I wasn't sure who was doing the better acting job, me or the interrogator, who had come up with an elaborate theory that I was somehow connected to the nation's best-known dissidents.

The interrogator pounded on the desk again. "Why is he taking it so personally?" I thought. Involuntarily, I started cackling with laughter, which further exasperated the interrogator. He walked over and waved his fist at me. I could smell his bad breath. The whole room had become a big filthy mouth. I cowered inside, hidden under its wriggling tongue to dodge its sharp teeth.

Once again, I turned my eyes toward the skylight. The sun was receding and the big universe was about to close for the day. My rear end felt icy cold. The newspapers I was sitting on were moist to the touch and had stained my trousers with ink. I ignored the chief interrogator's barking and struggled to stand up. When I wiped my nose and pulled at my trousers which were stuck to me, the interrogator's assistant looked at me with disgust.

Soon, the interrogator's shouting attracted attention. The director walked in and politely gestured for me to be seated on the floor. "Is there anything bothering you?" He leaned over and asked with concern. "You can tell me."

"Could you send another interrogator who is less agitated?" I said bluntly. The interrogator's face turned as purple as a pig's liver.

By the time I returned to the cell from my first interrogation session, it was past midnight. I trod carefully around the swamp of human flesh, avoiding my fellow inmates as if they were land mines. I found the tiny spot that was reserved for me, collapsed into the fishnet comforter and instantly fell into a deep sleep.

Before dawn, an unbearable itch on my back and legs woke me up. I removed my shirt and trousers, and discovered swaths of red bruises caused by hordes of lice. As a young boy, I had stayed with my grandpa in the countryside where lice, fleas, and other bugs were endemic, and I had learned how to kill them. The skill came in handy. A few minutes later, there were bloody carcasses everywhere and stains on my fingers and shirt.

As I was basking in my victory over the lice army, a hand gripped my shoulder — the antiques dealer sleeping next to me got up to use the toilet. He sat uncomfortably on the bucket. Every few seconds, he arched his back and then straightened it out. His brow glistened under the glow of the twenty-four-hour ceiling light.

Crickets chirped from outside, and waves of cold air sent shudders down my spine. I covered my nose to sneeze, and my body twitched. The surviving bugs started attacking again. The itch seemed to have seeped into my veins. No matter how vigorously I scratched, there was no relief. I felt the urge to rip off my skin. Fortunately, fatigue soon took over and I dozed. In the half-awake, half-asleep state, I saw the antiques dealer sitting on the toilet bucket, grimacing. Soon, the toilet bowl gradually rose from the floor to the sky. The old man was still constipated. The stars crunched under his feet like gravel. The night sky turned into a piece of badly scratched skin, twisty and curly . . .

Veteran inmates said new detainees typically suffered from constipation because the body was in shock. Fortunately for me, constipation, which caused severe abdominal pain, plagued me for only one week. However, stress from the interrogations caused ulcers in my mouth and took away my appetite. Depressed, I decided to go on a hunger strike.

My refusal to eat caused quite a stir. On the first day, people gaped at me strangely, as if I were an alien. At lunch, they took my bowls and laid them out outside the door to show the officers that I had not taken a single bite. When I declined dinner, the chief and other senior leaders, under instructions from the officer in charge, took turns persuading me to jettison my plan. When I persisted, they threatened me. In the end, the director came to get me himself. I strode into his office like a fearless Communist martyr and squatted on the floor. He patted me on my shoulder and pointed at a couch. "Sit over there. You and I are equal in spirit," he said and took off his cap, revealing a head of gray hair. "I have a daughter who is a university student," he continued. "She was also involved in the protest movement in Tiananmen Square. So I do have a little understanding of intellectuals like you."

I listened, but kept my head bowed.

"No matter what crimes they are charging you with, you need to take care of yourself. I don't have the right to release you. It's beyond my power. My job here is to ensure that detainees are held according to the law, stay alive, and do not create problems during their incarceration. If you were one of those regulars, my deputies would have handled your hunger strike differently. They would get several cellmates to pry open your mouth and feed you."

"Well, feel free to do whatever you see fit," I was determined to carry on with my strike, but my voice wavered a little.

"Don't worry. I'm not going to do that to you," the director assured me. "If you continue with your hunger strike, all I have to do is report you to my supervisor. It doesn't hurt me a bit. You are the one who will suffer. But you are still young and you have a future in front of you. Try to stay healthy and get out of here early."

"I've had the same advice from my interrogators," I said with cynicism. "They told me that if I follow their advice and confess, they will let me out in no time."

The director leaned closer to me and whispered, "You should speak the truth. Confess what you have done, but don't drag others into your mess."

His words surprised me because the other officers always asked for more names, trying to get me to implicate as many people as possible. The director stepped out and brought back a big bowl of steamed rice with vegetables on top. "Can I tell you something?" he said. "Don't believe what you have read in the propaganda books about defiant Communists staging collective hunger strikes or secretly sewing Communist flags in the Kuomintang prisons in the 1940s. They are pure fiction dreamed up to deceive kids."

He handed me the bowl. "Here, help yourself. I've added some lard and MSG. It tastes really good."

Just like that, the director sabotaged my hunger strike. The personal attention he showered me with boosted my prestige. Huang, the chief's number two, and Shi, the number three, gave me the thumbs-up sign and began playing up to me. We actually became friends. Since both were illiterate, I became their designated letter writer. The chief still nursed a grudge against me for undermining his authority when I refused his order to sleep naked. He also thought a newbie like me had gotten off too easily for staging a hunger strike. Whenever possible, he picked on me. One day, he ordered me to recite the *Guidelines for Detainees*. I refused. "The public security officers are the ones who should memorize it and follow the rules," I explained. "I'm a detainee. Why do I need to memorize them?"

The chief was speechless. "Are you staging a coup against me?" he roared.

The enforcers stepped up and twisted my arms behind my back. I scowled and screamed with pain, "Dammit, if any of your bastards dare touch me, I'm going to claim I am injured, and use that as an excuse to skip interrogation. For every punch I receive, I will get one day off."

The enforcers hesitated. As they were figuring out what to do next, I struggled free and lunged toward the chief. His lackeys subdued me and yelled for help. The officer in charge, Wen, heard the commotion and came into the cell. The chief accused me of refusing to memorize the guidelines and attempting to start a fight.

"I don't have enough space in my brain," I defended myself. "The interrogator has requested that I focus on my case."

Officer Wen fastened his angry eyes on me for a few seconds and then shook his head with resignation. "Chicanery seems to be your specialty. Okay, we'll extend the deadline and give you a couple of more days. But I want you to know that you have to memorize the guidelines."

Before the officer left the cell, a new interrogator came in to summon me. A short, stocky man, he spoke with a strong Fuling accent and introduced himself as Wu. He was the fourth one assigned to me over the past few days. Like a businessman eager to make a deal, he gave me a bear hug. "We grew up in the same city," he said, handing me a small bag of Fuling-made pickled vegetables. "Here is something to remember your hometown. We specifically bought this for you."

"I'm not from Fuling," I corrected him.

"Your wife is from there, isn't she?" Wu said. "Here is a letter from her. As long as you 'fess up to everything honestly, we can request a transfer on your behalf. We can even release you on bail so you can reunite with your family."

I took the letter from Wu's hand and immediately recognized A Xia's squiggles. "With our current situation, it's better that we go our separate ways," she wrote.

Wu noticed my distraction. Taking on the intimate tone of a relative, he asked, "Are you ready to talk?"

"What do you want me to talk about?"

"I want us to have a fresh start," Wu said.

"I don't know where to start."

"You don't have to follow a chronological line," Wu's assistant interjected. "I can follow along and jot down everything you say. I know poets tend to talk in a stream of consciousness. Say whatever you want, as long as it's related to your case."

"I really don't have much more to say. It looks like my wife wants to end our marriage. I guess I should plan on spending the rest of my life in a monastery."

"Once we have cleared up your case, you'll be free. You can go wherever you want," Wu reassured me.

"How do you clear up this life of mine? I've had enough of this world. Maybe you should join the monastery with me."

"Let's be serious and get down to business," Wu said, trying to put on a forced smile.

During the interrogation, I couldn't pull my mind away from A

Xia's message and sank into a deep funk. Several times, Wu left his chair and came over, reminding me to focus. When I blabbered away incoherently, the smile that had masked his face disappeared. "We are not interested in your bullshit," he warned. "Based on China's criminal law, you cannot refuse to answer questions from public security officers."

"If that's the case, please convict me according to the law."

Back in my cell, I read and reread A Xia's letter, which was obviously written under tremendous mental distress. What had happened to her? I wondered. At that time, I had no idea that she had also been detained because of me.

The dinner bell rang. Like a robot, I walked over to receive my food — rice with a thin layer of my favorite twice-cooked pork and green peppers. My eyes fixed on a white hair attached to a slice of pork. The food was getting cold in my bowl. I poked my chopsticks at the pork but had no appetite. A cart carrying a black-and-white TV was wheeled past our door. Number 2 stomped his feet. "Fuck, when is it our turn to watch TV?"

A drop of blood dripped onto the pork in my bowl; my nose was bleeding. Springing to my feet, I searched for something to wipe my nose. "Are you going on another hunger strike?" the chief asked scornfully.

I ignored him and stepped over a row of shaved heads, giving my untouched food to the toilet thief who was squatting by the corner. He was a migrant worker from Fujian and had been caught working without a proper city residency permit. In the few days I'd been in the cell, I had already seen the chief bully him mercilessly. The toilet thief was flustered by this unexpected kindness. He paused for a few seconds to make sure I was sincere and then snatched the bowl. The chopsticks clicked and the twice-cooked pork disappeared into his mouth.

What happened next was like a scene from a kung fu flick. An enforcer raised his leg and kicked the bowl in the air. Before I could react, the bowl landed on the concrete floor, bouncing up and down. Rice scattered all over. I heard the unwitting toilet thief choking.

"You must be the reincarnation of a pig," the chief chastised the toilet thief. "Do you want some more? Let's offer you a dish from our official menu. What about a plate of stewed pig nose?"

Half a dozen inmates pitched in to help with the "serving." I was shoved to the side. The toilet thief knelt, trembling like a duck with its wings chopped off. His upper and lower lips were tightly pinched between a pair of chopsticks.

"Start," the chief ordered.

The enforcer pressed hard on the chopsticks. The victim's lips were squeezed out, blooming like a bright red flower over his face. Amid the thief's moans, the chief smirked and turned to me with a look of triumph. "In prison, sympathy is a crime. Since you didn't taste the dishes from our menu, let him eat them for you."

He turned from me and issued another order: "Prepare for the second entree — a small portion of freshly ground tofu."

I stood there helplessly. But soon, an idea hit me. "You win," I said, pretending to back down. Slowly, I moved a few steps away from the chief. Then, I threw myself at the wrought-iron fence and shouted to a guard in the corridor, "Help!" All the inmates ran back to their spots and sat up straight with their legs crossed.

Within seconds, the torture chamber became a meditation studio. To my disappointment, it was Officer Wen who unlocked the door and let me out. Before he had time to ask, I reported to him what had happened. Wen looked straight ahead and said nothing. After we reached his office, he motioned me to squat against a wall in the hallway. He then pulled a chair out into the hallway and sat down, his legs splayed out in front of him.

"Now, tell me again what you just said."

Three other officers were playing cards in the office. As I was recounting the torture in my cell, Wen listened halfheartedly.

I waited. "Please go on, I'm listening," Officer Wen egged me on. But soon he became distracted again.

"Are you going to do something about it?" I couldn't help raising my voice, like a traitor who was ready to part ways with his master.

"What do you expect me to do?" Officer Wen shot me a glance impatiently. Before long, he wheeled his chair back into the office and joined the card game.

I was enraged by his indifference. My blood pressure rose. Like a child, I imagined myself turning into a warrior and hacking him into pieces with a machete the size of a crescent moon. But I had no idea how long I had to stay inside this brutal zoo. I had to find a way to survive, even though it would mean losing my dignity. After all, my asshole had already been poked with chopsticks. What else did I have to lose?

Like a dog, I squatted in wrathful silence. I was barely able to stay awake. An hour had passed and Officer Wen finally emerged from his office.

"Can I tell you something? Don't stick your nose into matters that don't concern you. It won't do you any good," he advised. "In a cell, there have to be rules. Without rules, nothing can be accomplished. I bet all prisons operate the same way, even under the Nationalist government, or the Qing Dynasty before that. Western countries also employ prisoners to manage their fellow prisoners — don't you think?"

"I have a copy of the menu. Don't you think the tortures are excessive?" I asked Officer Wen.

"Thieves have different ways of doing things. Now that you are one of them, stop whining about how badly people are treating you. Isn't it true that you are in jail because of your own excessive behavior? Everyone needs to know what fear is."

While delivering his lecture, Officer Wen took off his policeman's cap several times to brush off any specks of dust. With his neatly pressed uniform, he looked suave and sophisticated. However, his outward scholarly facade masked a wicked nature. He could probably kill a person while smiling, like those aristocratic military officers serving under Adolf Hitler. They were moved to tears by the music of Chopin and Mozart but had no compunction about exterminating Jews in the gas chambers. "Do you like music?" I couldn't help asking. Confusion came over Officer Wen's face. He replied, "Of course I do."

"Remember, don't mess around in other people's business," he said as he walked me back to the cell. "Now that people have seen that I have kept you outside and chatted with you for such a long time, they'll start to treat you differently."

Officer Wen was right. When I entered the cell, everyone was watching a TV that had been brought into the cell while I was out. All the senior leaders rose to offer their seat to me. Number 2 pointed at the TV and said, "We have to thank Officer Wen for this." He gave his spot to me and I sat next to the chief, who nodded at me as a sign of conciliation. The images on the black-and-white screen were grainy, but people did not seem to mind. "There is nothing there," I muttered.

The chief treated my mumbling like the holy uttering of an emperor. He yelled at his subordinates, "The counterrevolutionary said he can't see anything! Adjust the antenna!"

Two inmates stood erect behind the TV. One of them held the antenna with both hands, like the flag bearer leading the honor guards in Tiananmen Square. The other positioned himself solemnly next to the flag bearer, clutching a long cord. Number 2 clicked all the buttons, turning from channel to channel impatiently. Finally he directed the "flag bearer" to tilt the antenna to the left, to the right, a little more to the right and to the northeast. The TV acted like a capricious woman, occasionally revealing herself as the signal came in clearly, and then as everyone started cheering, she resumed her normal evasive self, and static took over the screen.

Infuriated, Number 2 kicked the TV cart hard. Miraculously, pictures appeared, but lasted only three seconds. In the end, the chief stood up and grasped the tip of the antenna. The picture became clear instantly, except for a black strip at the top of the screen, which was fluttering like the tail of a comet.

"No wonder people on the street used to call you a master pickpocket," Number 2 complimented the chief. "You are so smart." Then he shouted at the antenna holder, "Did you see how the chief does it?"

During the evening, the antenna changed hands three times. At ten o'clock, the whistle blared in the hallway, announcing bedtime. Someone had already made my bed. I had been elevated to the status of a senior leader. Later, when all was quiet, the leaders huddled near the corner, furtively drinking bootlegged liquor. Each time the chief took a sip, he would let it swill around in his mouth for a few seconds, so he could enjoy the full taste. After he swallowed it, he would hold his breath as long as he could to prevent the evaporating alcohol from escaping his body. It was fun to watch. One leader invited me to join them. I took a big sip and the chief frowned. It was hard to believe that a few days into my detention, I was sitting side by side with the big shots.

Song Mountain had a high turnover rate. Admissions and releases occurred daily. The high turnover sustained an underground postal system. Letters or messages could be delivered to family and friends by soon-to-be released inmates. Contract workers who cleaned the hallway sometimes smuggled bootlegged goods like cigarettes and booze into the cell. Many police officers turned a blind eye or were just careless. Crackdowns never stopped us from sending letters or obtaining things we wanted.

During my time at the investigation center, I had many letters delivered to friends with the help of the chief and his senior leadership. They would tuck my letters in their pockets and chat up the hallway workers through the wrought-iron bars, asking them to make the delivery. Many times we were caught and punished, but several of my letters found their way out successfully. In one of the contraband letters, I asked Yang, a literary critic friend, to warn people who had worked on *Requiem* not to admit guilt if they were summoned by police. After I was released, Yang told me over dinner that he had never done so out of fear, and this had added to the troubles of a number of my friends.

To reciprocate for small favors in prison, I provided my secretarial services to the leaders whenever they needed anything. As time went by, I became friends with Number 2 and Number 3, and they bared their hearts to me. Life at the cell became relatively tolerable.

The Confucian Policeman

AFTER INTERROGATOR WU GAVE up on me, a new one was assigned. His name was Qin, and he had white teeth and a dark, coarse complexion. He claimed to have years of experience battling criminal thugs on the street, a history that probably explained his overconfidence and warped, overactive imagination. At times, I even felt he was more of a poet than I. He approached my case like a third-rate detective-story writer, using his theory about my work to construct details of my crimes and deduce my intent. When I related facts that contradicted his version, Qin would attack like a hunting dog, shredding my story to pieces. Any attempt to correct him with the truth only fueled his suspicion.

"Think hard," Qin urged me one day. "Tell me the first time you got together with your friends and decided to make a film. Do you remember a person sitting next to you, scribbling in a notebook with a pen? Who was that person? During the gathering, you got up twice, once to use the bathroom and the other time to retrieve a copy of your poem."

"You sound like you were actually there with me," I said.

"No, but your friends shared this detail in their confessions and they all mentioned a plan that you hatched at the gathering. Be honest and tell us about it. Cooperation will earn you leniency."

I had no idea what he was talking about, but I lowered my head and pretended to consider his question.

A few minutes later, Qin barked at me, "Do you remember it now?"

I shook my head, and grinned like an imbecile.

Qin paced up and down the room, balling up his right fist and holding it against his chin. "On the second night of the Chinese New Year holiday, five people sat around a heating stove inside your living room. Your friend Big Glasses was the first one to propose that you make a film commemorating the 1989 counterrevolutionary riot in Beijing. He suggested you take advantage of the technician's connections as well as the recording studio in his language lab at the Third Military Medical University.

"Everyone would help raise money. Even though the film's name and theme had not been decided at that meeting, the nature of the project was clear. It would be a sequel to 'Massacre.' Your poetry was the unifying element in this big counterrevolutionary scheme. However, I doubt you and your friends did all of this alone. Who was manipulating things behind the scenes? Did anybody from outside your circle get involved? So far, all of your friends have blamed it on you, but it wouldn't be fair to you if I held you responsible for everything."

"Ah, I see." My face glowed with feigned enlightenment. "Based on your theory, I was merely a puppet. There was someone else who controlled everything. Is that correct?"

Qin was caught off guard by my sarcasm. He interrupted me: "Did you know that Michael Day was a foreign spy?"

"I have said this many times and I will say it again: he is not a spy."

"You are naive about him. You were blinded by your relentless pursuit of fame and provided lots of cultural intelligence to Michael Day. You gave him many of your illegally published poems and underground magazines. You introduced him to underground poets. You fell deeper and deeper in his trap, and even collaborated with him in recording the 'Massacre' poem. As a reward for all your work, he sent you nine hundred yuan and encouraged you to make the *Requiem* film," Qin recounted smugly, taking satisfaction in his eloquent recitation of the details of the "plot."

"He sent me money to pay for food he ate at my house," I protested. "He had visited me twice and lived with me for quite a while without pitching in a dime. He loves China and has spent eight years studying Chinese."

"He loves China? A Canadian spy loves China? What a joke!"

"His feelings for China are beyond your comprehension," I explained.

"I'm sure he loves you as well," Qin said cynically. "His love has led you astray and sent you all the way to jail. Do you need me to provide some evidence of his treachery?" Qin started to read off remarks that Michael Day had made to friends criticizing the Chinese government's crackdown on the student protesters.

"Those comments are taken out of context," I explained. "They merely reflect his views on the events of 1989, not on our country. He is not hostile to China. Like me, he doesn't agree with the way the government handled the protest movement. Even Premier Zhao Ziyang openly challenged the party's decision. If the premier was entitled to his view, why weren't Michael Day and I allowed?"

Qin pointed his finger at me. "Stop the nonsense. Your crimes were perpetrated *after* the party central committee had correctly defined the nature of the protest movement as a counterrevolutionary riot. Your action was driven by your past indifference to the Communist ideology. According to experts, in the 1980s, when Western bourgeois liberalism was rampant in China, you were a leading figure and published many political poems that attacked our party's rule. So, the 'Massacre' and 'Requiem' poems are the inevitable result of your past thinking."

It was futile to argue back. I simply stared straight at him. Soon, repeated interrogations like these cut into my brain like a blunt knife, damaging my central nervous system.

At one session, Qin tried to extract a confession about the true intent of the *Requiem* film. "On the morning of March 9, you and the film director had a brief conversation about the theme of the film. Do you remember that? You told the director that you wrote *Requiem* to commemorate the mobs who died on June 4, 1989, and appease their souls."

"That's not true," I defended myself. "In my film, *requiem* was a generic term. I meant to appease the souls of all the world's dead, both in modern and ancient times."

"Including the mobs who died in Beijing," Qin tried to put words in my mouth.

"You have no artistic sensibility. It's pointless to talk to you about my work," I retorted.

"I don't lack the ability to appreciate art. I understand your work perfectly well. Through your poems and film, you evoke sympathy for the mobs in Tiananmen Square. Following your conversation, the director went ahead and carried out your instructions for the film," Qin continued.

"My instructions? Then who instructed me?" I asked, alluding to my interrogator's claim of a broader plot.

"We'll find out. We have plenty of time. Why did you take such risks making that film? What was the purpose of your Beijing trip? Did you want to escape China?"

I had already responded to these questions many times and was too tired to answer.

Sometimes, the questions relating to my poems were pure tragicomedy. Literary critics used to dismiss some of my earlier poems as obscure material only good for bringing on headaches. Public security officers like Qin thought otherwise. They formed a study group to read my works. They became my most devoted readers, trying to decipher hidden antigovernment messages. Even after I was released, they would show up like packs of wolves with contrived smiles to snatch the fresh fruits of my labor, without even giving me a receipt or a "thank you."

Late one night, Qin tried to trick me again by putting words in my mouth.

"Let's have a chat. Everything we say will be off the record," he promised. "I've been studying your latest poems for the past several days. To tell you the truth, I'm becoming a big fan of yours. I personally think 'Requiem' is more interesting and subtle than 'Massacre.' Poems with subtle messages carry more weight. For example, in 'Requiem,' you wrote, 'A certain person possesses the soul of the Han Chinese. Immolating himself in a heavenly fire, he hovers, far removed from the people.' Many people in our bureau believe that you were talking about

Chairman Mao, but I think that you meant Deng Xiaoping. Is my interpretation correct?"

"I'm the only one who is entitled to interpret my poems," I declared. "I want to go to bed."

"No, you don't. I know all poets are night owls." Qin looked benevolent. "Have some snacks and you'll be in the mood to talk about another poem."

Qin interrogated me for over a month. The endless sessions took a heavy toll, gradually eating away my hair, which, before my arrest, was thick and lush, like a lion's. I noticed patches of baldness on the top of my shaved head.

Every now and then, when Qin was in a good mood, he would allow the guard to bring me copies of Chinese classics such as *Romance of the Three Kingdoms* and *Outlaws of the Marsh*. In addition to getting a confession, Qin had something else he wanted from me.

One morning, at interrogation time, a guard told me that the session would take place at the director's office rather than in one of the usual dark, dank rooms on the first floor. Standing in front of the director's door, I shouted, "Sir, may I come in?" Nobody answered. An officer came up behind me, ordering me to walk up and down the corridor three times. I saw a camera aimed at me like a machine gun through a transom window. I was baffled but did what I was told.

When I was let into the office, Qin sat stiffly behind a desk. He was all smiles, like a kind father. Following our normal routine, I squatted down in a corner like a dog. Qin jumped up and came over, pulling me up by my arms and gently steering me to the couch. I blushed like a shy teenager on his first date and sat awkwardly on the edge with gratitude. "Relax," he said with sympathy. "We are not interrogating you today." Then he started chatting with me about my life and family. How long had I been married? Did I have a child? How many books had I published? I answered them scrupulously. We whiled away half an hour on this bullshit. The sun moved up from the bottom to the top of the window frame. During our conversation, a cameraman kept interrupting us. "Your face is too dark, move this way," or, "There is too much sunlight on your face, tilt your head."

At one point, Qin sat by the window. The sunlight cut across him, bathing one of his legs in bright light and leaving the other one in the shade. Out of nowhere, I blurted out a question, asking Qin if he had arthritis.

Qin was surprised, but confirmed that he did suffer from the illness and his knee hurt when it rained. "I don't think it's arthritis. It's bone cancer," I said, grinning. I didn't know why but I couldn't stop laughing. I knew I was complicating his project — whatever it was. Mindful of the camera, Qin suppressed his anger. He bent over me, raised his face slightly toward the camera, and flung his arm out dramatically, like a figure in a Sichuan opera.

"Liao Yiwu, do you think you are worthy of your parents?" he crooned in a high-pitched voice.

I recoiled at his sudden change of posture and tone. Qin repeated his high-pitched rhetorical question several times. His waved his hands dramatically, his left hand slicing the air and his right hand pointing at my nose. "Are you worthy of your parents?" I sat there, stunned and speechless. Qin's emotionally charged performance went on for several minutes. Then the cameraman put down his machine and walked over to whisper in his ear, "We are good." Qin stopped reluctantly, like an actor who had been deeply immersed in his role.

Later on, I realized that I had played the supporting role in a documentary that portrayed Qin as a tough but fatherly official. Not long after the documentary was aired on television, Qin was promoted. His successful handling of my case was cited. His reputation soared. Nicknamed among his colleagues as a "Confucian policeman," he eventually moved up to a senior position at the Chongqing Municipal Public Security Bureau.

The series of interrogations ended right after Labor Day, which in China falls on May 1. One day, during our political study session, I came across a speech in the party newspaper by Jiang Zemin, the general secretary of the Communist Party.

> *A small group of our comrades spoke some wrong words or acted inappropriately without learning the truth of the Tiananmen protest movement. As long as they have realized their mistakes and learned their lessons, we should welcome them. For those who still haven't turned around in their thinking, we will continue to help them enthusiastically and wait patiently. . . .*

Mistakenly, I saw the party's time-honored carrot-and-stick trick as my chance for freedom. So I wrote Officer Qin a letter, in which I quoted the words of Vladimir Lenin: "When young people commit a mistake, even God will forgive them." Upon receiving my letter, Qin agreed to meet with me one on one, and during our conversation he encouraged me to work hard and reform my thinking without giving me any definitive answer. His ambiguity gave me some false hopes that the government would follow what Jiang had stated in his speech — forgive my transgressions and end my misery soon. After all, the law stated clearly that if a person wasn't placed under official arrest after forty-five days of detention, he would have to be released.

I began counting the days. Number 2 teased me for being naive, even though he himself harbored a similar hope. Number 2 was charged with rape, murder, abduction, and burglary, but he clung to the hope that his death penalty could be commuted if he cooperated with the investigation and confessed his crimes. I helped him write several pre-execution notes to his family, and we became close friends. Sometimes he called me "Counterrevolutionary" as a term of endearment.

Fantasies of Escape

AT THE DETENTION CENTER, the most popular topic of conversation —besides women and sex—was escape. One day, Number 2 asked if I was willing to try to escape if the opportunity presented itself. I told him I had thought about it many times, even in my dreams, where I flew over the tall walls or squeezed through a crack in the floor. While dreaming, I kicked and flailed my arms, leaving my neighbor, the elderly antiques dealer, with bruises.

"We are together day and night," I said with a hint of exasperation. "How would we get the chance?"

"If you try, there are opportunities," he reassured me.

Maybe he was right, I thought. "During our break yesterday," I told him, "I sneaked into the latrine to take a dump. It was right after the inmates emptied out their toilet buckets and the stench almost killed me. I stayed to check out the surroundings. The one vent on the wall is sealed with thick iron bars. The only hope lies in the pitch-dark holes on the ground where the shit goes. Those holes are connected to a large pit outside."

"Did you jump in?"

"I almost did," I admitted. "I squatted and stared into it so long and hard that it seemed my eyeballs would fall in. I forgot all about the stench. Human feces has never seemed so appealing. But, as I was struggling with the decision, I lost that window of opportunity. I think as long as you know how to navigate through the shit pit, you'll be able to get out that way. All you need is to hold your breath for three or four minutes."

"Thank heavens you didn't take the plunge," Number 2 smirked. "Someone successfully escaped that way once. Afterward, the authorities installed barbed wire underneath."

"Dammit. I'm dead meat then." I was quite upset.

"Don't worry, Counterrevolutionary. We'll find another way or we can cooperate in our next life," he winked at me. We looked each other in the eye, reaching a silent agreement.

The bathhouse was located opposite the latrine on the first floor. Usually, we were allowed to take a hot bath once every ten days. After dinner one day, all my cellmates were ordered to sit upright in our spots. The chief held a brand new towel, a new pair of slippers and a new bar of Lux soap, and stood quietly by the door. He was waiting for orders from "King Father" — the officer who was in charge of our cell. It was the chief's job to accompany the officer to the bathhouse.

Under usual circumstances, the officer would take his bath first and then we could use the leftover hot water in the boiler. The towel and the soap would be thrown out after just one use. Like a eunuch at an imperial court, the chief would rub the officer's back, cut his fingernails and toenails, and keep him entertained with gossip and jokes. "You can't imagine the hard work," the chief would whine afterward. "Even though my body was soaking in the warm water, I wouldn't dare wash myself. By the time King Father was done, I was all sweaty and my mouth was dry and thirsty. Dammit, he treated me a like a male whore in a Finnish bathhouse, except he didn't fuck me, thank God for that."

The chief sometimes took out the humiliation he suffered at the hands of King Father on an effeminate young man known as "Singer." The chief demanded Singer treat him as if he were King Father. He even went one step further — raping the young man after the bath and bragging about his sexual prowess.

The inmates' showers were in two rooms, a small outer one that we used, and an interior one behind it with showers that didn't work. There was a cloth curtain dividing the two. There wasn't enough room for everyone in the outer room, so inmates awaiting their turn had to huddle stark naked in the changing room. Members of the upper class went in first, the enforcers and the housekeeper second, the middle class third, and then the underclass. When Number 2 came out from his shower, I asked him to stand by and keep an eye out. Number 2 immediately caught on to what I wanted him to do.

He lined up everyone in the changing room and put me at the back of the queue. After a little while, the shower room was steamed up, and I was able to sneak into the inner room without arousing any attention. A lone ventilation window was positioned high up on the wall. I groped my way to the window. In the dusk, I could see a cliff outside, so steep that it looked like it had been carved with an axe. In the distance, the guards inside the watchtower looked like tiny nails.

The window bars were rusty. If one person stood on another's shoulders, he could easily pry them off. Once we got out, we would have to tiptoe for thirty feet, with our bodies pressed to the side of the cliff. Then we could jump over a low wall and enter the polytechnic school next door.

My heart beat wildly, as if I had found a slim chance of survival under the chin of a tiger that was about to attack me. I crawled back along the floor, brushing the floor with my leg, hunting for something hard or sharp to use on the bars. There was nothing available. I tried turning the switch on the showerheads one by one. Unexpectedly, the third handle came loose. By then, sweat oozed from the palms of my hands. I struggled to move the handle. A loud noise from inside the empty pipe scared me, echoing through my head. As I was struggling with the handle, Number 2 coughed loudly. I left grudgingly.

Back in the cell, I reported my spectacular discovery about the ventilation window to Number 2. We were both excited. Our faces flashed like two drunkards. Luckily the light in the cell was dim, or our comrades would have wondered what was up. Number 2 rubbed his hands and whispered, "You and I are tied together in life and death. If we succeed, I will make you my blood brother."

"There is really no need," I said humbly. "Once we are out, you and I will go our separate ways."

"No. The police know my hangouts like the palms of their hands. I have nowhere to go. I have to follow you," he said seriously.

"I don't have any connections and I don't even know where I'm going," I protested.

"Don't you dare get rid of me," Number 2 grinned maliciously. "I'm familiar with your background. A big counterrevolutionary like you always gets protection wherever you go."

"Wherever you go, you steal and kill," I replied. "If I allow you to follow me, I'll end up with a death penalty too."

"I promise that I will only steal from people, not kill them, and I won't steal from ordinary folks," he swore solemnly. "You are my guiding light, like Chairman Mao. I might be illiterate and stupid, but I can be a good bodyguard. I'll risk my worthless life to help you escape to Taiwan."

I don't know how he had gotten the idea that I wanted to escape to Taiwan.

In the following weeks, we were obsessed with plotting our escape. One day after dusk, Number 2 came back from an interrogation and told me excitedly, "Hey, Counterrevolutionary, I just helped police crack a big robbery-and-murder case. I gave out several names of key people involved. Since the party's policy has always been 'leniency for those who confess,' the interrogator has promised to commute my death sentence."

"You've been charged with one murder and two armed robberies. Each single one carries the death penalty. If he spares you in one, you still have two more."

"You don't understand," Number 2 lectured me. "The government is looking for a positive example to showcase the success of the 'Leniency for Those Who Confess' campaign. I'm sure they will keep their word."

I found it hard to carry on the conversation without letting him down. So I grabbed a book and retreated to a corner, but could not concentrate. During the break the next day, I stayed alone, gazing at the hazy mountain in the distance. Number 2 crept up on me. He paused for a few minutes and said, "Just to let you know, the interrogator asked me about you but I didn't tell them anything."

"There isn't much worth telling."

"I know you despise people like me. You probably don't know that I also participated in the student protest movement. I mingled with students and delivered water to them. In the end, the students kicked me out."

My heart warmed to him.

"You and I won't be able to get out of here by ourselves," he said in a low voice.

"But at least we can try."

"I've thought about it for several nights," he continued, his voice hoarse. "You know, you are right, Counterrevolutionary, my crimes are very serious. I don't want to implicate you."

After his previous shows of bravado, I was surprised at the defeat in Number 2's voice. He was not wrong about his fate, however; several days later, Number 2 was officially arrested. It was quite a scene. Twenty antiriot police were called for the occasion. The corridor was crowded with people. The cell door flung open and special agents burst in. Number 2 shouted at them, "Don't rush me!" He hunkered down on the floor, meticulously sorting a big pile of high-quality clothes that he had stolen or usurped from other inmates, and packing them into two suitcases. An agent soon became impatient and urged him to act fast: "You are not going to be around long. What do you need them for?'

Number 2 roared back, "None of your fucking business."

I stepped forward to help him pack and he silently accepted it. In return for my kindness, he gave me a pair of socks as a parting gift. It struck me that this heinous criminal would be gone forever, and waves of sadness washed over me. On his behalf, I had written several affectionate and sentimental farewell letters to his younger brother, who was imprisoned at a reeducation camp.

As Number 2 had confided in me, he and his brother had grown up as homeless orphans. In the big, cold world, their aunt was the only one who provided them some measure of care and parental love. Despite his dire circumstances, Number 2 took good care of his brother. Before his execution, he left him all of his possessions. As his trial dragged through the long, cold winter, I was told that Number 2 wore only a shirt and a pair of summer trousers. Even when he fell ill, he refused to touch the winter clothing that he had bequeathed his brother.

Confess and Report on Others

IN CHINA, POLITICAL CAMPAIGNS are the fuel that keeps the totalitarian machine running. It worked the same way in prison. At the Song Mountain Investigation Center, authorities rolled out at least two political campaigns per year — "Confess Your Own Crimes and Report on Others" and "Crack Down on Prison Bullies" were two that I remember from my time there.

For the first campaign, the authorities forced detainees to extract confessions from each other. When the campaign was launched, all the detainees were herded into the courtyard, where we dutifully sat on the ground with our legs crossed and our backs straight. Fully armed police enclosed the area as if they were guarding a war zone. Officials from the Public Security Bureau, the prosecutor's office, the court, and the provincial justice department sat side by side behind a makeshift podium. In order of their rank, they stood up one after the other to deliver their speeches.

The senior bureaucrats dabbled in abstract ideas and low-ranking ones focused on the details. Banners and posters with stirring messages hung all around us. We pumped our right fists and shouted slogans. When we filed back into our cell, the officer in charge presided over a discussion, encouraging inmates to confess and report on each other while the chief distributed paper and pens. For the next three days, silence reigned as everyone hunched over their confessions. Since the campaign aimed at regular criminals, the chief showed no particular interest in what I wrote. So I simply jotted down what I had already said during my interrogations. When we finished, the officer in charge read them and summoned the chief to impart secret instructions on helping authorities make breakthroughs with key targets.

The results of the campaign directly affected the officer's promotion and bonus. With tacit approval from the officer, the chief roughed up inmates thought to be withholding useful information or who had failed to inform on their fellow detainees. The same routine was repeated in every cell. Loud screaming rang out all over the center.

In my cell, the chief acted like a Supreme Court judge, perusing each written confession. He ordered the enforcer to cook up "dishes" for those whose reports didn't meet his requirements. One inmate, who had been the trade union chairman at a large military enterprise in Chongqing, was detained on suspicion of embezzling public funds. He was tough and stubborn by nature. No matter how hard the interrogators tried, they could not squeeze anything out of him.

In the end, authorities assigned the chief to break him. Since I refused to take notes for him, the chief assumed the role of both interrogator and secretary. For a whole morning, he ordered multiple "dishes" for the trade union chairman, but he got nowhere. After lunch, the chief became desperate and grabbed the chairman by the hair, dipping his head into the toilet bucket. The chairman's body went limp, slipping from the chief's grasp, and his head plummeted back into the bucket.

The irate chief commanded the enforcer to pull the chairman out and clean him with cold water before ordering "Ride the Motorcycle" from the menu — the chairman was forced to bend his knees slightly and hold his arms out in front of him as if he were holding the handlebars of a motorcycle. He held that position for more than half an hour but remained defiant. For the rest of the day, the chairman was reduced to the status of a whore, abused and trampled at the whim of the chief.

In the afternoon, a member of the upper class requested entertainment and asked the chairman to make a song out of a popular ditty in a liquor commercial:

> A fairy descends on earth
> Dragging me to share a stage and sing along
> I raise a glass to her and she raises a glass to me
> We sing and drink, red clouds flow on our cheeks.

To the amusement of the chief, the chairman came up with a tune immediately and began singing, his big mouth opening wide and his right hand tapping rhythmically on his hip.

"Pay attention to your facial expression," a senior leader barked at the chairman. "This is a song about liquor. You should look happy. The more you sing and drink, the happier you are."

The chairman didn't disappoint. He winked at the senior leader flirtatiously and forced a halfhearted smile. Following his crooning the whole cell burst into a chorus with the chairman conducting. The chief and his friends were delighted and applauded in approval.

"Who knew that we have a composer in our cell?" the chief complimented him. "Liao Yiwu is a poet. You two should collaborate. Life in our cell would be very entertaining."

As a reward for his good work, the chief brought out a packet of sugar-coated peanuts and beckoned at the chairman, "Mr. Composer, come claim your bonus."

The chairman bowed and stepped forward. "On your knees," the chief commanded while taking off his slippers to slap the chairman's face with them, back and forth, left and right. Amazingly, the chairman hardly winced.

"This bastard is a fucking robot," the chief said and the frustration was visible on his face. "Hey, let's take off his trousers and see if his body is made of flesh or steel."

One enforcer stripped the chairman, and pried open his anus while the other one shoved in peanuts with a pair of chopsticks. With each poking, the chairman's body would thrust forward. His mouth was open but no sound came out of it.

By the time all the peanuts had been crammed into his anus, the chairman's face was drenched with sweat. He crawled forward and reached out both hands, trying to grab the chief's legs. Startled, the chief stomped his feet on the chairman's claws, snarling, "This bastard must be a faggot."

One of the chief's friends bent over the chairman. "I don't think he is hitting on you. It looks like he wants to say something."

We all looked down. The chairman raised his head, two lines of tears streamed down from his swollen eyes. "I'll confess," he murmured.

Based on his confession, the chairman was officially arrested. When he left, he had three broken ribs and his body was covered with bruises. He also coughed blood incessantly due to possible injuries to his internal organs. We were told later that he recanted his statement during his trial, claiming that he was coerced. Since there were too many holes in the witnesses' accounts, the court was not able to convict him. His case dragged on for two years. In 1993, the Sichuan Provincial People's Intermediate Court sentenced him to death despite the scant evidence. The verdict shocked his lawyer, who petitioned the Provincial Supreme Court for a retrial. The chairman's death sentence was upheld. The doctor who shared the story with me at the investigation center said regretfully: "The government has spent thousands of yuan on medicine to treat his injuries. It's a shame that we are sending him to another world when he is just getting better."

The Song Mountain Investigation Center had a reputation for breaking hardened criminals. When an unruly suspect became too tough to control, authorities in the region would send the person to the center, where inmates did the job of the authorities, torturing the hell out of him.

Deaths from inmate beatings were common. I was imprisoned when the "Confess Your Own Crimes and Report on Others" campaign had just started to gather momentum. A week later, news came that a similar campaign at a detention center in downtown Chongqing had caused the deaths of several inmates. Worried about the possibility of scandals, the authorities called a halt to the campaign. Before we had time to adjust, the pendulum swung and a different campaign was launched in its place. Slogans that encouraged inmates to come clean about their crimes were scrubbed off and new ones were painted in their place about cracking down on jailhouse bullies.

Once again, a public meeting was held in the courtyard, and the same group of bureaucrats came to promote the new campaign in their speeches. This one was quite different: the chiefs from several cells had been singled out as bullies. They stood in front of the crowd with their hands cuffed behind their backs.

After the meeting, the bullies were paraded around, their feet shackled with chains weighing nearly twenty pounds. Each bully was led by a guard holding a rope looped around his neck. Another guard drove the bullies from behind with a bamboo pole. Like a cattle dealer, the guards would yell and beat anyone who moved too slowly. The heavy metal chains scraped on the floor and the deafening clanking sound lingered in the corridor. At my cell, the chief and members of the upper class were spared because the officer in charge protected them. When the parade started, they thronged around the wrought-iron fence door to watch. "Guys at Cell Eight overcooked the dishes and almost killed a thief," our chief explained. "As a result, the whole upper class is in trouble."

Two hours later, the bullies were still making the rounds. Every shackled step became a struggle, but the guards wouldn't allow them to stop and rest, and prod them on with the bamboo poles. At the entrance to each cell, they took turns shouting a prepared statement: "My name is [so and so]. I have been punished by the government for bullying my fellow inmates. I deserve the punishment. Please don't follow my example."

It was a poignant performance. Some choked up in midsentence. Others delivered it with heart-wrenching eloquence. Their ankles were bleeding. One person tripped and fell. He covered his head with both hands to fend off a thrashing and refused to get up. A guard dragged him off to be prodded with an electric baton. Then another prisoner fell. In the end, there were only two left. They kowtowed in front of their guard, "Please have mercy," they begged. "We can no longer move."

The campaign ended a week later. The director made an announcement over the loudspeakers. "The antibully campaign has achieved tremendous success." He emphasized that authorities would continue to encourage inmates to confess and report on others while cracking down on jailhouse bullies. The two initiatives, he said, were like interlocking waterwheels that "drive everyday life at the investigation center."

In the next few months, I became acquainted with a former enforcer named Cui, who was temporarily transferred to my cell after he had killed a fellow inmate during the "Confess Your Own Crimes and Report on Others" campaign. He was eventually given the death penalty. The day his verdict came down, he grabbed my hands like a drowning man clutching at a straw. "I killed someone and I deserve to die, but the officer in charge is the real criminal. He pressured me to extract a confession from the inmate. Without the approval of our officer in charge, who would have dared touch anyone?"

"How did the officer pressure you?" I asked.

"First, he gave us a target list," said Cui. "One of our targets was pretty tough. We ordered dishes from the menu and forced him to confess. But several dishes later, he still wouldn't talk. The officer in charge stood outside, his face all gloomy. He tapped his feet on the floor. When the chief heard the signal of impatience, he became nervous. He turned around and yelled at me to enhance the 'flavor' of each dish. I did and that was how I killed the guy. In every cell, the enforcer is always the scapegoat. If you are successful in coercing the target to give out new information, the officer in charge is awarded with a big bonus. The chief may also receive favors. The enforcers end up with nothing. But if something goes wrong, we are the first in line to take the blame."

I promised to write an appeal letter for Cui and hand it over to Officer Li, a short man in his forties, who was responsible for collecting and processing appeals. Cui and I met him in his office, where I jotted down Cui's statement and put it into the appeal format. "Hurry up," Li urged me while checking his watch. "I have to pick up my kid. It's already past six o'clock and I'm going to be late."

"Can I give the letter to you tomorrow?" I wiped the sweat from my forehead and asked. "I still have three pages to go."

"It's not like you are writing a novel. Just write it clearly. That will be enough," he said impatiently.

"But this is a matter of life and death," I argued.

"Bullshit! You have helped more than twenty people with their appeals. Have you ever saved anyone's life?" Li scolded me with unusual candor. "The Provincial Supreme Court has assigned a committee to review his case. They are discussing it next door."

"If they reach a decision before they even see the appeal, then what's the point of my doing this?" I was fuming.

"This is called 'going through every legal procedure.' I just need an appeal letter in his file to show that we have completed every necessary step."

The color faded from Cui's face. The next day, he and two other enforcers were hog-tied and sent away.

Killing Time

MANY PROMINENT POLITICAL PRISONERS enjoyed privileges in jail, especially top student leaders and nationally known scholars captured after the government's crackdown on the protest movement of 1989. Usually, they were allowed their own small cell. I was merely a poet and my name was known only to a small circle of people. I had none of the luxury typically granted to political prisoners and was tossed into one crowded cell after another, mixing with detainees of all social backgrounds. As time went by, I learned to survive and picked up all sorts of bad habits.

For example, I excelled in catching lice and fleas, and won the cell championship with a score of seventy-three lice in an hour. The honor did not come without a price. Those six-legged parasites, shiny like black sesame seeds, loved to nest in a person's genitals. When I first detected crabs in my pubic hair, I used a toothpick to pull them out one by one. However, according to Number 3, who suffered from a severe case of crabs, one had to shave off the pubic hair and use prescription medication to get rid of them completely. But there was no way a doctor at the investigation center would treat an inmate's crabs.

In the quiet of the night, the sounds of Number 3's scratching and groaning kept me awake all night long. Sometimes, the itch was such that he sat up screaming. His fingernails were smeared with blood. Two hairy thieves rushed over to scratch his crotch and comb his pubic hair. Number 3 dismissed all but one of them, a young, attractive one, to help. While his slave boy was busy catching crabs, he would grimace, like a person on a guillotine. Eventually, Number 3's family brought in a special type of shampoo and we managed to eliminate the problem.

During my incarceration, the monotony of the evenings was more unbearable than lice and crabs. Dinner was served at five and the bedtime bell rang at ten. There were five hours to kill. We were only allowed to watch TV a couple of nights a week. The rest of the time, we sat there with nothing to do. Members of the upper class secretly played mahjongg and cards, both of which were banned. If discovered, the players would be handcuffed and jabbed with electric batons. Even so, the inmates were undeterred. The mahjongg tiles were made from soap bars. We cut the soap into small cubes and put them in a string bag. They became dry and hard after being left outside the ventilation window for several days. Then we pasted papers around each cube and drew pictures and symbols. Cards were much easier to make. We had an inmate who was a skillful handyman. He could make a pack of cards in two hours using a ballpoint pen and pages torn from a book.

Under normal circumstances, mahjongg games involve money or liquor — depending on the rules, the losers will either cough up money or drink a shot of hard liquor as punishment. Since nobody had money to gamble, and bootlegged hard liquor was too precious a commodity in jail, we used water to penalize the losers — a person would be forced to drink a big bowl of cold water each time he lost a game. The chief and other senior leaders were exempt from the punishment. The chief always designated a hairy thief to gulp down water for him when he was defeated. One day, an inmate, who had been forced to drink water on behalf of the senior leadership, set a new record by drinking eight bowls without stopping. He soon lost his balance and his face looked like melted wax. A few minutes later, he started to vomit green bile.

On days when our officer in charge slacked off, the chief would organize parties, which featured singing, waltzing, and comedy skits. In the repertoire, there was a routine that depicted a hooker seducing a john near the entrance to a dancehall; it never failed to generate laughter. A pale-skinned inmate who played the hooker stuffed two rice bowls into his shirt as his "breast implants." The john would wrap his arm around the hooker, sauntering into the imaginary dancehall. The script for their conversations was vulgar and jarring to the ear. At a certain point, everyone hummed "Dance of the Little Swans" from Tchaikovsky's *Swan Lake* ballet, and the two actors would dance to the tune while kissing, fondling, and slapping each other's behinds. Often, the john would lift up the hooker's skirt, turn him around and mount him from behind. I remember two of the chief's friends got into a fist-fight once over possession of an inmate who played the hooker's part most ravishingly.

The investigation center lay adjacent to a polytechnic school. The ventilation window looked out over a lane through which female students walked after school. One of the chief's favorite hobbies was to stand on an inmate's shoulders and watch those young women. Their talking and giggling sounded as sweet as the singing of the Sirens' song. The chief drooled at the sight and yelled obscenities, sending the young women screaming. Sometimes, he became so excited that he would hold the wrought-iron bar with one hand and unzip his pants and masturbate with the other. Occasionally, he would jump off from the human ladder and order his slave boys to make a bed for him. Then, he and members of the upper class would lie neatly on their beds with their pants down and their private parts exposed. The slave boys, two for each master, would pounce on their dicks. It was a talent show and each slave boy displayed his own unique set of skills. They rubbed and squeezed, culminating in licking and sucking. Their loud slurping conjured up the image of starving peasants gulping down a bowl of hot congee.

The leaders moaned with their eyes closed, some murmuring the names of their fantasy women while directing the heads of their surrogate lovers to their crotches. After ejaculation, the slave boys lay flat on the floor, panting. Some shed tears when their masters forced them to swallow the semen. Anything dripping from the corner of their mouths had to be licked up. Afterward, wet towels were distributed. The slave boys wiped their own faces first and bent over like dogs to lick clean their masters' groin areas and patiently wait for the dicks to soften and shrink. Then they would dip small white towels in bowls of water and cleanse their masters' bodies.

Once the orgies were over, those poor sex toys would sit like wooden sculptures next to their masters, who lay down with their eyes closed, relishing the sexual release. Half an hour later, the chief would wake up, wave the boys off, and reign over the whole cell as if nothing had happened.

Occasionally, orgies could go awry. One day, a newbie found it hard to swallow the semen and threw up. Outraged, the chief ordered a "Sautéed Bear Paw with Tofu" from the menu to punish the sex toy. The enforcer struck the new inmate on the chest with an open hand until he coughed up blood. He was forced to lick and swallow his own blood along with his master's sperm. Even so, the chief wasn't satisfied. He plunged the newbie's head inside the toilet bucket repeatedly to "Watch the Goldfish."

Since I managed to maintain cordial relations with the chief, I was spared many of the tortures. As time went by, I became disgusted with the brutal, perverted lifestyle of the upper class and gradually distanced myself from the chief. Instead, I spent more time with members of the lower class. Out of curiosity, I chatted them up about their cases and heard many colorful stories. Once I tried to rally some disgruntled inmates to report the brutalities to the officer in charge. My efforts failed miserably. The officer leaked the information to the chief. Fortunately, my fellow conspirators were known for their loyalty. Nobody betrayed me, even after receiving harsh punishment.

A tidal wave of new arrivals swelled the population of my cell from eighteen to thirty-four. Since the upper class set aside a large area for their beds, the rest had to sleep on their sides, all facing one direction. The chief complained that the inmates were not wedged together tightly enough and ordered the enforcer to walk back and forth on top of the bodies, eliminating the gaps. In the hot summer, the air was choked with the odor of sweat and cigarette smoke. The person in charge of the toilet had the filthiest assignment but he was the envy of us all at night because he had more room. His body coiled around the toilet bucket like a snake and he could stretch freely when he needed.

I slept on the border between the upper and lower classes. The painful moaning from the downtrodden constantly interrupted my sleep. Out of desperation, I rolled up my bedding and moved to a spot in the corner facing the door, right between two enforcers.

The chief and his friends exploded at my defiance but I refused to back down and deliberately shouted loudly. An officer on duty whom I had not seen before, came in. I stood at attention and pointed at the inadequate sleeping arrangements. He was shocked and ordered everyone to get up and rearrange their bedding. All members of the upper class were kicked to the lower class side and their original spots were equally split among the slaves. Basking in my victory, I slept comfortably in a new spot next to a corner where books were stacked. The officer praised me in front of everyone. Before he left, he patted me on the shoulder and said with affection, "You damn counterrevolutionary!" Glancing out of the corner of my eye, I could see the chief was seething with anger.

The Artist

THE OFFICERS FOR CELL 2, where I was incarcerated, and Cell 3 could not get along. Their acrimonious relationship poisoned the way inmates from both cells treated each other. Hostilities between the two groups extended to the courtyard during breaks. Sometimes verbal insults escalated into fistfights. The guard would punish both sides evenly by shackling their hands. The next day, our officer in charge would remove the cuffs without a question asked and reward everyone involved with extra vegetables and meat.

One day, when our boss was absent, the officer for Cell 3 showed up during a break. Like a referee, he blew his whistle and ordered detainees from both cells to wrestle each other. With their boss looking on, the thugs from Cell 3 chased us around like eagles preying on rabbits. The officer laughed and applauded, and even joined in the chase himself. He swaggered around with his bamboo stick, trying to capture someone from our cell. I became his first victim. Grabbing me by the shirt collar, the officer sized me up and said with mock surprise, "You are the one who acted in that anti-party film called *Requiem*, aren't you? What a life you've had!" Taking me as a hostage, he placed me in Cell 3, under the custody of Mu Ming, the chief.

Although Mu Ming was a veteran thief, he possessed extraordinary

artistic talent. He was born into a poor family and joined the underworld at an early age. By the time he reached his teenage years, he had
been in and out of jail frequently. He attempted several prison breaks
and took great delight in bragging about them. "I worked hard to win
the officers' trust. They soon made me a purchasing agent for the labor
camp. An official and I took a bus to the market. When we reached
downtown, I got rid of him in lightning speed. I wandered around the
mountainous region for a week but never got lost because I followed
the electric poles. I ate whatever I could get my hands on — tree bark,
grass roots, raw potatoes, and frogs. It was worse than Chairman Mao's
Long March. Occasionally, when I ran into strangers, I would crouch
down, pretending to scout for minerals. With my dirty face and over-
alls, I didn't even need makeup to play the role of a geologist. Nobody
suspected that I was an escaped prisoner. One time, a peasant girl even
tried to seduce me with her singing . . ."

"I think I've heard this story before," I broke in.

"Oh, did I tell you that already?" Mu Ming said, without the slight-
est embarrassment. "I wish I had known you before I came here. You
might have given me a part in your *Requiem* film. Going to jail for
directing and acting in a movie sounds more glamorous."

"You'd be perfect to play an escaped prisoner," I teased him.

Mu Ming took offense. "Hey, don't underestimate me. Let me produce a show to impress you."

"You probably don't know," Cell 3's deputy chief interjected, "all the
popular songs and ditties that are circulating at our investigation center are written by Mu Ming."

I was impressed. I also realized that Mu Ming and his deputy were
the only two senior leaders in their cell. "How can the two of you manage this large group?" I asked.

"I'm sure the big bureaucracy in your cell is doing a better job," Mu
Ming replied sarcastically. "Those seven leaders are sucking everyone
dry."

"The more leaders you have, the bigger the burden on the rest of
the inmates," Mu Ming's deputy explained. "Like Chairman Mao says,
oppression leads to fierce struggles between two classes. We are all suffering in jail. If we can get by, we don't need to be harsh."

"How do you handle the 'Confess Your Crimes and Report on Others' campaign? Do you cook dishes for others in order to extract confessions?" I asked.

"Inmates torturing inmates for the benefit of police? That would ruin my karma," Mu Ming declared. "We are lucky that the officer in charge isn't relying on us to get promoted. He is just here for the job. As long as we don't stir up trouble in the cell, he doesn't care one way or another."

"Compared to our chief, you are an angel!" I complimented Mu Ming.

He blushed and said bashfully, "It would be nice if you could be transferred to our cell. You can teach me literature and I can be smarter and more cultured."

That evening, my status as a hostage ended. I said goodbye to Mu Ming and was delivered back to my cell. Ever since I ruined the chief's sleeping arrangements, he and his friends stopped talking to me. I felt very isolated and began to hang out in Cell 3 whenever I could. Initially, I acted with prudence and would quietly move over after breakfast and sneak back during the midmorning break. Gradually, I became emboldened, leaving after breakfast and returning after dinner.

Mu Ming put together variety shows every day—comedy skits, one-act plays, singing choruses, acrobatics, and sports competitions. For example, a teenage inmate grabbed a tube of toothpaste as his imaginary microphone and performed a song as if he were on TV. Mu Ming served as the program host, presenting the "teen star" to the audience with made-up stories in a style reminiscent of Hong Kong and Taiwan TV shows:

"This talented little kid comes all the way from the Juvenile Delinquency Center in Taiwan. At the age of nine, he dreamed of being a singer. But how can an orphan realize his dream? He had no option except to steal. He figured that if he stole enough money, he could fly to heaven and sing there. This kid, who wanted to sing for God, struggled for many years before getting enough money. So he bought a plane ticket that would take him abroad. Over the Taiwan Strait, he got up from his seat and was about to show off his singing talent when the flight attendants wrestled him to the floor, thinking he was a hijacker. Taiwan didn't want him back and he was sent back to mainland China.

His dream was dashed . . . No. Wait! It wasn't! Under the tutelage of Director Mu Ming at Song Mountain, his dream has come true!"

With that colorful introduction, Mu Ming motioned to the boy, who stood up and crooned. Mu Ming played his "air guitar" next to the boy:

> *At the age of eighteen, my heart is bleeding*
> *For the freedom I'm losing*
>
> *Life behind bars*
> *Harsh, tedious, and uninspiring*
>
> *Mother is expecting the son's homecoming*
> *Don't be sad, Mom, I'm only eighteen*
>
> *The gray sky, depressing*
> *The day of family visit approaching*
> *Losing your family, do you know the pain?*
> *Looking through the wrought-iron bars*
> *I could not see enough of my Ma*
> *My heart is bleeding*
> *Don't be sad, Ma, your son just turned eighteen.*

The cell was quiet and Mu Ming wiped his eyes with his sleeves, as if he had been moved to tears. The duo's performance was received with vigorous applause. The style might have been amateurish but I was touched by its authenticity. Mu Ming bowed and asked everyone to hold their applause. Then he roused everyone in the room for the last number — a song called "The Little Monks at Song Mountain." Maestro Mu Ming flung his arms out and conducted with a chopstick. The crowd burst into song. Inmates sitting in the front row stood and swayed back and forth in imitation of a group of dancing monks in a popular Japanese cartoon show.

Mu Ming was an expert at hand puppetry. On days when the sun was out, he would lie on the floor and hold his hands up in front of the rays, shaping his hands into different birds, with the wall as a screen.

"See, this is a swallow. This is a sparrow. Look, here's an eagle, his wings are flapping and flapping. He is swooping down on his prey."

I heaved a sigh.

Mu Ming paused for a few seconds and forced out a smile. "You certainly are grumpy. Why don't I get the fortune-teller for you? He's really good." He beckoned for a pockmarked man to come over. He was a vagrant from the city of Tianjin.

Pockmark shuffled his cards and placed them face down in front of me. Nervously, I selected one after another. Pockmark repeated the process three times, murmuring and calculating. Half an hour later, he still had no answer. Mu Ming became impatient. "Is his future that bad?"

Pockmark nodded despondently. "The prospects aren't good."

"Is he going to be in jail for a long time?" Mu Ming asked.

"Three years, at least."

"Three years, that's not so bad," Mu Ming consoled me. "You can stick it out."

"Good God!" I was crestfallen.

"I'm sure you'll get out soon," Mu Ming reassured me. "Even people from the dregs like me have hope. Be confident."

Under Chinese law, the authorities were allowed to hold a criminal suspect for investigation for no more than forty-five days. After my detention went over the forty-day mark, I began to dream, like many other inmates, that my case would be resolved and I could be set free. I fidgeted, like a thoroughbred injected with stimulants but not allowed to dash down the track. To release the pent-up tension, I increased the speed and frequency of my daily indoor stroll. During breaks, I jogged around in bigger circles.

From across the corridor, I could see Mu Ming was also waiting anxiously. The day after he finished the first month of his detention, he ordered his cellmates to organize a party and invited me over. When I joined him after breakfast, Mu Ming put on a suit and tie that he had smuggled in somehow and dressed up like a groom, with a tiny red paper flower on his lapel. He danced with his "bride," a feminine inmate adorned with colorful clothes, and offered everyone a toast by raising a wine cup made from aluminum foil. His fellow cellmates and

I repeated it in unison three times. As the sound of "freedom" lingered in the air, Mu Ming dropped to his knees, weeping.

The next morning, I stayed in my cell. Through the wrought-iron bars, I saw him bow three times in my direction like an ancient warrior and begin a sit-in. The next day he announced, "It's my thirty-second day," and the following day, he shouted, "Thirty-three!" Thus, he started a new routine, announcing the days of his detention every morning. After that, he wouldn't speak for the whole day. He tried to calm his nerves through meditation. He sat facing the corridor, his legs crossed and his eyes red from lack of sleep. The anxiety reduced him to a mere skeleton.

On the forty-seventh day, a court official arrived with a verdict. Mu Ming was sentenced to three years in prison for robberies. I watched him depart from across the hallway, but he avoided my gaze. I turned my eyes away from him and resumed my daily exercise. For the whole day, I felt distracted. The scene at Cell 3 stayed with me for many years. I don't know where Mu Ming has landed. He was a remarkable performer in the underworld, and better than any of the pop stars of the 1990s. Unfortunately, he never had the opportunity to entertain on a public stage.

Isolation

THOSE "ESCAPES" TO CELL 3 soon got me into trouble. One morning, my officer caught me and dragged me back. Incensed by my treachery, he awarded me a pair of tightly fitted cuffs that were painful to wear and was among the worst of the many punishments I received.

Seeing that I had lost favor with the officer in charge, my fellow inmates immediately began taunting me, changing their formerly friendly attitude. With both of my hands cuffed behind my back, using the toilet became a challenge. The migrant from Fujian, who was assigned to take care of the toilet bucket, had been under my protection for months. He volunteered to help me untie my pants. But then an enforcer came over and punched and kicked him. The chief the Fujian migrant a "human bench" — the enforcer stripped him of his clothes, forced him to lie down flat on the floor and the chief sat on him, leisurely picking his toenails. In our cell, a human bench could also be used as a washing board, an ottoman, or a pommel horse.

When the dinner bell rang, I joined the crowd and stood in line, but couldn't use my cuffed hands to receive food. An enforcer stepped up to carry the bowl for me. Once we were back in the cell, he made me wait until the chief and his friends had finished eating. Then, he tossed my bowl on the floor and kicked me, forcing me down on my knees. "Eat like a dog," he commanded. The senior leaders stood in a semicircle, yelling, "Come on, doggie!" I put up a futile resistance, but the enforcer clamped his claws around my neck and pushed down my head into the bowl. The scalding food stuck in my mouth and nose, triggering violent coughing.

I hugged my knees, my head pounding. My tormentors continued to imitate dogs barking. The chief laughed himself into a convulsion. Egged on by the reaction from his boss, the enforcer grabbed me by the neck and spat into my mouth. Again, he shoved my face in the bowl. I bobbed my head, trying to struggle free from his grip. He banged my head against the floor, my face turned into a flattened persimmon cake.

"Do you admit guilt?" the chief yelled.

I was silent.

"Do you admit guilt?" the chief's friends chorused. The enforcer pulled me up from the floor and someone spat cold water on my face.

"Dammit, I don't," I roared, but my head hung limp.

The leaders who grew tired of torturing me deposited me next to the toilet bucket and merrily started their card game. I propped my body against the wall, my head between my knees. I could hear the chief complimenting the enforcer on the way he treated me. Flattered and excited, the enforcer deliberately lost two rounds of card games to the chief and willingly drank two big bowls of cold water as the penalty for losing. "I deserve to lose," he said ingratiatingly and wiped his mouth. For two hours, I sat with my head down like a statue in mourning. Gradually, I was forgotten. Anger and humiliation washed over me. Little by little, I gained back my physical strength. I wriggled my wrists, trying to free my hands, but failed again and again. I persisted with inexplicable, fruitless stubbornness.

In the end, I successfully moved my left hand out of the shackle. I took a deep breath and hurled myself into the circle of card players like a battering ram.

None of the leaders saw it coming. My head butted heavily against the chief's chest. Number 2 and Number 3 were also bruised in the clash. I seized the enforcer around the waist and bit him hard on his nose. The enforcer lowered his head, trying to duck my attack but my teeth sunk into his forehead, ripping off a piece of skin. The enforcer let out a loud inhuman shriek. The room was in chaos. I fell under siege; it felt like thousands of hands were punching and grabbing me. The chief jumped on me. I bit his finger and he leapt back like a monkey. In the middle of the scuffle, the door clanked open. A guard popped his head in: "What's going on here?"

The chief got up and stood at attention. "We are just bored and playing a game," he lied.

"Fuck your game," the stern-looking guard bellowed. "Sit down."

The crowd dispersed and everyone returned to his seat. I wiped the blood from the corner of my mouth and spat out a tiny shred of the enforcer's forehead. No sooner had the guard left than the crowd regrouped themselves. I retreated to the toilet bucket, pretending to take a pee. I could hear my enemies closing in on me.

Quickly, I tore off the lid, lifted the bucket and turned around one hundred and eighty degrees. Like the martyred warriors who defended their cities against foreign invaders with cannons in revolutionary movies, I aimed the stinking bucket at my tormentors, and hurled it. "Fuck! I'm going to kill you!"

Human feces proved to be an effective weapon. The chief called a truce. My fearless fight brought me no triumph, however. My fellow inmates stayed away and talked about me behind my back. "That bastard, he certainly doesn't act like a suave political prisoner."

Even though I had brokered a temporary cease-fire with the chief, the vengeful leader and his friends were secretly plotting against me. They were looking for new excuses to punish me. A secret edict was issued. Nobody had permission to speak with me. For eight days, except for a couple of dry coughs, I hardly made any noise. The Fujian migrant resumed his duties and crouched next to the toilet bucket. Each time I looked at him, he lowered his head to avoid my gaze. Two weeks later, investigators found no criminal evidence in the case against him and released him. Before his departure, he promised to ferry me across to Taiwan when I got out. I still remember the name of his fishing village.

The endless rain of the season seeped into everything. Even my bones felt moldy. I sat in a corner miserably perusing a book. Occasionally I would raise my head to glance at the cliffs covered with green foliage outside the window. Even the words in my book seemed to have turned green.

At dusk one day, I strolled around the room as part of my routine physical exercise. The chief and his friends sat around bantering. I rolled my eyes, stuck out my tongue and made strange noises to get their attention. A couple of the chief's friends swore at me, asking me to stop, but he quieted them. "Just ignore him. He's approaching the end of his tolerance. I bet you he'll go crazy in no time."

I refused to give up. In imitation of a zombie, I walked stiffly up and down near the wrought-iron fence. The officer for Cell 3 happened to pass by. "You do look like a zombie," he said. "You are a good performer." He opened the door, and stepped in. His breath reeked of alcohol. He said to the chief scornfully, "I heard that you bastards are trying to isolate the counterrevolutionary. It's damn strange. None of you are his match, even if I put all of you together. On account of him, I'm going to let you watch a couple of hours of TV. Come and gather in Cell 3." I was too touched to say anything. Thus, the blockade against me was broken.

The Other Sex

IF CHINA WERE A PATIENT suffering from colon cancer, the city of Chongqing would be the filthy terminus of the colon, a diseased anus. The Yangtze River, choked with toxic foam, gushes out of the city, carrying waste from a large number of industrial plants. As a result, acid rain and fog lingers, which can extend the rainy season for at least two weeks. The pollution makes people in this formerly pristine mountain city impatient and irritable. A thick crust builds up in their eyes. It was during this rotten season that the authorities at the investigation center organized a general cleaning in anticipation of a visit from a senior official. We were supposed to sweep and scrub every nook and cranny of the building, and paint all the walls.

On that afternoon, I saw Big Glasses in the corridor through our wrought-iron door. I hardly recognized him without his long, unkempt hair. His shaved head looked like a tiny duck's egg. He wore the flower-patterned shirt that I had given him as a gift years before. I called out to him. He looked around furtively and came over to chat. I made fun of him as usual: "How come you look so ugly?" Before he even had time to get back at me, a guard passed by and Big Glasses immediately went back to work. He was sweeping the floor with a broom twice as tall as he was and pretended to sweep vigorously and even wipe his forehead with the sleeve of his shirt as if he were sweating.

After the guard left, we talked and laughed, forgetting temporarily that we were in jail. We were both overly optimistic about our cases, believing that we would be released soon. Over the course of our conversation, Officer Huang, notorious for mistreating inmates, scurried past several times, but ignored us. We were emboldened by his indifference and continued chatting for nearly half an hour. This was the only miracle that I encountered throughout my incarceration.

My turn to sweep the corridor came the next day. I dragged the broom and wandered around in search of Big Glasses, but he was nowhere to be seen. As I was turning a corner, I noticed a small crowd in front of a cell where female detainees were kept. The door was solid, unlike the wrought-iron fence in my cell, but the food delivery window was open. One inmate stuck his head in, begging, "Let me take one more look. I'll add another half bun in exchange." I heard a loud slap. The inmate pulled his head out. A second person stepped up and poked his head in unabashedly. "Let me touch your pussy with my eyes closed. I'll give you two buns in exchange." The woman stuck a burning cigarette butt in his face. He screamed and took his head out before more damage was done. A third man went up. Having learned a lesson from his two friends, he simply clasped his hands and shouted, "You are a tough bitch! I like that." Then, without a word spoken, he dug out three buns from his pocket and handed them inside.

"You seem honest and straightforward," said a voice from inside. "Poke your head in." Everyone was salivating, their legs weakened. They stood on their toes, hoping to catch a glimpse. The inmate with a slight cigarette burn on his face even yelled, "I can see her pussy dripping wet!" The lucky "lottery winner" immediately silenced him with an elbow.

I watched, laughing, but soon became bored. As I was about to leave, hurried footsteps could be heard on the stairway. Someone shouted in fear, "Officer Huang is here!" The crowd dispersed and fled like startled birds. Several cold buns fell to the floor.

Officer Huang strode toward us, carrying a big wooden stick. "You trash!" he roared at me and flung the stick at me. I tilted my head and the stick missed, rushing past my ear like a gust of wind. Officer Huang then ran past me to chase the others. Their footsteps rumbled in the corridor as if a minilocomotive were passing. A few minutes later, he came back and looked at me disdainfully. "Counterrevolutionary, don't lower yourself with stuff like this," he sighed, nodding toward the women's cell.

I blushed and tried to explain that I wasn't part of the vulgar game, but he waved me off and walked away. I was left to watch him disappear down the corridor. Somehow, his reprimand had shocked me, making me think about a poet's dignity, which I had long forgotten. "Dignity?" My heart tightened. "Do I need a policeman to remind me of my own dignity?" But sometimes one had to jettison one's dignity to survive. That was the only choice. While I stood there trying to pull myself together, a pretty face peeked out of the food delivery window. "Do you have buns?" said a soul-grabbing voice. "You can look at my pussy for one bun . . . for two, you can touch . . ."

Gambler Zhang

As the weather warmed up, people I had befriended left, one by one. Even the antiques dealer who slept next to me was released. This stubborn old man earned his release by refusing to confess, even under the threat of torture. The chief was sentenced to five years in a labor camp for aggravated assault and robberies.

At the beginning of June, I had been held for two and a half months, long past the forty-five-day legal limit. Officials from the Chongqing Municipal Prosecutor's Office came to interrogate me to determine whether I should be tried. As we descended the stairs, a big, burly official could not resist caressing my bald head. As a protest against this insult, I refused to answer any of his questions during interrogation. By this time, I could skillfully quote the country's laws and regulations, using them confidently to defend my case. Although my efforts were futile, I could at least maintain my dignity. My unwillingness to answer questions infuriated the other officials from the prosecutor's office. When they threatened me with beatings, I resorted to histrionics. Hearing my outburst, the director of the investigation center rushed in and berated me. But once I left the room, I heard him warning the officials not to use excessive force during interrogations. "You might kill someone."

Back in my cell, I stopped taking my daily stroll. Instead, I lay down and started reading again but had problems focusing. My cellmates changed constantly. I had joined the ranks of veterans. We had a new chief, an infamous gambler from Chongqing who was also an avid reader. Through books, we became friends.

Three days before my official arrest and transfer, an elderly man arrived. He was tall and thin, unbowed and upright even though we later learned he was over seventy. His gigantic feet aroused many curious stares. The minute he entered the door, he slipped out of his black cloth shoes, knelt down, gave us the palm-and-fist salute and kowtowed as a show of respect. Before we had time to react, he crawled his way rapidly to the side of the toilet bucket, crouched down with both hands over his head, waiting for his initiation.

Everyone was stunned. "This old fart really knows his place," the chief blurted out.

The enforcer rolled up his sleeve, walked up from behind and was getting ready for the initiation routine when the elderly man turned around and said, "Brother, my old bones are falling apart. If you have me go through the whole routine, you should be careful. I might not come out of it."

"Hey! We can't break the rules!" Number 2 yelled.

The old man cackled, "This is my fifth time here. Believe it or not, I made the rules."

That got the chief's attention. "Do you mean to say that you are Gambler Zhang?"

"Yes, sir. That's me."

The chief immediately helped him up. "Please rise."

"The enforcer said that we can't break the rules." Gambler Zhang laughed.

"Don't take us too seriously." The chief signaled to his senior leaders, all of whom immediately rose to apologize. "You are a veteran."

"Well, rules are rules. I insist that you treat me like everyone else." Gambler Zhang turned away from us and bent over. "Please go ahead."

We all regarded him with amazement. Reluctantly, the chief issued an order, "Pig elbows braised in herbs" — using an elbow to repeatedly hit a person's back.

The enforcer cautiously and gently elbowed Gambler Zhang's back like a masseuse. At the end of the ritual, Gambler Zhang stood up and was about to move to a corner when the chief grabbed him by his shirtsleeve. "Sir, please sleep in my place. Let me serve you."

The old man rolled his eyes and waved the chief off. "Brother, I wouldn't dare accept a favor from you. I have nothing to give you in return," he said. "Let me sleep in the underclass section. I have thick skin and don't mind the lice at all." With that, he strode over and squeezed into a spot next to me. A few minutes later, his eyes were closed.

In the afternoon, Gambler Zhang was taken away for interrogation. About an hour later, he returned, smiling from ear to ear. I chatted him up out of curiosity to find out what had buoyed his mood.

"The interrogator was furious with me," he bragged. "I think I'm going to be out of here in two weeks at most."

I must have looked confounded.

"You need to worry if your interrogator treats you with great benevolence," he explained. "If the officer acts like he were your father, it indicates that they are either ready to deliver you to another world or give you a deferred death sentence. When I was young, both the Nationalist and Communist police pulled that shit on me. Gradually, I've turned into a wily old bird. I am invincible."

Then he replayed the interrogation scene for us:

INTERROGATOR: *Zhang, you've been in a reeducation camp five times. We are embarrassed to send you there again. Aren't you?*

GAMBLER ZHANG: *Don't be embarrassed. Go ahead. This case will probably get me three years at most. I'm turning seventy-three this year. A stay at a reeducation camp is like retiring to a nursing home.*

INTERROGATOR: *You old poisonous scoundrel!*

GAMBLER ZHANG (CLASPING HIS HANDS): *I totally agree. I'm quite poisonous. I've been gambling for sixty-three years. I don't know how many people I have poisoned with gambling. Many have gone bankrupt, divorced, or committed suicide. When I was in jail before, my hand itched and I ended up gambling every day inside the reeducation camp. We used food and meat as currency. After several years, I had trained at least three skillful gamblers. Now that I'm getting too old, I can't wait to go somewhere where I*

can pass on my knowledge and skill to the next generation. I find
that there are more suitable candidates inside a reeducation camp
than elsewhere. I guarantee that I will be able to take several
students and turn them into gamblers this country can be
proud of.
INTERROGATOR (POUNDING HIS DESK IN ANGER AND RAISING
HIS HAND): *You . . . you . . .*

The whole cell fell under his spell. Number 2 gave him a thumbs-up. "Good story." The chief flattered him: "I hope both of us will be sent to reeducation camp together. I can be your last disciple."

Gambler Zhang shook his head. "I think reeducation camp is too much to hope for. It's very likely they'll send me home. I'm a bachelor, without parents or children. All I need to do is take care of myself. I'll just gamble myself to death."

Gambler Zhang left an indelible impression on me. He could gamble on anything. He even took a bet on me.

"Hey, chief, I think Counterrevolutionary will get out of here on the thirteenth of this month. Think I'm right?"

"How do you know?" The chief was skeptical.

"I know all scholars are afraid of number thirteen. In the West, it's considered an unlucky number."

The wily old bird's predictions turned out to be true. As a result, the chief lost two portions of meat to him at dinner.

On the afternoon of June 13, a police van drove me out of the Song Mountain Investigation Center. Drizzling rain sparkled in the heavy air. I sat in the rear of the car, with a big bundle of my quilt, my papers, and my books on my side. My right hand was chained to the back of the seat in front of me. As I raised my head, I noticed that Big Glasses was in the same van, slouched in the front seat. We were just a few rows apart but it felt like a great distance. His thin figure seemed to have shriveled even more. When the car hit a pothole or a bump, the top of his shaved head popped up from behind the seat back.

"Take a good look at the scenery," the escort policeman told me. "This trip will take you to a place even further away from the free world outside."

I was in despair. All hope had drained from my heart. The weather seemed to have turned treacherous in sympathy as the sun and clouds sent down a hot, impetuous rain that soiled the streets with a leaden hue. I pressed my nose unconsciously against the window, like a child tethered too long at home with illness. Women of this mountain city sauntered on the streets, some with umbrellas and others recklessly bareheaded. I felt numb.

I was tormented with the urge to smash the window with my fists and fight my way out. I wanted to run and find a place to hide under one of those colorful umbrellas. My spirit was roaming the streets, oblivious to my shackles.

Part III

THE DETENTION CENTER

June 1990–August 1992

The Living Dead

THE POLICE CAR SPED wildly, not bothering to slow down when making turns, nearly hitting the curb on a downhill slope, and sending scared pedestrians running. Other vehicles stopped or pulled over to let it pass. The reckless rascal of a driver slammed on the brakes just a few inches from the car in front of us, leaving my body to continue unimpeded; Big Glasses and I lunged forward like devils eager to plunge toward hell. We wove in and out of traffic, the shops on both sides of the street blurring into a colorful sliding stage, its curtains rapidly rising and falling. At last, we reached 15 North Shibanpo Street. I narrowed my eyes and caught the sign of the Chongqing Municipal Detention Center,* where I was doomed to await my trial.

The police officer in the car leaned out his window and handed a piece of paper to a guard wearing a steel helmet that came down almost over his eyebrows. The guard checked the paper carefully and motioned us into a meticulously landscaped compound filled with lush plants and blooming flowers. The car climbed uphill and cir-

---

* In China, the detention center incarcerates those who have been officially arrested and are awaiting trial. Some can end up at a detention center for years without a conviction. Convicted criminals with a one-year sentence or less also serve their time there.

cled around a soccer field where bare-chested officers were engaged in hand-to-hand-combat training. They wrestled each other on the ground or aimed kicks into the air, bellowing, "Kill and kill!" I shuddered like a nervous rat.

At the second entrance, an officer led me through the gate, then through a large parking lot flanked on both sides with tree-shaded stone paths. We stopped near a flower bed and I was ordered to wait while Big Glasses went ahead. Ten minutes later, I followed and trod on the same stone stairs. Farther along, the path meandered through meadows and more flower beds, surprising me with its air of a luxury resort, with stone tables and chairs placed here and there.

As we moved along the steady upward grade, the whistling wind blew against my cheeks. The city's largest detention center, perched at the top of a flight of steep stone stairs and hidden inside the forested hills, revealed itself ominously. At first glance, it looked like an altar. I straightened my back and stood at attention as ordered, but I couldn't resist turning back to gaze at the setting sun, receding like a tidal wave of light. The sprawling city below shimmered with the big dome of the Chongqing People's Hall perched in the middle. "The dome is the launch pad for a flying saucer," I thought. "I hope aliens will come abduct me."

The disarming scenery abruptly ended in the big hall, where I was greeted with a full-body search. Two officers on duty idled on a bench near the door, enjoying the cool breeze, while a small group gathered around two chess players in the middle of the hall. A Red Hair patted me down, examining every inch of my shirt and pants in search of hidden contraband. My comforter was slashed open; the cotton inside emptied out and swept into a garbage can. After every one of my belongings was thoroughly checked, the officer ordered me to sign a piece of folded white paper. I complied without knowing what it was. The next day, I learned from an inmate that it was my arrest warrant. More than three months into my incarceration, I was officially arrested. At the detention center, I was told to keep my old identity number, 0-9-9.

With my shaved head and big bushy beard, I looked like a scraggly old man in mourning. It was the beginning of summer but I still wore a winter sweater that my wife had knit for me. She had embroidered it with a pair of the Chinese yin and yang symbols in black and white on the upper right chest and on the right elbow. These ancient symbols are supposed to mean the polar opposites in nature: yin is closely associated with night, darkness, and the moon, while yang with day, light, and the sun. In the past three months, I had learned their true meaning — endless dark days without the sun.

The guard shoved me through a wrought-iron gate into a rectangular compound in the back. This was the core of the detention center, which held serious offenders waiting for their convictions. The compound was fenced in by thick brick walls thirty feet high. Watchtowers loomed at the compound's four corners. A gray square building in the middle of the compound looked as if it had been built with a gigantic version of children's building blocks. The guards called this square box the "warehouse for the living dead."

"New inventory for Cell Ten," my escort bellowed. Like magic, the thick metal gate to Cell 10 clunked open. A large group of shiny shaved heads greeted me. Two inmates stood naked in a corner, their manacled hands and feet indicating death row status. That was the first time I'd seen a death row inmate at such close range.

I maintained my composure, but seeing them triggered a scene buried deep in my childhood memory. When I was growing up in a small town in the mid-1960s, executions of criminals were major public events. One day, when I was nine, an execution notice was posted and the whole town turned out to view the proceedings. Thousands swarmed into the stadium where a public trial was supposed to take place. A criminal, hog-tied and gagged, was hoisted up over the side of the stage; a cardboard sign with a big X over the word *counterrevolutionary* hung around his neck.

I joined a group of fearless children and we squirmed our way forward like eels between the adults' legs, ignoring the risk of being trampled by the crowd. We wanted to crawl to the front to see the condemned enemy and throw rocks and fruit peels at him. People around and above me screamed, "Kill him!" Through a loudspeaker, the judge presided over the trial from a podium; his words struck the crowd like waves of thunder. The enemy's body was covered with cuts and bruises, his head bleeding and smashed out of shape by rocks.

Strangely, the mere spectacle of a man hog-tied and overcome with fear, his limp body propped up by armed police, excited me.

At the end of the trial, a police van arrived, forcing a path through the mob to take the convicted prisoner away for execution. We ran and ran, chasing the police car until it disappeared in the bright sunset. When we stopped, reluctantly, our faces were covered with dust. We were told that the actual execution would take place in a rugged mountainous region, along the lower reaches of the river somewhere. After the execution, the body of the deceased was wrapped in straw mats and sent away for cremation. Unlike adults, who avoided the criminal's family, we children gathered near the ominous house. Itching with curiosity, we snuck up to the doorway to take a peek inside. All of a sudden, a shadow stepped out. We turned around, dashing away to a busy intersection before we took a breath and looked back. Under the hazy streetlights, a tiny shadowy figure of a boy, who looked our age, came out of the doorway and wandered on the sidewalks like a lone ghost. The image of the boy who had lost his father to an execution stuck in my mind for many years.

China probably executes more people than any other country in the world. A friend of my brother's who clerked at the municipal court in Chengdu told me that between ten thousand and fifteen thousand people were executed in China in the 1990s. The death sentences were normally carried out fairly fast, within two weeks to three months. With rampant corruption in the court system, it is hard not to question how many of those on death row were wrongly convicted.

The two naked death row inmates that awaited me at the detention center, one short and plump, the other tall and lanky, were not as mysterious as I had imagined when I was a child. They stood there expressionless, like two wooden sculptures. As I was lost in thought, a loud voice from outside the cell brought me back to reality: "Water is ready for Cell Ten." The two death row inmates clanked their way to a concrete rack to grab their bowls and scooped up water from a sink, pouring it over their heads and bodies. They made a game of it, winking at each other and prancing up and down like two chained monkeys. Others soon joined in, creating chaos. "Hey, stop! Let the newcomer wash first!" a sturdy inmate with pasty skin yelled in a stern voice. He seemed to have appeared from nowhere. The other inmates shrank

away from the two "living dead," as they were called, and waited obediently off to one side. Quickly, I slipped out of my clothes and washed
thoroughly.

My undershirt and a small quilted mattress were swept into a corner as garbage. The rest, including my sweater and quilt cover, were
pressed by someone into a big metal basin. Then the sturdy man in
charge swaggered to the middle of the yard and shouted through the
wall for boiling water to kill any lice and fleas on my body. I stepped
into the basin, frantically jumping up and down for nearly ten minutes
while two inmates poured hot water over my head. I slipped and fell a
couple of times. My misfortune won a round of laughter. When they
pulled me up from the floor, I had been turned into a clean, naked
monk.

The sturdy man, Wen Zhi, was the chief. He ordered me to raise
both my arms while two other inmates took turns scrutinizing and
sniffing every part of my body to make sure that I didn't stink and that
no suspicious bugs lurked hidden in the folds of my skin. After the
health inspection, I was allowed to mix with the other sixteen monks,
all of whom filed into the inner sanctuary at the end of the break.

The cell's layout was straightforward — an electronic wrought-iron
fence divided the cell into a covered courtyard at the front and a back
room for sleeping. The courtyard, no more than five steps long and
wide, had a sink and a concrete rack for eating utensils. Inmates could
briefly stretch and wash in the yard. The ceiling resembled a gigantic sieve, interwoven with reinforced concrete beams. On sunny days,
rays of light shone down on the floor through the holes, square and as
big as rice bowls. As the day went by, those squares of sunshine slowly
crept up the walls. A smart inmate could calculate the exact time of
day, accurate to the minute, simply by checking the positions of these
sun squares.

The back room was twice the size of the front yard, with a massive sixteen-feet-long and three-feet-wide concrete bed dominating
the space. There was not much room left, except for a three-feet-
wide aisle. At the Song Mountain Investigation Center, each cell was
equipped with a toilet bucket. Here, however, we had a real toilet — a
concrete troughlike urinal and an open squat toilet in a corner. With
the overhead sieve at the front courtyard and a big iron-barred win-

dow in the back room, lighting and air circulation were well accounted for. Every part of the cell, of course, was fully exposed to the prying eyes of the guards. They dutifully carried out their twenty-four-hour patrol outside and on the roof, where a sheltered passageway had been built for them.

Inmates received their food from a small opening in the right-hand corner of a sidewall, like an embrasure in a fort. A big round peephole in the cell gate was used to monitor activities around the small opening during meal times. In other words, there was not a single blind spot inside the cell.

"This layout is an import from Czechoslovakia," the chief bragged.

I had never seen a Czech prison before, but I was familiar with animal cages in zoos, which displayed two or three tigers, lions, or chimpanzees in a fenced-in enclosure. In contrast, seventeen *Homo sapiens* packed together in such narrow environs was much too intimate.

Many years ago, I read the essay "Notes from the Gallows" written by the Czech journalist Julius Fučik. I recalled a sentence from it that described his cell in a Nazi prison: "Seven steps from the door to the window, seven steps from the window to the door." The Nazis seemed very generous, providing such a spacious cell for a journalist they had condemned to death. In our cell, seventeen prisoners slept side by side on the big concrete bed. As a newbie, I was told that I should have been given a spot closest to the open toilet. Taking into consideration my "status as an intellectual," the chief decided to place me in the middle of the bed, between the two living dead. All I could do was bow to the chief for his generosity.

Suicide Watch

AFTER SUPPER, THE CHIEF slouched on his "throne," a pile of quilts lined up against the wall, and lorded over his subjects. First, he shot me a volley of questions about my case, but my story bored him fast. He changed the subject to daily work assignments: "Your job is to clean the floors in the back room, the hallway, and the front yard. You need to clean the floors with that big mop three times — morning, noon, and night — I want them to shine so that I can see my reflection in them.

"In addition, the officer has ordered us to keep a twenty-four-hour suicide watch over the two death row guys. For nighttime, we have divided the job into five two-hour shifts. Since you are new, we'll grant you the honor of taking the graveyard shift from three a.m. to five a.m., as well as the two-hour napping period after lunch. It's part of your initiation here. You do it for one month and I'll put you on the regular rotation."

"What kind of initiation is this?" I made a long face.

"Cut the crap." The chief glared at me. "Roll out your bedding. It's TV time."

Suspended in midair at twice my height was a fourteen-inch black-and-white TV. Just like at the investigation center, the picture was fuzzy and the loud sound jarring. Nobody seemed to mind. They craned their necks and fixated on the TV screen until ten, when the bell for bedtime rang. Suddenly, the giant bed turned into a meat rack; hot bodies, sweaty and fetid, were crammed together, while thin cigarette smoke swirled in the air.

I sat on the edge to compose myself for a few minutes before diving into my spot — about sixteen centimeters wide. Lan, the tall lanky death row person sleeping on my right, gave out a painful "ouch." He lifted his shoulder to stretch — the manacles had crushed a big red bruise on his wrists. Dead Lan moaned incessantly. I turned around to face the other way but accidentally planted my lips right on those of Liu, the short, fat living dead. That nearsighted bastard whimpered with delight. "Nice!" He smacked his lips and I smelled his foul breath. His nostrils flared, like two big ant holes.

At the Investigation Center, I had a slightly bigger spot and did not have to sleep on my side. It was hard to get used to such physical intimacy here. I clenched my teeth and repositioned myself, lying down with my head on the opposite end of the bed. It did not work out as I had hoped. My head was wedged tightly between two big pairs of chained feet, jutting out into the air like fleshy promontories. I got up again, digging out from my sack all the books that I was allowed to bring and stripping my undershirt off to wrap them and make a pillow of them, so my head was raised above the threatening feet. The light bulbs dazzled and hummed on the ceiling, creating a pure white night — like those in northern latitudes. I closed my eyes and the world morphed into a colossal buzzing fly that I couldn't chase away. The chirping crickets outside heightened my sense of loneliness. Under an oval blue sky, I sank to the bottom of the sea and snuggled against the belly of a giant fish. It was so soothing that I never wanted to wake up and face the ugly reality of my imprisonment.

Clink, clink. The earth broke apart. I opened my eyes and jumped up. Dead Lan was turning in his sleep, his shackles jangling. I closed my eyes and drifted in and out of a dream — the factory that I had worked in after high school bobbed up in the river of memory. Inside an old metal workshop, a steam hammer rose and fell, pounding on my eardrums. I stuffed cotton balls into my ears to block out the deafening noise. Soon the steam hammer floated away and the workshop seemed big and empty. A handgun pressed against the back of my neck, and then my throat. I woke up only to find my neighbor's ankle chains digging into my chin.

Before dawn, a monster's claw tapped on my sweaty shoulder. I opened my eyes wide. A mammoth head hovered over me. I tried to get up but my limbs wouldn't move. Outside the back window, the yelling of the guard swirled in the air like a snake. The monster yanked me from bed with his gigantic claws and shrieked in my ear, "Time for your shift!"

I stepped off the big bed like a robot. The piles of human bodies drifted away. I dream-walked on the moon. I had never felt so tired in my life. I plunged my head into a basin of cold water and stood, dripping wet, in front of the wrought-iron fence. A light breeze blew on my face.

The moon shone through the fence. As I walked in place to fight off my sleepiness, I imagined my body shrinking, allowing me to squeeze through the wrought-iron fence and fade into a tiny shaded spot on the ground outside. The escape seemed effortless. I jumped from the moon to Mars, and found myself drifting inside to my memories of reading Gabriel García Márquez's *One Hundred Years of Solitude*. Colonel Aureliano Buendía loses his sanity, living for many years tied to a chestnut tree, under which he chooses to ignore the ugly reality and retreats deep into his mind. Clouds and sunshine freeze, transforming themselves into a ceiling of sculpted ornaments. People whom the colonel has encountered during his life return like cool breezes, greeting him like a long-lost brother.

I woke up briefly, stood still to urinate, and then resumed my walking in place. Colonel Aureliano Buendía and I became one person. I fell calf-deep into a swampland and was stuck. I tried to pull my legs free. When I opened my eyes, both my hands were pulling at the wrought-iron bars. My knees hit the concrete floor. Excruciating pain shot through my thighs.

"Stand up and don't move!" a guard on duty yelled from the peephole in the door. In a moment he softened his tone. "Hang in there. One more hour to go. The best way to stay awake is to raise both of your arms in the air." There was no need to raise both arms in the air. The sharp pain in my knees chased my dreams away. Not long after, I could hear a rooster crowing in the far distance.

The officer in charge of our cell was a young, muscular fellow named Ju, who had a high-pitched voice like that of a prepubescent boy. He conducted an interrogation the next morning as part of my introduction to the center's routine. I was required to answer some simple questions about my case so he could put together a file on me. By then, the sun had risen. A cool draft blew on the back of my neck. I stole a quick glance outside the window. The mountain town crouched under a massive veil embroidered with diamonds. I opened my mouth to swallow the view of freedom, and let my mind fly among the pigeons. Invigorated by the promise of the morning, I decided to take advantage of Ju's joviality, grouching to the public servant about my workload. "Isn't it a little unfair to assign the late-night shift to a new inmate for a whole month without a break?"

"I approved the idea." Ju laughed with a snort.

"But it's not fair, is it?" I persisted. "Sleep deprivation affects my ability to stay alert on duty and I don't think I can focus on your questions during interrogation."

"Did you doze off while you were on the suicide watch?" Ju snapped, and turned hostile. He reached out a hand to grab his stun baton from the corner.

"No, never." I immediately stood at attention and, changing my story, told an outright lie. "I'm suffering chronic insomnia. I was going to take over the late-night shift. It suits me well."

Night after night, I woke up at an ungodly hour to work my night shift, making sure the two death row inmates didn't kill themselves before the state had a chance to execute them. The shift strained both my mind and body to the limit. I began to detest talking and thinking. I was half-asleep while reading family letters and half-asleep when I walked. It was common to see me dozing off while standing against a wall. I soon devised a new trick to hide my drowsiness during the night shift: I'd grasp the iron fence with both hands and sway my body slowly with my eyes closed. From a distance, it looked like I was trying to memorize difficult English words before a test. In fact, I was deep in my dreams.

It was during those exhausting early hours that I established my friendship with my two neighbors on death row. While I was sleep deprived, they suffered from insomnia, and volunteered to stand guard for me. If the guard's footsteps sounded in the passageway, one of them would kick my thigh to rouse me from bed. I would jump up.

In return for their kindness, I wrote wills, letters, and appeals for them. Dead Liu was a butcher by profession. An avid reader, he spent his days and nights hunched over books, his face pressed close to the pages, as if he were sniffing each word with his bulging eyes. On hot summer days, Dead Liu crouched with his book on the floor in his sweat-soaked shirt and pants. Occasionally, he would laugh aloud over a joke or an amusing scene. His hearty laughter would attract attention — other inmates took turns pinching or rubbing his round belly.

A butcher for more than ten years, Dead Liu had had an affable temperament and taken every step in life with caution. But one day he got into a squabble with a customer who then slapped Liu in the face. Outraged, Liu grabbed a knife and stabbed the customer multiple times. When he picked up his glasses and put them on, he found the customer shaking uncontrollably in a pool of blood. With the help of onlookers, Liu slung the customer onto his back and dashed to the hospital. Halfway there, he felt the man's head pressing limply into his shoulder. The victim stuck his purple tongue out and threw up all over Liu's neck before expiring.

Dead Liu had been convicted of death twenty days before I arrived at the prison. He said he had lived his life free of adversity, but insomnia, an ailment that he had developed since his imprisonment, seemed insurmountable. He would throw a tantrum when others urged him to go to bed early. "I've spent the first half of my life sleeping like the hogs that I slaughtered. Now my eyes bulge wide open like a frog's and my body is telling me to stretch the days out and maximize my time in this world."

"There is a village in South America," I said, "where everyone sleepwalks. People conduct their business at night — planting, trading, shopping, and cooking. The whole village is lit up like it's day. When dawn approaches, people begin to yawn and enter their dream world. Some travelers who stumble upon the village during the day notice that people walk around like zombies. Often, when villagers run into each other on a narrow path, they move to the side at the last minute to avoid collisions. Even the dogs fall under the spell. They look awake but when they open their mouths to bark, no noise comes out."

"I must have lived there in my last life," Dead Liu joked. "I'll return there soon."

"Fuck those dream walkers," Dead Lan added, giving us a dirty look. Even though their days were numbered, the two never ceased fighting. "When a person dies, he is as worthless as a bucket of shit," Dead Lan said.

Ignoring Lan's bitter remarks, Dead Liu lamented, "I've finished all the books that I could get in our cell. I've already read your *Romance of the Three Kingdoms* three times. I think I'm going to start all over again tonight. The main character has been my favorite since I was a child."

A cold wind rose that night. The temperature indoors dropped precipitously. Inmates brought out their quilts. Since the stuffing in my quilt had been swept away on the first day, I shivered under a quilt cover. Dead Liu took pity on me and offered to share his comforter with me. I turned down his offer and lay down with my head on the opposite end of the bed. Dead Liu simply grabbed my legs and pulled them toward him. We clutched each other's legs for a long time. I could feel the metal shackles warm up against my chest. Strangely enough, I slept particularly well that night, despite the smelly feet pressing into my face.

Before dawn, I woke up for my nightly shift. Dead Liu was devouring *Romance of the Three Kingdoms*. At one point, his eyes were sparkling. I had no idea which chapter engrossed him so. He tossed the book aside, sat up in bed, and smashed his handcuffs against the wall. "Butcher Liu," he addressed himself, "you come from a long line of virtuous people. How did you end up here? What a tragedy!" He then heaved a long sigh with his face toward the ceiling and belted out an aria from a Sichuan opera. His singing broke the predawn quiet, plunging the cell into chaos.

"Are you nuts? What time is it?" Fellow inmates rose and shouted. The guard was called and Dead Liu was escorted out for electroshock.

Dead Liu's final moment came soon after he was transferred to Cell 5. One of his cellmates described it to me with relish. That morning Dead Liu hunkered down in a corner, waiting as usual for an inmate to bring him his breakfast. He cupped a bowl of congee awkwardly with his shackled hands. The hot sun shone through the windows, yet the dank walls oozed a chill. The cicadas blared and sparrows perched on the electric lines, leisurely tending their feathers.

"Liu," the familiar high-pitched feminine voice of Ju, the officer in charge, sounded in the doorway. Dead Liu had just taken a gulp of congee from his bowl and stuffed a piece of bread in his mouth. He instinctively backed into his usual corner and dropped his congee bowl on the floor. His breakfast partner quietly moved to the side.

The cell door glided ominously open. Ju stepped in with his hands crossed casually behind his back. He stopped by the metal fence, looking pensive, as if he could not bear to disrupt Dead Liu's last breakfast. Like a disobedient child, Dead Liu continued to retreat. Shaking his head in displeasure, Officer Ju marched into the inner room and motioned with his fingers. At this signal, two Red Hairs behind him slowly moved in on Dead Liu. One held out his hands gently, palms up. "Hey, don't resist. Behave yourself." Before Liu could respond, the two suddenly scooped him up. The terrified Liu was firmly ensconced in a sedan chair made up of four human arms. His cellmate said he had his eyes closed. He would never have to suffer hunger in his next life — his cheeks were puffed out with food when he was carried out the door like a bag of sagging mud. . . .

My other neighbor, Dead Lan, was a convicted bank robber. Several days before he was sent away for execution, Dead Lan developed sore and swollen nipples — within a few days, his breasts swelled up like those of a girl in puberty. His nipples reddened like fresh cherries. The inmates ridiculed him every day about his physical transformation, but Dead Lan chased and kicked those who mocked his misfortune. While running after one of his tormentors, he slipped off the bed and banged his head on the floor. He suffered a gash to the forehead. As he gasped for breath and struggled to get up, blood mixed with the tears that streamed down his face.

The doctor, who came in with the guard, found it hard to suppress a chuckle at the sight of Dead Lan's red nipples and big boobs. Calling it an "inexplicable illness," he could not come up with a diagnosis. He merely stitched up the cut on his forehead to stanch the bleeding and spread an herbal ointment on Dead Lan's swollen nipples. He adroitly formed three bra-shaped patches out of a roll of gauze to cover the cut on Dead Lan's forehead as well as his nipples, cautioning about possible infection. Soon after the doctor and guard exited the room, the cell exploded in laughter. Poor Dead Lan was besieged by his cellmates, who cackled, "Baby, how did you end up with three boobs?"

The doctor advised Dead Lan to change the gauze daily. When he forgot, his breasts would bloat and become sore. He always had his shirt buttoned, even in the unbearable heat of the cramped cell, and kept his arms crossed in front of his chest to keep unwanted hands away.

Despite his sore, bloated breasts, Dead Lan liked to sing. Every now and then, he would raise his head and launch into one of his favorite pop songs. I was the only one who never poked fun at him. In return, he looked out for me when I dozed off during my midnight shift. Before he was led away, he even gave me a picture of his daughter as a gift. "She is a beautiful girl," I complimented him.

"My wife left me and I've given her up for adoption." He heaved a long sigh. "She should have a father like you."

"I'm not a good parent either," I said awkwardly. "I can't even take care of my pregnant wife."

"You are smart." He giggled. "Once you plant your seed, your woman will wait for you at home, regardless of how long it takes."

"Only heaven knows," I muttered distractedly, my mind entangled in the past.

On the morning Dead Lan departed, I awoke early to assume my suicide watch over him and accidentally spotted a stirring inside his underwear. He let fly like a small mortar, making a large wet patch. Dead Lan wiped his crotch with a mortified look. I handed him some toilet paper and dug out a clean pair of underwear from his bag. "It's so disgusting," he mumbled, his face blushing. I left him alone and turned my back to him to rest my eyes.

Just as I was dozing off, Dead Lan tapped me on the shoulder. I turned around and he was gesturing for a bowl. I jumped out of bed and went to get him a bowl from the rack in the front yard. Thinking he was thirsty, I filled it with water, but he asked for an empty one. Confused, I dumped the water out and handed the bowl back to him. He quickly ripped off his "bra," put his right hand around his left breast and started to pump milk into the container. I couldn't bear to watch him grimacing with pain. He kept at it for half an hour, until his breasts sagged like empty pouches. I took the bowl from him — the thick yellowish-white liquid smelled like dead fish. Seeing the look on my face, he said apologetically, "It won't be long, I promise you! I can't wait for it all to be over."

After lunch, the temperature shot up. Dead Lan's breasts swelled up again. He pushed his way to the water tank and requested a cold shower, but the chief shot him down because the other inmates had to wash their eating utensils first. As Dead Lan waited in line and the water in the tank was disappearing, he turned desperate. Breaking through the human wall, he ran naked to the tank and scooped up a bowl of water. The chief seized his wrist, and knocked his bowl to the floor. Dead Lan stood there, stunned, his tall figure streaked with sunlight; the veins on his head bulging and his swollen breasts trembling, ready to explode. At that moment the cell door opened and let in a light breeze. The familiar womanly voice called from the outside, "Lan, step out for a minute."

The air suddenly froze. Dead Lan's spirit left him in a wisp of smoke, swirling up into the sky through the sun-filled squares on the ceiling. I picked his shirt off the floor and handed it to him. He was too distracted to even hold it. The shirt fell to the floor again. Officer Ju and two Red Hairs materialized in the cell, pushing all the other inmates into the back room. Bank robber Lan went on his journey stark naked. He had intended to take a shower and cleanse himself before turning into a ghost, but even this trifling request was mercilessly denied.

The Unrelenting Sun

TWO WEEKS AFTER I entered Cell 10, I got into a fight with a fellow inmate and ended up with my hands tied behind my back. Sympathetic to my situation as a counterrevolutionary, the doctor fitted me with large handcuffs but clamped a much smaller pair on my opponent's wrists. Half an hour later, my arms felt a little sore, but my foe's hands had swollen up like two hot steamed buns. The metal cut into his flesh; by the next day, pus oozed out of the welts.

At break time, an inmate folded up his quilt and bedding, and piled them up against the wall so I could lean against them and alleviate the pressure on my back. At night, drowsiness enveloped me, but I couldn't sleep. Sometimes, I could bite my right shoulder and the momentary sharp pain would distract me from the dull discomfort of my pinioned wrists. At midnight I got up and strolled around near the fencelike door. Quietly, I slipped my hands out of the oversized handcuffs, furtively raising my arms in the air for a quick stretch and yawn. An officer on duty, with the ironic name of Tender Lao, caught me.

"You're a little too comfy in there, aren't you, Mr. Poet?" he said in a sardonic tone that also exuded a tinge of sympathy. I felt relieved that I had fallen into the hands of Tender Lao, a thin, bony man in his thirties. On my second day at the detention center, Tender Lao secretly called me into his office and listened to me recite "Massacre." He looked visibly moved after I finished.

I thought I had gotten away with my breach. The next morning, however, Officer Ju summoned me into his office. A pair of smaller, tight-fitting handcuffs awaited me on his desk. He declared that I would have to remain handcuffed for two additional days. The last of my trust in apparently sympathetic police officers was smashed to pieces. "You don't look very happy with my decision," Ju mocked me. "Your cellmates will feed you food and hold your pants when you shit. You'll live the life of a king."

I begged him for leniency, but Ju rebuffed me. I refused to go back to the cell, and sat down on the steps outside the building. "You are a well-known poet and I'm a low-level prison officer," Ju said sarcastically. "I wouldn't dare force you. If you choose to sit here, why not help me keep watch on those three standing in the sun." He nodded at some other inmates. "They merely started a singing contest in their cell. In comparison, their offense is a minor one."

The eaves sheltered me from the sun. Three prisoners, with bare heads and feet, stood wilted inside a chalk circle in a corner of the compound. The blazing sun had almost dried their perspiration, and a thin crust of yellowish salt was accumulating on their shaved heads. At noon, one crashed to the ground. Officer Ju ordered a Red Hair to pour a big bucket of cold water over the heatstroke victim. A cloud of steam rose from him.

"Our great leader Chairman Mao once said, 'What a pleasure to fight with heaven,'" Officer Ju encouraged the violators with humor while fanning himself furiously. He then turned to a Red Hair. "Reward each one with a bowl of cold water so they can continue to enjoy the pleasure of fighting nature."

Out of generosity, a Red Hair poured a bowl of water down my throat. Within minutes, hot sweat slithered down my body like biting locusts. My shackled hands twisted around behind my back, trying to scratch my spine, waist, and buttocks. Meanwhile, I lowered my head to my knee to wipe away the sweat that stung my eyes. The itching ground through my armpits. I raised both arms and jabbed my chin under there, trying in vain to rub it against the hairy skin. For spots that I couldn't reach with my hands, I scraped myself greedily up and down against the rough surface of a wall like a lazy dog. Soon, the itch on my back turned into stinging pain as salty sweat washed into the bloody scratches. Officer Ju clasped his hands. "It's so much fun to watch. On this side, a bunch of barefoot monks are dancing in the sun. On the other side, an intellectual is rubbing his itchy back against a wall."

Hurt and humiliated, I asked to be sent back to my cell. The sun gradually moved west. The three prisoners were ordered to shift locations. As their bare feet touched the burning concrete floor, they jumped up and down like desperate frogs on a dry, cracked field.

Many years later, I suffered constant bouts of itchiness all over my body. A doctor attributed it to animal allergies, but I disagreed. I was certain I had gotten it from prison. Each time I had my hands tied behind my back, I most feared the itching. With itchy spots on accessible parts of my body, I rubbed incessantly against the rough surfaces of walls or on the edges of the concrete bed. My crotch, armpits, and the backs of my knees were the hardest — gnawingly itchy but unreachable. With the departure of my two death row pals, I had to rely on the mercy of others. For help on a special part of the body, an ingratiating smile and a bow never worked. Financial incentives were needed.

"Hey, Brother, could you lend me your hand, three yuan per scratch."

"No fucking way! I'm not touching that, that's disgusting."

"Oh, come on!" I said. "I'll double the amount."

"I'll scratch your balls and armpits for ten yuan."

"Fuck, that's too expensive."

"You think I want to do it?" he said.

I wanted to walk away but the gnawing itch begged me to stay. "Okay, I'm flexible on the price."

"So, you agree to pay that amount?"

"Okay, ten yuan. It's a done deal."

His fingernails scratched my armpits. Nothing ever felt so good.

A New Neighbor

THE MONTH-LONG TORMENT ENDED. The chief allowed me to join the regular rotation on suicide watch. My change in status coincided with a change in officers. The newly appointed officer was a handsome young man, politically ambitious and reform-minded. His first day on the job, he walked into our cell and shook up the pecking order by revoking the privileges bestowed on seasoned prisoners like the chief.

Without the predawn shift, I could finally sleep through the night. Heat waves ravaged the mountain city and continued unabated at night. We all slept naked on straw mats, which stuck firmly to our sweaty bodies after we lay down. Each time I rolled over, it felt like peeling a bandage off my skin. A ceiling fan hummed noisily right above me, and when I closed my eyes a colossal humming machine hovered in my dreams. The multiple ceiling fans circulated the dry, filthy air, parching our skin and lips. Once the fence was shut for the night, the small bucket of boiled drinking water ran out fast. Veteran inmates set aside an extra bowl of water to cool off on the windowsill for themselves. New inmates had no such privileges. When the boiled water dried up, we turned to the concrete tank that stored unsanitized water for washing and flushing the toilet. Once that water was used up, the foul stench from the toilet permeated the air.

I was assigned a new neighbor — another man on death row. Like my two previous neighbors, he also had problems sleeping at night. Each time he closed his eyes, he said, he could hear gunshots in his head. He constantly sat against the wall, his eyes fixated on me like a pair of needles. A few days later, I discovered his gaze was not directed at me, or at anyone else. I learned to ignore it.

His name was Zhang, and he was an accomplice in a major drug-trafficking case. His cooperation with the government won him a reprieve and he was able to avoid the death penalty. But life was full of surprises. The chief culprit filed an appeal, determined to drag him down. "We are good friends. If we die, we'll go down together so I won't be so lonely in the netherworld," said the key defendant. The appeal succeeded. The Sichuan Provincial Supreme Court concluded in its second review that the prosecutor's initial arguments to commute Zhang's sentence were based on questionable facts and ordered a retrial. The intermediate court complied and reinstated Zhang's death penalty in the subsequent trial.

The new verdict devastated Dead Zhang. He had barely turned thirty but his hair had gone completely gray. He was full of self-pity, comparing himself to Wu Zixu, an ancient Chinese scholar and military strategist whose hair had turned white overnight after the crown prince in the kingdom of Chu murdered his father and brother and sent troops to hunt him down.

Late one night, Dead Zhang prodded me with his fingers, trying to strike up a conversation. I rolled over and ignored him. He tempted me with a bag of snacks.

"What do you want to chat about?" I mumbled, with my eyes half-closed.

"Did you know my hair turned gray within one month?"

"Yes."

"In the first half of that month, when my death sentence was initially commuted, I burst out crying, pleading with an officer to withdraw money from my bank account and buy tinned meat for everyone in my cell. Little did I know that excessive joy could be so harmful, whitening half of my hair. Then, in the second half of the month . . ."

"I know."

"Like the ancient saying goes, excessive joy leads to sorrow, and even an early death."

"I know."

"You don't know shit," he cursed at me and startled me by singing an aria from a Sichuan opera at the top of his voice: "Wu Zixu fled his country, with deep hatred for his enemy; his mane turned white overnight when he was stuck at Shaoguan."

It was like being drenched with a bucket of ice-cold water — I came to with a start. In Dead Zhang's frightening face I recognized the specter of Dead Liu, who also loved humming Sichuan operas. I shivered.

Dead Zhang had woken everyone else as well. My hair stood on end. Was it pure coincidence or did Dead Liu's spirit attach itself to another man on death row? I could almost hear the two of them talking with the same voice.

To distract myself from Dead Zhang, I befriended a cellmate, Wu, who had been a police officer in charge of city residency permits. He was thrown in jail after seriously injuring a resident during a street fight. We became closer after I learned that he had been locked up in the same cell with my friend Chen Dong, the director. Wu loved literature, and before their departure, Chen Dong had even gifted him a copy of *Remembrance of Things Past* by Marcel Proust.

I engaged in long talks with Wu about poetry, prison, and my new literary fantasy: "Someday, I hope to perform my poem 'Massacre' in Tiananmen Square, broadcast over more than a hundred loudspeakers, enough to make the earth vibrate."

"I'm sure the government will reverse its verdict against the student movement of 1989," he ventured. "Unfortunately, it will take a very long time."

"I don't care."

"And we'll be very old."

That line struck me in the heart. I shuddered and almost teared up. "Since the first day of my detention, I have rehearsed and rewritten

'Massacre' in my head a thousand times." I struggled for words. "It is my only reason to live."

My passion apparently did not impress Wu, who advised me, "There are many reasons for a person to live. Only a lunatic clings to a set rule."

Officer Gong

In August, the heat reached its peak in Chongqing, China's furnace. The detention cells were the heart of the furnace. The ceiling fan spun noisily all the time but failed to bring down the sizzling temperature. Heatstroke hit half my cellmates. Each day, two or three would collapse on the floor and be hauled off to the infirmary. The doctor force-fed them with bottles of herbal water and then abandoned them, leaving them to regain consciousness on their own. The rest of us stayed awake all night long, like rabbits in heat; eyes, ears, and noses turning purplish. My steely skeleton was rusting away with sweat and my temper erupted sporadically like a sudden burst of firecrackers. For each altercation or fight with the other inmates I was penalized by having my hands tied behind my back for as long as a week.

Fortunately, Gong, the new officer, acted like a patient animal trainer, taming his tiger with great humanity. He treated me as his favorite, delivering letters from my family on time and updating my visiting wife and relatives on my situation at the detention center. He never missed an opportunity to discuss politics with me, even when my hands were cuffed behind my back for breaking prison rules. "I agree that the verdict against the student movement will be overturned someday. But, when that happens, what will that do to our country?" he said with concern.

"We can learn from the Soviet Union," I said, stretching my swollen shoulder slightly.

"We don't have a Mikhail Gorbachev in China. Party Secretary Zhao Ziyang tried to be one but he lacked Gorbachev's political will," Gong disagreed gently. "If we are not careful with political reforms, our country could be in chaos. It's scary to think about it."

Officer Gong rose from his chair, pacing up and down the length of the room. As he went on about his views on world affairs, I sat there sweating, tormented by an unbearable urge to scratch the itch on my back. Tears and snot had run down my face. I raised my knees to wipe my nose on my thighs. My awkward attempt caught Gong's eye. He stopped his monologue and mopped my face with an immaculate white towel. The tender gesture emboldened me. I begged him to remove my handcuffs. Officer Gong was noncommittal and sent me back to the cell, his face pensive.

Breaking news came across the TV that evening—the conservatives within the Communist Party had launched a coup d'état in the Soviet Union. The whole prison tensed up. The number of guards outside our cell doubled, as if the political uncertainties in our socialist neighbor could spill over to China. The bell rang and prisoners were asked to go to bed earlier than scheduled. The next day, prisoners' outdoor breaks were cancelled.

A week later, I was taken out of the cell to have my handcuffs removed. The first assignment after my limbs were freed was to mop the floor. The mop was made of rags from two pairs of used pants. With my butt in the air, I crawled about the floor, pushing the mop at full speed, back and forth, left and right, until the concrete floors in the courtyard and the back room shone. My fanatical devotion to the job irked many, including a newly arrived member of the living dead who preferred to sleep on the cold, wet floor. "You've scrubbed the surface so many times that it's burning," he whined. "I'm going to pour water on the floor to cool it off."

"Don't you dare mess up my clean floor!" I flashed my fist in front of him.

He scooped up some water with his bowl, and I kicked the bowl out of his hands.

"Well, well, if you pick a fight with the dying, you're up against the whole cell," the chief warned me.

"You're the one behind all of this," I roared. "If you have the balls and want to cut my head open, do it then."

"You're being overly sensitive," the chief said with his signature sly chuckle.

To defuse the tension, the chief had other inmates clear the aisle. Then he seized another living dead, a former peasant, who was sleeping like a hog in his pool of dirty water. The chief ripped the peasant's underwear off. Other inmates mobbed him, tying a piece of string around his big dick and parading him around the room. Some clinked their bowls with chopsticks, others stomped their feet, cooing and clapping their hands. The peasant boy did not mind the teasing and basked in the attention. He proudly flaunted his member and yelled, "Your loss if you don't look at it. The world's biggest dick, thicker than those foreigners'!"

Watching the show, I forgot about my grievances with the chief. But he didn't. That night I realized that my usual spot had been taken by the chief's new boy toy, Big Dick. The others sat off to the side, waiting for the show to begin. Big Dick, who was normally shy and timid, lay flat on my straw mat and moaned with pleasure as the ceiling fan blew cool air onto his face.

Politely, I told him to get up.

"No, this is where I sleep," he answered defiantly.

Blood surged to my head. I grabbed his pillow and tossed it toward the fence. Big Dick got off the bed and brought it back. I tossed it again and raised my fist. A patrolling guard on the top clicked his gun and the electric fence popped open. My clenched fist froze in midair.

Officer Gong and a big, bearded guard arrived, each carrying electric batons that could deliver a fierce crackling spark. Several Red Hairs thronged behind them. Big Dick and I were shoved out of the cell and ordered to squat at the bottom of the stairs, putting ourselves at the mercy of the guards. Officer Gong walked over to ask the cause of the commotion and Big Dick cried foul, claiming that he was bullied. Ignoring the histrionics, Officer Gong tapped Big Dick on the head with his baton. He jumped like a frog, his screaming was loud enough to shatter the earth.

Officer Gong called the chief into the courtyard to inquire about what had happened. I was left with the guard, who touched me with his baton and pulled the trigger. Bright blue sparks stretched out into an arc. The electricity ground through my scalp as if it were pulling out all my nerves and battering my brain with a cudgel. Instinctively, I buried my head between my knees to cover my ears. The electric current surged from my neck to my feet, and my body trembled uncontrollably.

"Who started the fight?" the guard asked.

My tongue stiffened.

There was another jab on the right side of my ribs. I jumped as if I had been poked by a burning poker and reached out to snatch the stun baton. The Red Hairs closed in on me, seizing my hands and feet. I fell, my chin hitting the concrete floor. Someone helped me up. Through a haze, I recognized the face of Officer Gong. With a stern look, he twisted both of my arms behind me and handcuffed them. Meanwhile, Big Dick swaggered back to the cell.

The cell gate opened, revealing a dazzling hole of light, like the bloody mouth of a lion. I prostrated myself near the entrance and refused to enter. I knew my cellmates were grinding their teeth, waiting to eat me alive.

"Go in. We'll talk tomorrow," Officer Gong advised.

"No." I was adamant. Two or three stun batons were thrust in my direction. Crackling sparks flew and my body convulsed violently. The stars in the sky blinked, shining like razor blades, weaving a sprawling net above me and poking holes all over my body. "You are so pigheaded," the guard bellowed. He dropped his baton, stood over me, and smacked me from left to right. The old-fashioned blows sent me running.

The Red Hairs laughed loudly. They caught up with me, wrestled me down, and more shocks followed. I do not remember when they loosened their grip on me. When they propped me up, I had no clue where I was.

"The door is there," I heard someone say.

"Aren't you going to admit your wrongdoing?" It was Officer Gong's voice.

"No, I won't." I slurred my words. After what I had gone through, I had to say no.

All was quiet. Still dizzy from the blows, I lay wilted against the metal fence inside Cell 10. For a poet, harsh tortures may provide a cure for delusions. Only when our flesh suffers can our spirit keep alert and free amid the confusion and constrictions in our lives.

The Model Cell

THE NEXT MORNING, OFFICER Gong came in with the news that I would be moved to a different cell. "A new environment will be good for you," he unlocked the cuffs behind my back and said in a concerned tone. "Wash your face and change into some clean clothes. Try to forget what happened last night."

I suppressed a surge of bitterness. When we were out in the corridor, Officer Gong handed me a stack of letters. "Take all of them with you," he said. "You have more letters than anyone else. When you think of all the people outside who really care about you, you might feel better and calm down a bit."

The sun was spewing fire. The moss on the tall wall had baked dry and curled up. From a distance, it looked like ringworms on a scalp. With both hands around my bundle of clothes and books, I followed Officer Gong through four black gates. Perspiration ran down my nose, but I felt cool inside. Officer Gong ordered me to stop at Cell 5. He lifted the latch and let me in. "This is your new home," he said.

I crossed the front yard and hesitantly reached the inner cell. A gaggle of shaved heads immediately swarmed around me. A young man with big eyes took the bundle from me and placed it at the end of the big concrete bed. "My name is Chen Dejian, a counterrevolutionary," he declared proudly.

"We all call him Chairman Chen," a thin, dark-skinned inmate joked.

"Officer Gong mentioned that you are a poet. Is that correct?" Chairman Chen asked. "We have lots of talented people here."

At that moment, I noticed a death row inmate named Chang sitting in the middle of the bed. He had a big head, with bulging fish eyes. There was a deep groove between his eyebrows, perhaps a grotesque wound — I couldn't tell. Dead Chang smiled as if he could see through me. "Do you have any books with you?" he asked.

I handed over my whole collection. Surprisingly, he picked an atlas and buried his head in the maps. Meanwhile, two portly old men, fully shackled, stared at me. One introduced himself as Sun and the other, Sui. I stepped up to greet the two living dead and both nodded at me warmly. It looked like I was going to be with a less regimented group — everyone seemed to get along. A calendar that marked each person's dates to clean the cell was pasted neatly beneath the detention center regulations. Chairman Chen borrowed a pen from a passing Red Hair outside and added my name to the calendar.

"Officer Gong is determined to reform the system here. He started a pilot project at our cell." Chairman Chen deliberately raised his voice so the guards could hear his praises. "The new and old are treated equally."

Around lunchtime, Chairman Chen distributed bowls and chopsticks to everyone. Each shackled living dead was assigned a cellmate to help with his food. Even though the pumpkin soup was not appetizing, everyone cheerfully gulped it down. At naptime, I followed tradition for newbies in my previous cell and put my pillow next to the toilet. Dead Sui stopped me, claiming that the spot was specifically set aside for him. He asked me to pick a nicer spot on the bed. I was so overwhelmed by his generosity that I was at a loss for what to do. "I didn't know Dead Sui could be so noble and altruistic like a model Communist," a dark-skinned inmate quipped.

The next day, I brought out all my unopened letters and started reading them, making my other inmates jealous. By noon, I still hadn't finished and continued in the afternoon. Most of the letters were from A Xia, who used to keep a journal and write an entry every day. Tears that she shed for each departure and reunion stained the journal pages, which had yellowed prematurely, making them look like writings from a different era. Following my arrest, all of her journals had been confiscated, along with a large number of letters, photos, and antiques her father had left her before he died. The police had perused all of her writings line by line, and technicians had even made special marks on the margins of the letters, looking for hidden messages. With police constantly raiding my house, my wife stopped writing in her journals, but she had gotten into the habit of writing me one letter per week. For a while, her letters were filled with news about our unborn baby, in the hope that the prospect of being a father would cheer me up and inculcate a sense of purpose in me. She was well prepared for motherhood. Each time she felt a kick in her abdomen, she would obsessively record it and compose a long, sentimental letter. Without me at her side, the unborn infant became her constant companion.

My friend Zhong also wrote to me. He had been detained for only a brief period and was released after the police failed to find any evidence about his direct involvement in my film project. Zhong frequently sent me money and food, and he hired a lawyer for Hippie Poet, who, among all those implicated, seemed to have the most hope of early release. More pessimistic about *my* prospects, Zhong consulted a fortune-teller to see what lay ahead of me. "You will spend years drifting around the world," Zhong quoted the fortune-teller.

One afternoon, all the inmates were ordered to file out into the compound for our routine haircut. For each haircut the officer gave, he could could get 1.5 yuan in bonus pay. Therefore, all the officers were present with clippers to participate in one of the world's grandest hygienic operations. Nervous detainees hunkered down on the ground, forming a large patch of black hair. Bare-shouldered officers were as skillful as chefs slicing melons and chopping vegetables. "Next. Step up," they commanded. Within an hour or so, the garden of black hair was harvested, and in its place were more than one hundred and sixty melon heads.

Officer Ju emerged as the haircut champion. A compulsive cleaner, he kept an upright posture and maintained a cautious distance from the detainees. "Stay away, because each criminal is home to a kingdom of germs," he warned his colleagues. Thereafter, all the "barbers" followed his example—they put their left hands behind their back and their right arms stretched out rigidly. The only moving parts were their right hands, which operated the clippers. Every haircut involved a few quick strokes up and down and left and right. Occasionally, they would call out instructions like a real barber: "Tilt it to the right," "Raise your head," or "Lower your head."

Right before his turn, Chairman Chen quietly moved away to a different queue for a veteran officer, who, after years of practice, had become really good at what he did. Officer Liu spotted him. "Catch that slippery eel!" he hollered and ran after Chairman Chen with his clipper. Clamping Chairman Chen's head with his left hand, Officer Liu buzzed away with his right one. Chairman Chen tried to struggle free from his grip and plunged onto the ground in the process. Instead of pulling him up, Liu kicked Chairman Chen hard on his buttocks.

I had a thick beard, and previous haircuts had left me bleeding as if I had been slashed by a murderer. On that day, the officer must have pressed the clipper too fast or the tool had become blunt and rusty. The teeth of the blade burrowed into my flesh and ripped a piece of skin off the back of my head. The officer-barber simply pulled a tissue from his pocket, tore off a corner, and stuck it on the cut. To wipe off the blood from his "weapon," he rubbed it against my bare shoulder.

"Don't fuss over the cuts," Dead Chang comforted me after we returned to the cell. "Injuries are unavoidable. It's better than having someone play a practical joke on you and leave several spots untouched. That would make you look like a lunatic."

"What's to be afraid of if you have a bad haircut? It's not like you are going to date a woman here," argued a pale-skinned inmate whose nickname was "Scholar Yang." "Look at those punks in the West. They all have weird hair."

A Preliminary Hearing

AT THE END OF August, Director Li from the Provincial Prosecutor's Office came for more interrogation. He was harsh and unrestrained with me. I refused to be intimidated and argued back fiercely. My newly gained confidence came from months of researching China's Criminal Procedure Law. In the lingua franca of the government, I was "using the weapon of law to protect myself."

"In keeping with the legal procedures of our country, this is a preliminary hearing," Director Li explained. "Unlike a trial investigation, you can take back your previous statements if you think they strayed from the truth."

I refused to take the bait and stuck with what I had said in earlier confessions. The questions remained the same — what were the true motives of my writings? Did I attempt to attack the party for its crackdown on the "counterrevolutionary mobs" in Tiananmen Square? Who were my secret supporters?

In contrast to my previous reticence and denials, I chattered on. Employing the rhetorical device of repetition, I went on in circles. As the number of interrogations increased, I lost track and couldn't tell them apart. I no longer racked my brain to find ways to cover my trail, and I improvised as I went. Since I was the supposed ringleader, my confessions carried a certain weight. Director Li jotted down everything I said, even though much of it was simply sarcastic nonsense that was used to counter his threats and cajoling.

I would pay a price for my capricious improvisations during the preliminary hearings — prosecutors used them as new evidence against me. At the same time, the court also convened more than twenty well-known scholars from key cultural organizations in Chongqing to review my poems "Massacre" and "Requiem." Seven professors in Sichuan submitted their opinions in writing, accusing me of venting hatred against the party through my literary works.

One hot, rainy afternoon two weeks later, Director Li, with sweat running down his cheeks, handed me a stack of papers and solemnly announced, "Here are the minutes. From testimonials and the confessions given freely by you during previous interrogations and by your accomplices and relatives, we have concluded that the criminal charges against you are based on indisputable facts and that the investigations were conducted in accordance with the law. Therefore, we will submit our recommendation for prosecution. Please sign on these minutes that were taken during our hearings."

"This is a trap," I protested. "I refuse to sign."

Director Li ignored me. "Liao Yiwu, I advise you to take a more cooperative attitude. Resistance and denial are futile. If you cooperate with the authorities, it is still possible to have your sentence reduced."

In the semidarkness, I signed my name on the minutes, waiting for the rain to stop. Occasionally, Director Li would engage in idle chitchat to ease the boredom. I felt like I was trapped in the cabin of a ship struggling in the heart of a stormy sea. The world outside flitted past. I had been in police custody for nearly six months. When would this imprisonment end? Would I survive?

The rain outside showed no sign of letting up. With a sigh, Director Li stood up, buttoned his shirt, and stepped out first. He paused under the ledge above the entrance. "The sky must be leaking. Go ahead and run back to your cell in the rain."

Without a word, I dashed down the stone stairs. Halting in the middle of the parking lot, I stopped and looked up at the sky — so big and majestic. The shifting clouds were galloping forward like a pack of wild horses, their manes flying and their hooves kicking up claps of thunder. My spirit was riding on horseback, soaring in the bright night sky. I stared at the cars parked around me. Escaping in a car had long been a recurring fantasy of mine. I touched the window of a brand-new Volkswagen Santana; a trembling fear coursed through me like an electric current. I looked around, my heart pounding.

The fantasy soon dissipated, as quickly as it came. The watchful eyes of Big Brother were everywhere, and the parking lot was no place to linger. Covering my head with my hands, I returned to the cage. Silently, I thanked the heavenly god for granting me the enjoyment of those solitary twenty minutes in the rain. The freedom, however fleeting, was costly — I was sick with a cold for a week.

Back in my cell, many inmates surrounded me, asking questions. When Dead Chang found out that my interrogator was Director Li, he paused for a few seconds, straightened his back, and cleared his throat. Like a judge in court, he pronounced, "Fifteen years in jail," as if reading out a judicial sentence.

It nearly knocked me out, as if I had been hit by a thick cane. I crouched down helplessly.

"Many have died in the hands of Li," continued Dead Chang, who had friends at the prosecutor's office. "If the case is not serious, he normally doesn't come in person."

My forehead was covered with a sheen of cold sweat.

"You are the prime culprit in a major counterrevolutionary case," he said. "So, I would say you'll get at least fifteen years."

"That number is probably too conservative," Scholar Yang said, further fueling my fears.

"According to the Criminal Procedure Law, one gets five to ten years in jail for the crime of instigating counterrevolutionary propaganda," Chairman Chen disagreed. "In my case, seven of us have been arrested. So far, the chief culprit has only gotten seven years."

"Well, we shouldn't forget the new regulations relating to counter-revolutionary activities. Based on these new rules, those with serious violations could get life imprisonment," Dead Chang observed in feigned sadness. "Criminal 0-9-9 perpetrated his counterrevolutionary crimes after our government had cracked down on the student protest movement. In addition, he utilized equipment set aside for the military to achieve his goal."

"I think I read about it in the newspaper," added a young man nicknamed "Dark Skin" for his tan. "His case has implicated more than ten poets."

"Let me officially announce the verdict against criminal 0-9-9." Dead Chang stood at attention like a judge.

His performance triggered uproarious laughter. The festive noise stirred the guards on the second floor. Officer Yu, who was on duty, rushed over with his electric baton.

"You stinky scumbags," Officer Yu said, reaching his head in from the food delivery window.

"Yes, we are scumbags," Dead Chang responded.

"Did I ask you to respond? You son of a bitch! Move your head over here," Officer Yu ordered.

Dead Chang did as instructed. Officer Yu's stun baton landed squarely on the back of his head and shoulders. His belly and legs convulsed violently. After Officer Yu walked away, total silence descended upon the cell. Dead Chang's face was purple. He sat down in a corner for quite a while, limp as a drunkard. He asked a cellmate to help him take off his sweat-soaked undershirt. "The jabbing is good treatment for my cold," he murmured with a halfhearted laugh. The sinister groove between his eyebrows became more pronounced.

At bedtime, Chairman Chen, who slept next to me, whispered, "Don't take things seriously. They're just teasing you."

"What a cruel joke," I mumbled grudgingly. "Fifteen years in jail? That would destroy my whole life."

"I think Scholar Yang and Dark Skin are going to get tougher sentences," Chairman Chen continued. "Deep down, they hope you will get more years than they do."

"Why do they care how many years I get?" I shook my head.

"When people are in despair, they want to drag others down to make themselves feel better. As you probably know, half of the people in our cell have committed crimes that are eligible for the death penalty."

A cold draft looped around my neck, piercing my brain. I could feel a crisis lurking.

In the middle of the night, my throat hurt and I began to feel feverish from the exposure in the pouring rain during the day. Dead Chang got up to use the squat toilet. I peeked at him and noticed his face turning purple from constipation. Noticing my scowl, Chairman Chen turned his body sideways to block my view. The stench floated in the air. We dabbed toothpaste around our nostrils. It was a stark reminder of my wretched life in hell.

The Death Squad

As I was waiting anxiously for news from the prosecutor's office, the verdicts were handed down for three of my fellow inmates — Scholar Yang (convicted of larceny), Dark Skin (first-degree murder), and a nineteen-year-old whom we called "Little" (robbing and kidnapping). All were sentenced to death.

The three newly convicted huddled together with Dead Chang, and vowed to be blood brothers in the next world. At dusk every day, Dead Chang would lead his "death squad" in a military drill. They formed a single line, goose-stepping to one end of the wall, turning around in unison, and marching to the other end. The shackles around their hands and ankles clashed and clanked, and the noise turned our cell into a blacksmith's workshop. Sometimes the drill buoyed Dead Chang's spirit, and he would randomly belt out a song written by a Communist martyr: "Parading down the street in chains, bidding farewell to family and villagers." At this prompting, Dead Chang's friends chorused the second part, their shackled feet tapping the floor: "I'm not afraid of putting my head under the knife, as long as my faith is alive. / If you kill me today, more followers will come."

Among the four death row inmates, Little took the pending execution the worst. One night, he suddenly let out a piercing cry before springing to his feet and hitting his head against the wall in an apparent attempt to kill himself. "Nobody calls the guards," Dead Chang warned everyone. Scholar Yang clutched Little to his bosom, wiping the blood off his forehead. Dark Skin also dragged his shackled feet over to console his friend. "My good brother, take it easy," said Dark Skin. "Our fate is predetermined and you were not meant to live long in this world. Once the gunshot is fired, you won't feel or know a thing."

"He is right." Scholar Yang nodded approvingly. "Our life is filled with perilous thresholds. Imprisonment is one such threshold that we have to cross. Execution is another one."

As everyone buzzed around Little, the guards upstairs overheard the noise. Soon, guns were clicking and the guard yelled, "Stand up!"

The four "death squad" members rose as ordered and shifted uneasily under the humming fan. Little's suicide attempt, if found out, would be seen as a serious offense at the detention center.

"What's happening here?" the guard asked.

"Nothing," Dead Chang said with fake cheerfulness. "The kid is having a nightmare."

"Liar." The guard snorted.

"Please don't report us," Dead Chang cried desperately and dropped to his knees. The shackles around his ankles clanked loudly. "Soldier! Little Brother! We are going to die soon. Please let us get away with it just once."

"Well, you asked for it," the guard scoffed. "You made your own bed and you sleep in it."

"You are right. We deserve to die," Dead Chang sobbed. "But even bad people have feelings. We are human beings raised by caring parents. Kindness should be our second nature. Please give him a break, Brother. He's only nineteen."

The other three were also down on their knees, begging. "Please, soldier. Have mercy on us."

The tears must have softened the guard's heart. "If you want me to keep quiet, you'd better follow the rules and behave yourself while I'm on duty," the guard said. "It's not easy for us either."

"He couldn't handle things just now. I swear I'll take care of him," Dead Chang promised. "I don't sleep much. Brother, go ahead with your patrol. I promise he'll be okay. If anything happens, beat me and kill me. I deserve every bit of it."

Silence followed. From the overhead window in the concrete ceiling, I could see the guard's cigarette stub blinking in the darkness. Finally he sauntered away. His footsteps, which seemed laden with worries, gradually faded into the distance.

I awoke after midnight. In a corner lit up by hazy moonlight, I saw Little's friends cluster around him. They apparently were taking turns cuddling him like loving fathers. The next morning, before Little had time to wash away the traces of sleepiness from his face, he was escorted out. An hour later, he came back fully shackled. It was hard to believe this tiny, skeletal boy had committed multiple heinous crimes involving robbing and kidnapping.

"It's funny that I didn't get to live a good life until now," he sighed. "Now that I'm going to die, so many people take care of me. I don't have to worry about food and clothes. When I was outside, I begged on the street and robbed people because nobody would offer me a job."

Over the next few weeks, Chairman Chen adopted him and put him under his meticulous care.

"Little has put on weight and his face has started to have color now," he said proudly. "When he first came here, he was so emaciated that he could not even stand straight."

Scholar Yang agreed. "Chairman Chen gave him some clothes and bought three meat dishes for him during his first lunch. He ate it all and ended up having terrible diarrhea."

"That poor thing! It was certainly understandable." Chairman Chen beamed. "Little was transferred from a city in Jiangsu. They were fed with pig feed. That was why he was so emaciated and dizzy all the time."

"You certainly have a good memory." Dead Chang laughed.

"Of course, I do. Now that Little is getting plump and healthy, I'm taking my share of the credit."

"You've been bragging about it a lot; aren't you tired of it?"

Dead Chang's rude remarks stunned Chairman Chen, and his face colored. Words stuck in his throat. "So? So what if I have told the story several times?"

"You are a livestock keeper and feed a bunch of pigs," I couldn't help joining the fight on Chairman Chen's side. "Now the pigs are biting the hands that feed them."

"Yes, you are right. I am a pig," Little sobbed. "Now that you have fattened me up, they'll send me to the slaughterhouse. You counter-revolutionaries are evil."

The enraged Chairman Chen was shaking.

"You have given me your clothes, your pillowcase, and your shoes. Take them back if you want." Little threw the stuff at Chairman Chen. I picked up the articles from the floor one by one. The other inmates cheered, reminding me of a public denunciation during the Cultural Revolution.

Slave Labor

IN EARLY FALL, LOUDSPEAKERS blasted out an announcement that all detainees would be required to perform physical labor. We were told that the work involved making handicrafts. Minimal skills were required, but the job would be demanding, and strict rules would be enforced to evaluate it.

Nobody knew that the "handicrafts" were cardboard boxes of medicine packets. We were required to glue the packets one by one. Thus, a ten-hour day began. The work seemed endless.

In the morning, three inmates went out to cart cardboard boxes into the cell and pile them up high along the wall. The aisle was narrowed to a slit, just wide enough to walk through. A fully armed officer who supervised the project lectured us on the rules. Our job for that day, he said, was to make paper packets for a variety of medicine powders. We were taught to spread a thin layer of glue over the edge of a piece of paper and then carefully fold it into the shape of a packet. Once the glue dried, a quality control person would check and pack them.

Many local factories had long abandoned such repetitive manual work. Prison authorities sought it out, however, and contracted the work, using free prison labor and splitting the profits among police officers. Each of us could generate five hundred to six hundred yuan per month for the detention center.

As compensation, we were each given, free of charge, a big bowl of stewed tofu. Some veterans would eat half and save the other half for dinner. In addition, authorities also relaxed the rules on cigar smoking, which had been banned. In the afternoon, a Red Hair came to the window, taking orders from people who were interested in purchasing cigars at the price of twenty-four cents a packet. The smoke from the cigars smelled no less pungent than explosives. When a dozen or so prisoners lit up after lunch each day, a thick smoke fogged up the room. I felt like I was stuck in a gas chamber, struggling to breathe. Fortunately, a patrolling guard stumbled upon the scene. Shocked at the air quality, he granted us an exception by opening the fence and kicking the smokers out into the courtyard.

Smokers had their nicotine fix, but for us nonsmokers, the choking air disrupted our nap. Work resumed at full swing in the afternoon. We were divided up, two or three to a group. In the first three days, an officer came to demonstrate the necessary skills, and we were allowed to fumble around at a leisurely pace. Once our "internship" period was over, the quota for each individual was set at five hundred packets per day. Soon it increased to one thousand and then to fifteen hundred in the following week. A month later, the daily number jumped to three thousand. Through the loudspeakers, officers motivated everyone to scale new heights: "For those who exceed their quota and achieve remarkable results, we'll document their good work. The court will use it as the basis to commute their sentences." This promise, illusory though, worked like psychostimulants, prompting some detainees to set superhuman records by gluing and folding seven thousand packets all night without a wink of sleep.

The heavy workload temporarily alleviated the tension among inmates. The "death squad," led by Dead Chang, followed its own pace and rules. The quotas for death row inmates were hardly enforced; Dead Chang and his friends could afford to work for a few minutes and then stop to chat.

"0-9-9, do you need help?" Dead Chang inched over one day.

"What do you want? You want to borrow my atlas, don't you?" I joked, barely lifting my eyes from the packets.

"Kind of." He rolled his fish eyes. "Looking at maps is the only hobby I have left in this life," Dead Chang reminisced. "Look, I used to follow a certain route to transport heroin. I got the stuff in Ruili in Yunnan and delivered it to Chongqing. It was a long trip of thousands of kilometers. Besides, I had to pass countless checkpoints."

"No matter how good you were, you still got busted, though," Chairman Chen pointed out.

"Well, the goods had already reached their destination, but my partner ruined the whole plan. He was careless and drew the attention of the police. He was the one who got us all into trouble. Even so, he still intends to betray us to keep his own life," Dead Chang moaned.

"Ah, I know your partner. He was with me at Cell 10," I said in half-mockery. "His hair has gone gray from the trauma. He doesn't want to leave this world. He thinks you should travel there alone. Why would you need a companion?"

"That's what I thought initially," Dead Chang explained. "You know, we had been neighbors for years. We grew up together and were very close as kids. Since he was willing to spend the rest of his life in a miserable jail, I agreed to help him by taking all the blame. But after I came back from the court and my hands and feet were shackled, I changed my mind."

"How come?" I persisted.

"I don't know. I guess I felt so empty," Dead Chang replied. "I needed to hang on to something. If I had a companion in the other world, I wouldn't feel so lonely. So I filed an appeal, claiming that I had been wrongly convicted. The court reopened my case, and changed my partner's deferred death sentence to immediate execution."

"Now that you've gotten your wish, do you still feel empty inside?" I asked.

"I feel better, but the wait for the execution is way too long."

"Is that why you want to borrow the atlas and relive your past glory?" I wisecracked.

"I'm preparing for my life as a wandering ghost," Dead Chang said with a dreamy look. "I get lost quite often in this life. I don't want to repeat those same mistakes in the other life. When I turn into a ghost, I'm going to visit many of my favorite places. I might bump into you. You'll never know."

My limbs were quivering.

"Are you okay?" Dead Chang asked and let out a sinister laugh. The deep crease between his eyebrows seemed to have opened up like a mouth, ready to swallow me.

The Wife Killer

EVEN THOUGH HIS HANDS were cuffed, Dead Chang proved miraculously fast with packet folding. He agreed to help me, and his generosity enabled me to relax and think. It had been a while since I had time to contemplate my future. Had my family contacted two well-known literary critics and invited them to be my literary defenders as I had suggested they do? I wondered.

Since my case was related to literature, I felt strongly, and perhaps erroneously, that it would be appropriate for literary critics to defend me in court. "Even though their defense may have minimal or no impact, having friends speak for me in court will certainly boost my confidence," I told Chairman Chen, who happened to be pondering his own case. A factory worker, he had rallied support for the student protest movement by forming a Workers' Democratic Party. "I don't think I'm going to be here long," he said. "I filed my appeal six months ago. I should hear something pretty soon."

"I heard your lawyer got into a verbal fight with the judge and he was almost kicked out. Is that true?" Dead Chang jumped into our conversation.

"Yes, my friends and I hired a lawyer from academia," Chairman Chen replied smugly. "He is young, energetic, and sympathetic to the student protests. He knew the law very well and dug out every existing governmental rule and regulation to challenge the prosecution and defend our actions. The judge was exasperated. For example, my lawyer argued that the so-called political organization we had formed could not be considered an authentic political entity. We had copied everything word for word — the name, the mission and the guiding principles — from articles that people had posted on the street. According to this thinking, we were just simpleminded workers who hadn't founded our own group but had been tricked by others."

"Your lawyer is a mere bookworm," Dead Chang interjected with his typical bluntness. "What's the point of arguing with the judge? In this country, we all know that a lawyer applies his skills outside the court. Decisions are made behind the scenes."

That was true, I agreed, but my family did not share my view. In her letter, A Xia revealed that my family had hired a veteran attorney called Sun, who was said to be well connected politically. My elder brother had found him through a retired judge who had served as president of the court. Sun agreed to take on my case only after the retired judge implored him to do so several times on my behalf. I remained skeptical; Attorney Sun might be experienced, but I wondered aloud what kind of pull he had in a political case like mine.

"I never trust those crooked lawyers." Chairman Chen raised his voice. "I can't afford to hire a lawyer who has clout with the judge. What's wrong with having a bookworm? Do you think those so-called first-class, well-connected pros have the guts to speak honestly and seek justice for a counterrevolutionary like me?"

I was stunned by his candor. "You are absolutely right. Not so many people dare to defend those who were involved in the protest movement," I said. "It's too bad that I didn't have your luck and meet a good lawyer."

"We'll see. I'm sure your appeal will be rejected," Dead Chang said to Chairman Chen in his usual harsh tone. "Judges take offense at lawyers who challenge them."

"We pissed off both the judge and the prosecutor," Chairman Chen added. "In his appeal, one of my friends requested that the prosecutor be excused from the case because he described people with crude, animal words like *bark* and *howling*, and attacked our character during the indictment."

"Damn, that's certainly news to me that you can't use that language in an indictment," Dark Skin said. "In my court ruling, the judge described me as 'animalistic and having the impulse of a brute.' Only intellectuals pay such close attention to words."

"We have to pay attention to the exact meaning of each word. That's what law is about," I rebuked him.

"Debt is repaid with money and life repaid with life. There is nothing unclear about it," Dark Skin said and turned his back to me. He jumped off the bed, moved a box of paper packets to the entrance, and started working there alone.

"Our case has been submitted to the authorities in Beijing. According to our lawyer, there is a good possibility that our verdict could be overturned," Chairman Chen went on.

Dead Chang wasn't too pleased. Once again, the groove in his forehead turned ugly. Tossing aside the packets he was folding, he gave a sweeping look around the cell and said, "Anyway, the judge is nothing but my parrot. I'm the one who delivers the preliminary verdict for each person in this cell."

The air in the room suddenly chilled. Four death row inmates raised their heads in unison, staring at Chairman Chen and me with hostility. Chairman Chen, oblivious to the changing attitude, continued chattering but I pinched his arm forcefully to stop him.

The hushed sounds of paper folding evoked the sound of silkworms nibbling at mulberry leaves. The silence became unbearable. We could feel the tension building up between Dead Chang and Chairman Chen.

All death row inmates were powder kegs. If we didn't handle them right, they could explode at any moment. For example, before he was convicted, Dark Skin would hug his knees near the entrance, reading or gazing at the wall. He hardly slept at night. While I was on suicide watch over Dead Chang, I chatted with Dark Skin a few times. During our conversations, I was astounded to learn that he had hacked his wife, who was a head taller, to pieces. The judge was so appalled by the brutality that he reached a verdict halfway through the trial.

When Dark Skin returned from his trial, he seemed to have gone through a personality change — the humility evaporated from him. In its place was bitterness and conceit. He despised those with lighter sentences. "My wife taught me how to be a real man with her flesh and blood," he bragged. "When she was alive, I bowed to her every wish and whim but she still hated me and cheated on me. That really pushed me over the edge. Even after I slashed her with a knife a dozen times, she refused to beg for mercy. I prodded her with live electric wire and choked her with a rope. She never said a word. I was so beyond myself that I didn't even know that my own palms had been seriously burned by the electric wire as well. I admired her. I praised her in court. She was a good wife, but I was suffocating under her care. I had to kill her to grow up. From now until my execution, I want to live with dignity, free from humiliation."

Chairman Chen was equally shocked when I shared with him what I had heard about Dark Skin. "I thought he was an altruistic, humble person," Chairman Chen said in a hushed voice.

After Dark Skin was shackled, he became more temperamental. One night, we were watching the popular TV show *Desire,* and the leading actress, who played a virtuous wife and loving mother, somehow sparked off a strong emotional reaction from the inmates. Many watched her with misty eyes.

In the middle of the show, bouts of uninhibited laughter arose from the cell next door. "Ha, ha, bullshit! How come I've never crossed paths with pretty women like her?" a hoarse voice shouted.

I could tell it was my friend Hippie Poet. "Why don't you make her your godmother!" I could not help shouting.

"Obviously, even your accomplice next door can't stand the bullshit on TV," Dark Skin said, trying to pick a fight with me. "The script writer must be your colleague."

"I'm not as lousy as he is," I said.

"You are even worse!" he yelled at me. "You couldn't even make up this shit."

Scholarly Yang stepped in to fix the spat. "Okay, okay. The actress is our shared lover. Some people think she stinks and others think she is so goddamn hot. Regardless, you ought to admit that she is the creation of stupid writers like you."

I wanted to slap him but Chairman Chen stopped me. Similar confrontations went on for a few more days until Dark Skin's final day.

One golden afternoon, as the "death squad" members sat around as usual, folding paper packets, Scholar Yang brought up the topic of wife killing again. "You keep telling us how henpecked you were. But why did you kill her?"

"I have no idea," Dark Skin answered indifferently. "Once I picked up the knife, I totally lost it and don't remember a thing."

Dead Chang grinned. "It's like sex. Once you are on top of a woman, you just forget everything."

"That's more like it," Dark Skin concurred. "The difference is that killing is more orgasmic than sex. You can have sex with a woman many times, but you can only kill her once. In the past, that bitch liked to ride on top of me and her big boobs were suffocating. On that day, we switched position and I took full control of her. The knife became very handy. Blood spurted out after my first stab, sending my head spinning. I felt like I was floating in the clouds. I hacked at her with all my might. The knife was stuck between her shoulder blades. I grabbed the weapon with both hands and tried to pull it. But I couldn't. I lost my grip and fell backward, head over heels."

"Your love for her is bone deep," Scholar Yang quipped. "I'm sure your wife will be waiting for you at the other end of the bridge in heaven."

"0-9-9 is a writer. We should get him to write a book about you," Dead Chang suggested.

"He is a poet. He only knows how to write ditties." Dark Skin wasted no time belittling me. "Those ditties suck. Remember when we were in high school, we had to memorize poems like 'Many times I dreamed of visiting the revolutionary holy land of Yan-an / Hugging with both arms the tower of Baitashan.' Why do you want to hug a tower? Isn't it more fun to hug a fat woman?"

"Let me write a poem about you," Little said to Dark Skin in his high-pitched tone. "The tigress blew a fart / Dark Skin sniffed and swallowed it like a tart."

The room exploded in laughter and Dark Skin thrust himself at Little, who ducked and ran away. The two "death squad" members thrashed around in the cell, their shackles clanking. Little hid behind

Dead Chang and continued teasing Dark Skin: "The tigress takes a dump / Dark Skin licks her rump."

Our stomachs hurt from laughing so hard. As the two were horsing around, four guards suddenly appeared above on the ceiling. "Jin Tong," one of them said in a chilling voice, calling Dark Skin's name. He was taken aback at first and then composed himself. "Yes, sir." He stood at attention for a few seconds. Then the door opened. Realizing that his final day had come, Dark Skin closed the lid of a cardboard box and hopped off the bed. "I'm going to see my wife," he cried happily and dashed out.

Dead Chang, who had sent off several living dead before, was the first one to recover from the shock. "Dark Skin," he called out, "put on your new shoes before you go." He snapped off his own shoes and ran to give them to Dark Skin. But it was too late. Dark Skin's small, thin figure was nowhere to be seen. In frustration, Dead Chang tossed his shoes at the wrought-iron door as it was closing. One shoe flew out, and the other hit the door and bounced back into the cell. Dead Chang stood barefoot in a daze. At dinnertime he still held that shoe, looking lost. "That poor kid didn't even have the good fortune of wearing a pair of new shoes before he left," Dead Chang mumbled to himself. "The road to the other world is long. His shabby shoes won't carry him far."

"I heard that when we become ghosts, we jump around on one leg," Little said innocently. "One shoe is enough for Dark Skin."

Dead Chang's Departure

IN THE EVENING, THE inmates were grief-stricken. For the first time, nobody craned his head to watch TV. Dead Chang suddenly turned sentimental. "Goddamn it, it's like a dream. There were four of us last night. Now we only have three left. There may be two the night after. If you want to say something, put it in writing. That way, we won't march off hastily like Dark Skin, leaving important things unsaid."

Little was quiet, but Scholar Yang said, "Both of us are bachelors. We don't need a will."

"Don't you want to leave the world without being rushed?" Dead Chang asked.

"Of course I do," Scholar Yang said. "But I don't think it's under my control."

"Before they come get me, I'm going to sing us a farewell song," Dead Chang promised solemnly. "For the last time, let me look you in the eye," he sang, crooning a popular love song. "I'll etch you in my mind."

"Too bad all the people in the cell are male," Little lamented. "But there might be some female mosquitoes and spiders."

"Who gives a damn if we are male or female?" Dead Chang retorted.

"Even mice have feelings for each other if they grow up in the same hole, let alone people. 0-9-9, don't you agree?"

"I do," I nodded.

With true reverence, Little walked up to Chairman Chen and bowed deeply, thanking "Brother Chen" for taking good care of him. The flustered Chairman Chen helped him up, apologizing for being too narrow-minded.

Humanity was in the air. In the next week, all the inmates were caught up in the spirit of compassion. Chairman Chen and I used our own allowances to purchase cigarettes and canned meat for members of the "death squad." Whenever we had a free moment from the busy, labor-intensive schedule, we would fight for the chance to do chores around the cell. I helped the living dead with their laundry and changed bandages around their ankles to prevent wounds from the shackles. Seeking an illusory sense of selflessness, I drove myself to utter physical exhaustion. One day, as I was polishing the wrought-iron shackles around Dead Chang's ankles, he looked solemn and told me to stop. "There is no need to clean them. National Day is around the corner. It's normally time for another round of executions."

I didn't know how to respond.

"I doubt you are going to be next," Chairman Chen said to Dead Chang.

"I've been shivering with cold lately." Dead Chang shook his head. "My body is telling me that time has come." Slowly, he stood up and hollered at the guards upstairs. "Hey, Soldier Brother, I'm going to dance!"

"Don't make trouble for yourself!" the guard warned. "I'll have to report you if you do."

Dead Chang roared with laughter while Scholar Yang took a jibe at the guard. "You are not a three-year-old who reports everything to his kindergarten teacher. Do you tell your teacher after you get fucked in the butt by your playmate?"

The guard stomped his feet and walked away in anger. A few minutes later, the door flung open. The two troublemakers were carried out for a bout of beatings and electric baton prodding.

"Damn, it felt good," Dead Chang boasted, even though his body was drenched in cold sweat. "I had held my pee for two days. When the baton hit me, it all came out in my pants."

"I think you have a death wish. That's why you are provoking trouble," I observed calmly.

Dead Chang staggered and swore at me: "You fucking idiot. You don't understand because you haven't gotten this far yet. It's much better to ask for death than waiting for it."

Dead Chang's premonition was correct. The Red Hairs came in to get him the next day. Before stepping out, he turned around and smiled at all of us. His mouth was moving but no sound came out. I wondered if he had forgotten his promise to sing us the farewell song. When we heard his name again, Dead Chang leaned forward and rushed out like Dark Skin, as if he could not wait for the moment to come.

The two remaining living dead looked at each other, first in silence and then breaking into loud sobs, like children who had just lost their loving father. Chairman Chen and I gently lugged them back to the edge of our bed. "I hope he doesn't get the bullet today," Little blubbered.

"I doubt it," I said. "If they summon someone in the afternoon, they will normally grant him an extra night. He'll be tied up in a special bed. If he's lucky, he can probably watch videos and have a sip of liquor."

"He has left everything to me." Little started to weep. "I didn't even have the chance to thank him."

"Well, if you thank him now, I'm sure he can still hear you," Sun, the chubby inmate in his sixties, said in all seriousness. "That is called a 'spiritual connection.'"

"He won't have time for me." Little shook his head. "Time is pressed and he has too many things to think about."

"You are probably shedding more tears than his wife," Scholar Yang said in jest. "If you love him so much, he'll be reincarnated as a woman and marry you in your next life."

"Is there a next life?" Little asked.

"Of course," I spoke with true conviction. "When you die, the soul departs the body and can roam around. When they shoot him tomorrow morning, Chang's soul will officially say farewell to its stinky earthbound shell and experience complete freedom."

"He is right," Scholar Yang added. "You and I are better off dead than alive. Think about it: You are nineteen. How was life in your home village? Do you remember ever having a nice, filling meal? The amount that you have robbed was relatively tiny, but for that they've sentenced you to death. I'm in the same boat. I was locked up at a juvenile delinquency center at the age of ten. After I came out, I had a grand time for two years. Now, life is so worthless. Brother, it's better to be reborn."

The next day, nobody talked much. The air was stifling. Claps of thunder could be heard outside, but there was not a drop of rain. From the tiny window, I could see the sky brooding with gloom and heavy clouds detached from the heavens like charred canvas. The room darkened. The walls were sweating like a patient with chills, though still hot to the touch. We stripped to our waists. "The Indian summer is really fierce." Chairman Chen wiped his forehead with an arm. "Could it be that Dead Chang's spirit won't dissolve and has come back to bite us?"

"At midnight, the bowls on the rack will make noises," Sun patted his fleshy stomach and said with certainty. "Dead Chang's spirit will come back to visit us."

Before he finished speaking, the cell suddenly lit up. "The damn hot sun is out again," I cursed.

Chairman Chen took a peek at the sky through the window. "The late afternoon sun casts the color of baby's shit on the wall."

"Baby poop? That's disgusting," a voice suddenly sounded outside the door. Dead Chang was standing there cackling, his body bathed in the setting sunlight. We were scared out of our wits.

The three living dead huddled together in tears. Then Dead Chang extricated himself from their embraces and tottered around like a drunkard. When Chairman Chen handed him a wet towel, he ignored him and pushed away the crowd around him. He climbed into bed and curled up in a corner. "Please leave me alone," he burbled.

Dead Chang stayed in shock for two days—sleeping, sitting, or dream-walking. His face had a tinge of blue. At lunch, his eyes gazed into the distance while his mouth moved mechanically. It wasn't until three days later that he gradually came to his senses. "Bring me the glue," he ordered Little. "I want to fold the medicine packets."

"What happened to you?" I probed.

"They summoned me by mistake," Dead Chang uttered feebly. "The other person and I have the same family name. We were both convicted of drug smuggling."

"How could it be?" We were taken aback by his assertion and listened attentively to his story.

"On that day, two Red Hairs carried me away. We breezed through the checkpoints and arrived in court in no time. I was paralyzed with fear. I collapsed and couldn't even stand on my own. The Red Hairs held me up by my arms. I made it through the judge's final pronouncement and was lifted in the air again, with my face toward the sky. The next thing I knew, I had landed in a warehouse. The police tied me down on a torture bed and my mind went blank.

"In a blur, I heard someone swearing at me, 'He's a piece of useless shit. He peed in his trousers . . .' I was in and out of consciousness. A few hours later, I could feel a needle injected into my arm. It felt as thick as a shot glass and soon turned red. I woke up and realized they were drawing blood. I simply lay there, with no desire to move. I felt my body was sinking and then floating again. I could hear thunderstorms in the distance. The rumbling seemed nonstop. When I tried to open my eyes, I couldn't. Someone's hand pressed my eyelids, and I briefly saw the person's white coat. He was a doctor who came to do a blood test. For the past several days, I dreamed of the doctor in a white coat, as if he had been part of my body . . ."

As Dead Chang was blabbering away, we could no longer make sense of his words.

"Well, when the prison harvests your organ, they will sell it to the hospital," he explained with chilling matter-of-factness. "You should take comfort in the fact that you could still make some contribution to another person's health. Otherwise, your blood and organs would be wasted."

The Living Dead Ponder Death

AFTER THE DRAMATIC TURN of events with Dead Chang, members of the "death squad" slowly became immune to the threat of death. "Life and death are neighbors. They visit each other often," Scholar Yang mused over a piece of paper and called the two lines he uttered part of his "newly composed poem."

"This is my maiden work," he bragged. "It's quite a good start, don't you think?"

"What do you mean 'visiting each other often'? You make it sound too easy," Dead Chang said disapprovingly.

"It is called art." Scholar Yang wouldn't back down. "If you don't believe me, ask 0-9-9."

"It's not a bad idea to make death sound easy and pleasant," I defended Scholar Yang. "We all have to go through it. In ten or twenty years, those who have executed other people will also visit death and end up in the same place."

"I call that a long vacation," Dead Chang corrected me. "By the way, I heard that police who carry out an execution need a vacation afterward to recover from the killing. That way, they can prepare themselves to kill again. I think being an executioner becomes a profession, similar to being a butcher who slaughters pigs and goats."

"Don't you think some will take their break and never come back again?" Little asked. "It's hard to imagine that a person can carry out executions all the time."

"They might find it hard at the beginning, but after a while they'll start to enjoy it," Dead Chang surmised. "You know, killing can be addictive. I think Dark Skin knew that better than anyone."

"It's easier to kill humans," Chairman Chen said, joining the discussion. "Pigs and goats struggle, but once humans accept their fate, they give up any attempt to fight. In ancient times, many persecuted scholars stuck their necks out when they faced the executioner's blade and many had their relatives offer bribes so the killers could make a clean job of it."

"That wouldn't work for me. I think I'm going to struggle no matter what," Scholar Yang said loudly, as if the knife were already hanging over his head.

"It is useless to put up a struggle." Chairman Chen waved him off. "In the old days, the executioner would grab your hair with one hand and hold the knife with the other. Then, he raised the knife and *thwack*, your head would tumble down to the ground and roll around like a ball. Sometimes, while the head was spinning on the ground, the tongue would stick out to lick the dust."

"Let's not bullshit about ancient times," Scholar Yang said, "Tell me, how can I stay clearheaded and remember the moment they kill me?"

"Don't fool yourself," Dead Chang said. "It is impossible to stay clearheaded. Take me as an example. I planned to sing a farewell song to all of you. Guess what? After the doctor drew my blood, I turned into a sack of soft mud. Besides, before they take you to the execution ground, they hog-tie you with ropes. Every part of your body will be tied up except your asshole."

"Next they will dig a hole in the ground and force the prisoner to kneel down at the edge." Scholar Yang parroted Dead Chang's tone. "I think you've repeated this shit seven times!"

"It's still not enough!" Dead Chang yelled back. "Only when you are familiar with every detail can you make sure that your journey goes smoothly."

"How deep is the pit?" Little asked.

"About a foot and a half or so. Once you have plunged head over heels into the pit, your legs jerk and then stiffen. That's it."

"What if I were still breathing?" Little wouldn't give up.

"The forensic investigator normally carries a small instrument, which he pokes inside the bullet hole. If the needle on the instrument is still moving, another bullet will be fired to kill the person off." Scholar Yang took over the narrative, imitating Dead Chang's voice. "Then, a stench rises in the air. The two legs kick like those of a chicken until they are straight and stiff. A piece of dry turd is probably stuck in the asshole . . ."

Dead Chang tried to get back control of the conversation, but Scholar Yang's tone turned harsh. "When are you going to stop?"

Dead Chang ignored Scholar Yang and continued unabashedly: "My last question is: Does the bullet pierce your heart or the back of your head? If the bullet hit your heart, you could still turn around and smile at your killer. That would scare him shitless."

Scholar Yang threw himself at his friend-turned-opponent. The two were literally at each other's throats, rolling around in bed. While a couple of inmates dashed to the door to watch out for the guards, others tried to break up the fight. In the end, Chairman Chen and I managed to pin them down and separate them.

"Hey, meat will be served at lunch. Why don't we eat first and fight later," Sun jeered at the two fighters.

"We are truly despicable beings," Little wiped the dirt from his head and responded. "I used to think that I wouldn't want to eat anything before my execution, but now my appetite has grown enormously."

For some reason, the remark dissolved Dead Chang's anger. "You are so worthless," he jested. "All you think of is food!"

There was no meat at lunch, but at dinner, we had twice-cooked pork with green peppers. The three living dead bought five dishes to share among themselves and devoured them all. Scholar Yang acted jovially, as if there had never been any fight with Dead Chang. "0-9-9, why don't you perform one of your poems for us?"

I felt flattered by the request.

"Liao, come on, do a couple of good ones to enlighten us," Chairman Chen also encouraged.

I lowered my head to contemplate for a few minutes before straightening my body and chanting:

A starlit night is a skull riddled with bullets
We discuss death inside the brain marrow
Under the perpetual glare of the lightbulb
We discuss the ritual of execution
Did he depart the world kneeling or standing?
Did the bullet pierce through his heart or the back of his head?

When the bullet hits, in which direction did his brain splash?
The moment the soul runs off
Did he have time to blink and smile?
When he plunged into the pit head over heels,
Did his legs stick up like flagpoles?
Chains clattering, like the spattering waves of a river in the
 netherworld

If, on the eve of the execution
The prison doctor drew half of the blood from your body
You will feel high, your body floating
Your heart will beat like you had played basketball in space
A dog bigger than Saturn, whimpers and attacks

Why are you waiting?
Enjoy your high, so comforting
You have long exhausted what you intended to say to this world
The world should leave a will to the dying
This damn mute called "God"
Wasting that tongue in his mouth

The tongue that licked clean the blood
Only those who were spat out from a mouth don't have feelings
We, who slipped out of our mother's vagina
Know the pain
Even a bad person has a mother

Death is a ray of dazzling white light
An endless tunnel
The romantic train resembles a penis
Shooting out a bullet at the height of its climax
If the bullet misses, the person suffers
Soft as cotton
Your hands, which have grown into cotton
Cannot grasp anything
The last piece of turd is squeezed out into the sun, a big toilet

The anus talks, claiming
It's a virgin
Without being violated by heaven

My fellow inmates listened as if their heads were in the clouds. Scholar Yang yawned. "It sounds so familiar. You haven't plagiarized anything, have you?

"He quoted what we were just discussing," Dead Chang said.

"What does 'A dog bigger than Saturn' mean? Are you making fun of us, calling us dogs who 'whimper and attack'?"

As I was fretting over how to respond, Chairman Chen came to my rescue: "It's a misty poem, quite obscure. They are very popular among young people these days."

"A Black Hand and Evil Adviser"

BEFORE OCTOBER 1, NATIONAL DAY, the detention center conducted its routine search, ransacking our bedding and personal possessions for illegal weapons such as knives and screwdrivers, and for bootlegged liquor. The usually lackadaisical guards on the second floor became more vigilant. They stood with their legs apart, aiming their machine guns at us. "This is how we celebrate our holidays," Chairman Chen grumbled to me.

We had all expected the search and didn't care. The door burst open and in came Officer Gong flanked by several fully armed policemen. They blocked the fence and started frisking each inmate before allowing us to move to the courtyard. We raised our hands up in the air and our bodies were patted and squeezed from head to toe. Afterward we squatted outside, four people in a row, with both of our hands clutching our heads. Soldiers carrying rifles and machine guns stood posted inside and outside the door, and around the courtyard. Officer Gong, who wore a big surgical mask, rummaged through our mattresses and luggage, tossing out ropes, letters, books, and magazines that friends and relatives had smuggled in. A leather belt that A Xia had sent me was confiscated. The yellow buttons on one of my jackets and a pair of metal zippers from my trousers were ripped off with pliers.

The search went on for two hours. After the police left, our cell looked like a landfill. All of our personal belongings were piled up in the middle of the room. Inmates dove into the pile like firefighters dashing through smoldering debris to rescue babies. Some even scuffled with each other.

Things quieted down after National Day. Inmates spent most of their time in solitude, gluing medicine packets. When I wasn't working, I had learned to distract myself from the painful reality by thinking of my sister Fei Fei or by focusing on my surroundings. I would gaze at a spider for fifteen minutes, observing its movement in detail.

The arrival of letters from home was much anticipated. At night, I would deftly pull them out of the envelopes and peruse the text at my leisure. I remember the pleasure of fixing my eyes on the photos of my daughter, who came into the world on September 17, 1990. I never tired of looking at her, even though her red, wrinkled face made her look like a tiny old man. It was hard to believe that I was the father of a baby girl. I didn't even get to grow up myself.

Soon after my wife became pregnant, I had known intuitively that we were expecting a girl. I wasted no time finding an appropriate name for her, and the characters I came up were Miao Yi. The Chinese character *Miao* means "youthful and smart," and *Yi* represents the Chinese number one, which a fortune-teller once said was my lucky number. A friend of mine recommended keeping *Miao* but removing *Yi,* and I took his advice. Looking back, it was a mistake. The Chinese character *Miao* is made up of two parallel parts. The left part means "woman" and the right part, "young." In other words, *Miao* means "woman at a young age." Young women can be vulnerable. With one, my lucky number, added to her name, she would be well rooted and protected by her father. But I could not fight fate. Later on, A Xia attached another Miao to her name; thus she became "Miao Miao," or "Two women at a young age." The thought that two women who were destined to spend the rest of their life together spooked me.

The letters also tired me out. When I couldn't sleep, I closed my eyes to contemplate the upcoming trial that bedeviled me. My elder brother had hired a lawyer for me. Our first meeting took place in late October. Before the lawyer sat down to review my case, he quickly cautioned me, "A political prisoner has no control over his fate." He might be right. Based on what I had read, defense lawyers for major political cases must be recognized or directly appointed by the court's Political and Legal Commission. That way, they wouldn't dare challenge the prosecution. All of my accomplices felt the same way and none put much trust in the system. "You can't take your defense lawyer seriously," said Big Glasses during a chance meeting at the detention center. "Defense exists in name only. You want your defense lawyer to get you out of jail? Go on dreaming."

In his letters, my brother regaled me with stories about my lawyer's prowess. But the shriveled, inert old codger in front of me was completely different from the image that I had constructed in my mind. In fact, I detested him. He handed me the indictment, which I skimmed through, reread silently, and gave back to him. In the next two hours, while he was lecturing me on how I should cooperate with the government and admit guilt, my mind kept wandering. I hardly remembered anything he had said. At the end of our visit, I decided to get something practical out of him. So I asked, "Sir, I'm quite famished here. Could you bring some extra food when you come next time?"

The old man looked fiercely at me. I immediately followed up with an explanation: "It won't get you into trouble. Other lawyers always bring food for their clients — an interrogator even got me some pickled vegetables once."

"Based on what I have heard," my attorney said in his insincere voice before walking away, "the food served here is the best among the city's prisons. Look, your face looks radiant."

"I guess I'm just excited to see you," I said hopelessly.

Back in my cell, Dead Chang greeted me with all smiles. "Has he brought any cigarettes?"

I shook my head.

"Any beef jerky?"

I did not reply.

"Your lawyer must not be paid well enough to curry favor with you," Dead Chang groaned. "Political cases are just not profitable. No wonder lawyers like to handle economic cases."

"You are certainly in good spirits," Chairman Chen ribbed him.

"If they send you away to another cell, I would be in better spirits," Dead Chang responded. "I'm sure everyone here feels the same way."

"Stop it," I intervened. "The lousy weather sours our mood."

After dinner, many inmates puffed on their cigarettes. I waited near the fence door for the poisonous gas to dissipate before climbing into bed. When the TV came on, Chairman Chen and I retreated to a corner in our big bed, folding packets while conversing secretly like two spies swapping intelligence at a public place.

"I've done so much for those three bastards. None of them seems to appreciate it," Chairman Chen whined.

"The living dead are moody and it's hard to fully comprehend what they are going through," I tried to console him.

"At this stage, you would think that they would be more enlightened," Chairman Chen said. "It's hard to believe their desire for power in this life is still unabated."

"Why don't you let Dead Chang be the chief in our cell?" I proposed. "You should tell Officer Gong tomorrow."

"I can't do that. Having a death row inmate take charge? There is no precedent for that," Chairman Chen replied.

"Why don't you simply resign? Let Officer Gong appoint someone else," I said. "You'll be here for another two months at most. If the appeal succeeds, you'll be out of here."

It was too late for Chairman Chen to give up his power voluntarily; his opponents were already plotting to get rid of him. Half an hour after our conversation, Little abruptly accused Chairman Chen of stealing his comforter. Surprised by the allegation, Chairman Chen roared furiously, "All the comforters look the same. What makes you think I have stolen yours?"

Dead Chang watched from the side, looking for opportunities to instigate a fight. "You are so corrupt," he said, pointing at Chairman Chen. "Thank God you are merely the head of a cell. What would happen if you held an important government position?"

Scholar Yang jumped in, lashing out at both of us: "You counterrevolutionaries are controlling everything in this cell. You are deceiving the government and the people. It's high time we straightened things out."

I sat there, astounded by the coordinated attack. Knowing that they had set a trap, I urged Chairman Chen to stay calm, but the chief had lost his cool. He pushed me away and jumped off the bed. "If you want to have it out with me, come on over," he said, leaning his body on the door fence and flashing his two big fists. "I promise you I won't call the guards. The guards have just walked away. If you want, come on up, you three dying bastards!"

Shackles were clanking, and the cell once again sounded like a busy blacksmith's workshop. Little marched ahead of the others. I galloped over to Chairman Chen's side, hoping to stop him, but Little hit my chin with one of his cuffed hands. I fell, my face contorted with pain.

With me on the floor, Chairman Chen found himself surrounded by Little and Scholar Yang. A mild and benevolent person by nature, he was reluctant to punch his opponents. Instead, he simply seized Scholar Yang by his handcuffs and, with extraordinary strength, thrust him away. Little attacked Chairman Chen from the side, but ended up getting kicked in the balls. He fell to the floor holding his crotch, groaning with pain.

The officer on duty happened to be someone known for his prejudice against those who had been involved in the 1989 student protest movement. Between three death row inmates and two political prisoners, he chose to believe the words of the former. Chairman Chen was powerless to defend himself when the officer accused him of being a jail bully. He was hogtied, beaten, and pummeled with electric batons for the entire night. The next morning, he came back in handcuffs, his body covered with bruises. A Red Hair picked up his belongings and he was transferred to a different cell.

Using Chairman Chen as a scapegoat, authorities at the detention center broadcast a denunciation session over the public address system. Leaders from the Public Security Bureau delivered speeches to condemn Chairman Chen's illegal activities. All the previous good deeds that he had done were transformed and perverted. For example, he used to dig into his own pocket to buy meat dishes for the living dead. Now his beneficiaries accused him of being a loan shark, who had lent them money to buy meat and charged them high interest.

I, too, was implicated. The authorities bestowed upon me a new title — "a black hand and evil adviser." In their view, I was a more perfidious enemy than Chairman Chen. "Most detainees are willing to start a new chapter in life and cooperate with the government," the detention center's party secretary solemnly proclaimed, pointing his finger accusingly at me."If you want to sabotage our efforts, we want to make it loud and clear that we will not stand idle and let you get away with it."

Three weeks later, I was also transferred to a new cell. I knew that it would happen sooner or later. Before my departure, I also got into a fight. In fact, I fought more spectacularly than Chairman Chen. When I noticed that Dead Chang was planning to attack me from behind, I preempted him by dumping a big bowl of glue on his head, and then smashing his pig head repeatedly with it.

Welcome to Cell 6

I ENTERED CELL 6 FULLY shackled. To keep the last few shreds of my dignity, I refused dinner. My new cellmates were watching the last episode of *Desire* on TV that night. As usual, they squeezed together, craning their necks as the show entered its grand finale. Suddenly Wang Er, the chief of Cell 6, sprang to his feet in excitement. He unzipped his trousers and aimed his fully erect penis at the TV while blowing a kiss at the heroine: "I love you, my crazy wife."

An inmate nicknamed Big Kid joined in, letting out a loud, orgasmic scream. People roared with laughter, which inevitably attracted the attention of the guards. Guns clicked on the rooftop. Wang Er patted his chest and shouted, "Uncle Soldier, feel free to shoot here!"

"You again!" a guard thundered.

"No, it's not me. It's Huifang on TV," Wang Er replied. "Do you know my ex-wife's name is also Huifang?"

"Damn you for pulling the same old shit," the guard cackled.

My hands shackled, I sat on the edge of the bed with my head turned at a ninety-degree angle. I still couldn't see anything, but I simply followed the crowd and occasionally giggled like an idiot. Nobody talked to me. A sense of overwhelming grief and emptiness swelled inside me. I could survive tonight, but what about tomorrow? A person without his hands had no dignity; I had to debase myself and beg for help for every single human need.

Along the aisle, another group, in dirty and tattered clothing, hunkered down on the floor, folding packets. They were members of the lower class, who rustled around like a pack of rats. At bedtime I was assigned, as expected, a spot next to the toilet. Since stir-fried onions had been served at dinner, a pungent stench of onions and human feces rose from inside the squat toilet. Tears pricked my eyes. At one point, I walked over to the cell gate for some fresh air, but Wang Er barked at me from behind. "We don't have people on death row here at the moment," he said coldly. "There is no need to stand guard."

Reluctantly, I returned to my corner and leaned against the wall. Using my teeth first and then my feet, I pulled the comforter over me, trying to rest my eyes. A stream of people lined up near me, waiting to relieve themselves. The sounds of their urine stimulated my own desire to make water. I heaved a long sigh, holding my urine as long as I could. Gradually, the footsteps around me faded into a blur of white noise.

In my dream, I turned into a big chamber pot. Inmates took turns pissing into me. My stomach was ready to burst. I bit my teeth hard and squeezed my mouth with my hands to hold the urine inside. "I need to open the floodgate!" I yelled. "Let me empty my stomach."

I woke, stood up, and fell headlong onto the floor, bumping my head against the edge of the urinal. Bolts of excruciating pain coursed through my brain. I struggled to get up but felt powerless. One person pulled me up and changed my soiled clothes for me while several others came over to watch, making fun of my downfall. Soon, a small crowd had gathered around me.

"If you want to take a leak, you should let us know. There is no point in committing suicide," Wang Er scoffed at me. He assigned a young prisoner to help me.

I was still in a cloudy daze when I heard the sound of loud spattering water coming from the front courtyard. "Oh shit!" Wang Er yelled. "The damn guard is peeing into the water tank from the rooftop."

"How could he dare aim at our water tank?" another inmate bellowed. "Fucking bastard."

A few minutes later, a head came into view from the window. It was Tang, the officer on duty.

"The bastard is drunk." Wang Er shook his head, looking disheartened.

Soon two Red Hairs hauled the inebriated Officer Tang into our cell. He looked silly with his police hat askew. Wang Er lodged our complaints about the urine in our water tank, but Officer Tang was too drunk to comprehend. "I want to drink as much as I want and piss wherever I want," he mumbled. "Don't make such frightful noise at this late hour. If you want to sleep, go back to bed . . ."

Wang Er was planning to reason with Officer Tang, but the drunkard gave out a loud stinky burp and tossed a half-eaten chicken drumstick onto the floor. He waved Wang Er off: "Go away."

After Officer Tang staggered out with the Red Hairs, Wang Er bent over and picked up the fried drumstick. His face was beaming.

"Hey, Counterrevolutionary, since you didn't have dinner tonight, do you want it?" He waved the drumstick in front of me.

I looked straight into his eyes. He took a bite. "I know you won't take it because it's Officer Tang's leftover," he said. "Like the saying goes, a man of integrity would rather die of starvation than bow down for a bowl of rice. You would rather starve yourself than bow down for a drumstick. But didn't you just fall headlong into the urinal?"

I opened my mouth. "I don't have any pride. If you give the drumstick to me, I'll eat it."

The inmates were taken aback by my reaction. Wang Er smirked and handed over the drumstick. I tilted my head forward and bit one of his fingers. He drew back his hand fast. I growled like a cornered animal and hurled my head against his chest. Wang Er ducked and smacked me on my cheek.

"You are a lunatic!" people cried. Two inmates pounced on me and covered my head completely with a blanket. They were about to punch me when the guard on the rooftop shouted, "What's happening?"

"Drunkard Tang is on duty tonight. He's plastered," I heard Wang Er say to the guard. "Go ahead and report us. He won't be able to do a thing. To tell you the truth, Officer Tang and I are pals. All three times I've been here, Officer Tang has always been my handler. Like the saying goes, no matter how close your parents are, the party and the police are your closest relatives."

"Okay then, I'll report it to the director tomorrow."

"Don't be a bore." Wang Er pulled the guard's leg. "You must be new here. If you have nothing better to do, go have some fun like Officer Tang and pee into our water tank. I'm not going to drink from there, anyway."

"You bastard," the guard spat at Wang Er.

"Soldier, did you just call me a bastard?" Wang Er continued jeering at him. "Yes, that's my first name. How did you know that?"

The guard walked away. Wang Er ordered his lackeys to take the blanket off my head. "Bravo, you have certainly lived up to your reputation."

Like a frog that had escaped from the cook's hot steamer, I gasped for air, spitting lint from my mouth.

"I used to be cellmates with your friend, Chen Dong, the film director," he confided. "You have more guts than he does."

I tipped back my head and sighed. "More guts? I'm fucking useless. I'm just lucky to be alive."

"Please Insert Me Back Into Your Womb"

THE NEXT AFTERNOON WE had a new officer, a pallid-looking chain smoker. He brought me to his office to unlock my cuffs and in a soft, feminine tone, laid out his ruling philosophy: "There is one thing about me that you should know. I'm quite lazy. You should learn to manage yourself and stay out of trouble, okay?"

I nodded vigorously.

"There is a whole stack of letters for you." He tapped on his desk. "But I can only give you one because you've been punished many times for flouting the rules. You seem to be incorrigible. Intellectuals like you worship individualism. You use your mental stamina to overcome physical pain. I want to teach you a lesson this time. Even though I have unlocked your handcuffs ahead of schedule, I am going to keep all these letters to cut off the source of your spiritual support."

I held that single letter and returned to the cell despondently. It was from my mother. I washed my hands thoroughly before pulling it out of the envelope.

"Yiwu, I've been thinking of what to write, but haven't come up with anything. I only want to tell you one thing: Mother misses you very much."

I smacked my lips, savoring every word that my mother had written. My eyes moistened. I looked inside the envelope and flipped it upside down like a greedy thief in the hope of finding more cash from a stolen wallet. At dinnertime, I took a couple of bites distractedly and put the bowl down. Then I took out the letter and reread it. Wang Er noticed my preoccupation and said curiously, "You've been poring over the letter for hours. It must be good stuff."

I gave him a blank stare. He grabbed the letter from me and spent a while trying to decipher my mother's scribbled notes. "Your mom certainly loves you. How many poems have you written for her?"

"None."

"I don't believe you," he said. "Poets love to write about their mothers. I'm sure you have written many that start out, 'Oh my mother, my great mother.'"

"My mother never reads poetry," I protested, the frustration showing on my face.

Wang Er pointed at the letter in my hand and contended, "But that is a remarkable poem, don't you think?"

His sincere observation made me laugh. It may have been the most extraordinary moment of my imprisonment. I never expected my mother's letters to win praise, especially from a criminal. After all, she never understood or cared about my literary works. When my poem "The Big Basin" was published to great acclaim, I remember showing it to my mother, who spent a whole afternoon studying it, in the same way I later pored over her note. When she finished, all she could say, grumbling in her usual way, was that the lines were too long and they gave her problems breathing. "Son, this poem you have written is like a long, thick rope, and I feel that you are trying to strangle me to death with it."

Despite our shaky start, I knew that Wang Er and I were destined to become friends. A shared love for our mothers would help us transcend our daily tribulations. "Please insert me back in the womb," I said to myself as I curled up inside my quilt that night and jotted down the lines of what would be my first poem for my mother.

Please Insert Me Back Into Your Womb

You always complain that the lines in my poems are long-winded,
But now, fate has compressed your son

Into a short phrase
The phrase is still being shortened
Until there is nothing but a bag of bones
Or a word that has been raped and defaced

Is it a noun? It can't even be categorized
I'm only a complicated character
With too many strokes, it's always misspelled

I've aged,
I look older than you are
When I return home some day
Will the bald-headed me still be able to call you Ma?
Do I still have the strength to experience love like
The tenderness of the gentle gust?

I finished the poem at three o'clock in the morning. Before going to sleep, I glanced in Wang Er's direction but detected no movement inside his comforter.

Of all the prisoners I knew, Wang Er enjoyed sleeping the most. Occasionally, he would stick his head out to cough, spit, or smoke. A few slaves would fawn over him, helping with whatever he needed. He liked to chat while blowing smoke rings into the air. During debates, Wang Er displayed extraordinary eloquence and no one was his match. He took delight in the fact that I was a writer. "In the future, it will be your job to swap books with the other cells."

In addition, Wang Er assigned me to a five-man work group, one more than the usual four. "I'll do you a favor by having your teammates fold the medicine packets for you." He winked at me before disappearing inside his comforter. "Go ahead and read your books."

Elated and flattered, I did not know how to thank him.

The Epileptic

A WRITER BY TRADE, I was just intrinsically clumsy and slow when it came to rote tasks. In the previous months, I had gone into overdrive to fold and glue those medicine packets, but I still couldn't fulfill my daily quota. Wang Er's assistance in this area was invaluable; I could not believe my good luck. I sprang off the bed and picked up a Chinese novel in a corner.

Before opening the pages, I stole a furtive glance at my teammates, all of whom looked disgruntled because of the privilege granted to me. Wan Li, a squinty-eyed young man on my right, did not hide his anger well. His face was contorted and red with rage. In the next few minutes, he accidentally tore several packets while folding them. Seeing that his wrath was directed at me, I put down the book, moved over to join other team members. Wang Er noticed and spoke to the young man in a soft, yet firm voice: "Hey, are you challenging my authority?"

Wan Li raised his head; his limbs were trembling as if he had been in electroshock therapy. "I was actually planning to give you a promotion and let you supervise the lower-class section," Wang Er continued, using a tone that reflected his disappointment. "But you have let me down. No wonder our great leader Chairman Mao used to say, 'Educating our peasants is a big challenge.'"

"Let's apply the rules," commanded Old Bai, whom everyone respectfully addressed as the Foreign Minister because he was a big talker and often represented inmates in their negotiations with officers and the guards. Without a word, Wan Li dropped to his knees and slapped himself repeatedly on the face as a form of self-punishment. The other three members on my work team followed suit. The Foreign Minister paced around, counting the number of slaps. The four culprits, their eyes glazed, whacked their faces robotically like soldiers in a military drill. I begged Wang Er to stop them, but the whacking accelerated and got harder. Wang Er giggled. Satisfied with his minions' self-inflicted beatings, he plopped down and resumed his hibernation. The room fell into a tense silence.

"Should I read or work?" I lowered my head, debating my next move. Wan Li's unintelligible murmuring caught my attention. Thinking he needed help, I went over to him, but he suddenly fell and the back of his head hit the floor. Within seconds, his body stiffened as if he had been struck by lightning. His limbs jerked and thrashed against the floor like big raindrops in a torrential downpour. Inmates assembled quickly, cheering and applauding. They circled around, singing in unison a tune from a candy commercial — "Happy, Happy, Jumpy Candy."

I realized that Wan Li suffered from epilepsy.

In the middle of this commotion, Wang Er tossed a shirt to the rowdy mob and shouted, "Cover his mouth with this!" It was too late. White foam oozed out from the corners of his mouth. The pungent stench assaulted our nostrils. One inmate caught the shirt from Wang Er and wrapped it around Epileptic's face, but he bit the sleeve and started chewing it with his teeth. Worried that Epiletic might swallow the sleeve and choke himself to death, Wang Er ordered the inmate to seize the shirt by the collar and pull it with all his might. Eventually, it took five people to extract the remaining strips of cloth from Epileptic's mouth.

Epileptic's eyes rolled back in his head and the convulsion lasted a few more minutes before he let out a loud breath, followed by a gust of foul-smelling air. Then his body relaxed, and he gradually calmed down.

I pinched my nostrils and looked up at the rooftop guard. He grimaced and spat out a mouthful of phlegm, which landed squarely on our courtyard floor. "Your cell stinks like a toilet," he groused, holding his nose.

I pleaded with him to help.

"Nobody is around," the guard answered. "The stench has driven everyone away."

Several people giggled. Wang Er shot me an angry look. "Don't report to the officer," he said. "That's not how I manage things here, okay?"

His words reverberated in my ears. I felt like I was hanging awkwardly in midair without knowing where to land. Inmates resumed their work and Wang Er went back to sleep. Epileptic sat in a daze and then moved about like a sleepwalker. Half an hour later, he joined our work team and grabbed the colored paper packets, folding and gluing frantically. When he noticed that I was also working, he screamed at me to stop.

I reluctantly abandoned the packets, but the incident made me keenly aware that I had to accept the role that Wang Er had assigned to me. That snake, lurking inside his comforter, carefully observed every movement of his subjects, pouncing on anyone who dared encroach upon his authority. When a political prisoner, deprived of his independence, had to choose between a bandit and the government, the choice was obvious. I found myself trapped in an invisible kingdom ruled by blood and iron.

A few days later, I made an attempt to leave the five-person work team and go solo, but my fellow team members implored me to stay.

"I don't need your help, seriously," I said. "I would rather die of overwork."

My remarks triggered a round of good-hearted laughter. The Foreign Minister mocked my hypocrisy: "You sound like a Communist. It makes me wonder if you are a true political prisoner."

Not long after Epileptic recovered, he fell into the hands of the new officer in charge. Nicknamed "Pervert Liu, the officer acted more like a perverted poet than I did. He was sentimental, misanthropic, absent-minded, and imaginative. He was also a sadist.

One day Wang Er instructed Epileptic to step on the shoulders of another inmate known as Running Nose and change the default channel on the TV. Pervert Liu caught them red-handed and ordered both Epileptic and Running Nose to stick their tongues out and lick his electric baton. To the surprise of Pervert Liu, Epileptic sucked on the head of the baton as if it were a popsicle and his body was immune to electric shock. Pervert Liu frowned. He went out and came back with five Red Hairs who stripped Epileptic, pressed his body flat on the floor, and ran two stun batons up and down his body. There was still no reaction. "Your body is a damn insulator," Pervert Liu said, wiping sweat off his head. "The baton fucks you but you don't reciprocate."

Frustrated by the baton's failure, Pervert Liu brought two sets of cuffs and tied Epileptic and Running Nose together. Thus, conjoined twins were born in our cell. With their hands bound together, the two hapless victims faced each other twenty-four hours a day and had to do everything jointly. At meal times, one person would hold the bowl first while the other tried to scoop the rice into his mouth. When one person squatted on the toilet pit, the other had to crouch down face-to-face with him. At the end of the bathroom break, each person would bend forward with two legs parting, waiting for the other person to reach underneath to wipe his partner's butt. As one can imagine, mishaps occurred frequently, giving rise to bitter recriminations.

The conjoined twins provided endless entertainment for our cellmates. Anyone could creep up from behind and kick them in the butt. Sometimes, when one person turned around to fight back, he would drag the other to the floor. The most awkward and yet funny moment came around midnight one night when Epileptic urged Running Nose to get up so he could use the toilet. We could hear the handcuffs clanking. The two of them ambled forward like two villagers carrying a sedan chair between them. At the urinal, they helped each other unzip. When they closed their eyes to relieve themselves, urine shot out onto their shins and feet. They glared at each other.

Another night, something unusual happened — a fat white rat snuck into their comforter and nibbled on Epileptic's stinky foot. The startled Epileptic leapt up and screamed, dragging along his conjoined twin, who was sleeping like a log. The latter banged his head hard on the edge of the bed. Meanwhile, the old white rat darted forward blindly to the end of the aisle, spun around a couple of times, and scurried back. Before we had a chance to catch it, the rat disappeared outside the fence.

The cell was thrown into chaos. Wang Er, who had a phobia about rats, squealed. "The rat must be the reincarnation of a former inmate who used to hate me," he proclaimed. On the floor, the twins were locked in a fistfight. Epileptic tried to raise his foot to check the rat bite. Repulsed and frustrated by the tortures in the past twenty-four hours, Running Nose spewed out a big lump of phlegm, which landed squarely on Epileptic's face. Stunned, Epileptic raised his arm to fight back, but his opponent effectively thwarted his attack by dragging their cuffed hands down together. The twins began wriggling their arms and hands like two Tai Chi practitioners doing their "push-hands" moves. Neither could get the best of the other. Out of desperation, they resorted to spitting and biting, while panting and wrestling with each other on the cold floor.

Inmates stood around, cheering and applauding, until Wang Er ordered them to stop. "That was a great performance. Stop and let's continue tomorrow," he snickered.

Four days after Epileptic and Running Nose became conjoined twins, we had a new transfer, whose hands were cuffed behind his back for violating rules at Cell 7. Pervert Liu's imagination ran wild. He tied all three together, making them triplets. Pervert Liu's sadistic joke had gone too far. The emotional stress triggered Epileptic's illness. He let out a loud scream, his face contorted, and his limbs stiffened. As his body twitched violently, Epileptic yanked the other two down from the bed and they were piled into each other, mouth to mouth. The two healthy triplets were frightened out of their wits and maneuvered themselves into kneeling positions, crying loudly for help. Several minutes later, Officer Liu appeared with the doctor. By then, Epileptic had lost consciousness, but his body still jerked forcefully, hauling along his partners, who were sobbing helplessly, their bodies covered with bruises.

The doctor rolled up his sleeves. His left hand held Epileptic's left shoulder while his right hand pinched an acupuncture point on his upper lip. The patient moaned for a few minutes and relaxed. White foam bubbled out of his mouth. The doctor withdrew his hands in disgust and slapped Epileptic's dirt-smeared face hard. Epileptic's mouth opened and a gust of filthy, malodorous air shot out. His bloated stomach sagged. The doctor held his nose and said to Pervert Liu, "He's okay now."

Pervert Liu unlocked the cuffs for the triplets in a gesture of grudging benevolence. Epileptic's two partners broke out in tears. They carried Epileptic's wilted body to bed and bowed to Pervert Liu in gratitude. The sadist was not amused. "Cut out the feudalistic ritual," he said angrily. Wang Er shrugged his shoulders and whispered as Pervert Liu swaggered out of the cell, "I've messed around in the underworld for years and I think I'm pretty tough. I'm certainly no match for that brute."

In the next few days, I gradually picked up some information about Epileptic's background. He was a peasant who had been jailed on murder charges. Based on the stories Epileptic shared with us, he had gotten into a squabble with a friend over a postage stamp. The friend, in a moment of anger, slapped Epileptic on the face. In response, Epileptic picked up an ax and hacked his friend more than twenty times. But the brutal hacking didn't satisfy his bloodlust. He dashed over to the friend's house, planning to set it on fire. Fortunately, his mental agitation set off his epilepsy, and he fainted before reaching the house.

"If you play the epilepsy card and have a seizure in court, the judge will spare you the death penalty," we advised him. Epileptic took our suggestion to heart and began to practice feigning a seizure.

As the saying goes, good luck waits for the survivor of disasters. Epileptic's suffering did not go unrewarded. After his recovery, Wang Er appointed him as head of the underclass section, which consisted of seven peasant inmates. After the announcement was made, Wang Er urged others to donate nicer winter clothing to Epileptic, who, as a consequence, took on a completely new look.

"From now on, you have officially ended your life as a country hick and become a member of the urban elite," the Foreign Minister teased. "Drop on your knees and thank Daddy Wang for the favor."

Overwhelmed by the kindness, Epileptic bowed and knelt in front of Wang Er, who ordered him to discard his old filthy clothes.

Epileptic, who was in his early twenties, had never held any official post before, so he took the appointment seriously. For two days, he observed Wang Er from a distance, carefully imitating his demeanor and the way he lorded himself over other inmates. Then he turned around and applied his knowledge to the exploitation of his subordinates. During working hours, he no longer bothered to glue and fold the medicine packets, but instead flashed his fist and ordered others to work on his quota. If anyone dared to resist his orders, he punched them.

At lunchtime one day, Epileptic lined up seven of his subordinates and moved them to the courtyard. They stood in a circle, waiting for his teachings. "We are one big family and I'm your daddy," he said, imitating Wang Er and assigned a role for each one to play: "You'll be my wife, you will be the eldest son, you the second son, you the third, you the eldest daughter . . . In this new family of ours, we'll share our happiness and suffering. I want you all to follow the traditional virtues and respect your elders."

His new family members glowered at him, but Epileptic ignored them and continued, "Daddy has a bigger stomach and will eat at least three bowls of rice. It means you have five bowls of rice to share among yourselves. Be sure to let your mother and sister have more. We should respect women, okay?"

However, on Tuesday, when meat was served, Epileptic kept all eight dishes to himself. When his subordinates complained, he castigated them like Wang Er: "Don't salivate over the meat dishes. Daddy is turning eighty-four this year and he doesn't have much time to enjoy in this world. You guys are still young and will have lots of tasty meals in front of you."

"Brother Wan, please have mercy," one inmate begged. "Don't eat all of them. Leave us a little."

The words infuriated Epileptic, who whacked the inmate's head with his chopsticks. "Damn you. You don't show any fucking respect for your daddy."

Fed up with Epileptic's ruthlessness and greed, the "wife" punched him in the face. The new tyrant, who was hunched over his food, did not see it coming and fell flat on the floor. Fortunately, Wang Er arrived and pulled Epileptic to the side. "Do you have a death wish? If you continue like this, they'll kill you."

"Daddy, I'm merely following your example," Epileptic retorted, his face daubed with grease from the meat.

"You are doing a much better job than Daddy," Wang Er said sarcastically.

"I'm flattered." Epileptic smiled like an idiot, failing to grasp Wang Er's sarcasm. Irritated, Wang Er raised his hand, but stopped in midair. Instead, he held back his fury and forced a smile. "Good job, Mr. Supervisor."

At that point, we all knew that Epileptic had lost favor with Wang Er and that trouble awaited him. The next day, Wang Er teamed up with the Foreign Minister and Da Long, the enforcer, to fix Epileptic. The two brought out a handmade Chinese chess set from under the mattress. The Foreign Minister invited Epileptic to a game, which thrilled him. To our surprise, Epileptic was a genius of Chinese chess. The uneducated, backward peasant boy had won the county Chinese chess championship at the age of nine. God must have endowed him with this talent to compensate for his epilepsy.

"We don't have money to gamble on chess," Wang Er, the self-designated referee, announced. "I want each of you to pledge two bowls of meat as deposits for your losses."

Epileptic looked invigorated and elated. He patted himself on the chest and bragged, "Daddy, if I win the meat dishes, I will share one with you."

At Wang Er's cue, we surrounded the two Chinese chess players, blocking the view of the rooftop guards. The Foreign Minister, who had the red pieces, moved first, and Epileptic followed up quickly with his own move. Five minutes into the game, he captured a chariot. When the Foreign Minister hesitated, Epileptic glanced around at the scene, anticipating his victory, but he soon realized that he had paid a hefty price for his brief absent-mindedness.

"My horse captures your chariot. Check!" the Foreign Minister yelled gleefully.

Epileptic's narrow eyes opened wide with surprise: "How come the pieces have moved? Where are my cannons and horses?"

"You've already lost your horses," Wang Er brushed off his skepticism. "Accept your defeat."

"No, no, someone moved my pieces!" he yelled like a child. "I remember my horse was right over here. The chariot and the cannon were on the same row. My elephant was about to take your pawn."

We all chuckled. Enforcer Da Long had moved the pieces so fast that I hadn't even caught it. Knowing that he would offend everyone in the room if he persisted, Epileptic reluctantly agreed to a second round. From the beginning of the game, he lowered his head and fixed his eyes on the chessboard. The Foreign Minister soon suffered heavy losses. Wang Er tried to distract him with a cup of tea. The chess genius had learned his lesson and refused to take his eyes away from the chessboard. Soon, he was on the verge of winning. Wang Er's face fell.

Da Long had a new idea. He grabbed a wet towel, wrung out the water and handed it over to Epileptic. "Use this to wipe your sweat," he said. When Epileptic refused, Da Long tried to dab his forehead with the towel. As Epileptic jerked his head to dodge Da Long, Wang Er bent over, quickly moving several pieces. The whole game changed.

Within a half hour, Epileptic had lost four rounds — the worst performance of his life.

"As punishment for your losses, I'm going to take away your meat dishes for one month," Wang Er ruled.

"I didn't lose," Epileptic teared up. "You guys were heartless. Your consciences have gone to the dogs."

"I think you have lost your meat dishes to dogs," the Foreign Minister scoffed. "Your chess skills suck."

Having been deprived of the right to eat meat, Epileptic soon found himself in a harsh situation. In the fall and winter, pumpkins, which were cheap and easy to store, became the staple dish at the detention center. The cooks cut them into chunks and tossed them into hot water to make pumpkin soup. Before serving, we would mix in some salt. This sweet-and-salty, gluey soup, which had no nutritional value, weakened us, giving us oral ulcers. Every day, the cell reeked of fermented rotten pumpkin from our breath and feces. As the market price rose for pork, the kitchen almost never served meat dishes. The only source of protein came from a few thumb-size fatty pork slices in stir-fried vegetable dishes, which were only offered twice a week.

Without access to those precious pork pieces, Epileptic was stuck with pumpkin soup every day. Soon his stomach was bloated like a drum and he was hit with violent bouts of diarrhea. His body weakened fast. A week later, he could hardly walk without leaning against the wall. On days when stir-fried vegetables with pork were served, Wang Er would steer members of the lower class to the courtyard, where their former chief was eating alone. The inmates would swarm around Epileptic, flaunting their steamy meat dishes. They would swallow the fatty pork, pucker up their oily lips to air-kiss Epileptic, and make satisfied throaty noises. Epileptic would close his eyes and lean his head against the wall. Once, he wept silently; tears and rice got stuck in his throat. He began coughing violently. Oblivious to his pain, inmates danced around him with their bowls in their hands. Epileptic eyed one bowl furtively and reached out his big hands. He snatched a slice and stuffed it into his mouth. He chewed and swallowed greedily, his eyes widening like bronze bells. Inmates swooped over him, and one shouted, "Pry open his mouth!" When one inmate jabbed a chopstick in, Epileptic bit it hard and broke it with his teeth. In the end, he swallowed the meat and a quarter of the chopstick.

In addition to restricting Epiletic's meat intake, Wang Er also initiated a denunciation campaign against him, just like the authorities had done with other incarcerated bullies. Wang Er encouraged victims to stand up and condemn Epileptic's crimes. Several people even stripped Epileptic of the clothes that they had donated to him a month before.

"That underwear is mine but I'll let him have it," one inmate joked.

It was the dead of winter. A cold wind blew through the cell. Epileptic shivered in a corner, his hands crossed over his chest. He screeched at Wang Er: "You told me to throw away all my own clothes. I want them back."

"Your dirty clothes have long since become fertilizer in the field," Wang Er answered.

"You . . . you," Epileptic stammered, his eyes turning white. I went up to Wang Er, trying to prevent him from going too far with Epileptic. "Don't overdo it. We could be playing with fire, if you know what I mean."

Wang Er took the hint and ended the farce with a "generous" proposal. "Okay, now that the bully has admitted guilt, Counterrevolutionary believes that we should help him in the spirit of revolutionary humanity."

Epileptic managed to get hold of a shirt and a pair of trousers, but they were not enough to keep him warm. A few days later, I saw frostbite on his body and suggested giving Epileptic a pair of socks and some long johns. Wang Er was displeased: "Are you suffering from sympathy syndrome again? Why don't you let him call you Daddy?"

Chinese New Year

IN JANUARY 1991, I spent the first Chinese New Year behind bars. A week before the holiday, everyone wanted to write home.

Since the birth of Miao Miao, A Xia wrote to me more frequently, filling each one of her letters with news about our baby daughter and always enclosing a thick stack of photos. Her letters made me feel that prison was merely an extension of our home. In my letters to her, I wrote like a martyr, sparing no details of life in the cell.

According to an unwritten rule, each detainee was given one piece of paper for one letter per month. There were eighteen detainees in our cell, and Pervert Liu only provided us with one pen. He also limited our collective time with the vital instrument; we had to take turns writing and hand the pen back to him in two hours. The piece of paper was a palm-size recycled notification form detainees used to request clothing or money from families. Several years before, when no letters were allowed at all, the form was the only means for detainees to communicate with their families. During my time there, authorities relaxed their control due to Western pressure on the Chinese government to improve the country's human rights situation. We could write letters on the back of the form, which was big enough for about one hundred words. I always packed in two to three hundred. A Xia had to read it with a magnifying glass.

During letter writing time, Wang Er designated me as the ghost-writer for seven members of the upper class. That was the only time when I could get my fix as a writer and enjoy an illusory sense of dignity. I would write furiously in the hope of finishing the assignment in the first hour and saving the next hour for my own letter.

Seeing that I wouldn't have time for them, members of the under-class looked unhappy. Some begged me to help fill out the notification forms with items they needed from their families. Epileptic, who suffered tremendously without winter clothing, requested two cotton-padded coats, a pair of cotton-padded trousers, and thirty yuan from his mother.

The day before New Year's Eve, the director and other officials delivered their annual greetings through the loudspeakers. The much-anticipated menu was announced at the end of the long and dull speeches — from December 31 to January 4 (Chinese lunar calendar), a meat dish would be served for free every day. For New Year's Eve dinner, there would be eight dishes for each cell, including chicken and fish.

Wang Er, unwilling to share a table with his peasant pals, devised a new way to distribute eight dishes among sixteen inmates. He wrote the names of the dishes on tiny pieces of paper and organized a drawing of lots. I got "twice-cooked pork" while Wang Er and the Foreign Minister both had the "sweet-and-sour pork." They swapped their lots with two peasant boys who happened to get the chicken and fish dishes but preferred pork.

When the New Year's Eve meal started, inmates divided themselves into two groups — urban folks spontaneously gathered at one end of the bed whereas those from rural areas sat together in a circle at the other. The rural folks cleared their plates fast and fought over pieces of fatty pork. In my group, we used water as liquor and toasted each other for fun. The chicken dish contained two legs, traditionally a sought-after treat. As the supreme leader, Wang Er inevitably took one and gave the other to me. "Counterrevolutionary, you did a good job with those New Year letters," he complimented me with a toast. "As a poet, you never put on airs and look down on scums like us. Here's to your future."

I was flattered and immediately poured chicken soup into everyone's cup and replied humbly, "We are all in the same boat. There are no such things as scums or intellectuals. Let's drink to our future."

Wang Er began to wax poetic. "I've been in and out of jail since I was ten. I used to be locked up with many death row inmates. In those days, the review period for a death penalty case was quite short. Once a person was convicted, he would be shot in ten days. To prevent the death row people from acting up, the prison guards would shackle their hands and feet together. They curled up like meat dumplings; they could not stand, walk, or lie down. One day I befriended a death row inmate. He wanted me to help him take revenge on his enemy in the cell. I was kind of stupid. I used all my strength to carry him over to where his rival slept, lifted him up, and put him on the rival's chest. We almost killed his enemy. I was only sixteen. I figured if I killed someone, they wouldn't shoot me because I was underage."

Soon, the wind rose and blew through the room. The leftovers on the plates were getting cold. We scrunched up our shoulders, shivering. Ma Yun, a living dead, began sobbing. "This is my last New Year's meal."

Da Long, the enforcer, consoled him. "You go first and I'll be next. We are both in the same boat."

The Foreign Minister protested, "Hey, don't ruin the holiday. The earlier you die, the faster you reincarnate. The grease is starting to freeze in our bowls. Let's finish up."

"Let's lie down and watch TV," I proposed.

After the dishes were cleared away, Wang Er gave me a pair of paper binoculars made from toothpaste packages as a gift. Through the pinholes on the paper cylinders, I could see the pictures on TV clearly for the first time. "This is so valuable," I thanked him profusely. "What do you need from me?"

"Nothing," he said.

A group of inmates snuck over to the door to puff on cigarettes. Wang Er smoked inside his comforter, and I was suddenly hit with an idea for a gift.

"What if I buy you a packet of imported 555 cigarettes?" I asked.

Wang Er thought about it for a few minutes and answered, "I do like 555 cigarettes, but there is a rule among us thieves — no trading during the New Year's because it's bad luck."

"Can't we have just one exception?" I persisted.

"An exception to the rules will ruin your luck for the coming year."

Around midnight, firecrackers blasted outside. Smoke penetrated the high walls and wafted into our cell, blending with the hazy winter fog. Soon things started to quiet down. Sporadic sounds of firecrackers in the distance punctuated the silence. Wang Er jumped out of bed stark naked and knelt down toward the north. He kowtowed three times and sobbed, "Mom, I'm wishing you a happy New Year." Then he dove back into his quilt and covered his head.

His outburst was contagious. The other inmates started kowtowing to their parents and crying. I felt like I was visiting a funeral home. The guard banged the butt of his gun on the ground and shouted, "Hey, hey, don't get too carried away!"

The midnight uproar soon died down. The night sank deeper into the abyss. The glaring lights of the cell illuminated the desolation. We were frazzled but no one was sleepy. We wrapped our bodies in our comforters. Our eyes were wide open, and each of us was preoccupied with the future. The moon traveled west across the sky. The guards moved in the shadows cast by its glow, as if strolling through the galaxy.

The Woodcutter

THE DAYS WERE ENDLESS, and the early-spring drizzle added to the forlorn mood. My lawyer visited more frequently, but not once did he bring any snacks to appease my rumbling stomach. I stopped asking for food and pestered him instead for more extraneous things. "Do you have a mirror?"

"Why are you always making fun of old people?"

"Sir, I'm not joking with you," I answered. "I haven't looked at myself in a mirror for over a year. I just want to see how I look and if I have lost weight."

He sized me up. "They are treating you well. You look healthy and have put on weight."

"But my legs feel weak," I said.

"I'm not your doctor. Let's focus on business." The old man looked annoyed. "It's raining hard outside. I can't stay here forever."

"Wait, wait." I sprinted to the window and examined my reflection in the glass darkened by the bleak weather; my complexion was somewhere between that of a deathly ghost and a heavily painted mask worn by opera singers. "Is this what you call 'healthy and fat'?" I asked him.

"Come back and sit down," the old man demanded.

I was livid. "You've never bothered to bring me any food and you put too much trust in the system."

"Bringing in food is a violation of prison rules." The old man banged on his desk and stood up to leave. "Didn't you and the students oppose government corruption in 1989?"

I was speechless. Why did fate send this worthless old fool to represent me?

Sometimes I shared an umbrella with my attorney or with the policeman guarding me as we walked down the stone stairs in the pouring rain. Unconsciously we held on to each other. Yet I frequently thought of pushing one or both of them down the steps and escaping. I let many such opportunities pass by and the desire to escape also invaded my dreams.

According to a superstition that prevailed at the detention center, a spider landing on a person's head brought a run of good luck. So late one afternoon, when a big cherry-size red spider accidentally fell and dangled in the air, we all watched anxiously. Unfortunately, a blast of cold air swept it away. The inmates were visibly disappointed.

"Cell 6, receive new inventory," a voice roared from outside. The fence door opened and in came a middle-aged man with a stocky build. His eyes were cast downward and he was mumbling to himself.

"Supervisor"— Wang Er gestured to Epileptic—"teach him the rules here."

Epileptic, overwhelmed by the power granted to him, nodded briskly. He picked up a rag and led the newbie to the courtyard. "Mop and polish the floor five times," he directed him. When the newbie got down on his knees, Epileptic stepped on his butt and issued orders, gesturing wildly with his hands. "Make sure to cover every nook and cranny. I want the floor to be as clean as a mirror so you can see your reflection."

The newbie glared at Epileptic but clenched his teeth and started mopping. Half an hour later, he was finished and straightened up to wait for further instructions.

"Now, there." Epileptic pointed at the inside cell. Before he finished his sentence, the new robot lunged forward and smashed into Epileptic like a speeding locomotive. The jolt knocked Epileptic off balance. While Epileptic was swearing and trying to recover, the newbie stepped over his body and resumed mopping the floor back and forth. We could hear his teeth grinding. He never moved around people; instead, he pushed straight through them.

Infuriated by such open defiance, Wang Er signaled his troops to teach the newbie a lesson. Inmates jumped on him, dragging him to the bed and pummeling him. The newbie bellowed like a tiger before springing up and spinning around like a tank, whacking the crowd with his fists. One of his punches struck my chest and prompted me to join the mob.

The newbie proved a fierce fighter. He waved his arms wildly in the air, keeping his attackers at bay. Enforcer Da Long ran to the courtyard and came back with a basin of ice-cold water. He poured it on the newbie, soaking him, but the newbie shook it off quickly. Nobody could subdue him. Scared and helpless, we shouted, "Help! He's going to kill someone!" The guards roused themselves from their daydreams. Officer Yu entered the cell and jabbed the newbie in his ribs with a baton, until he recoiled in pain and then collapsed.

"Sir, he's a lunatic," Wang Er gasped, his voice trembling with fear.

"You just figured that out?" Officer Yu snorted. "We know he's a lunatic. That's why we sent him to your cell."

The psychotic man, whose family name was Zeng, was a woodcutter in a village deep in the mountains. All his life, he knew nothing except how to hew logs, a skill at which he had become expert. One day, for no reason, he slashed his wife's head in two like a piece of wood. According to the story, blood splashed out of her skull and scalded his eyes. After his wife died, the cold-blooded murderer carried her body several miles to the police station "My wife was too thin and she looked like a bundle of wooden sticks," he reportedly explained. "When I see wood, I want to chop it."

"I'm quite thin, why don't you come and cut me?" the interrogator mocked him.

The murderous woodcutter stood up and laughed. "Get me an ax and I'll show you."

Before taking him to the hospital in Chongqing for a mental checkup, the police brought the woodcutter to the detention center so they could prepare his paperwork.

On that infamous first day, after subduing the woodcutter with the baton, Officer Yu went out to get the roster for the bedtime roll call. Each time an inmate's number was called, he was expected to say "Yes, sir." The Woodcutter's number was 0-1-9, disconcertingly close to my own. Officer Yu shouted "0-1-9!" three times, but the Woodcutter wouldn't respond. The angry officer smacked him on the head with the roster. The Woodcutter was confused: "My name is Zeng, not 0-1-9."

"The number 0-1-9 is your code name here. It's like a nickname."

"But my nickname is 'Ax.'"

"You are such a stupid pig," Officer Yu scolded.

When the bell rang at ten o'clock, everyone lay down to sleep. The Woodcutter stood by the wall with a blank gaze. When silence fell, he crept up next to Epileptic and lay down fully clothed on the ground. I crawled to the edge of the bed and took a quick peek. When Epileptic and the Woodcutter were sound asleep, they actually looked like twins.

I have no idea when I dozed off. In my bleary state, I felt a cold knife against my neck. I tried opening my eyes but couldn't. The blade cut into my skin and my breathing stopped. I tossed my head to free myself from the knife . . . When I awoke, the Woodcutter hovered over me, his piercing eyes gleaming. "What the hell are you doing?" I screamed.

The Woodcutter grinned and shuffled away. He moved to another inmate, circled one hand around the person's neck and made a cutting gesture with the other. I reached for my jacket and swung it at him. Startled, the Woodcutter left the inmate alone and quietly slipped back to his spot.

The next morning, still reeling from the nightmarish experience, I dashed to the courtyard and dipped my head in a basin of cold water to sober up my thoughts. The Woodcutter followed, imitating me. I glared at him. He smiled back and raised his thumb in the air. "You are the captain!"

"What about me?" Wang Er stepped up to question him.

"You are the ship's floor sweeper."

Insulted by the Woodcutter's comments, Wang Er threatened, "Wait until lunch! This floor sweeper won't give you food to eat."

The Woodcutter frowned. "Why? I'm a sailor."

I intervened: "Okay, okay, we are all sailors. Have you been on a ship before?"

"I'm on a ship now," he said with a full look of innocence.

"We have already pulled into shore." The Foreign Minister patted the Woodcutter on the shoulder. "In a little while, the officer will take you to see a doctor. If he thinks you are healthy, you don't have to be on a ship anymore."

During breakfast, Wang Er put his legendary thieving and sabotaging skills to work. He first mixed some glue from a can with a packet of over-the-counter laxatives that he had gotten from the prison doctor. Then he poured the concoction into the Woodcutter's congee. No one noticed, and the Woodcutter gulped it all down. Wang Er dispatched other inmates to occupy the squat toilet while he monitored the Woodcutter's reaction to the toxic glue. Half an hour later, the moment that Wang Er had anticipated arrived. The Woodcutter lurched out of his chair, looked around and rushed over to the toilet. Wang Er yelled in his resonant voice, "Hey, hey, get in line. It's my turn next!"

"No, no, I can't hold it anymore!" The Woodcutter was panting heavily.

"We can't hold it either!" Others thronged around, imitating him.

The Woodcutter opened his mouth wide, breathing with difficulty. People moved out of his way, and the Woodcutter scurried back and forth in the cell like a rat in heat. Soon, he began to perspire profusely.

"Big Daddy, please let me take a shit, just once, okay, please," the Woodcutter stopped by the toilet and pleaded.

Epileptic, himself a former victim of Wang Er's cruel jokes, squatted over the pit, with a copy of *People's Daily* in his hands. "My legs are asleep but I still can't shit," Epileptic pretended. "I'm constipated."

"Without discipline and rules, the revolution will not succeed," several inmates teased by quoting Chairman Mao. "Go get in line."

"I'm going to shit in my trousers," the Woodcutter grabbed his belt and begged. Epileptic ignored him. Out of desperation, the Woodcutter clambered on top of Epileptic, who was squatting with his trousers around his ankles, and pulled down his underwear. Within seconds, the Woodcutter let open his squalid, digestive floodgates and covered Epileptic with shit.

Six days into his detention, the Woodcutter was sent to a mental hospital for a checkup. The doctor diagnosed him with schizophrenia, which spared him the death penalty, but life was no better than death. Days of severe diarrhea reduced the former invincible tank to a pile of scrap metal. On the day of his release, the emaciated Woodcutter ambled along in our cell. Epileptic, still livid from the memory of his shit bath, struck the Woodcutter on the face with a basin. His victim crumbled to the floor, his face a bloody mess. Wang Er applauded Epileptic's heroic move but feared punishishment for bullying the Woodcutter. On the spot, Wang Er came up with a story. "Help! The lunatic is committing suicide!" he shouted loudly, feigning panic. Predictably, several Red Hairs arrived with dispatch and fetched the Woodcutter.

Outside, we could hear the Woodcutter screaming from the jabs of the stun baton.

Wang Er's Verdict

WITH THE WOODCUTTER'S RELEASE, the noisy excitement and intrigue were replaced by silent boredom. The pattering rain outside never seemed to stop. The cell was crammed with cardboard boxes. All day long, we hunched over, folding medicine packets. In those long and monotonous days, I would put my elbow on the windowsill and my chin on my fist, gazing at the strands of raindrops cascading off the roof.

In the cell, people no longer harbored any illusions about our days ahead. Before Wang Er could relish his conquering the lunatic Woodcutter, his own indictment came down. The court upgraded him from an accomplice to a main culprit, charging that he was the mastermind of a big theft ring. With that charge, he could face the death penalty. "My life is over," he said with a doleful expression.

By early summer, Wang Er's case remained unresolved and he was overtaken by anxiety. He would frequently sit on a pile of quilts, calculating the possible date of his trial with his fingers. There didn't seem to be much hope for him. Meanwhile, the biennial "Confess Your Own Crimes and Report on Others" campaign started with great fanfare. Pens and papers were distributed to each inmate for confessions. I was ecstatic and immediately used the paper to write a new poem. While I was deep in my poetic mood, Wang Er came up to seek my advice.

"What do you expect an idiot like me to tell you?" I said.

"I'm serious. I want to find out a way to get off death row."

"Oh, really." I lifted my face and studied his. "Are you planning to provide important leads for major criminal cases or do you intend to return the money that you have stolen?"

"I've been trying to retrieve some of the money and turn it over to the government since last winter, but my buddies have all fled and disappeared," he said. "I don't want to burden my mother and wife."

"You have a family?"

"Yeah, not really a happy family, though. My wife and I used to live in the same neighborhood. We were childhood sweethearts. In our teenage years, her family moved away and we didn't see each other for a long time. I later learned that she had graduated from college and worked at a research institution. One day, the heavenly god arranged for us to meet on the street. We were married and had a daughter, but for years I lived a double life. At home, I acted like a decent husband and father, but behind my wife's back, I was robbing and stealing. Each time we went to visit friends and neighbors, I wouldn't even dare open my mouth for fear that I would accidentally give away my secrets. In those days, life was sweet and suffocating."

"Did you ever think of giving up stealing?" I asked.

"Of course, but before I washed my hands of it, I decided to go on a spree. I needed money to support the family. One day, I was caught pickpocketing in a department store. One of my wife's colleagues happened to recognize me and told her about it. I was in big trouble. My wife ripped off her own mask of a sweet and well-educated intellectual, and revealed her true violent nature. She chased me out of the house, carrying two bricks, one in each hand. I ran past the busy shopping center and snuck into a small lane. She saw me hiding behind a car and tossed the bricks at me. The bricks missed me but flew through an open window, knocking the driver unconscious."

"Did she file for divorce?"

"No. I slit my wrists, vowing to turn a new chapter in the next life. I copied that from a movie. My wife took me to the hospital. We huddled together, crying, and reconciled."

"But you soon returned to your old life?" I said.

"That's right. Since I was detained, my wife has been writing to me every month, promising to borrow money and pay back what I stole from people. Apparently she doesn't want to be a widow," Wang Er confided.

"I would think twice before paying the money back." I slipped into the role of a judge. "Chinese laws are like a rubber band. The judge can stretch it or shrink it back to its original state. It all depends on if he likes you or not. You may be eligible for a lesser punishment, but if the judge doesn't give it to you, there is nothing you can do. Why don't you ask your family to visit the judge at home and offer the money to him as a bribe?"

"What if the judge takes the bribe but still won't reduce my sentence?" Wang Er wasn't convinced.

"If that happens, you are truly out of luck. You know how corrupt judges are." I raised my hands helplessly.

"That means that I'm doomed."

"Whether you are doomed or not, bankrupting your family to keep your life won't work." I felt the need to be honest with him. "Even if you manage to keep your life, you will still stay in jail for twenty years."

"You're full of shit," Wang Er said, dismissing my remarks. "If I die, I'll leave my wife and daughter to you. She is pretty."

"Knock it off."

"I've been around in the underworld for a while. I have done and seen a lot. Nothing surprises me. I know you look down on me and feel sorry for my wife."

"That's true," I admitted.

"Okay then. Let me tell you some more embarrassing stories about me. For a while, I had too much sex and I became impotent. Even so, I still went with my pals to visit prostitutes. One day, a hooker made fun of my dick, saying it looked good but didn't do much for her. I ended up burning her pubic hair. Another time, when I couldn't do it with my dick, I fucked a hooker with a beer bottle. She loved it, screaming and scratching my back."

"Great story." I clapped my hands disdainfully.

"You want me to slap you?" Wang Er blew out his cheeks in exasperation.

"Do you want to slap my face or my ass?"

"You fucker!" Wang Er seized me by the collar. Da Long and the Foreign Minister immediately came over to break up the fight. We stared each other in the eye, unblinking, with the tips of our noses almost touching.

"You think I won't slap your ass?" Wang Er dragged me to the toilet area, and his friends automatically dispersed to watch out for the guards. At that critical moment, I heaved a sigh: "If you dare do anything to me, our friendship ends right here."

Wang Er's face twitched and his eyes moistened. He tossed me against the wall and let go. Turning around, he seized an inmate nicknamed Big Mouth. Wang Er ordered Big Mouth to face the wall and bend over. He ripped off the victim's trousers, spat into the victim's butthole, and raped him from behind. As Wang Er thrust back and forth violently, Big Mouth yelped in pain. Blood trickled down his thighs and the back of his knees in two distinctive lines. Inmates stood around, astonished. I sat on the edge of the bed and tears welled up in my eyes for the first time in a year. The sexual violence touched a raw nerve in me.

After the cruel violation, we were quite surprised that Big Mouth fell in love with his attacker. For the next week, the two became inseparable. They found a spot near the aisle and moved their mattresses together. Big Mouth fawned over Wang Er with exaggerated feminine mannerisms. He swung his hips and cat-walked, ate with his pinkie sticking out, and flirted with other inmates. The excessive coquetry repulsed everyone. Soon, Wang Er's impotence returned. During a spat, Wang Er whacked Big Mouth on the face and ended the love affair.

A Suicide Attempt

"THE CONFESS YOUR CRIMES AND REPORT ON OTHERS" campaign continued for two weeks before gradually cooling off. As usual, the loudspeakers declared the campaign a spectacular success, even though we had no idea how many confessions authorities were able to extract from gullible inmates with their false promises. Around this time, Old Xie, a tall, scrawny, middle-aged man, arrived from Cell 9. He had a pallid and sickly face, but glowing eyes. Old Xie was a graduate of a well-known military academy and could speak two foreign languages. In fact, he had served as a secretary to a deputy mayor. He was in jail on charges of embezzlement and stealing cultural relics. Officer Tang had high hopes for this mild-mannered former official. He carried Old Xie's belongings, announcing his decision to unseat Wang Er and make Old Xie the chief of our cell. The title came with many privileges — Old Xie would be entitled to the best spot in our big bed and he did not have to fold medicine packets.

We avoided Old Xie like a land mine for the first few days, treading around him cautiously. He attempted to strike up a conversation with me once: "I have a message from your friend Chen Dong."

I did not respond for fear of isolating myself from other inmates, who remained loyal to Wang Er. Old Xie did not push, either. He simply went back to reading. I peeked at him and saw that he was reading a pocket-size Bible. I found it a miracle that the authorities allowed him to keep a Bible in jail. From a distance, it looked like he was committing passages to memory. Every few minutes, he would close his eyes, his face flush with excitement.

One day, Old Xie pulled out a bamboo stick from the straw mattress. He held up the tiny, sharp weapon and examined it carefully. Then he began pricking the tip of his left middle finger with the stick. After dripping the blood into a small container, Old Xie dipped the bamboo stick in the blood and wrote on the back of his Bible. A few days later, I got to see the words that he had written:

> We are all aliens on this planet, our bodies the graves of our souls. We cannot destroy our bodies to liberate our souls because they are God's possessions. When we are lost, God's sheep pen appears on the horizon. Lightning flogs my crooked back like a tender whip . . . God's footprints are everywhere in nature.

Time seemed to have congealed like blood. I was entranced and drew closer to him. On the timeless stage of my dream world, he and I performed together, shoulder to shoulder. We were our own audience.

In the evening, I discussed Old Xie with Wang Er, requesting permission to cross the picket line and end his isolation.

"I can understand since both of you are intellectuals. But I'm afraid that he might be a mole," Wang Er said.

"Did you ever think that I might be one, too?" I fumed.

Wang Er was speechless. He defused the awkwardness with a joke. "Okay, I'll make you the political commissar. Your job is to get in touch with our enemy and see what you can find out. Don't leak any secrets about us."

The bedtime bell rang. All inmates lay down on cue, but Wang Er rested his elbows on the edge of the bed and cupped his head in his hands. He cautioned me about my desire to know Old Xie.

"Don't be too bookish," he whispered. "Remember what Chairman Mao said about class struggles — never let your guard down against your class enemy."

A voice outside interrupted our talking. "0-9-9, stand up!"

I rose, stark naked. Wang Er immediately withdrew his head into the comforter like a turtle.

"You are chatting and blabbering during bedtime." Officer Yu stood outside the window and reprimanded me. "Go stand outside the door for two hours."

I swallowed my pride and folded my arms tightly across my chest. "Sir, can I put on my clothes?"

"Permission denied."

"I might get a cold. I'm afraid of the cold air." I wouldn't budge.

"If you keep bugging me, I'm going to have your underwear removed so you can have a grand time," Officer Yu replied.

"Sir, you can't insult my dignity."

"You are a criminal. What fucking dignity are you talking about?"

"How dare you swear at me!" I became incensed. "Are you a policeman under the Communist rule or the Nationalists?"

"So what if I say I'm a rude Nationalist?" Officer Yu flew into a rage. "Stand still!"

Officer Yu left. A few seconds later, the door was kicked open. "0-9-9, step out!"

People stuck their heads out from under their comforters, watching with indifference as I walked out, my head high and chest out like a Communist martyr.

A group of Red Hairs leapt on me, twisting my arms and delivering me to a hallway inside the administrative building. Under Officer Yu's order, they fitted me with cuffs and tied me up with ropes. Bai, another officer on duty, was sitting on a long bench with bare feet and shoulders. He was fat and round like a pig.

"What the hell are you doing on a day like this?" He gave me a dirty stare and grumbled.

"Officer Bai, don't you want to help me out? Some exercise can help you lose weight," teased Officer Yu. "Look at you, it's only twenty degrees centigrade and you are already perspiring."

"The mere sight of this garbage makes me sweat." The porcine Officer Bai turned his back on me. I got a glimpse at the starlit sky. The mountain city was cloaked by a gigantic piece of black velvet, and I yearned for wings that would spirit me away.

Too soon, my soaring imagination melted into a pot of stewed flesh as electric batons tore at me like the sharp claws of crows. When Officer Yu started to jab at my armpits, I literally bounced around. Officer Yu's laughter echoed in the cavernous hallway. The jabbing accelerated, and I rolled around on the floor like a lump of chewed-up food on an invisible tongue, trying to break free so I wouldn't be swallowed and digested. "No, no!" I shouted.

"Officer Yu, you . . . you and I have no past grievances against each other. Why are you doing this to me?"

"I never hold any grudges against anyone. Don't forget, a Communist official is like your parent. When a son doesn't behave himself in front of his parents, he deserves punishment."

The Red Hairs giggled. The humiliation was so great that I wished I could drill a hole in the ground and disappear into it. Life officially lost its meaning. My mind was as chaotic as a busy construction site, with the ramming machine pounding twenty-four hours a day. I shriveled and my body instinctively recoiled like a flattened spring. I wanted to end that miserable life. Springing up, I hurled myself against a wall.

In my lifetime, I have written several times about car collisions — the speed is abruptly intercepted, the sun seems to be hacked by a cleaver. After a moment of surreal, supersonic euphoria, dark blood gushes out. On that night, my first suicide attempt happened so fast, like a fleeting inspiration. Before I had time to think and perhaps even savor its final possibilities, it was already over.

Embarrassingly, the crash did not even knock me out. My bound limbs diminished the force of the thrust. The gate to hell vibrated slightly but remained closed to me. My heroic act of preserving dignity through death turned into a contemptible farce. The prison doctor came to treat the cuts and stem the bleeding. Officer Yu walked away disdainfully while Officer Bai spat on the floor with disgust and commented, "Using suicide to threaten us? It doesn't work. Many people have tried this before you."

The Red Hairs also joined the disgruntled chorus. "Even political prisoners play this dishonest card. It's so pathetic."

Their remarks angered me. "You are right! I'm going to play the card until I win."

The officers and guards pummeled me afresh. After the Red Hairs vented their fury, Officer Yu returned and pulled my chin toward him. "You bastard! Why don't you take a good look at yourself in the mirror? You want dignity? How much does it cost per pound? I could lock you away like I normally do with the other criminal bastards out there! As we say in China, a tiny louse is not strong enough to overturn a heavy quilt. Committing suicide to escape punishment doesn't do shit for you."

"Okay, I am a piece of shit. But this piece of shit didn't do anything wrong and you punished him for nothing. If you won't unlock the cuffs for this piece of shit, why don't you kill him now?"

"Shut up and go back to your cell now. I'll talk with you tomorrow."

"I won't go back until you remove my handcuffs," I persisted.

"If you refuse to go, someone will carry you back."

"Okay then. Come and collect my corpse tomorrow morning," I threatened.

"You have no shame," Officer Yu said.

"I don't even want my life anymore. What do I care about my shame?"

"You can stay here as long as you want," Officer Yu said. "The cold draft might clear up your head. We are going to bed now."

"You are on duty tonight. It's illegal for you to sleep on the job."

"You are such a loathsome son of a bitch," Officer Yu roared and raised his fist but stopped in midair. He then shook his head, grinning helplessly. "You scumbag. I'll let you win tonight."

"I'm not a ruffian. I'm trying to gain back my dignity."

"You have the dignity of a dog, that's how I see it. What am I going to do about you?" Officer Yu signaled a Red Hair to unlock the cuffs.

I returned to the cell in triumph. The inmates had all heard the commotion. They mobbed me, checking the wounds on my forehead. Wang Er flashed me a thumbs-up and praised me: "Counterrevolutionary, I didn't know you were such a good performer."

"I wasn't performing. I was truly desperate."

"I don't believe a word you say," Wang Er argued, smiling at me knowingly. "The cut you got is right in the middle of your forehead, which is the most solid spot. The most you'll get is a cut. It will heal in a few days. You educated people are such good actors. You managed to get yourself covered with blood without causing any real damage to your body."

Angry at him for belittling my suicide attempt, I started cursing: "I swear it was for real. Otherwise, you can have American imperialists fuck me in the ass."

My desperate and crude defense aroused some good-humored chuckles, but people still refused to believe me.

"Then, what is the effective way to kill yourself?" I asked.

"First, you find a sharp corner of a wall and hit the temple against it," Da Long, another veteran detainee, advised. "The temple is one of the most vulnerable spots. You can easily poke through it with a chopstick. When you smash it against the wall edge, your brains will pour out."

"Counterrevolutionary is now eligible for a doctoral degree from the prison university," the Foreign Minister joined in the taunting. "He's all thunder but no rain. He knows exactly where to hit his head without damaging his brain. Congratulations on the success of your first suicide attempt."

The whole cell pretended to toast me.

I spun around, ready to seize the Foreign Minister and kill him, but Old Xie hushed everyone. We took the cue and jumped back to bed. The guard passed by like an apparition. Exhaustion gradually dissolved my anger, but the humiliation and the gnawing sadness of my suicide attempt stayed with me for years.

The Feast of Imaginations

THE ENDLESS ACID RAIN outside carried on like a long, boring play, and sunny days seemed as rare and as brief as an intermission. Summer was approaching. We learned from the party newspaper, the *People's Daily*, that severe flooding battered parts of Anhui and Jiangsu Provinces, forcing farmers to abandon their fields and retreat to high ground. Prison authorities made it abundantly clear to us that, in the face of such difficulties, the party and the people still generously managed to feed and shelter social dregs like us. Therefore, it was necessary to tighten our belts as an expression of remorse for our crimes and gratitude to the party and the people.

As part of the belt-tightening, our already-meager food rations were reduced, but fortunately we could still have some pork twice a week. I soon developed a special way to savor the precious pork slices. First, I carefully sorted out the pork morsels and put them aside. Second, I tackled the vegetables and rice, gobbling them up fast. Third, I rinsed my mouth thoroughly and washed my bowls and chopsticks. Last, I brought out the previously sorted pork slices, putting a small piece in my mouth one at a time. I masticated noisily like an old toothless lady chewing hard candy. As my mouth moved vigorously, I didn't allow my nose to idle. I inhaled greedily the rising fragrance of meat.

At the same time, I stopped my daily exercises to preserve energy. At lunch, I sat next to Old Xie, whom I had gradually befriended. With dark circles under our eyes, we looked like a pair of excavated artifacts. At lunchtime one day, Old Xie refused to touch the pumpkin soup and simply stared stoically into the distance. I raised my bowl and tried to entice him by gulping down my soup in one breath as if I were pouring a cup of bitter Chinese herbs down my throat.

Wang Er came by and energized us with a piece of exciting news: "I just asked the cook why the lunch portion was so small. He said we are going to have treats at dinner."

The excitement was palpable. When we resumed work in the afternoon, we found it hard to concentrate. In the dim light, the Foreign Minister stood on tiptoe near the window and reached his hands out toward the falling rain. "I can feel the rain!" he shouted excitedly and quickly licked his fingers. "It's greasy and tastes a little salty."

"It must be raining meat broth now," Wang Er joked. "Didn't the Bible claim that God is a fat chef?"

Old Xie was not a baptized Christian but drew his inspiration from the Bible, which a friend had given him before his arrest. He bowed his head and prayed deferentially: "God, please forgive us for our ignorance and blasphemy."

The Foreign Minister followed Old Xie's example and bowed. "God, if you bring me meat, you'll make a believer out of me."

By five o'clock, work stopped. We washed our hands and sat eagerly in bed. "You look like survivors of famine," Wang Er teased.

"Okay, Mr. Insider, what on earth are we having tonight?" Enforcer Da Long asked Wang Er.

"It's top secret and I can't disclose it," Wang Er said in a lowered voice, like a special intelligence agent.

"I think we are having steamed pork buns," the Foreign Minster licked his lips and said. "Four per person."

"I wouldn't mind if those buns had vegetable stuffing," I interrupted. "If a bowl of real bok choy soup comes with it, it would be heavenly."

"If I could be spared the death penalty, I would donate all my pork buns to you," Wang Er said. "I would be willing to remove one of my legs, chop it into fine meat, and mix it in the stuffing of the buns."

"I call that a true selfless hero," Da Long commented. We all applauded his generosity.

The much-anticipated dinner finally appeared and our joy and excitement evaporated without a trace. The "treats" were actually steamed sweet potatoes, two per person — one big and one small. When the cook handed me mine, I smelled something strange. So I broke the big one apart and saw that the inside was rotten. Grudgingly, I tossed it away. I noticed that Old Xie had gotten one as long as a thousand-year-old ginseng root. Wang Er's sweet potato was big and fat. His smaller piece was shaped like an egg.

Our disappointment was indescribable. Epileptic covered his face and sobbed. Wang Er went up to the fence and swore at the cook for lying to him. The officer in charge came and brought an extra piece of sweet potato to buy his silence.

Despite the grumbling, we wolfed down the sweet potatoes in no time. After dinner, Old Xie voiced his concerns: "Sounds like the flooding is worse than what we have read. If that's the case, I guess we'll have to have sweet potatoes for every meal."

Wang Er immediately dropped down on his knees and started praying. "Dear God, please take back what Old Xie has just said." Then he turned toward Old Xie. "You have such a foul mouth. So far, none of the good things you have predicted has happened, but every single one of the bad things has come true."

Fortunately, the good-humored Old Xie seemed to take Wang Er's insults in stride. It was a long evening. After the nightly roll call, everyone lay down, but nobody could sleep. Someone recommended that we should have a mental feast. The suggestion sparked a heated discussion over gourmet food. Like a magician, Wang Er fished out a pack of cheap egg-and-sweet-potato chips from under his pillow and called out to everyone, "Let's play some games and whoever wins can take these prizes. Anyone who has snacks hidden in their bag can join the game."

Nobody took up his offer. Wang Er threatened, "I'll have to conduct a search."

His threats produced results. A few reluctant participants contributed some soft candies, a dozen biscuits, and a few more packets of crispy egg-and-sweet-potato chips.

"Let's start," Wang Er proclaimed. "The person who can name a high-end dish that is both tasty and unique will be awarded all the snacks."

The Foreign Minister rubbed his hands and was the first to go. "I would like to have diced pork in clay pot. It has dozens of different exotic spices and ingredients."

"I'm craving the Big Nine Bowls, a popular set of dishes in my hometown," Big Mouth, Wang Er's former prison "wife," chimed in. He stood up and described it with expressive hand gestures. "Each piece of pork is as big as your palm. They come in different shapes — round, square, triangle, and twisted. Each bowl of pork is cooked differently, stewed, grilled, stir-fried, and steamed."

"I like the Chongqing hot pot!" an elderly inmate shouted. "You can dip everything in the broth — fish, shrimp, crab, chicken, beef, and pork."

"I like the hot pot," Wang Er agreed. "But my favorite one is called grilled camel. You empty the camel's innards and stuff a skinned horse in there. You remove everything from the horse's stomach and fill it with a lamb. You then fill the lamb's stomach with chicken and chicken's stomach with eggs. After that, you concoct a big pot of special sauce with spices and pour it inside. You sew up each layer nicely and set it on a pile of wood and roast it for days. This dish alone can feed several hundred people."

We salivated over his vivid description, and Wang Er reached both hands out to snatch the prizes, but the Foreign Minister stopped him. "What you just described is a well-known feast for the Muslim Hui people. None of us has tried it before. Let me suggest something that all Han people have tasted — Imperial Feast with Han and Manchurian Courses."

The Foreign Minister's words were met with total silence. Soon several inmates began to nod in agreement. "It is by far the best," one person voiced his vote.

Seeing that we were warming up to his dish, the Foreign Minister bowed to all sides and went up to Wang Er to claim his winnings. "Wait," said Wang Er, "I have another dish — Chicken for the Beggars." Wang Er held the Foreign Minster's hands, keeping him from taking the prizes.

Several people snickered. The Foreign Minister shook his head. "That's a fictional dish from a martial arts story. If we are allowed to use fictional dishes, our contest will go on until tomorrow morning."

Wang Er scratched his head and defended himself. "There is such a dish in real life. It's a whole chicken marinated in spices and wrapped in leaves and mud."

Nobody responded and Wang Er quickly turned to me. "You are the scholar. Help me out here."

"For a starving scholar, how many gourmet dishes do you think he has tried?" The Foreign Minister was willing to attack anyone who dared challenge his victory.

There were loud murmurs in the cell. Old Xie, who seldom aired his views in public, stepped up to support the Foreign Minister. "No dish in the traditional cuisines of Beijing, Shandong, Sichuan, and Guangdong can match the Imperial Feast with Han and Manchurian Courses."

At that moment, I could not help but sneeze.

Wang Er banged on the edge of the bed. "Wait, I'm not ready to admit defeat yet. As you can see, Counterrevolutionary has been struck with inspiration."

Under watchful eyes, I wiped my nose and uttered in a feeble voice, "The slop bucket at the imperial kitchen. The bucket contains all the delicious dishes you have just mentioned."

Mine was the final word. Everyone applauded in unison except the Foreign Minister. "You can eat slop?" he asked skeptically.

"Of course you can," several people answered for me simultaneously. "The emperor's slop is the best cuisine," one person added.

The Foreign Minister shut up. Wang Er ostentatiously unwrapped a soft candy and handed it over to me as a reward.

Staging a Funeral

AT THE END OF June 1991, Wang Er scheduled an appointment with his lawyer. About half an hour later, he came back, looking grim. The police were not able to use the information he provided during the "Confess Your Crimes and Report on Others" campaign to crack a major robbery case. "My lawyer said the chances for a commutation are not good," Wang Er groaned. "I'm done."

The bleak prospect of his case exacerbated Wang Er's brutal temperament. He acted as if he were the chief and organized a marathon boxing match, forcing everyone to participate. When the boxing match bored him, he amused himself with a game called Cracking Down on the Black Market — one person would sit blindfolded while others lined up to punch him on the head. The victim had to identify his attackers. If he guessed right, he would be freed and another would take his place. If not, the person had to suffer another round of beating.

A new arrival, worried that Wang Er would single him out as a torture target, claimed to be the housekeeper for the kingpin of the Ax Gang, a notorious secret society. His lie worked and Wang Er spared him the initiation ritual. However, a week into his detention, his indictment came down. We found out that he was a convicted rapist and murderer, and had nothing to do with the Ax Gang. An irate Wang Er ordered his lackeys to hold the "housekeeper" upside-down and dip him in the toilet pit to eat feces. "My dear housekeeper," Wang Er pulled his hair and said, "now that you are stuffed with shit, go do some work."

Around that time, Jin Hua, who had been jailed for his leadership role in the 1989 protest movement, was transferred to our cell. Since both Old Xie and Jin Hua had been friends at Cell 9 and both knew my friend Chen Dong, the three of us bonded.

Jin Hua used to be a high school art teacher and a literary aficionado. In 1989, he took to the streets and joined the student protesters in Chongqing, but didn't play a prominent role. Following the government crackdown in June, Jin Hua crossed the border and landed in Hong Kong, where he sought political asylum. Upon discovering that he was not a student leader on the government's most wanted list, immigration officials deported him. Jin Hua was first detained in Shenzhen for three months and sent back to his hometown on charges of illegal border crossing.

A year later, Jin Hua was suddenly seized with the urge to write. He created a poem — a rhyming political statement, to be exact — called "Commemorating the First Anniversary of Our National Tragedy." He printed several hundred copies and circulated them throughout Chongqing. One day, he brazenly walked into the municipal government office. "I was told that there was going to be an important meeting attended by several senior officials. So I snuck into a meeting room ahead of time," he recounted. "The staff members were too busy to notice me. I put a copy of my poem under each bureaucrat's teacup and left quietly. When I got home, I was so happy with myself. That night I dreamed that I fled to Hong Kong again and authorities immediately granted me my political asylum."

"What happened later?" I asked.

"I tucked copies of my poem into a bag and planned to take a train south. I was hoping to try Hong Kong for a second time. But on my way to the train station, I noticed that I had been tailed. I got on a bus, and so did two undercover agents. Before the bus reached the train station, I jumped off abruptly. The agents tried to follow me but were stuck. By the time they got off the bus, I had already boarded a different one. I could see them running after my bus. I was so proud of myself that I even flashed them a V sign. Little did I know that police in the 1990s were already equipped with cell phones. They dialed a number and someone else was waiting for me at the other end.

"And then?"

"They caught me and put me here. Ironically, the interrogators were the same people who questioned me after my first escape to Hong Kong," Jin Hua lamented.

Meeting Jin Hua and hearing his story was an unexpected pleasure. "It's good to meet a fellow poet," I said, shaking his hand. "We are everywhere, aren't we? Why don't you read a couple of verses from your poetic pamphlet?"

Jin Hua's pallid face reddened. He stammered out a couple of lines and stopped. "It's not that good. I wrote it on the first anniversary of the bloody crackdown. I just felt it was wrong to stand idle and pretend that I was deaf and mute."

Wang Er interrupted him: "Don't read your poem. Nobody here understands it. That big counterrevolutionary doesn't want to listen to your poem either. He's just poking fun at a small counterrevolutionary like you. In addition to poetry writing, what other talents do you have?"

"I can draw," Jin Hua admitted shyly.

"But there are no pens," I said.

"I can make one."

"You can make pens?" several inmates exclaimed. My heart stirred with excitement.

"You are a talented guy," Wang Er said in admiration. "When you have made your pen, could you draw a portrait of me?"

"How big?"

"This big." Wang Er indicated the size with his hands, stretching his arms out wide and then above his head. Seeing that the artist was still confused, he added meekly, "You know, like a portrait we use for memorial services."

"We are not having a memorial service, are we?" Jin Hua looked a little surprised. "I'll draw you a smaller one, in any posture you like."

Wang Er insisted on having a big one. "I want it for my memorial service," he said.

We were taken aback by his words. I probed further. "Do you have a fever or have you lost your mind? I've never heard of a memorial service for a living person."

"After I die, there won't be a chance for a memorial service," Wang Er replied calmly. "I've given a lot of thought to this. I've even lost sleep over it. I want to be accorded the same memorial service as a senior Communist leader."

I voiced my concern: "What about the guard? He will report us if they find out."

"I can bribe him with an expensive sweater of mine. I'm not going to wear it anyway," Wang Er said confidently.

I contemplated his request and was fully aware of the risks, but I found it hard to resist. Jin Hua enthusiastically embraced it and even proposed that we establish a Funeral Preparation Committee like the party did with Chairman Mao. I volunteered to take up the important task of drafting a eulogy and the VIP condolence letters.

After dinner that day, preparations for Wang Er's memorial service were in full swing. Jin Hua took a brush that we used to paste glue on the medicine packets. Fortunately, it was an old-fashioned broad brush. Jin Hua carefully dissembled the bamboo handle and picked four of the smaller brushes. Then he cleaned out the hollow inside of each pen shaft, plucked out the brush, and fitted it with writing points, or nibs, made from wood. Finally, Jin Hua spent a whole afternoon carving and grinding the nibs. By the end of the day, we had four pens whose tips could lay down lines of different thicknesses.

Wang Er and I hatched a scheme to get some ink. During the prison doctor's routine rounds, Wang Er scraped his ankle hard with a bamboo stick and blood trickled out of the cut. The Foreign Minister shouted for help. The doctor, who was treating an inmate next door, kept us waiting for quite a while before coming in. We crowded around him, begging for different kinds of medicine. The even-tempered doctor doled out a few aspirin, herbal cold-medicine packets, and digestion pills as though he were distributing candy to kindergarten children. The Foreign Minister volunteered to help Wang Er rub some gentian violet, a bactericide, on the cut with cotton balls. While the doctor was talking to another inmate, Wang Er deliberately knocked over the Gentian Violet bottle on the windowsill. The doctor's face darkened. He picked up the empty bottle and walked away, leaving a pile of cotton balls on the floor.

The Foreign Minister cautiously soaked up the puddle of gentian violet on the windowsill with cotton balls and gave them to Jin Hua, who slowly and meticulously stuffed the "ink"-soaked cotton balls into the hollowed pen shafts. Thus, before the officer came in for the nightly roll call, Jin Hua was officially able to present four pens to the Funeral Preparation Committee.

The next morning, Wang Er put on his white shirt and a pair of navy blue trousers. The outfit made him look like a Hong Kong movie star. His face glowed. At the command of the painter, he changed his pose. The portrait session lasted several hours. Jin Hua tore off several pieces of wrapping paper from the big cardboard boxes piled up along the wall. He drew six sketches but wasn't happy.

A gaggle of half-naked inmates stood around behind Jin Hua, gawking at the well-dressed gentleman. Wang Er put on a funny face to ease the awkwardness and asked the spectators to go away. "This is not a zoo, okay?"

Before dusk, the workaholic Jin Hua presented a standard-size portrait to the "deceased" amid universal praise and went on without rest to review the eulogy and condolence letters that I had composed. At the same time, the Foreign Minister and I personally directed and arranged every detail for the ceremony.

Following a dress rehearsal the next day, we were ready. In imitation of a government official, I announced the start of the ceremony:

> The memorial service for Comrade Wang Er was solemnly held inside Cell 6 of the Chongqing Municipal Detention Center at three o'clock in the afternoon. Placed in the middle of the bed was the casket (a cardboard box draped in black cloth). Comrade Wang Er's body was lying in state next to the casket on a pure white sheet, a symbol of his spotless and uncorrupted character. His face, coated with makeup, radiated health and peacefulness. A Communist Party flag (a red comforter) was spread over Comrade Wang Er's body, which

was surrounded by seasonal flowers (a cluster of colorful sweaters). *The military band of the Chinese People's Liberation Army played the sad yet uplifting mourning music* (a small group of inmates stood along the bed, playing air trombones, trumpet, and French horn, and squeezing their noses to hum the well-known Communist mourning tune).

When the music stopped, the Foreign Minister stepped on the stage (he came from the direction of the toilet and climbed up on a pile of comforters that we used to form a makeshift podium) and proclaimed in his sad baritone voice,

> *Comrade Wang Er, a great proletarian revolutionary, military strategist, and social activist, the Chinese people's great son, an outstanding model for all the pickpockets in the world-famous mountain city of Chongqing, and an outstanding robber and bandit, died on a gloomy day in 1991 from gunshot wounds at a shooting gallery on Chongqing's Geleshan Mountain. He was thirty years old.*

"You are reading too fast," Wang Er growled from his deathbed. "Slow down and pause after every comma. Your voice could be deeper. Try to imitate the voice of TV anchor Zhao Zhongxiang."

"Shut up!" I yelled at the corpse. Giggling could be heard among the "mourners." The eulogy continued:

> *At an early age, Comrade Wang Er developed a passion for money, and he was known in the neighborhood as a money-grubber. Over the years, he was determined to make it big in the world and honed his pickpocketing skills. The road to success was not always paved with easy cash and beautiful women. He was in and out of the Public Security Bureau numerous times and was first imprisoned at a reeducation camp. But Comrade Wang Er remained undeterred. Four times, he escaped or attempted to escape from detention, thus enriching our cutting-edge capabilities in frontline combat with the police and helping us accumulate a wealth of experience. His tireless work earned him the "legendary thief" medal title from the Chongqing municipal government.*
> *With the rising crime rates in recent years, the police force is ex-*

periencing a severe shortage of staff. The government has attempted to mobilize the masses in their pursuit of criminals and has started a "people's war." In response to the new situation, Comrade Wang Er, inspired by stories from foreign movies, came up with the "cops and bandits are one family" theory. He urged all criminal rings in the city to bribe police and avoid direct combat.

There is a saying that goes, "You are doomed to encounter a ghost if you constantly travel at night." Unfortunately, this is what happened to beloved Comrade Wang Er, who was ambushed by undercover agents and shot multiple times. The mountains and rivers are crying, and the whole nation is in deep sorrow. Today, we are here to mourn the passing of Comrade Wang Er. On behalf of the Communist Party Central Committee, the State Council, and the Chinese People's Congress, I confer posthumously on him the titles of Chairman of the Mountain City Pickpockets Association, Honorary Chairman of the Communist Party Central Committee, and Honorary President of the People's Republic of China.

The spirit of Comrade Wang Er lives forever.

When the eulogy was over, the nasal military band played the Chinese national anthem. Jin Hua stepped forward to read "letters of condolences" from world leaders. The letter from former British prime minister Margaret Thatcher said, "Shocked to hear the terrible news. The whole world is in deep grief." Li Teng-hui, the president of Taiwan, lamented, "I'm deeply saddened by the passing of Chairman Wang, the father of all thieves in Chongqing. He was indeed an anti-Communist hero and a pillar of our society." Current president of the United States, George Herbert Walker Bush, praised Wang Er in his message. "Why didn't we think of sending him over to Iraq to steal Saddam Hussein's head?"

The mock senior Chinese leaders such as party General Secretary Jiang Zemin, Premier Li Peng, and Foreign Minister Qian Qichen ascended the bed one by one to pay their respects. They circled the martyr's body and offered condolences to Wang Er's trembling widow (a scared young peasant boy who wore a loud-colored bandana and had two bowls inserted into his shirt as breasts).

The ceremony concluded with a powerful rendition of the "Internationale." All inmates stood around the bed and bowed three times to the dead.

"You missed the bowing at the beginning of the ceremony." The guard's muffled voice coming from the rooftop surprised us. "The portrait should be placed on top of the deceased."

"Why didn't you say that earlier?" Wang Er sat up and yelled.

"Mr. Chairman, I was busy guarding your memorial service," the guard replied, standing at attention and saluting Wang Er. We all laughed. The guard put his gun down and commented in his lazy tone. "Overall, it was not bad, but the party flag looked a bit crooked from this angle."

Two weeks after Wang Er's "state funeral," he was convicted of leading a criminal ring. The court sentenced him to death.

"Counterrevolutionary, our time together will be over soon," he said, adjusting the shackles around his ankles and smiling bitterly. It was a stifling morning. Wang Er and I sat next to each other in the courtyard. The others were working inside the cell.

"Please forgive me if I start to act badly in the next few days," he continued.

"Don't act out. They could transfer you to another cell and you'll suffer more," I admonished him. "I have written an appeal for you. No matter what the outcome will be, we should stick together until the end."

"My fate is in the hands of the heavenly god," he said despondently. "When I feel miserable, I want to drag another person down to share my misery."

"You've pretty much tormented everyone in the cell already," I pointed out. "When I'm released someday, I'll go find your daughter. What do you want me to say about you?"

"You tell her whatever you want," he replied.

"I don't believe that humans can completely turn into beasts. Don't try to prove me wrong," I said. "You don't have to have the whole cell turn against you and hate you before you die."

"But I don't want to die. I've only had thirty years in this life. I wanted to stay longer in this world," Wang Er said.

"Spending your long life in a labor camp? What's the point?"

"I can risk my life and escape, or I can settle down and serve out my sentence," Wang Er mused. "If they put me in jail for twenty years, I would be released at the age of fifty. I can still get a wife."

"So, you would rather suffer twenty years to gain back an ordinary life?" I asked.

Wang Er's face reddened with anger. "I want to live."

The Lunatic

THE NEXT WEEK, THE authorities suddenly issued a general cleaning order. We swept and scrubbed the floor even more than usual. Drunkard Tang, who had never bothered to monitor any activities at our cell, showed up at the door and personally supervised the cleaning. He insisted that we scrub the water tank and the squat toilet with toothbrushes. Wang Er rolled up his sleeves, pretending that he was working hard, but when Drunkard Tang wasn't looking he winked at me and whispered, "We must have visitors."

He was right — the day after the cleaning was completed, Drunkard Tang came in, ordering us to clear out the cardboard boxes on our bed and sit cross-legged, reading *People's Daily*.

"We had a banking delegation last time," the Foreign Minister reminisced. "I wonder who is coming this time."

A steady stream of people in colorful outfits swarmed into the second-floor corridor and flitted by the back window. Some visitors stopped to get a quick glimpse or pointed at things that interested them.

"Have you bought entrance tickets?" Wang Er suddenly yelled, triggering squeals and giggles among the tourists.

"Hey, do you have a death wish?" A guard pointed his gun at Wang Er.

"Women's screams always turn me on," Da Long said. "I'll have something to fantasize about when I jack off tonight."

I noticed Old Xie hiding in a corner, burying his head between his knees. Even so, a visitor, who peeked his head in from the window, recognized him. "Old Xie, come over to the window," he hollered.

Old Xie hesitated a moment and ambled his way over.

"Do you know who I am?"

Old Xie narrowed his nearsighted eyes and apologized nervously, "Sorry, I don't have my glasses. Would you tell me your name?"

"You are so forgetful." The visitor let out a scathing laugh. "You finally have your comeuppance. Prisoner Xie, I hope you can reform yourself thoroughly."

"Yes, yes," Old Xie stammered, his body slumping onto the floor. I stepped over and held him steady.

According to Old Xie, the visitor used to work for the municipal government. When Old Xie was secretary to the deputy mayor, he turned down a request for a favor from the visitor. "Since I was too principled and refused to grant favors, I made a lot of enemies," Old Xie sighed. "That's why I was made the scapegoat when the deputy mayor was implicated in a corruption scandal. But I'm at peace with myself. The Bible helps me cope with my agonies."

"Damn, this seems endless," Wang Er interrupted our conversation. "How many new faces have we seen today?'

"Several hundred, I would think," I answered.

"Look at these law-abiding people," remarked Wang Er. "They come here to visit a prison on such a hot day, like it's a big holiday. Some are dancing with joy. It just shows how bored they are with life."

I nodded. "It's better to die than to put up with a meaningless life."

After the visitors left, work resumed, but the oppressive heat slowed down our pace. A few days later, we were told that the factory had rejected the packets we had glued due to poor quality. We had to redo them. As punishment, the authorities withheld all our letters and denied us access to TV, cigarettes, and snacks.

The news sent tempers flaring. Jin Hua and I argued fiercely over a variety of philosophical questions. Meanwhile Wang Er continued to beat up people to satisfy his sadistic impulses. Sometimes he would try to strike up a conversation with the inmates next door by banging an inmate's head against the wall to get their attention. When our neighbors heard the loud banging they would "answer the telephone." Most of the inter-cell chats were about sex. For example, one person next door would yell: "Hey, where are you?" Wang Er would shout back, "I'm in Shanghai, fucking your wife in your bed."

None of our unruly behavior went unpunished. Except for Old Xie, who was spared because of his political connections, all of us were cuffed or jabbed with the baton. Even Officer Gong, known for his leniency, became so frustrated one day that he dished out electroshocks for the whole group.

For me, reading books was a pleasant distraction in the burning hell, even though dizzy spells came on after flipping only a few pages. In the ancient classic *The Romance of the Eastern Zhou Empire*, a fictionalized account of events in China's Zhou Dynasty in 1100 BC, there were lavish descriptions of state banquets. Many times I felt tempted to tear out the passages describing roasted beef and lamb, and chew the pages in my mouth.

I was not the only one who craved food. One night, we discovered that some greedy mouth had licked the glue bowl clean. Worrying that the glue could sicken the thief, Wang Er investigated all day but turned up no clues. Another night, an inmate caught a big rat. He ripped it apart, skinned the poor animal, and ate it raw.

In addition to food, we were also starved for sex. Wang Er launched what he called a "soft sports game" — masturbation contests. Those who could ejaculate the most would be awarded a piece of candy. I did not participate in the masturbation contest but fancied a type of testicular exercise that I had learned from an elderly herbal doctor at Cell 5. He taught me to massage each of my testicles three hundred times in the mornings and evenings. The practice, which he claimed originated one thousand years ago, could help strengthen sexual energy, enhance memory, curb urges of hunger, and improve skin complexion. His arguments were so convincing that I had started practicing it. One night, as I was sitting against a wall, holding my breath and exercising my balls, a beam from a flashlight shot straight down at my rising private parts. "Hey, I've finally caught you red-handed!" a voice shouted at me.

"Officer Bai, what are you taking about?" I answered innocently.

"Masturbation is a violation of prison rules," Officer Bai snarled from up on the roof. "You son of a bitch! I won't let you get away with this disgusting behavior."

"This stuff belongs to me. I can touch it whenever I want. What law have I broken?"

"You . . . you," the officer stammered. "How can you claim to be a poet? You are such a dick."

Our sparring happened on the night of a rare partial lunar eclipse. It must have been the beautiful sight of the eclipse that changed the officer's mind — I didn't hear from him the rest of the night.

My complacency led to other disasters.

One day I clashed with a new inmate who was assigned to clean the courtyard. The Foreign Minister sided with me and punched him. The scared new arrival shrieked for help. All three of us were ordered out of the cell.

Pervert Liu did not even bother to find out whose fault it was. He simply handcuffed us all. When I protested, Pervert Liu directed five Red Hairs to wrestle me to the ground. I fought back, but I was out-numbered. My arms were twisted behind my back and my wrists were tightly cuffed. I was in excruciating pain and roared like a lion, biting the hand that clamped around my mouth.

No matter how hard the other Red Hairs thumped on me, I wouldn't let go of the three fingers in my mouth. As a baton jabbed my temples, I sank my teeth deeper into the fingers and could taste blood in my mouth. The piercing screams of the poor Red Hair sounded like the most beautiful music in the world. He shook his arm violently but couldn't maneuver his hand out of my mouth.

Pervert Liu rolled up his sleeves and poked a slender finger of his into my nostrils before tugging it upward abruptly. I could hear the tearing sound of my flesh around my nose. Blood darted out, smearing my face. My clenched teeth finally loosened.

"0-9-9, you are an animal," Pervert Liu cursed.

I was out of breath, my face was battered like a flattened rotten peach. "All policemen are beasts," I declared.

The Red Hair rumbled over with his fingers bandaged and kicked me hard in the head. I raised my head and shot him a lump of spittle.

Pervert Liu yelled from the side of the room in his high-pitched sissy voice, "You are doomed!"

In the end, I was thrown back into my cell like a bag of garbage, with my hands cuffed behind my back. All my cellmates sat around me in mourning. The newbie who triggered the incident had been brutally beaten by Wang Er. He crawled over to me like a dog, begging for forgiveness. I kicked him away arrogantly, like a master with his slave, but he came back again. My bruised eyes darted around the room in defiance. I saw Jin Hua at a corner with a look of pity and disgust. I deserved his reproachful look; years of living with the thieves, murderers, and rapists had transformed me.

I was suddenly seized with the impulse to scream. Wouldn't it be nice to go crazy? I wondered. An insane person could howl and scream without the normal restraints and could even get away with murder. "Am I a crazy performer or a true lunatic?" I asked myself.

Soon I lost control of my mind. A long, beastly howl shot out of my body. I started chanting "Lover," a poem about a wolf cub ripping apart his mother's body and devouring her flesh. The screaming sent my fellow inmates fleeing, as if they were running for cover from an aerial bombardment in wartime. I cried and howled with abandon, dragging each syllable out as long as I could. I felt like I was flying through time and space and was back inside the studio where we filmed *Requiem*. I stretched my neck like a wrathful rooster and filled the space between each segment with a dense drumbeat of swearing.

The officer on duty came in with the doctor. Old Xie clutched my waist, and his dry, shriveled chest muffled my voice.

"I think there's something wrong with his brain," the doctor said. "His blood pressure and heartbeat are normal. The insanity is triggered by trauma."

"Prescribe some sleeping pills to shut him up," the officer in charge sneered. "This is the first time I've heard a singing donkey."

The Jail Bully

THE NEXT MORNING, THE loudspeaker blasted a message condemning prison bullies, and, predictably, I was the key target. In contrast, my opponent the newbie was transferred to another cell and received praise from officials. Meanwhile, the authorities launched an investigation to collect evidence against me. A special work team, led by the head of the detention center and monitored by a prosecutor in residence, summoned my fellow inmates for interrogation. Wang Er's turn came on the third day. He was out of the cell for merely thirty minutes before an officer hurled him back inside. He gesticulated with his shackled hands and joked, "Counterrevolutionary, they urged me to rat on you. I almost wavered and gave in to their request."

"I don't care," I responded coldly while trying to reposition my cuffed hands behind my back.

"They have gathered a thick stack of materials on you — enough for at least eight years. They encouraged me to expose your crimes and even promised me a commutation."

"Do whatever you want. I don't care."

"If they allow me to live, I would do anything and incriminate you in all sorts of crimes."

"Go away."

"No, I'm not going away because you are the last friend in my life," Wang Er said, grinning.

I looked him in the eye and noticed new patches of gray hair on his head. I tried to touch his hair but the pain in my shoulders reminded me that I didn't have the use of my hands. I thought of the story of Wu Zixu, the ancient Chinese military strategist whose hair turned white overnight while he was pursued by his enemies. "Wu Zixu . . ." I hummed.

"What are you singing? An operatic tune?" Wang Er grabbed my shoulder but tears welled up in my eyes. My mind was so muddled I could not carry on a normal conversation. For days Wang Er had fed me large doses of cold medicine that he and other inmates had gotten from the doctor. I was in a perpetual dreamlike state that shielded me from the brutal reality. I slumped to the floor in a corner of the cell like an abandoned mop; my chest and stomach burned, bitter-tasting acid backing up into my throat.

An hour or so later, someone patted me on the back. I popped my eyes open. It was the Foreign Minister. "Interrogation time," he reminded me, and pinched my face with his shackled hands. "Be tough," he added.

Inside the interrogation room, I sat on an unforgiving stone bench made for prisoners. The detention center director conducted the questioning, and the fat, pear-shaped Officer Bai took down the minutes. By then, the effects of the cold medicine had started to wear off. Bursts of cold surged through me and my teeth chattered. "He looks like a fucking opium addict," the director mumbled to Officer Bai. Turning to me, he roared, "0-9-9"

I widened my eyes for a few seconds and squinted to focus. It was to no avail. The officers blurred into two meatballs, one taller and the other shorter. "The policemen are so well-fed," I thought. "Inmates have been reduced to bags of bones, like sweatshop workers in movies from the 1930s."

"Don't squint," the tall meatball ordered.

"This is what nearsighted people do when they don't wear their glasses," I remember muttering.

"You don't deserve to be nearsighted," the short meatball spat out. "Most people are nearsighted because they are well educated. You are such a disgrace to the intellectual community."

I kept quiet. When the interrogator started grilling me with questions, I stubbornly denied every allegation — a trick that I had learned from veteran prisoners. In fact, I turned into such a liar that I could deny my past as a poet and, if necessary, my own existence.

The cuffs had cut into the skin on the back of my hands and smelly brown pus oozed out. Both of my arms had swelled up, like an injured weightlifter.

"I can't think with my hands cuffed behind my back," I protested when the two meatballs castigated me for failing to answer their questions.

"On the contrary, the handcuffs will force you to focus and think," the short meatball said harshly.

"If you don't cooperate, we'll leave them on for a long time, maybe a year," the tall meatball added while unbuttoning his shirt collar.

"According to the law, there is a time restriction on corporal punishment," I pointed out. "As the director here, you are knowingly violating the law."

Both meatballs guffawed in unison. "You sound like a high school student," the tall meatball lectured. "To tell you the truth, we used to double-shackle the death row inmates from a couple of months to a couple of years. By the time of their executions, their muscles had shriveled and their arms were thin as sticks. Even if we removed their shackles, they could scarcely move their arms or shoulders. Maggots infested their armpits."

I shuddered involuntarily. Seeing that they had conquered me, the two meatballs immediately followed up with more questions. As the session progressed, I realized that no matter how much I denied them, I would not be able to escape the jail bully charges. I threw up my hands and gave in by admitting to most of the allegations. At the end of the session, the meatballs pressed my inked finger on the minutes of the interrogation and delivered me to the office of the prosecutor in residence. Li, the prosecutor, had a square-shaped head, bulging eyes, and big gold teeth.

Sitting behind his big desk, Gold Teeth wove a stack of documents that contained accusations against me. His questions were stern and clear-cut. I nodded or shook my head. Occasionally I became distracted and my eyes shifted to the overcast sky outside.

In jail, my life was as worthless as an ant's, but I was unwilling to accept that fate. When the harsh reality trampled me like a big boot, I raised my antennae unconsciously, poised for a fight. As a child growing up, I would imagine retaliating against the bullies or my enemies after they hurt me. In later years, my enemies in each phase of life had faded away. Time was my best revenge. I no longer had to encounter those bullies, who had slapped me on the face in broad daylight or forced me to paste big character posters on the walls condemning my father as a counterrevolutionary during the Cultural Revolution. Time corrodes the passion that fuels old grievances, and heals old wounds. Would I ever be able to move on with my life and forget about my experiences in jail. Could I somehow obliterate this day when I faced Gold Teeth?

A towering shadow stood over me, jolting me out of my reverie. I strained my eyes and recognized him. It was Officer Zhao, who had crept into the prosecutor's office without my noticing. I greeted him. He walked over to me and lifted my chin with his gloved hand:

"Are you the one who bit someone's fingers the other day?" he asked while straightening his palm. He smacked the side of my face hard with his open hand. My teeth clattered. I felt like I'd been decapitated; my head somersaulted through the air and landed on my shoulders. I choked on my own blood and a violent cough tore my vocal cords.

I plummeted to the floor. Officer Zhao forced me into a corner, where I curled up like a hooker awaiting a blow from an angry client. Flames of fire shot up from my throat. I gathered enough strength and protested, but my voice was as feeble as that of a bee's. I whimpered, "This is the prosecutor's office. How could you do this?"

"Are you trying to say something?" Gold Teeth rose from his seat and came over between me and Officer Zhao. "Do you want to confess and admit guilt?" he whispered. "What you have done in the past couple of days is pretty hideous."

I twisted my shoulders and turned my head away from him. Opening my mouth wide in pain, I struggled to stand up, but Gold Teeth pressed me down. He moved over to Officer Zhao, gave him a thumbs-up sign, and gleefully walked him out the door. When Gold Teeth re-turned, he bent over with a stern expression and grabbed my shackled hands. "Put your fingerprints on these documents," he ordered.

Trembling from the pent-up anger, I exploded like a time bomb whose last second has expired. With a loud wail, I crashed into Gold Teeth, who was caught off guard and fell aside. Then, with one foot stepping on a chair, I clambered onto Gold Teeth's desk. I shattered the window with my right foot and thrust the left one into the air. Gold Teeth reacted fast and seized my right foot before I could jump down. In yet another cartoonish moment, Gold Teeth's mouth struck the windowsill, and blood splashed on his glittering gold teeth.

Pervert Liu and a group of Red Hairs burst in. One raised the elec-tric baton, but Pervert Liu stopped him. "Don't waste your energy. It doesn't do much to him." Gold Teeth grimaced and pressed a towel over his teeth. He warned me in front of everyone, "0-9-9, don't even try. We'll never allow you to end your life and escape punishment under the law."

I returned to the cell covered with bruises. Wang Er was gone. In addition, the Red Hairs had shackled the Foreign Minister's hands and feet. Each time he walked, he had to bend over like a crooked old man.

Faint sobbing and moaning came from next door. "An inmate is writing a letter to his mother," the Foreign Minister whispered. "The guy is a robber and requested a pen but the officer in charge ignored him. So he has pulled out a tiny stick from the bamboo mattress to poke and scrape his belly, and uses the blood as ink."

"His mother might faint if she gets a letter written in blood. Isn't he worried about that?" Jin Hua questioned.

"There is no need to worry. The authorities will never allow the let-ter to get out." The Foreign Minister shrugged his shoulders. "Some-times, I wish I could write a similar letter, but I don't have a wife and my parents died young. You poets are different. You can moan and groan over anything."

His words suddenly reminded me that Wang Er had dictated sev-eral farewell letters to me. I stood up and rummaged around under his bedding. There was nothing there.

"Wang Er brought the letters with him," the Foreign Minister said. "He is as sentimental as a poet."

I glared at him, but Old Xie stepped over to help smooth things over. "Don't feel too sad. The letters will keep him company when he enters another world."

I lost my voice for two weeks. Hunger gnawed at my stomach but the pain of swallowing deterred me from taking food. Luckily, I had Old Xie to feed me. He was always smiling, encouraging me to take more. Each act of chewing and swallowing was a torment. Often, a meal took one and a half hours.

Feeding me was as labor-intensive as blacksmithing. Old Xie's arms became sore, but he never gave up on me. I used to ask my gentle mentor if his facial muscles hurt from all the smiling. "It's part of my nature," he said, smiling.

On the twenty-third day, the Foreign Minister declared that he could no longer stand it. "Let's surrender," he said, his eyes sunk so deep in their sockets that two eggs could fit inside.

"If we surrender, it means that we have admitted our guilt. There is a possibility that the court could add time to our sentence," I said.

"I don't care. As long as they unlock the handcuffs and let me leave this hellish cell, I'm willing to accept eight or ten extra years," the Foreign Minister sobbed. "I haven't changed my underwear for a month. The stink there makes me sick to my stomach."

The two of us slunk out of the cell like dogs and requested papers and pens to write our confessions. When the officer in charge and several Red Hairs came to remove the shackles, I blew a big stinky fart, and my handlers moved away with their noses covered in disgust. I had been constipated for eight days because I could not overcome my inhibitions to let someone else unbuckle my trousers and wipe my butt.

The Foreign Minister and I spent the next two days in an office writing self-criticisms and reflecting on the crimes we had perpetrated during our detention. In fact, I listed more than twenty of them, both big and small. Drunkard Tang skimmed through the papers and looked at me. "You know, Wang Er's execution date is coming up."

"So it won't make a difference to him if I let him take most of the blame?" I asked.

Drunkard Tang smiled knowingly: "You still need to be truthful."

"Okay, I will be very truthful," I answered.

Based on Drunkard Tang's suggestions, I revised my confession, filling each paper with self-condemnation while blaming some of my transgressions on Wang Er. My writing passed muster, and our limbs continued to heal after staying shackled for twenty-four days. The Foreign Minister and I strode back to our cell, throwing our arms around freely. Our cellmates held a celebration party for us. Giddy from the experience, we straightened our backs and talked our heads off. At night, I stretched my limbs and sank into a deep slumber. As I was taking a cold shower the next morning, I felt as if I were on the top of the world.

Fortunately, the prison bully charges didn't adversely affect my sentence. After nearly two years in police custody, the court had postponed deliberating my case again. Incredibly, the authorities at the detention center did not add any new charges to my file.

On the first day after I was freed from the shackles, a big red spider fell and dangled precariously from the ceiling. "A good omen!" the Foreign Minister shouted like a child. "Let's see whose head the spider touches. Whoever he lands on will be able to walk out free."

Old Xie dismissed that as pure superstition. "All of us here are facing serious charges. Unless we receive a general pardon, I don't see how anyone of us can get out of here."

"Jin Hua is likely to get a light sentence," I teased. "He has already filed an appeal. He might be the lucky one."

"Why don't I sit on a spot directly under the spider?" Jin Hua took my words seriously.

"Too bad, the wind has blown it away," the Foreign Minister informed us with regret.

At that very moment, the fence door slid open. Like a flock of geese, we all craned our necks, thinking that miracles were about to materialize. "Receiving inventory," a Red Hair's voice sounded in the corridor. The disappointed geese retracted their necks.

The Robber

"HELLO EVERYONE," A HALF-NAKED robust fellow said. He stood by the door, his shackled legs parted slightly. His straight posture reminded me of an ancient knight. Bowing around to everyone, he introduced himself. "My name is Mao Shengyong. I've gotten the death sentence on robbery charges. The forty-five-day review period has long passed. Considering that I don't have too many days left to live, please forgive me if I offend anyone."

Inmates stared at him indifferently. I couldn't help applauding. "Excellent performance!"

"What do you mean?" The fellow looked puzzled.

"The little monologue was dramatically delivered against the silhouette of the fence door. In the future, I'm going to copy that," I said.

Mao bent his body slightly and sprang forward, his shackled body landing at my feet. "Brother, are you also waiting for death like me? What did you do — Steal? Kidnap? Murder?"

I flinched while the other inmates burst out laughing.

The Foreign Minister teased, "He's more dangerous. He wanted to overthrow the government."

"Are you a counterrevolutionary?" Mao asked in admiration. "No wonder you sounded so poetic."

I looked at Mao closely. He wore only a pair of burgundy underwear. "Where are your clothes?" I queried.

"Oh, after my verdict came down, I gave everything away," Mao said proudly. "I came to this world naked and I want to leave naked. In this way, I can avoid a body search from the guard in hell."

Noticing my skeptical expression, Mao unpacked a magazine-size bundle tucked under his arm, revealing a neatly folded shirt and a pair of trousers. "I'm wearing these on the day of my death," he explained earnestly. Then he pulled two pictures out of his shirt pocket and handed them to me with both hands as though they were valuable antiques. "This is my family picture," he said as I looked at a group photo. "Everyone is here except my sister. That's her," he said, pointing at the second photo. "Isn't she pretty? Many people thought she was my girlfriend."

"That's all your belongings?" Old Xie said with sympathy. "It's late fall and can get very cold at night. Let me apply for a quilt for you."

"I appreciate your kindness." Mao balled his hands before his chest. "But I'm scared of lice. I prefer to sleep without a quilt."

After a few days, I became attached to Mao. He was smart, and his toughness and agility impressed me. He practiced high jumps every day like a trained gymnast, and his feet landed effortlessly and elegantly on the middle of the bed. When he slept, he lay on his back, straight and stiff as a gun.

As my new friend, Mao offered to fulfill my daily work quotas — three thousand packets, no more, no less. I was flattered but found it hard to accept his kindness.

"You are a scholar and I'm a warrior. I'll do the heavy labor and you offer ideas to help me sort through this mess."

"I get the impression that you have sorted it all through."

"I have no choice. I was a robber. I don't have any other skills. It's fate."

"So, you think you were destined to be a robber?"

"In the ancient Chinese classic *The Outlaws of the Marsh*, it was called robbing the rich to help the poor. All the rebels and heroes were robbers or bandits, don't you think?"

"That's a wacky theory," I answered.

"When I was young, my family was poor. I dropped out of school to support my sister's education. Later on, the whole family depended on me — my brother, who was retarded, and my aging parents."

"Other than robbing people, did you have another means of making a living?" I asked.

"Look at my fingers. They are rougher than wooden sticks. I'm a born robber," Mao bragged.

"Tell me about your case," I probed.

"I operated independently for several years and was never caught. My targets were mostly department stores. So I found it hard to do those big stores without a partner. I recruited a young fellow. One rainy night, we picked a target and broke into the building from the roof. I crept up behind an employee who was working late, overpowered him, and pressed a knife against his stomach. I ordered him to lead us to where the safe was and to open it. Most people would have been scared shitless. I mean, it was public money anyway. Who would want to risk his life?" He sighed. "But it was different with that idiot. He started calling, 'Thief, thief!'

"We later found out that he was the head of the department store and a loyal Communist Party member. I was so touched by his devotion to public property that I pushed half an inch of the knife into his body. I did it tenderly and slowly, thinking that the bleeding could weaken him and shut him up. In this way, I could wrap up my knife, grab the money, and run. But that old man became crazy and he grabbed me with both hands. I pushed another inch into him. The heroic old man fell against a wall and his face contorted in anger. His mouth was wide open but he made no sound. I lifted his shirt, wrapped it around the blade, and pressed it back into the wound. When I slowly pulled the knife out, the blood was stanched by the shirt, inside his body. It was a beautiful and clean job. With regret, I held him by the shoulder and lay him down on the floor." Mao finished up his story with an ironic flourish: "May his revolutionary spirit live forever!"

I could feel chills run down my back. Old Xie interjected, "You even keep your sense of humor when you kill people."

"That's part of my nature," Mao said with modesty. "How can you live without humor?"

Late one night, Mao woke me up and pointed at the guards. The shackles around his limbs clanked in the quiet. "Look, they have doubled up the guards," he whispered.

"What does that mean?" I asked, with my eyes closed.

"This is my forty-ninth day. My time will be up shortly."

I looked at him, speechless.

"Don't you want to say something to me? In the West, before a person is executed, a priest will come say a farewell prayer."

"But I don't believe in God," I said.

"Yes, you do," he persisted.

"Nobody in China believes in God."

"But you do," he insisted.

"Okay, I'll start believing in God," I said, yawning. "It's all useless. You'll probably feel better if you just go without thinking too much about it."

"I want to know everything before I die." Mao tightened his grip on my shoulder. "I want to discuss life with you."

"Don't get too deep. This is a big question and I don't think we have time," I quipped, brushing him off. "You won't feel lonely when you go down there. There will be one billion ghosts waiting for you. It's a crowded and noisy place," I reassured him.

Mao paused for a few minutes and bleated, "Dammit, you are so cruel. I didn't realize scholars can be so callous. Since I don't have much time left, I'm going to keep my eyes wide open every second now."

"They are not coming to get you tomorrow." I yawned again and lay down. "I know it."

I drifted between dreams and reality. I heard the electric fence door slide open. The officer in charge, flanked by Red Hairs, walked in with his hands behind his back. He waited patiently as Mao clumsily changed into his white shirt and navy blue trousers. A sleeve was stuck inside his handcuff. Mao turned his hands around, pulling it, but couldn't get it out.

What happened to him? I wondered. He had been so brisk and agile. Suddenly, his head fell off, but his mouth was still moving . . .

The morning bell rang. I awoke and other inmates jumped up like broken springs. With the nightmare still vivid in my mind, I looked quickly to see if Mao was there. He had changed into his death outfit.

After breakfast, the sun broke through the clouds. Heat waves rose, turning the cell into a hot grill. We bared our shoulders and began our daily routine of folding packets. "This damn weather," the Foreign Minister cursed. "We haven't seen any sunshine for two weeks. When the sun finally comes out, it attacks us like a warrior."

"My underwear is all wet," Mao complained. "My dick has been fully cooked."

"Then why the hell are you all dressed up?" I mocked him. "You look so dapper in that shirt. If you wear a bowtie, you can go to a cocktail party like those nicely dressed Western gentlemen in the movies."

Mao wiped his sweat off with a piece of toilet paper and hopped down, taking up a spot near the fence door. "I'm going to stand here. It's quite airy." Then he turned to me. "Counterrevolutionary, I can't do the job for you today. Sorry."

Old Xie switched the topic by commenting on the weather. "It's already fall. The heat won't last. It will be over in a few days."

"I can't even last for another hour," Mao brought the topic back. "Counterrevolutionary, could you make me a cup of tea?"

I dug out a pinch of tea leaves and stirred them in a bowl of hot water. Mao took the bowl from me with both hands and put it on the floor next to me. Then he lit a Treasure brand cigar.

"I'll finish this cigar before I leave," he said to me happily.

"No, this cigar will never burn out," I encouraged him to talk about the future. "What are you going to do when the weather gets cooler? You've already given everything away."

"After the soldiers blow my brain out, cold won't mean anything."

"You idiot!" I became upset. "I dreamed about your death last night, but dreams are the opposite of reality."

"Okay, let's place a bet on it," he said. "If I'm still here at lunch, you can have my meat veggie dish. If I'm gone by then, Old Xie can take yours on my behalf."

"I don't want to take that meat veggie dish," Old Xie pitched in.

"If you don't want to eat it, you can put it on the back windowsill. My spirit will come back to taste it." Mao said. "Dammit, don't they even offer me a nice meal before they kill me?"

Mao took a puff on the cigar hungrily. Before he had time to exhale, a loud rumbling sounded at the end of the corridor. Mao froze in fear, choking on the smoke. His violent, heart-wrenching cough could not cover the rhythmic and thunderous footsteps that were advancing toward us like big bowling balls rolling down an alley.

Every few minutes, the footsteps stopped and resumed again. We pricked our ears. From the murmurs and the clinking of fence doors, we understood that the grim reaper was harvesting souls during those silent intervals. We listened attentively and counted, "Cell 13, Cell 12, Cell 9, Cell 8 . . ."

"Wang Er is probably among this batch," the Foreign Minister mumbled. I slapped him on the forehead to shut him up and went down to add more water to Mao's tea bowl. Mao gazed into the distance, pinioned by his thoughts, and, after a moment, he raised the bowl to his lips. It trembled in his unsteady hands. Beads of sweat rose across his forehead. His shirt, soaked with sweat, clung to his muscular frame.

"They are in front of Cell 7 now," some inmates called out.

Mao abruptly put the bowl of tea down on the floor. "Our cell will be next!"

"This is a large group. At least, you won't be lonely," Old Xie said. Mao ignored him, pushed my hands away, and stood next to the fence door. The cigar had long been snuffed out by his sweat but he kept sucking on it.

The normal departure routine was being played out next door, but there was no heavy clanking of shackles. Jin Hua tried to defuse the tension. "This guy next door is tough. He doesn't need the Red Hairs to carry him."

"I'll do the same and walk out myself, with their help," Mao responded.

The silence that followed felt longer than one hundred years. We waited nervously but our fence door remained closed. Soon the rumbling noises moved past us and stopped at Cell 5.

"I won!" I shouted ecstatically. "The meat veggie dish is mine."

Inmates bumped each other with their foreheads in celebration. Mao stripped off his good clothes. "I can live to eat tomorrow's meat dish," he said with relief.

Return to Cell 5

I DIDN'T HAVE THE OPPORTUNITY to see Mao off.

On that afternoon, Drunkard Tang summoned me and the Foreign Minister to his office. Both of us would be transferred out of Cell 6, he said. We weren't even allowed to go back to get our belongings; two cellmates packed them and brought them out.

The Foreign Minister and I went our separate ways. I moved next door to Cell 5, and he left the detention center to serve his fifteen-year sentence in a reeducation camp. "We'll probably never get to see each other again in this life," I thought as he straightened his back and disappeared at the end of the corridor. To my disappointment, he didn't look back.

Suddenly, time had been sundered and my life in Cell 6 dissolved. Even though Old Xie, Jin Hua, and Epileptic were only separated from me by a wall, they seemed as far away from me as aliens on Mars. Our future encounters would only take place in my writings or dreams, I remember deciding.

It was hard to believe that I had lived in Cell 5 just six months earlier. I hardly recognized anyone. Nobody greeted me when I walked in. They chatted with one another in hushed voices while their eyes focused on the medicine packets. My eyes darted around looking for familiar faces. I spotted Sun, a veteran detainee, sitting solemnly on the chief's seat, with his round belly protruding. An inmate named Yao, with whom I'd had a fistfight, was also there. He avoided my gaze.

I felt oddly homesick for Cell 6; now I was living under someone else's roof. I went up to pay tribute to my new chief. He lectured me in a formal, austere tone on a routine that was hardly new: "You have bullied others in Cell 6. I hope you can behave yourself. Tuck your tail between your legs. Officer Li is in charge of our cell. He has specifically instructed me to treat you like new inventory. Your sleeping spot will be next to the toilet. Every day, you need to clean the toilet and its surrounding area.

"Last, but not least, the work quota in this cell is three to five thousand packets per person per day. If you can't fulfill your quota, you can choose between cuffs or the stun baton. If you end up with your hands cuffed, you will have to work overtime to make up for the missing work after your hands are freed. Receiving punishment is not an excuse to escape reeducation through labor."

"But we are not serving in a labor camp here, are we?" I questioned. "We are not even convicted yet."

The chief was speechless and stared at me with contempt. I got the hint and shut up. I slept on a narrow stretch at the end of the big concrete bed. If I wasn't careful at night, I could easily roll over and fall into the toilet pit. So I always scrubbed the toilet area nice and clean. I rinsed it with soapy water first, mopped little by little and then hosed it down with another round of water. For the urinal, I would squeeze toothpaste in there and brush that "big foul mouth" thoroughly with a broken toothbrush. I even spent some of my own money on toothpaste for the urinals.

Thus, I gradually turned into a clean freak, and I hated it when people squatted on the pit right after I finished cleaning. It was torturous to see the results of my work stained and ruined in front of my eyes. Of course, I dreaded Friday night, when the kitchen served stir-fried onions with pork. Not even toothpaste smeared beneath my nose could drive away the stench of the toilet.

My hideously mundane and repetitive tasks of cleaning the toilet and folding medicine packets consumed all my time during the day. I hardly had time to read or think. Soon my waist thickened. To many Chinese, loose fat dangling around the belly was a sign of prosperity and a stress-free life with good food. A prisoner's protruding belly pointed to the opposite. Like a robot, my hands moved mechanically to make the packets during the day, and the work intruded into the world of my dreams.

Every now and then, I thought of my friends in Cell 6. One night, when I was guarding two death row inmates, the bowls on the rack rattled in the wind. I stared at the rack, half-awake and half-asleep. The sound stopped. I couldn't help muttering, "Wang Er, is that you who have snuck back from the other world and come to see me? I'm sorry that we didn't even get to say good-bye."

The rattling resumed. Cold air blew on my back, and my teeth were chattering louder than the vibrating bowls. I begged Wang Er, "Please leave me alone. You are a ghost now. Don't drift back and forth between the two worlds."

To keep Wang Er out of my mind, I shook my head vigorously, trying to remain alert. I moved a big cardboard box out of my way and approached the toilet to pass water. As I pulled up my pants and turned around, I was startled by another inmate standing quietly behind me. I lost my balance and fell into his arms. Fortunately, I grabbed the person's shackles before our mouths touched.

I could not have picked anyone stranger to nearly embrace. It was one of the death row inmates, who was nicknamed "Cross-Eyed Killer." His eyeballs were malformed. As a result, he had problems focusing on the person or object in front of him. As a robber, the birth defect proved deadly. During an armed robbery, he had accidentally killed his own masked comrade. Now, as we met in front of the toilet, Cross-Eyed Killer tilted his head sideways and eyed me closely: "I wouldn't mind a kiss," he joked, while trying to untangle himself. I regained my footing and helped him with his bathroom needs. By then, I was wide awake.

Readers may have noticed that I have made numerous references to human feces. In *The Unbearable Lightness of Being*, the Czech writer Milan Kundera famously defined totalitarian kitsch as "the absolute denial of shit." He made shit the theme of a remarkable book of satire. Unfortunately, I am not capable of elevating human feces to a higher level and imbuing it with political, historical, and religious meaning. In this ordinary memoir of mine, shit is shit. I keep mentioning it because I almost drowned in it.

As I write, I am still living in the shitty pigsty called China and I yearn to cleanse my soul thoroughly. To do so, I have to transform myself completely — an agonizing process, which is much harder than scrubbing a toilet with a toothbrush. I am a witness created by this particular social and political enviornment, and it is important that I stay free from the fetid stains of the feces.

Hearing stories related to feces reduces us to our most primal, but such stories are also perhaps the most instructive about prison life. One notable inmate, a former banker whose name was Jiang Wei, struggled with severe constipation. He had been accused of embezzling a large sum of money from a state bank. His pampered life did not prepare him well for prison, of course, and he could not force himself to shit in front of other people. This virtuous habit in a civilized world was beyond the understanding of other inmates, who saw it as an idiosyncrasy. The banker's constipation lasted for ten days. He had foul breath and terrible skin eruptions. His eyes reddened like those of a female rabbit in heat. Sadly, the painful, humiliating circumstances of a wealthy, suave gentleman provided ample entertainment for the inmates, who otherwise lived a monotonous life behind bars. Fellow prisoners took turns harassing him, at first talking loudly in front of him about the great catharsis they felt after taking a shit. The banker's face and body would twitch violently in reaction to their vivid descriptions, but the minute he squatted on the pit, a gaggle would gather around like hungry dogs eager to sniff feces and shout in unison, "Go, boy, go!"

The banker covered his face in embarrassment. Tears soon poured from his eyes and sweat oozed out from between his fingers, but the inmates were merciless with their jokes. One patted him on the shoulder and said, "Don't get too emotional. We know you are thankful that we keep you company here, but this is the least we can do to help." Another person "consoled" him in an extremely concerned manner. "I know this is your first child. It'll be a little difficult, but not to worry. Take your time. Push hard, push . . . it will come out eventually."

On the eleventh day, the banker, whose forehead broke out in a rash, finally squeezed out a little. Worrying that the constipation drama would end soon, inmates immediately rushed over to stop him. The chief was among the crowd. I seized his arm. "You are over fifty. Why do you act like a child?"

He bristled at me. "Why the fuck do you care?"

The mob split into two groups. One group squatted on the edge of the bed, their buttocks aimed in Jiang Wei's direction and pretending to shit. The other group approached the victim, pulling his ears and cheering, "Go, friend, go." The banker experienced severe rectal bleeding. The blood further excited the savage crowd.

Another inmate hypothesized that the blood was the banker's menstruation. "When did you have your sex operation? I can see your dick is shrinking."

The exasperated banker pulled up his trousers and tried to rise, but two people pinned him down again. "Don't leave. You are an aristocrat. You need a lot of people to entertain you while you do your business."

"Please have mercy on me," the banker begged. "When the kitchen serves pork, I'll buy a dish for everyone. It will be my treat, I promise."

The inmates sang in unison, "Thank you, thank you, but we are monks. We don't touch meat and pussy."

The banker held his trousers and didn't know what to do. Then an idea hit him. He turned around unexpectedly. His big white buttocks proudly faced the whole group.

We were stunned. The chief roared, "How dare you turn your big fucking white ass toward us? It's insulting."

Ye Ya, a former petty thief, also chastised the banker: "Where are your manners?"

Several inmates dashed over, seized the banker by the shoulder, and forced him to change his posture.

"No, no, don't touch me! It's coming out!" the banker screamed.

The petty thief slapped the banker on the head and pushed him around.

"It's gone back in," the banker said in disappointment and burst into sobs.

Feeling bad for what others had done to the poor banker, I dug out a pair of long johns, jostled my way through the crowd and handed them to him. "Put this over your head. When you can't see anything, it will be easy. Imagine yourself taking a shit alone in outer space."

The banker inserted his head inside the long underwear. There was an explosion of laughter. "Counterrevolutionary is really smart," observed the petty thief.

The rowdiness in the cell caught the attention of the officer on duty, who happened to pass by the back window. Seeing the long johns over the banker's head, he thought he was witnessing a suicide attempt. "You bastard! How dare you!" he barked.

The crowd immediately dispersed. The banker froze — his head hidden inside the long johns.

"I'm not going to let that happen," the officer blustered. "Chief, peel that mask off from his face."

The banker grasped the long johns and wouldn't let go. The officer was fuming: "I'm not going to let you die so easily. I'll make you suffer first. Tell me, do you want to show your face?"

After a moment of silence, the banker sprang to his feet, and his legs, thin as sticks, trembled. From a distance, he resembled a big frog that had been skinned. His penis was erect and pointing directly at the officer. Slowly, the banker removed the mask with his left hand while his right hand reached into his anus. He pulled out his blood-smeared hand and screamed hysterically, "You want my shit and blood, take it!"

The officer rewarded the banker by beating him with his baton. The aristocrat yelped and screamed in pain, as would the rest of us low-class citizens. Then the officer fetched the doctor, who prescribed several doses of a laxative.

Once his bowels were cleared, the banker found it hard to keep anything in his stomach. Whatever he ate came out right away. A few days later, when he suffered severe dehydration, the doctor sent some antidiarrhea pills. Following two rounds of extreme treatments, the banker became a mere shadow of his former self. The well-mannered and fastidious man in him had disappeared, and in its place was a listless and slovenly hulk who never bothered to wash or comb his hair. His eyes brightened at the sight of food, and he devoured it like a starving beggar.

The banker's insatiable hunger proved dangerous. At mealtime, after the kitchen staff wheeled the cart from door to door and stopped to ladle out rice, soup, and vegetables, they would sometimes return to split the leftovers.

The petty thief would take most of the "profits" and share the rest with the chief and his friends. The banker salivated at the prospect of getting more nourishment. Without bothering to negotiate, he simply elbowed his way to the window, trying to get his bowl filled. When the petty thief shoved him away, the defiant banker raised his arm, shouting, "Down with the prison bully!"

Annoyed over the altercation between two of his subjects, the chief stepped forward to arbitrate. "I have to play fair," he declared. "Why don't I ask each of you three questions? Everyone else here will be the judge. Whoever gets them right will be given the chance to get the extras."

The petty thief was impatient: "We don't have time. I can hear the food cart coming this way."

"Okay then, you go get this one. The banker can step back and wait for the next meal," the chief said.

The banker was reluctant to obey. The chief pulled him away and reassured him, "I'm going to make it up to you."

Before the chief finished his sentence, the cart wheeled past. "They are not going to stop. No leftovers to share today," the petty thief uttered in dejection.

I egged him on by saying, "I'm sure they still have some leftovers. They are just lazy and don't want to stop. Use your street smarts to change their minds."

The petty thief looked around hesitantly at first and thrust his arm out with a bowl, his face pressed against the dark greasy wall near the window. Puckering up his strength, he let out a long, heart-wrenching yell: "Please, please, I'm hungry. Give me a bowl of soup."

The sound of his begging reverberated in the empty corridor. The guard sauntered over but made no attempt to stop the beggar. The rumbling food cart paused for a few seconds, but moved away again at a steady pace. Seeing that his last hope was slipping away, the petty thief began wailing while hitting his head on the wall. I could tell it was not acting. "Please give us some extra. I beg you, brother . . . have pity on us."

It so happened that an elderly officer overheard the tearful plea. He heaved a long sigh and called the food cart back. The cook scraped the bottom of the container and filled the petty thief's bowl with pickled vegetables and rice noodle soup.

The chief and his friends were ecstatic at the unexpected gain. They each took a slurp from the bowl.

The banker watched silently, scratching his head in resentment. "You can't monopolize the leftovers," he grumbled. "You beg on behalf of Cell 5. We should each get something."

"Bullshit," the petty thief snapped. "My appetite is three times bigger than yours. Otherwise, I wouldn't do this humiliating job."

"My stomach is at least five times bigger!" The banker patted his chest vehemently to go the petty thief one better. "You might be taller but it doesn't mean shit. Let's have a contest if you don't believe me."

"I don't have any food to compete for," the petty thief said.

"Didn't we just purchase snacks yesterday?" The banker wouldn't let the petty thief get away with his lie.

"Let's do the crunchy fried salted horse beans," someone suggested. "The loser will buy two bags for the winner."

"The banker hasn't received a monthly allowance from his family yet. I don't think he can afford the bet." I politely discouraged the game, but the banker rolled up his sleeves and was ready. "Don't worry, I'll borrow money first. Mine will come in soon."

"Okay, on your mark," the chief commanded.

The inmates started humming the Chinese "March of the Athletes" tune. The two contestants sat cross-legged face-to-face like dueling Japanese samurai. They looked each other in the eye with hostility, and smirks tugged at the corners of their mouths. The chief appointed himself the referee. He wrapped a white towel around his head and solemnly put four one-pound bags between the two contestants, opened them up, and shouted, "Get set, go!"

The contestants' cheeks wriggled and the crunchy sonata played on for half an hour. Half of the broad beans were gone. By then, both contestants had red blisters on their lips. When they swallowed, they leaned their heads forward and tilted their chins upward. From a distance, their Adam's apples bulged like big tumors. Their eyes misted up from the spicy peppers.

Two inmates who waited on them wiped their necks and sponged up the sweat off their heads with toilet paper. As the competition accelerated, the contestants' perspiration thickened, and the tissue paper disintegrated into pulp.

The contestants ground their teeth vigorously. Bloody saliva oozed from the corners of their mouths. Initially, they sat calmly, samurai-style. One hand lay on the lap while the other one fed the beans into their mouths. Then the banker switched strategies. He jumped off the bed, walking around and stretching his limbs. Eventually, he simply knelt on the floor and rested his chin on the edge of the bed. "Throwing in the towel?" The petty thief grinned.

The banker ignored him, and the petty thief soon noticed that his opponent had modified the technique. Spreading the beans evenly along the edge of the bed, the banker lowered his head, sucking up beans like a hog snuffling food in a trough. The new method proved to be faster and the petty thief immediately imitated his style.

Unfortunately, the new posture gave the petty thief stomach pains. He jumped back onto the bed reluctantly and resumed his former method of swallowing. The banker charged ahead fiercely — crunching, slurping, and sucking. At ninety-three minutes, the two were locked in a dead heat. Even though the petty thief set a remarkable personal record by swallowing 1.8 pounds of beans, his progress slowed. The banker, however, continued eating voraciously. To my amazement, he had guzzled down 1.97 pounds of horse beans, setting an unbreakable record at the detention center.

At the last minute, though, a mass of beans spurted out of his mouth as if a dam had burst.

People covered their mouths in disgust and fled. I tossed the banker a rag so he could clean up. The loser clutched his pregnant belly in agony; the pain gave his face a waxen appearance. He was bedridden for several days.

The court delivered the banker's death sentence three months later. On the morning of his departure, the sewage was blocked, affecting the toilets in several cells. The officers racked their brains but couldn't find a way to fix the problem. The banker, who saw a golden opportunity to have his sentence commuted, volunteered to go down into the pit and to clean out the sewage with his hands. It was deep in the winter, and the formerly pampered banker stepped out of the cell under the gleaming bayonets of stern-looking guards. He removed his sweater, coat, and trousers, and crawled down into the filthy manure pit in his underwear. One by one, he plucked out the filthy objects that obstructed the sewage and tossed them up to the surface. The stench almost suffocated him, but he persisted.

Inmates and guards looked on, deeply moved by his brave and altruistic act. After the banker finished and stepped out, he trembled uncontrollably but still insisted on cleaning up the mess outside the pit. The officer in charge stopped him and asked the Red Hairs to give him a hot shower and a cup of hot tea. At that very moment, the court summons arrived. He would be executed after all. The banker stood there, stunned and transfixed. Upon returning to the cell, he took a quick shower and hastily changed into his clean clothes.

Guards waited outside impatiently. Our officer in charge was sympathetic but helpless. Before the banker left, his body still reeked of feces. He gave us a bitter smile. "I have just been to hell. I don't have to be afraid anymore."

Permission to Read

IN 1991 THE DETENTION center experienced a high turnover rate. At its peak, twenty-six inmates were cramped into a space designed for only twelve. People slept everywhere — along the aisle and in the toilet section.

The sleeping arrangements exacerbated tensions. People in the aisle lay on top of each other. When they woke up, they shoved and pushed, swearing and cursing. Fistfights over space broke out at midnight. Sometimes, inmates beat each other up while they were only half-awake. The winners obtained the right to stretch their legs, and the losers could only curl up, their hands clutching their knees.

Unexpectedly, the arrival of two death row inmates from Ba County brought a ray of sunshine to my otherwise dark, drab prison life. Initially, the inmates fawned over the two fully shackled new arrivals as if they were VIPs. Since death row inmates were exempt from fulfilling work quotas, many attempted to enlist these two available human machines to reduce their workload. People swarmed around the new inmates, carrying their luggage, bathing them, and polishing their shackles. However, the two did not appreciate the VIP reception. They retreated to a quiet spot near the fence door, scanned the cell several times, and whispered to each other, trying to decide which work group they wanted to join. In the end, to the dismay of their many suitors, the two living dead walked slowly toward me. "Are you nearsighted?" the older of the two asked. Before I answered, he took the cardboard boxes from my hands and started working.

Their shackled hands moved with dazzling speed. In a little while, a small mound of glued and folded packets appeared. Other inmates were green with envy. Even though I lowered my head, I could feel the flames of anger licking at my face. Taking a deep breath, I kept my cool until the chief came over.

"Hey, you can't monopolize both of the living dead."

I sprang to my feet to confront him. My fists tightened but I restrained myself; I couldn't afford to court trouble again. A packed crowd soon surrounded us. I held myself in check, responding, "I don't know what you mean. I'm in charge of cleaning the toilet. As the toilet king, I only know how to monopolize shit."

"These death row inmates are not shit." The chief tried to use the opportunity to provoke a fight. "Those two people are nice enough to help you. How dare you swear at them?"

"You are trying to instigate trouble," I said.

"Wherever you go, you never change," the chief rebuked me.

"Neither do you. You are always a mole for the guards wherever you are," I retorted.

The chief's face convulsed. As our quarrel escalated, my new friends came to the rescue. "You are being unreasonable, old fart." The younger of the two hopped up like a leopard and stood firmly between me and the chief. "We want to help whomever we choose. It's none of your fucking business."

"I'm the head of this cell. If you don't show respect and obey orders, I'll have to report you," the chief threatened.

"Grandpa, what's the point of getting upset?" said the older newbie. He gave a look to the younger one to step back, put his arm around the chief's shoulders and whispered something to him that made the chief's dull and listless eyes sparkle with fear. When the conversation was over, he waved everyone away and withdrew to the inside of the cell.

I was still standing there pouting, but my new friends took me back to my place. "Sir, go read your books." The younger one smiled charmingly. "The alarm has been deactivated."

I was touched and at a loss for what to say. My eyes moistened, and I stammered, "I'd better work on these packets."

The younger friend gave me a contemptuous stare while the older one looked around and spoke to me with his hands cupped around his mouth: "Don't worry. That grandpa won't dare do anything. I told him that we've done a lot of killing already — why not one more?"

They had given me the most priceless gift. I resumed my old reading habits. As other inmates glared, I read rapaciously, from Chinese classics such as *Dream of the Red Mansions, Journey to the West,* and *The Romance of the Eastern Zhou Empire* to novels by Milan Kundera and a memoir by Boris Pasternak, the author of *Dr. Zhivago.* I was surprised to find these good books in the prison library. Also, after repeated pleas, I was granted the opportunity to leave the cell and choose books for my cellmates at the library. I was exceedingly happy. Outside, the cloudless sky was pleasantly blue. Even the shouts and curses occasionally emanating from our supervisor, Officer Yu, sounded like music to me. As if by appointment, I even saw three of my accomplices in the *Requiem* film lined up with three other inmates outside the library, waiting to be called. I sprinted over, joining the reunion. "Don't move or talk to each other," Officer Yu warned.

We whispered to each other nonetheless, our heads bowed and eyes fixed on the ground so as not to attract attention. "Our case could be decided soon," Hippie Poet briefed us.

"Well, be prepared. We could get at least five years," said Chen Dong, the director, in his lethargic tone.

"Five years? That won't work for me," Big Glasses scratched his bald scalp and said. "My wife hasn't visited or written to me for quite a while. I need to get out earlier to save our marriage."

"Chen Dong is lucky. His family visits all the time," I joked. "I heard they even sent roses."

"I've been pretty lucky with women," Chen Dong boasted. "You guys have ugly male lawyers. My family got me a young, attractive woman lawyer. The first time I saw her, I totally fell for her. Throughout our meeting, I couldn't take my eyes off her boobs. I don't even remember what stupid things I said to her."

We giggled. Officer Yu raised his electric baton. "Didn't I warn you not to talk? It's a violation of the rules to talk here. Bend your heads over; I'm going to scald them one by one."

"Sir, I have heart disease." Chen Dong launched a mild protest. He reached into his shirt pocket and brought out a medicine bottle. "Here is a bottle of fish oil that my girlfriend sent to protect my heart. It's the famous Treasure of Heart brand."

"Treasure of Heart, the gel for lovers," we all crooned, imitating the TV commercial. "You should take it daily, monthly, and yearly."

Officer Yu couldn't keep a straight face. He burst out laughing.

"Big Glasses Liu, it's your turn," a Red Hair called at the library entrance.

"Could you let someone else go first? I need to get some sun," Liu said brazenly. "My body is all moldy and fleas thrive on it."

Officer Yu thrust his baton at Liu, who jumped to his feet and ran. The rest of us stayed in a line, watching. The two of them circled around us several times before Officer Yu caught up with Big Glasses, lifting him by the collar like a chicken.

"Sir, you are so strong and have excellent martial arts skills," Big Glasses begged, with his lips puckered. "Don't punish me."

Officer Yu kicked him, and Big Glasses fell to the ground. Undeterred, Big Glasses rolled around on the ground and got up. "Sir, if it makes you feel better, feel free to kick me. This is much better than getting jabbed by the baton."

Officer Yu stopped kicking and turned around to grab his fully charged electric baton from his toolkit. The contrite Big Glasses shuddered with fear and immediately dropped down on his knees, pleading for forgiveness. "My kind and benevolent police officer, please don't do that. Come squeeze my bones. They are quite fragile. I admit I'm a smart-ass, but I do this to entertain you and help you beat your boredom."

"But I'm not bored."

"I feel so bad for you. You spend days and nights keeping us company. It would be one thing if we were all young, attractive women, but we are not. That's why I want to make it up to you," Big Glasses rattled on.

Officer Yu turned around to suppress his laughter. In the end, he simply waved Big Glasses away and said, "You are not allowed to exchange books today. Go back to your cell."

My name was soon called. At the library entrance, a Red Hair was flirting with a pallid-looking young female prisoner. I walked in and was astonished to see my friend Ba Tie, the screenwriter for my *Requiem* film. Due to his cooperative attitude, authorities at the detention center had assigned him to manage the library. I approached him and said teasingly, "Looks like you are having a pretty good life here. You should try to get your wife transferred and start a family here in prison."

The screenwriter dropped his work and came to talk to me between two rows of bookshelves. "I apologize to you," he said. "We were too naive then. We are up against the government and we'll never win."

"Forget the past. Let's move on and think about the future," I consoled him.

The screenwriter's lips twitched. He attempted to say something but stopped.

Officer Yu stepped in and urged me to leave. On my way out, I noticed that the female prisoner was staring at Officer Yu, who made a clicking, salacious sound in the back of his throat, as if he had stuffed too many delicacies in his mouth. The woman passed him and stepped out. She turned her head with an alluring smile that would melt the bones of any tough guy. I tucked the books under my arm and followed her, but Officer Yu wouldn't allow me to take his delicacies from him. He caught up with the woman and pinched her swinging bottom. Startled by the sudden unwanted attack, the inmate quickened her step and escaped.

Pathetically, Officer Yu's lewd behavior gave me an immediate erection. Upon returning to my cell, I thought about that episode for a long time before calming down to focus on my books.

My cellmates snatched most of the books I had taken out from the library. I picked up one that nobody wanted — George Orwell's allegorical political novel *Nineteen Eighty-Four*. Reading the book was like walking through a gallery where there was no difference between art and life. On the page was an imaginary prison, while all around me there was the real thing. George Orwell's prescience about the future of totalitarianism shocked me.

Winston Smith, the novel's protagonist, admits to the crime of harboring doubts about the country's leadership. To save himself, he implicates all his friends and relatives. Unsatisfied by his superficial confessions, his cold-blooded interrogators use physical torture to destroy his emotions and feelings of love. In the utopia of totalitarianism, individuality perishes. If any citizen dares to possess a small space in his mind that he claims as his own, and derives pleasure from it, the leadership sees it as the beginning of a crisis on the horizon. It is like a tiny bug that causes a small tear in an intricate and massive spiderweb. If the tear is left unrepaired, it will spread fast, destroying the integrity and structure of the entire web. The leadership fits Winston Smith's face into a wire cage containing hungry rats—his most primal fear. As the rats are about to reach Smith's face, he shouts, "Do it to Julia!" thus betraying the only woman that he had loved in life. His tormentors stop to laugh while Smith lies paralyzed beside the cage, feeling depraved and broken, like a human rat. If a woman can fall in love with a rat in the form of a human being, she must be a rat herself. Human feelings can be debauched and corrupted, Smith thinks. After the torture, Smith repents to the invisible leader, accepts his punishment, and reintegrates himself into the national collective.

"I'm glad the protagonist defeats himself and ends the darkness of life by capitulating to power," I said to myself cynically. I put the book down and closed my eyes. A few minutes later, the cell door slid open. My two friends who had generously picked up my workload were taken away. The last rays of sunset sprayed the courtyard with gold and blood. Our cellmates sat there quietly, watching the two walk to their last stop in life's journey toward death. I stood up to clean up their legacy—piles of nicely glued and folded packets for painkillers. I spent half an hour placing them neatly inside big cardboard boxes. With the work they had accomplished, I would be able to stay idle and read my books for another week.

For a Song and a Hundred Songs

IT WAS MY SECOND winter at the detention center. Snow fell, blanketing the courtyard with several inches of radiance. Inmates curled up in bed to preserve energy and body heat, but I was unusually hyperactive. My mind ran wild, and unknown, mysterious waves of heat coursed through my body. Every morning, I was the first one to dash over to the water tank to pour a basin of ice-cold water over myself. Fragments of ice left tiny scratches on my skin, but I was oblivious to the cold and pain. I jogged vigorously on the spot, galloping and panting like a horse. Soon the white courtyard blurred into green pastures. In my mind's eye, I traversed the country, from Chengdu, Beijing, and Guangzhou to Inner Mongolia and Tibet, from rice paddies in the south to wild desert in the northwest. My mental and physical gymnastics helped to liberate me, at least temporarily.

One morning I was so hyped up that I could not put a brake on my gallivanting feet. Every nerve of my body was struggling to jump out for cold, fresh air. Finally, I collapsed on the ground. Wang Han, a convicted robber who had just moved into our cell, helped me up. "Don't exercise to death," he admonished. "Take it easy."

My kneecaps swelled up and jogging was soon out of the question. The robber taught me to stand on my head with my back against the wall. "If you do it twice a day, it will clear up your head because it promotes blood circulation to your brain," he said.

I stood on my head and the world looked upside-down. A few squares of sunlight filtered through the tiny window into the cell. Inmates dropped their packets and thrust themselves into the sunlit areas, their pale shaved heads glittering. Since there was not enough sunlight for everyone, fistfights broke out. The chief towered over all of us. He stood on tiptoe and stretched his neck, putting his head right inside two precious squares of sunlight. Meanwhile, he balled up his fists and was ready to punch anyone who dared to challenge him. The sun cast a brownish light on the chief's face, making it look like an egg soaked in tea leaves. Despite his efforts to keep as much sunlight to himself as possible, the sun was moving away, climbing over his chin, his lips, and his forehead. As the light dimmed, the chief let out a long wail. His tongue darted out, running around his lips as if he were trying to lick off every tiny drop of sunlight like it was jam. "Calm down. You are no longer a kid," I chided the chief as I came down from my routine headstand. My face was reddened and my body energized.

The chief ignored me. As the sun moved high up on the wall, the crazy old man leapt up and down to touch the bright spots. The robber said furiously, "In the future, you can't monopolize the sunlight."

Our arbitration over portions of sunlight ended abruptly when the officer in charge burst in with a small squad of armed officers. A stream of cold air followed them.

It was time for the annual pre–New Year search.

The armed police took our belts away and chased us into the courtyard. We clutched our heads and crouched down in the cold. Soon, our bodies were frozen stiff. After the cell was ransacked, the police frisked each one of us. When we came back in, the floor was covered with our belongings. I scoured around, frantically picking up my clothes and books. "When will this life come to an end?" I thought bitterly.

In the afternoon, I sat around, depressed, and absentmindedly singing the words of a fitting, popular tune called "When Will This Life Come to an End?" Officer Yu happened to pass by and overheard. He paused for a few minutes outside the window and clapped his hands when I stopped.

"Excellent," he complimented me in a smarmy tone and invited me to come out and give a show. Frightened out of my wits, I apologized profusely. Officer Yu flashed his fake smile and said, "No, you didn't do anything wrong. Don't be too modest. I remember hosting a 'concert' for you last summer. You know I'm a big fan of yours."

Officer Yu referred to a notorious incident the previous August when I was caught singing and severely punished. "I'm sorry. Those shitty songs you heard are too crude for your taste. You deserve something better," I answered ingratiatingly.

"No, I'm a crude policeman and I especially love shitty songs." Officer Yu toyed with his electric baton. "You were able to sing us fifty-one songs last summer. Why don't you make it to one hundred this time?"

I was forced to squat in a corner of the yard, racking my brain for all the songs I knew, from the strident Red Guard songs of the Cultural Revolution to the soft love songs of the 1980s. I even performed several Russian folk ballads that had been introduced into China in the 1950s.

My repertoire was endless. As my voice grew hoarse, the Red Hairs crowded around me, cheering and jeering. Officer Yu sat in a wicker chair with his eyes closed and his feet tapping to the rhythms. The sky darkened and the electric wire on top of the high wall buzzed. I performed the songs mechanically; my face was expressionless and my voice emotionless. The cold wind felt like iron nails in my mouth.

"Your voice is as stiff as a blacksmith's hammer," Officer Yu complained. "Here's a love song. Soften up and sing like this . . ." He rose and hummed in his falsetto voice a popular song about how a wife missed her soldier-husband posted in a remote border area. Then Officer Yu ordered me to imitate his style, as he belted out,

> I'm at home and you are at the border. We both shared the same full moon. On this quiet night, I miss you and you miss me. I'm home taking care of our baby while you are away guarding our motherland.

The Red Hairs applauded Officer Yu's performance but he did not find the applause flattering.

"I know damn well how badly I sing, okay?" he castigated the lackeys.

I asked for water, but Officer Yu refused. "As a star, you need to know how to protect your voice. It is your most important asset," he said, faking a look of concern. "You've done thirty-nine songs. I'm sure your throat is burning like an iron. If you pour water down your throat now, you could end up losing your voice forever."

"Officer Yu, what have I done to deserve this? Why do you hurt me like this?" I finally asked.

"Oh, no. It's nothing like that. You don't understand. I'm a talent scout, trying to discover a purebred race horse. It's disappointing that you've cracked your front hoof after galloping for a few kilometers," Officer Yu said as he smacked his lips.

I had no choice but to continue. The members of my audience, the Red Hairs, were shivering in the cold wind. They scrunched themselves down like turtles and tapped their feet on the ground to keep warm. I hugged myself. My throat was dry, as if a large ball of cotton were stuck in it. I squeezed out one song after another. Soon my mouth was moving but there was no sound coming out of it.

The electric baton landed squarely on top of my head. I jumped up and down in pain. Out of desperation, I grabbed the tip of the baton, pulling it toward me. For a few seconds, sharp, wringing pain pierced through my heart. The smell of burned skin wafted through the air. When the juice in the baton ran out, Officer Yu ordered the Red Hairs to bring him another one.

I was wrestled to the ground and my trousers were stripped off.

"Are you going to sing or not?" Officer Yu asked.

I could feel the baton on my butthole, but I refused to surrender. The tip of the baton entered me. I screamed and whimpered in pain like a dog. The electric current coursed through my flesh and burst out from my neck. I felt like a duck whose feathers were being stripped. I clenched my teeth and puckered up enough strength and bellowed out the famous Red Guard song:

> The East wind is blowing, the war drums are beating. In our world today, who is afraid of whom? The Chinese people are not afraid of the American imperialists. Rather, the American imperialists are afraid of the Chinese people.

Officer Yu was stunned I could still sing. He burst into laughter: "Okay, I'm afraid of you."

The Trial

ON JANUARY 11, 1992, the prosecutor's office rescinded my indictment. I later found out that human rights activists pressured British prime minister John Major, who personally intervened and urged the Chinese government to review my case. The situation changed dramatically. By mid-March, the Chongqing Municipal Public Security Department released all of my accomplices from prison, although most of them stayed in police custody for two more years. I, the alleged ringleader, was the only one remaining at the detention center.

Chen Dong had a relatively easy life during his incarceration. Tapping into his talents as a painter coupled with his shrewd personality, he had quickly adapted himself to his new surroundings. Managing to win the sympathy from the officer in charge, Chen Dong was appointed the chief of his cell. He took advantage of his position and sketched many portraits of his cellmates. Those distinctive portraits were smuggled out and, years later, earned Chen Dong a windfall. While most of us had our heads shaved, Chen Dong was able to keep his poet's shoulder-length hair intact.

Still, he was not exempt from searing experiences. Chen Dong's most-repeated story from his time in prison involved forced mutual face-slapping with another inmate. The practice was an often-employed method of punishment at our detention center. Initially, the face-slapping between Chen Dong and the other inmate was polite and gentle. But for the guards, the relatively soft touches were not up to snuff. The two had to start all over again. Chen Dong and his cellmate pretended to be angry, but their tender feelings for each other remained the same. They slapped each other like lovers engaging in foreplay. Finally, the exasperated officer stepped up to demonstrate what he wanted, sending Chen Dong reeling with two smacks across the face.

The gloves were off, and heavy, blood-spilling blows followed. Chen Dong flung his arms and punched at his friend, now his enemy, who responded in kind. Their faces were pummeled into unrecognizable pulp. In the end, the two collapsed on the floor, like two exhausted prizefighters who threw knockout punches at the same moment. Even so, their legs still wriggled around, kicking each other. . . .

Upon Chen Dong's release, I was told that he was paralyzed by the dazzling world outside. He was too afraid to cross the street alone, and each time he saw a police car he couldn't help running away. It took a long time before his friends were able to help him get adjusted to freedom. In later years, Chen Dong entered the commercial publishing business, and swore that he would never allow himself to be on the other side of the law again.

My other artistic accomplice, the long-haired Hippie Poet, was not as fortunate. He was the last one to leave jail before me. The rules stipulated that he return to his hometown of Qiuyang, but authorities there were reluctant to pick him up in faraway Chongqing — the trip takes two days and two nights by train and boat. On the cold, drizzling morning of March 4, 1992, I banged on the wall to send a signal to Hippie Poet and pressed my ears against the wall, waiting for an answer. His voice came through and my heart pounded loudly.

"Yiwu, I'm going to leave here soon. It's a pity I won't be able to keep you company in the courtroom," he said in a muffled tone, and his voice broke occasionally. I felt as though something was stuck in my throat, blocking my airway.

"Do you need me to take any messages? Tell me fast."

"No."

"Not even for A Xia and the baby?" Hippie Poet asked.

"Go and visit them for me," I answered.

"By the way, could you spare twenty yuan so I can buy some liquor on the boat?" Hippie Poet asked. At least he had not lost his lust for alcohol.

"Okay, I'll tell the officer and transfer the money to your account."

"Two police officers will escort me home. They only pay for food, not liquor. Even if they did, I don't want to drink their liquor," he explained.

"You haven't touched any liquor for two years. Be careful," I advised.

"I will. Take care."

Complete silence followed. The brief conversation depressed me. I looked at my fellow inmates who sat there like sculptures, as if they would outlive the cell. About an hour later, I heard the fence door clink in Hippie Poet's cell. The vagrant poet left for good.

My own case stretched on. Following some long and turbulent investigations, the country's so-called largest counterrevolutionary case, involving thirty writers and poets, dissolved into a simple individual case — mine. I received a fresh indictment. The crimes remained the same, but I became the only criminal.

With the trial pending, my lawyer, who had disappeared for a while, visited me frequently. During his previous visits, he had been stern, taciturn, and inscrutable, like a typical lawyer, but when he reemerged he had turned into a new man, regaling me with news about the government's latest effort to revive political and economic reforms.

Encouraged by my lawyer's rosy descriptions of a political thaw, I wrote up a twenty-thousand-word self-defense relating to the "Massacre" poem and the *Requiem* film. Even though I was willing to take responsibility for everything, I categorized my writings merely as having the status of a "political transgression."

My lawyer put on his reading glasses and perused my confession. Frowning, he sighed and said, "Why don't you admit guilt? Do you still stick with the view that it is wrong for the government to lock you up? Remember, in a political case, the government will never admit wrongdoing. You have to take the blame."

I reminded him it was possible that the government would change its verdict and admit its own mistakes. "Weren't you labeled a Rightist by the government in the 1950s? The government under Deng Xiaoping acknowledged mistakes."

"Don't forget that the verdict was reversed many years later," the lawyer argued. "In the 1950s, the government never believed it did anything wrong. That's my point."

I was speechless. To strengthen his point, the lawyer produced a stack of letters from my wife, my mother-in-law, my father, and my friend Zhong, all of which tried to persuade me to admit guilt. In his letter, Zhong wrote, "No matter what is going through your mind, you should confess as a formality and try to avoid criminal charges and gain your immediate release at the trial. All of your friends are out now. Remember Liu Shaoqi was the president of China and he was persecuted during the Cultural Revolution. One day, the Red Guards forced him to crawl through a tiny hole for dogs. He complied in exchange for his life. Why can't you?"

A Xia also tried to persuade me to follow the lawyer's advice. "Freedom is not only important to you but also to us. Don't forget that your daughter hasn't seen her daddy yet."

I stepped out of the office where the conversation with my lawyer took place and sat by a stone table in the garden, gazing blankly at the soaring walls. Through the sinewy tree branches, I could see sparrows jumping and somersaulting between the electric fences. The sun broke through the clouds, and narrow shafts of sunlight hit the ground in a pattern that resembled hordes of heavenly sparrows flitting across the ground. "What do I want?" I asked myself.

Suddenly I remembered the powerful words I had seen on the back of Old Xie's Bible:

We are all aliens on this planet, our bodies the graves of our souls. We cannot destroy our bodies to liberate our souls because they are God's possessions.

I had no idea where he had found that passage, just as I was clueless as to where God came from. Those words touched me over and over again. Standing outside the office at the detention center, I felt unknown forces pulling at my heart. I broke down.

My trial took place in early May. On that day, I put on a white shirt and a pair of navy blue trousers—the first time I had worn street clothes in almost two years. Two policemen cuffed my hands behind my back and hustled me into a van. "Behave yourself!" the shorter policeman warned me while the tall one flashed a sinister grin. He toyed with his mini–stun baton to underscore his warning; its tip occasionally sparked with arcs of blue light.

I bit my lips and lowered my head silently to suppress my anger. My imprisonment—having dragged on for nearly two years—might come to an end in a few hours. I could not afford to solicit more trouble. I needed to return home with my body and mind intact.

The police van sped wildly on the hilly street. The turbulence churned my stomach. When I stumbled out of the car and stood at a playground in front of the Chongqing Municipal Intermediate People's Court, my heart beat violently like a ferocious person pounding on a door.

I used the excuse of a toilet break to compose myself. No sooner had I come out than the policemen put the cuffs back on. I protested and was soon shoved into the courtroom, which was actually a theater with nearly a thousand seats. The stage stood six and a half feet high. The judge, three members of the jury, a court clerk, the prosecutor, and my attorney sat behind a long table on the stage. Looking up at them from the well of the auditorium, I felt like a food particle trapped in a big empty mouth.

The two police officers quietly walked away from me. A cold draft seemed to have risen from the empty seats behind me, biting the back of my neck. Scanning the empty theater, I was acutely aware of another courtroom high above in the clouds, where the Final Judgment was about to take place. Looking around, I felt as though mounds and mounds of transparent skeletons of the dead, along with the sparkling stars of the universe, would receive judgment from God.

The prosecutor began reading the indictment in his drab professional voice. His words reverberated in the empty space. Every now and then, he would tilt his body to salute the judge or smile at his imaginary audience down below the stage. Is he talking to the angry ghosts of 1989? I pondered.

The investigation proceedings began.

THE JUDGE: Defendant Liao Yiwu, do you agree with what the prosecutor has stated in the indictment?

DEFENDANT LIAO YIWU: Yes, I do. The prosecutor cited extensively from my journals and personal correspondence in the indictment, even though according to our country's criminal law, private documents such as journals and personal correspondence cannot be used as criminal evidence for public conviction and sentencing. In the law, at least, a person cannot be punished for exposing his own thoughts in his private journal. In addition, the prosecutor insulted my character in the indictment by using loaded vocabulary such as "savage," "yelping like a dog," "swollen with arrogance," and "evoking the spirits of the devils." Those words were reminiscent of the language used in big-character posters during the Cultural Revolution. I hope that the judicial departments can eliminate the vestiges of the Cultural Revolution and reiterate the seriousness of the law. Lastly, if the prosecutor thought that my poem "Massacre" had fabricated facts and that no one was killed in the 1989 student movement, why did he accuse me of "invoking the spirit of those who died in 1989?"

JUDGE: I want to warn the defendant not to dwell on specific wording. Once again, I want to ask you, do you admit committing the alleged crimes?

(I held my head high in silence.)

JUDGE: Please bring out the evidence.

(A police officer stepped up and held the manuscripts of "Massacre" and Requiem *as well as their audio and video versions under my nose. I shrugged my shoulders. With my hands tied behind my back, I could not touch my own precious possessions. Sadness washed over me as I identified the "criminal evidence" that had been made with blood and sweat, and watched the officer take it away.)*

LIAO YIWU: I have submitted my self-defense to the court. I take full responsibility for all the literary works.

JUDGE: There is overwhelming evidence to show that no one was killed in Tiananmen Square on the early morning of June 4, 1989. In your "Massacre" and *Requiem,* there were numerous

references to "murderers and butchers." Did you refer to the
Chinese People's Liberation Army which was sent to Beijing to
enforce the martial law?

DEFENDANT: Yes, I did. However, there were two different voices
within the Party Central Committee relating to the imposition
of the martial law . . .

JUDGE: You are wrong. When it came to the decision of cracking
down on the counterrevolutionary riots in Beijing, there was
only one voice within the Party Central Committee. Clerk,
please record this statement.

In the end, I confessed all of my crimes and pleaded guilty. In post–
Tianamen Square China, all political cases were predecided and the
trial was just a formality. In that secret trial, there were neither witnesses nor an audience. There was no point in wasting more energy.

As the judge was lecturing me, a bout of itchiness struck the right
side of my waist. I tried to reach the itchy spots, tilting my body and
reaching around myself with my cuffed hands. The female clerk giggled at my posture, which must have looked comical, but a police officer kicked me on the shin, ordering me to stand straight.

Finally, my lawyer began defending me. He sounded like a patient
with chronic asthma. Over the course of his defense, the judge and the
prosecutor left their seats to use the bathroom. The others looked relaxed and occasionally whispered to each other. Only the three jurors,
all of whom were old men, continued to sit there attentively, like Buddhist statues. Jurors in China were mere decorations; I had been told
that many of them were retired judicial workers who had been paid
some extra money to attend trials several times a month.

"Defendant, do you have anything else to say to the court?" asked
the judge when he had returned from the bathroom.

"Oh, nothing," I responded.

Two weeks later, I appeared in court for the second time to provide
fingerprints for my confessions as well as a stack of legal documents.
Without any clear guidance, the court arbitrarily handed me a four-
year sentence, including the two years I had spent at the detention
center.

For several days, I sat by the wrought-iron fence and stared outside. The freedom that had almost landed in my hands had flown away. How was I going to manage the remaining time in jail? My brother wrote to me, saying that he had asked my laywer to file an appeal on my behalf. A convicted robber advised me otherwise. "Don't even waste your time. There is really no point. Be patient and get ready for the labor camp. Life is much better there."

Political Power Grows Out
of the Barrel of a Gun ·

AS I WAS WAITING impatiently for the court to review my appeal, the acid rain season came to an end. The sweltering summer hit without any warning.

"I wore a thick woolen vest yesterday," said Inmate 1-4-7, a newbie from Guizhou. He put down his work and fanned his face with his right hand. "It's getting so hot. I'm going to go naked."

"Stop the nonsense. Keep folding," the chief chided him. "We need to hurry up. After we are done with this small pile, a whole big box is waiting. We can't swagger like ducks and lag behind other cells."

Inmate 1-4-7 was not willing to back down. "In this cell, the dog is barking louder than his master," he wisecracked.

The chief shook with anger. With the help of two lackeys, he thrust his chubby body at Inmate 1-4-7, who was quite swift and agile. His tiny thin body wove in and out of the piles of boxes in the narrow aisle without toppling anything or tripping.

The chase soon stirred up a cloud of dust. The chief panted like a dog chained in the sun on the hottest summer day. Seeing that Inmate 1-4-7 was beyond his reach, the chief called the guard. The gate opened and in walked Dwarf Li, who was on duty. He stood in the courtyard, calling 1-4-7 to step out. From far away, the courtyard looked like a fishbowl, and Dwarf Li's silhouette a big shark sinking to the bottom of a muddy river. Without a word, the shark opened its jaw and bit 1-4-7 with his stun baton.

That afternoon, 1-4-7 was escorted out for interrogation, but he returned after only half an hour. Dwarf Li followed him in and announced somberly, "From today on, Inmate 1-4-7 doesn't need to fold the cardboard packets."

Inmate 1-4-7, whose real name was Liu Xiaoyue, sat stiffly in bed. Dwarf Li moved over and lifted Liu's chin and hurled an angry threat at him. "You bastard, I admire your guts today. I'm not done with you. We'll see who gets the last laugh."

That breathtaking scene stunned us. At night, the robber and I quietly probed him about what had happened. "I told the interrogator that we have a ten-hour shift every day. With such a stressful work schedule, I had no time to focus on my case. The interrogator said, 'Why don't you report this to leaders at the Public Security Department? This is a detention center, not a prison or reeducation facility.' I said that police at the detention center care more about money than case investigation. If we don't work, we'll get beaten. The interrogator became mad as hell because he couldn't extract information from me. On my way back, I could hear him rebuke and swear at the police officer. Even the director was called in to explain the situation."

Authorities at the detention center did not allow Liu's brazen whistle-blowing to go unpunished. A month later, they intercepted and confiscated all his family letters, and began taking Liu away late at night to beat him up. One time when he came back, his face was nearly unrecognizable from the swelling and bruises. It was painful to watch that hideous face.

"Don't court more trouble," I advised him.

"I'm not." His smile froze and a row of his sharp white teeth glinted in the light. I admired his guts in battling the police, but it seemed pointless to fight back against them. Seeing how I felt, Liu blamed me for being too jaded and shook his head in disappointment. "You weak scholars."

If I had been ten years younger, I would have challenged him to a fistfight. I had been a writer and poet for the better part of my life.

With thick glasses and extra pounds around my belt, I felt with a tinge of melancholy that my destiny was to make a living from my writing for the remainder of my life.

"What do you expect me to do?" I raised my voice at him. "I'm imprisoned for writing 'Massacre' and *Requiem*. I feel like a tiny ant facing a gigantic meat grinder. We are small people. It's fucking useless to fight. You are just asking them to kill you."

"A little person can have big dreams," Liu lectured me. "That was my friend Lao Ji's motto. He and I met for the first time last year. I knew martial arts and used to be a member of the Chinese Army Special Forces. But Lao Ji won my mind and heart with his intelligence. I willingly served as his bodyguard and helped him sneak across to Hong Kong three times so he could connect with leaders of various human rights organizations. He wanted to seek their support. The discussions eventually ended badly. The democracy activists in Hong Kong are a bunch of cowards who crave fame but are afraid of death.

"In the end, Lao Ji declined their offer to keep him there as a political refugee and came back in frustration. He proposed that we establish secret organizations in mainland China and overthrow the government with force, like the revolutionaries did with the Manchurian dynasty at the beginning of the twentieth century."

"Who is Lao Ji?" I asked.

"He had a master's in Marxism and Leninism from the University of Guizhou, and became the executive vice president of a big company in Shenzhen," Liu stated proudly. "He was a big intellectual and I was a low-class veteran. He never looked down on me, though, and we became sworn brothers. We had another friend. His name was Zhao San. The three of us formed the Organization for Promoting Democracy in China. Lao Ji was the president and I was head of the assassination department. Zhao San was responsible for organization. Our first plan was to bomb the Jiuquan Satellite Launch Center in the northwestern province of Gansu. We hoped that the blast could trigger a political earthquake. When I was in the army, I was stationed there for four years. I knew the area like the palm of my hand — I mean the terrain and the troop deployments. So we made connections with a secret society in Pingyuan County, Yunnan Province. We bought guns, some ammunition, and detonation devices from a widow whose husband fought in the China-Vietnam War in 1979. To prepare for our mission, we conducted several dry runs deep inside the forest to make sure the bombs worked properly."

I felt like I was falling into the land of the Arabian Nights. Other inmates also pricked up their ears while folding their medicine packets. "You certainly led a much more interesting life than I did," one convicted robber said.

"Hey, let me finish," Liu continued. "After we had trained for two months and gotten much better at making bombs, we decided to go north for the Lunar New Year. Before we left, we separated and went home to prepare for the trip. We agreed not to contact each other for a month. About ten days later, Lao Ji breached our agreement and visited me at home. He told me to come with him immediately. It turned out that Zhao San had been arrested and had leaked our plan to the police. I still don't know how the hell we caught the attention of the police. Lao Ji and I fled Guizhou and took an overnight train to Chongqing. But the police were right behind us and no matter how hard we tried, we couldn't get rid of our tails. One day, we found ourselves in a shadowy dell on a mountainside. The two of us huddled together and cried. 'I never thought we would end up like this,' Lao Ji said. 'It's our fate and the heavenly god is not on our side. The only way out is to kill ourselves.'

"We took out our guns and pointed them at our heads. I silently counted one, two, three. The cold wind was blowing hard and the stars blinked and shivered. Soon we could hear the rumbling sounds of police motorcycles. Lao Ji paused for a few seconds and chastised me. 'Why the hell did you stop?' I threw my gun on the ground and said, 'I'm a trained soldier. We can't be so useless and die without a fight.'

"Lao Ji agreed. So we got up and ran. We ended up at a place on the outskirts of Chongqing. In the course of our escape, we shot two policemen and snatched a motorcycle. We drove north for a whole day until we ran out of gas. Then we parted ways and decided to meet each other at a small hotel in Qiuquan County. We also agreed that if one person got arrested, the other would take his own life."

"Then what happened?" the convicted robber asked, swallowing hard.

"You've seen it." Liu balled up his fist. "I'm here and Lao Ji ended up in another jail. But I'm not willing to accept this fate yet."

All the inmates were in awe of him. Even his nemesis, the chief, said sympathetically, "When you realized that you wouldn't be able to bomb the satellite launch base, you should have at least blown up a gas station. You knew you were going to get caught and die anyway."

"Revolution through force doesn't mean that you can use violence indiscriminately," Liu said seriously.

A few days after the summer solstice, Liu was charged with a number of crimes including murder, robbery, counterrevolutionary armed uprising, and counterrevolutionary incitement. In total, he received two death sentences, one life sentence, and one fifteen-year sentence. The day he was shackled, it was already dusk. I bathed him, helped him change into his clothes, and fed him. He put himself at my mercy and acted mechanically like a puppet.

Over the next few days, I helped Liu prepare his appeal and wrote several letters to his family members. I vowed to spend more time with him in the last days of his life. There were three death row inmates in our cell. Under normal circumstances, it was everyone's duty to help them with their food and bathroom needs. I volunteered to be Liu's sole caretaker. In return, he folded the medicine packets for me. Liu loved to sing but he had the world's worst voice. His "specialty" was love songs sung in a folksy style. When he sang, the veins on his neck throbbed. Each time the word "baby" came up, he would drag it out and follow it with "oh yeah, oh yeah." Several inmates covered their ears. In the end, the guard came over and finally stopped him by pointing a gun at his head.

Liu licked his lower lip and looked discontented: "You hummed a Cossack folk song last night. I want to sing it," he said to me. "You told me the song is about how a Cossack had a fight with his girl and left to wander around the world. Many years later, he returned home and found his beloved milking a cow in another man's farmyard. I think the same thing will happen to my girlfriend. My beloved girl doesn't know how to milk a cow, but I think she will end up in another person's bed and give birth to a big fat baby."

"Stop having these sad thoughts," I counseled him. "It's better to leave this world in a good mood."

"I don't know. I don't regret most things but I made some bad mistakes. For example, when Lao Ji and I were on trial, he claimed responsibility for everything. He told the judge, 'Liu is a crude and uneducated person and he knows nothing about democracy, human rights, or opposition parties. He is merely a wooden stick in my hand. He just did what I told him to do.' Lao Ji's words made me furious. I pointed right at him and shouted, 'How dare you insult me publicly! Yeah, I'm crude and uneducated, but I knew what I was doing. I was the one who killed the police. I was the one who snatched the motorcycle. I was the one who taught you how to shoot.' Lao Ji stomped his feet in frustration and swore at me, 'You stupid idiot! I was saving you!' I shot back, 'No, I'm not stupid. I'm a real man. I want to live an honorable life and die with a clean name.' Lao Ji carried on, 'What's the fucking point of dying? Nobody will remember us. So long as one person lives, there is hope.'"

Fascinated by his story, I nodded. "He was right. If one can survive, there will be hope."

"This is fate," Liu sobbed. "I just didn't think of that."

Toothpaste

IN EARLY AUGUST 1992, the heat wave reached its peak. The over-crowded cell turned into a slow-roasting oven that cooked each of us as if we were chickens on a spit. Out of his "respect" for me as a scholar, the chief "upgraded" my sleeping arrangement by moving me to the center of the bed. I soon found out why I was given the special treatment. He put me smack between two death row inmates. On my left was Mou, a nineteen-year-old boy who suffered from a serious form of sexually transmitted diseases. In the middle of the night, his scratching jarred my ears and I had to get up and sit with my back against the wall. Pus and blood oozed down the young man's thigh and toward my own space. I curled up and tried to stay as far away as possible. I finally dozed off at dawn. In my dream, I saw a snake that gently licked my butt, its tongue icy cold. I woke up and realized that I was sitting on a small puddle of Mou's pus. Furiously, I kicked Mou hard. Mou rolled over and his mouth landed squarely on another inmate's leg.

Early next morning, I poured some salts into the water and thoroughly cleaned my butt. The other inmate wasn't aware that Mou had "kissed" his leg for several hours. Three days later, an itchy spot appeared on the unwitting inmate's leg and the redness quickly spread like a blooming rose.

I lodged a strong protest to the chief, who sheepishly admitted he was in the wrong. As a special favor, he allowed me to open a cardboard box, empty out all the unfolded packets and use it to shield myself from Mou, who was upset about what he called my "discriminatory practices." When he was about to attack me, Liu knocked him down to the floor.

Meanwhile, the extreme heat became unbearable. While brushing my teeth one day, I was suddenly hit with an idea to cool off. I took off my trousers and urged everyone to follow my example—squeezing toothpaste into my anus. A shocking chill shot up my spine and neck, and reached the back of my head. My new cooling method was widely adopted. In a few minutes, all the inmates, more than twenty of them, blocked up their anuses with toothpaste. The chief crinkled his ass and complimented me, "You educated folks are never short of crazy ideas."

Unfortunately, the toothpaste lost its cooling effect very quickly. Many began suffering from severe anal itching. I poked my fingers in there and realized that the high rectal temperature had dried up the toothpaste. Soon, everyone had to scoop it out with their fingers.

In the evenings, the heat continued unabated and the cell felt like a pressure cooker. The officer on duty happened to be one known for his frugality. About eleven o'clock, he turned off all the ceiling fans to save electricity. It was as if he had poked a hornet's nest. People jumped up naked, screaming and cursing. The guard and several police officers teamed up and suppressed a potential riot with the threat of force.

We sat down helplessly. Desperate times called for desperate measures. Once again, we resorted to toothpaste. Many squeezed it into their anus several times a night. As a result, scooping the stuff out took longer and became more painful each time. Many inmates experienced rectal bleeding. "If your finger is too thick and dirty, you could cause bleeding and rectal infection," I cautioned everyone and suggested that we use a bamboo stick pulled from the straw mattresses on the bed. "You should poke your ass like you pick your ears," I demonstrated to them.

The stick proved much superior to human fingers and many enjoyed it tremendously. Several became too impatient, though, and ended up poking too hard. I could see their faces grimace as they convulsed in pain.

The heat wave assailed us for two weeks, during which time many of us suffered from terrible hemorrhoids, but no one came down with heat stroke.

Torrential rain finally drove away the heat but brought its sister form of torture: flooding. Water poured into our cell. We moved all the cardboard boxes of medicine packets onto the bed and then huddled together like a gang of wet monkeys. The officer on duty waded through the water and came in to make sure the boxes were dry. Under his direction, we shoveled the water out and reinforced the threshold. Before we had time to take a break, more boxes of medicine packets arrived with a tighter deadline. Seeing that everyone was grumbling, the officer on duty sent a Red Hair to go out and buy a big cake, which most of us hadn't tasted in a long time. Each inmate was given a slice. Even though it tasted stale and too sweet, we devoured every single crumb. After we, the "work machines," were fueled up with sugar, the officer decreed that nap and TV time would be temporarily repealed. Inmates were encouraged to work an extra shift at night.

We scurried around like locusts. I was fortunate to have Liu as a helper and fulfilled my quota easily. The officer on duty carried his stun baton and patrolled each cell frequently. It was impossible to read my books. Around noontime one day, Liu told me to take a short nap and promised to cover for me. I had just closed my eyes when we heard loud, piercing screams in the cell next door. The officer was punishing an inmate who was asleep on the job. By then, I was fully awake and set quickly back to work.

Meanwhile, personnel changes were taking place at the detention center. With the retirement of the director and several veterans, a new crop of guards was taking over. Dwarf Li, the officer in charge, moved up the ladder and became an especially harsh supervisor. Six tall and strong young officers were assigned to him for training, and the nightly roll call turned into a harsh exercise of power. Dwarf Li used the occasion to teach his apprentices how to conquer the hostile inmates with force. When a newbie was slightly slow to respond when his name was called, one of Dwarf Li's star disciples struck the inmate on the neck. His teacher nodded with approval. Emboldened by Dwarf Li's encouragement, the disciple smacked more inmates in the next couple of days and soon earned the nickname "Iron Palm."

A week later, I was caught napping after lunch. Iron Palm dragged me out of the cell and stung me with his baton. When I remained defiant, he rolled up his sleeves and slapped me five times on the face. Officer Bai, whom I had bitten earlier, passed by and kicked me hard in the ribs. The fatty pig's martial arts skills surprised me. With extraordinary pain, I slowly got up from the floor and glared at him.

Seeing that I refused to bow down, the pig gave me two more kung fu kicks. I stepped aside and he missed. He yelled at me in exasperation, "0-9-9, you are incorrigible!"

Iron Palm urged the veteran to take a break and sneered at me. "Let me handle this notorious jail bully."

His slaps rained down on my face. I stood there motionless like a wooden stake planted firmly in the ground. I looked at him as if I were trying to bore a hole in his face. Iron Palm roared, "How dare you look at me that way!"

Fatty Bai pitched in: "That face of his is made of wrought iron. I slapped him twenty times last year and he hardly moved."

My stare locked onto Iron Palm. I wanted to swallow his face with my eyes, dissolving him into my blood and bones. As a scholar, I did not have the power to exact blood-for-blood revenge, but I believed I could use the witchcraft of language to condemn my tormentors to hell.

Fury contorted Iron Palm's face. He leapt up and whacked me harder. "If you continue to look at me with hatred, I'm going to gouge out your eyeballs."

The stinging pain blurred my vision, but I kept my eyes focused on my enemy's face. I might have died or gone blind, but I still never blinked. I hurled my dilated eyeballs like two harsh pebbles at my enemy.

"You still hate me, huh? So damn boring and hopeless!" Iron Palm said. The slapping gradually subsided. The heavy smacking was reduced to soft touching, like the intimate kisses of two pieces of soft flesh. In my semiconscious state, I heard a sagging and disappointing voice. "I wonder what he is made of? He must be the reincarnation of a monster."

Iron Palm finally released me and told two Red Hairs to bring him some rubbing alcohol to sterilize his hands. I staggered away and then someone called me from behind, "Hey, you are going the wrong direction. The cell is this way." I turned around and could hear uproarious laughter.

A warm hand reached out to me like a blind person's guide dog. The next day, I found out that the warm hand belonged to a scholarly looking officer who had been assigned by Dwarf Li to take care of my cell. His name was Cao, a man who wrote poems while in college and had become very sympathetic to political prisoners.

"I was also involved in the student protest movement," he whispered to me one day and dug out a couple of my books from a suitcase in a corner of his office. "I have read many of your poems. They are remarkable. I have seen some of your pictures in *Writers* magazine. It's hard to reconcile those pictures with the real person."

"I'm getting old," I joked. "I'm old enough to be your father."

"No, I didn't mean that. I meant that you used to look like a lion. You had a full head of hair, and your eyes were serious, clear, and kind. But now, you are going bald and you have the beginnings of a belly. I feel sad at what they have done to you here. I shouldn't have taken this job," Cao said, flashing a sad smile.

"Many people are envious of your job." I forced out a laugh, which triggered pain in my face. "It's hard to find a job like this these days."

"You think so?" Cao asked in surprise. "That's exactly what my father has said to me."

I looked at him in silence.

"Your eyes are fierce and cold. You shouldn't provoke them. In this circle, the police are just as crazy as the inmates."

I started to say something but refrained.

"I'm trying to resist this professional insanity and refuse to use electric batons and cuffs to punish people. Do you know I'm becoming a laughingstock because I don't know how to operate an electric baton?"

Footsteps passed outside. Cao stopped the chitchat and stood up. "Let me walk you back to the cell."

Dwarf Li came in. Cao nodded at his boss and we walked out.

"Officer Cao, do you know a famous line from the Bible that could fit my situation?" I asked on the way back.

"If someone slaps you, turn the other cheek," Officer Cao answered without hesitation. "Too bad God is not Chinese."

My earthly governing body, the Sichuan Provincial Supreme Court, was Chinese, however, and at the end of August 1992 they rejected my appeal. I left the Chongqing Municipal Detention Center for Sichuan No. 2 Provincial Penitentiary.

Part IV

THE PRISON

August 1992–January 1994

The No. 2 Prison

IN HIS BOOK *The Gulag Archipelago*, Aleksandr Solzhenitsyn included a map that showed the locations of labor camps in the former Soviet Union. Every camp was represented by a mark in the shape of a sentry. The marks covered the vast country so densely that the map resembled an X-ray image of a lung riddled with tuberculosis scars. Through the X-ray image of this gigantic lung, Solzhenitsyn gave his diagnosis: the lethal disease had reached its final stage and would cause the death of the world's largest totalitarian empire.

In China in the 1990s, police and court officials called me and my cellmates "society's cancer cells." They weren't entirely off the mark. In a way, with our alleged crimes and sometimes-savage behavior, we were eating away at the totalitarian system, scarring its tissue and threatening its life.

On a sweltering summer day in August 1992, several of our "cancer cells" metastasized. With our guilty verdicts handed down, we were officially escorted out of the detention center and sent to the Sichuan No. 2 Provincial Penitentiary.

The police van zoomed in and out of a web of streets in the historic mountain city of Chongqing. My body felt like it was locked inside a stone grinder, bouncing up and down. I closed my eyes. "Hang in there. We are almost there," a policeman said from the front seat, his hands tightly grasping a handgrip on the ceiling.

The No. 2 Prison squatted in a section of Chongqing called Tanzi-shi, on the south bank of the Yangtze River.

The guards checked our pass and opened the gate. The van drove right into the courtyard, which, to my surprise, resembled a park, with blooming flowers, tree-lined walkways, neatly maintained lawns, and even a shimmering swimming pool for the guards. It reminded me a bit of my initial view of the investigation center on Song Mountain Road. People with angelic smiles walked about briskly in the summer breeze. When a butterfly miraculously landed on a car window near me, I puckered my lips and plastered my mouth against the glass to kiss it. That was probably my sole romantic gesture during my incarceration.

Our heavenly tour proved brief. The van stopped in front of the administrative building and an officer jumped out and ran in to take care of our transfer papers. Meanwhile, another officer led me and three other inmates to the prison clinic for blood work and chest X-rays. By the time we came back, the officers from the detention center had left, and two new officers were waiting for us. We were ready to enter the inner section, they said ominously.

With its formidable stone walls, the inner section looked like a gray castle. At the entrance, we lined up single-file and stood like soldiers at attention, shouting in unison, "Yes, sir! Can we come in?" The big wrought-iron gate glided open.

Inside the double high walls waited many smaller sections, isolated from each other, which kept inmates in one section from having contact with those from any other section. I was told later that many prisoners had lived in their own circumscribed areas for decades without stepping outside. On my first day, I was assigned to Section 8, a prisoner training center that lay at the prison's far end. I followed an officer and we passed section after section. At the entrance to each one, a guard would frisk me thoroughly. After the sixth time, I became so adjusted to the routine that I dropped my belongings and voluntarily stripped my trousers and bared my butt before the guard even ordered me to. My Pavlovian baring of my rear triggered hearty laughter from a group of Red Hairs crowded around me. One questioned me curiously, "How many times have you been here?"

"First time," I answered.

"What are your crimes?"

"Counterrevolutionary."

"Shame on you," he spat at me.

The supervising officer picked up my belongings and we moved further inside the maze. Soon we were walking through a yard. I looked up and around — the sky seemed so high and wide. The tall walls appeared to meander inside the clouds and merge with the surrounding mountains outside. I could feel the presence of small villages nestled between the wall and the mountains, and hear cows mooing in the distance. I staggered forward. By the time we passed the last checkpoint, I was mentally and physically exhausted. The officer handed me over to my new group leader. Looking around, I found myself inside a big yard with a green tarpaulin canopy. Indistinguishable shaved heads bobbed up and down around me. My new cellmates' faces looked a ghostly pale green.

After lunch, I went with a large group of new prisoners for head-shaving and then to surrender my finger- and footprints. Upon returning, I was ordered to unpack, and discovered that all of my underclothes were printed with a round seal bearing the name of my new prison. My jacket and trousers were spared the seal, but they had to be stored in a mildewed warehouse, along with my atlas. In their place, I was issued a set of prison outfits — navy blue shirt, a yellow vest, a pair of trousers, and a white badge with my picture, name, and group number. After I donned the official suit, I felt fully assimilated into the big, formidable family of inmates.

Every new prisoner was required to commit to memory the fifty-eight provisions in the "Rules of Conduct for Prisoners." The group leader informed me that there would be random checks by police officers, and those who didn't etch the rules into their brain would be severely punished.

Unlike at the detention center, a new prisoner at the penitentiary had to undergo six months of training and pass stringent physical and mental tests before he could join a regular group. A central part of the training modules involved physical labor — folding medicine packets like I did at the detention center. In 1992, senior Chinese leader Deng Xiaoping had issued his call to deepen China's economic reforms.

The whole country was mobilized to "get rich fast." Prison personnel never missed a beat and were quick to take advantage of the free labor to fatten their wallets. Our hefty quota was three thousand medicine packets per day for each inmate. While working on the packets we were also required to listen to political lectures. During breaks, we dutifully read *Reeducation News,* a weekly newsletter put out by the prison. Every morning, regardless of rain or sun, we had to gather on the playground to do mandatory jogging and group aerobic exercises. The total training, we were informed, would reform our thinking and increase our physical stamina.

Thus our daily routine was overloaded with activities. At night, I stayed up late to fold packets while trying to memorize the "Rules of Conduct for Prisoners." Physical exhaustion left little room for insomnia, and I slept soundly. Shrill whistles dictated our daily routine. They called us to the playground for morning exercise, for lunch, for dinner, for midday breaks, and for roll call, which were conducted before every activity. In the first month, I hardly had any time to nurture my own private thoughts. My body became so attuned to the collective rhythm that each time my name was called, I instinctively stood at attention and responded with a loud "Yes, sir!"

Initially there was not enough room to accommodate the large number of new arrivals. I slept on the floor in the corridor. Forty days later, I was thrilled to learn that I could have my own private bed — the top bunk of a standard metal-frame bunk bed. It took a while to get adjusted to my new bed, which sometimes kept me awake until after midnight.

A seventy-year-old man, a hunchback, slept underneath me. Nicknamed Old Ostrich because of his long neck, he suffered from severe asthma. At night, his wheezing and bouts of violent coughing rocked the bed like ocean swells tossing the hull of a ship. I prayed for him to stop. One morning at dawn, he suddenly became eerily quiet. I looked down, alarmed, and saw that his lips were blue and his mouth was wide open. He had apparently lost consciousness.

I called out, and several inmates rose and helped me carry the old man to the prison hospital. Fortunately, the doctors managed to bring him back to life. Three days later he returned to us. I was told that he had been a drug trafficker and it was his second time in jail.

Late one afternoon, a notice went around summoning all prisoners to the yard. The group leader instructed me to keep an eye on Old Ostrich during the meeting. In the fall breeze, I clutched his elderly arm and towed him forward. Armed guards were posted every few steps. The dregs of society poured out from all sections of the prison like currents in the Yangtze River; they converged on the playground and were surrounded by a forest of fully loaded guns. The aerial view must have been breathtaking.

Flanked on both sides by shiny bayonets, Old Ostrich and I followed the dusty trail of the mighty prisoners' army. By the time we arrived, the meeting had started. The yard was illuminated like a theater. Dazzling lights focused on a makeshift stage where a dozen bureaucrats sat in two rows. Onstage, the leaders looked meager in number and strength compared to us, their enemies, who were densely packed down below.

"All rise!" the moderator roared into his handheld microphone. The air vibrated with loud rumbling. Our first item on the agenda was singing "Without the Communist Party, There Would Be No New China." Other inmates around me opened their mouths wide and belted their hearts out. I felt obligated to mouth the words as well, and gradually the volume of my voice also rose:

> The Communist Party pointed the people along the road to
>   liberation
> It leads China toward brightness

With each line I bellowed, I involuntarily lifted my body upward, as if an invisible hand pulled my head from above. Since my right hand was clutching the old man's left arm, he synchronized himself with my movement as he belted out the song like a punk rocker.

The song of praise to the party helped to release our pent-up energy. When the song stopped, the moderator motioned for us to stop and the playground fell into total silence. The warden came to the podium to deliver his opening speech, which recognized the model prisoners who had excelled in folding medicine packets and condemned the few bad eggs who had attempted to escape. He urged prisoners to embrace their verdicts and warned that appeals would not provide an easy way out.

While the warden lectured us from the stage, Old Ostrich lowered his head and mumbled, "I don't want a way out. Prison is much better than a nursing home. At least I don't have to pay for it out of my own pocket."

Next, a bunch of bad eggs were hog-tied and paraded onto the stage. The shamed inmates stood with their heads down; each had their arms held by two armed officers who punched them if they moved. Meanwhile, an equal number of model prisoners stepped onto the stage one by one to denounce the escapees and extol the virtues of reeducation through physical labor. Since model prisoners would be rewarded with a reduction in their sentences of one to two years, they were particularly passionate in their condemnations. At the end of each denunciation, the audience responded with uproarious slogan-shouting. Feelings ran high both on and off the stage.

Soon a somber-looking official stood up and delivered a stern warning to those who harbored thoughts of escape: "For those who dare go against the government's reeducation policy, we will not hesitate to send you to the dark cells. You can commit suicide or dig a hole to escape. Nobody cares. You could be made of steel and iron but the dark cells will reduce you to a heap of rusty scrap."

I shuddered involuntarily. I had heard from other inmates that the infamous dark cells, designated for escapees or those who seriously violated prison rules, were known as "prison within a prison." Each cell was about seven feet long, three feet wide, and three feet high. Once a person entered, he would never see the light of day. Like a four-legged animal, the inmate could assume one of only three positions — crawling, sitting, or lying down. Every activity was confined to that tiny space, including eating, exercising, and using the toilet. After a year or so, the dark-cell dweller's skin turned pale, his bones fragile, and his hair white as frost. The skin became so transparent that one could see the blue veins.

"I'm halfway to the grave. Why should I be worried about getting rusty?" Old Ostrich continued to mutter. He turned to me. "I once stayed in a dark cell for two years. Patches of white hair grew on my shoulders; they were longer than my beard. My bones were so rotten that when I tried to walk on the day of my release, my backbone broke."

I nodded at him halfheartedly while listening to the official on stage.

"If you are tough, you might be able to survive one or two years, but after that, you'll be completely destroyed." The officer took a sip from his teacup and continued with his threat. "Let me use someone as an example. Some of you probably know or have heard of him. He strongly resisted the government's reeducation efforts and attempted to escape twice. Both times, he was captured. The court added six years to his sentence and locked him up in the dark cell. During the first couple of months, he screamed and threatened to kill himself in the darkness. We simply ignored him. After a few months, he quieted down. In the first two years, I would occasionally go see him. He wouldn't even talk to me at first, but at the beginning of his third spring down there, he dropped to his knees, begging me for mercy.

"We ignored his request, and he stayed there for five years and seven months. By then, he went completely blind.

"One day, when I was down there inspecting work, he clasped my legs and begged me to get him out of there. In the end, we gave him a chance to come back to the world of the living for humanitarian reasons."

"That guy was in my group," Old Ostrich whispered to me in his wheezing voice. "It's true — his muscles had shriveled. At the sight of the sun, he would drop to his knees in fear. He was never really able to walk again."

I shifted my attention back and forth between the speaker on the stage and Old Ostrich. Images of the old man languishing in the dark cell flashed through my mind.

"This has been a very successful meeting," the moderator declared at the end. "I want every section to go back and divide up into smaller groups to discuss what you have learned today. Every person is required to share his thoughts."

"I can't wait to share mine," Old Ostrich kept on. I grabbed him tightly and lifted him up to his feet. Prisoners exited in an orderly fashion, from the front to the back. We stood there, waiting for our turn, but before it came, Old Ostrich suffered another severe asthma attack. His eyes rolled back in his head until only the whites were showing.

"Do you want me to take you to the clinic?"

"Take me to the morgue," he murmured.

He was right. Late that night, my bunkmate's illness worsened and he had to be hospitalized. Three days later, Old Ostrich died.

Prison life moved on. Before National Day on October 1, 1992, the prison authorities launched a "Socialist Labor Contest," which required everyone to give up their naps and free time in the evenings to fold medicine packets. At the peak of the contest, a convicted rapist broke the prison's record by tripling the three thousand quota. At mealtimes, he stirred the food in his bowl to cool it and then buried his head in the bowl, gulping down the soup and rice in a few minutes. To save time, he also reduced the number of his bathroom breaks, suppressing his urges as long as he could. Even when he was squatting on the pit, he would bring work with him. When he stepped out of the toilet section, his pockets were bulging with neatly folded packets.

We were so overworked that several inmates passed out. I operated in a constant state of bleariness. The schedule reminded me of my days monitoring death row inmates on the night shift. After midnight, my hands still moved in work, but my eyes struggled to stay open. Each time I was about to doze off, I felt as though someone was rocking me from behind, reprimanding me for being slow and lazy. In reality, nobody at the penitentiary had the time and energy to spy on others, or even to gossip about them. Our group leader was an old man who was exempt from work. He wore his reading glasses and spent his day reading newspapers and practicing his calligraphy with a brush. During breaks, he would occasionally check up on a prisoner to see if the person had memorized the rules of conduct. Unlike us, he could sleep and get up on a normal schedule.

Since my incarceration, I had glued and folded thousands of medicine packets, enough to fill several empty rooms. The repetitive schedule sickened me. Soon I began to throw up. The mere sight of the medicine packets caused severe spasms in my stomach. Fortunately, the group leader took pity on this pathetic nearsighted poet and divided my quota among several new arrivals. He showed me several old issues of the *Reeducation News,* asking me to imitate them and draft some articles about how our cellmates were "enthused" about the contest. My writings were accepted, and our officer in charge even complimented me in front of everyone. It was nice to get back to writing, albeit as the author of propagandistic party pablum.

We had two days off to celebrate National Day. Inmates lazed around, playing cards and chess, which were permissible, or watching TV under a plastic canopy in the yard. I was in no mood for group leisure and crouched in bed instead, reading and reciting Walt Whitman's *Leaves of Grass*, which A Xia had sent me two weeks before.

As I quietly recited the familiar "Out of the Cradle Endlessly Rocking," tears welled up in my eyes. I had first come across this poem ten years before, when I started exploring Western literature. The poem describes a young boy's literary awakening, his reaction to nature, and his maturing consciousness. In a foreign land bathed in moonlight, on a beach, the boy speaker notices a bird crying out to its mate which has suddenly gone missing. The air reverberates with its call, and the moon droops in the sky with sympathy, heavy with tears.

Whitman's physical condition — he was paralyzed by a stroke — did not diminish his great capacity for love. His work inspired me as a young man to pursue the beauty of nature and literature. I lost interest in fame and money and dreamed, instead, of living the life of an eternally free man.

The lunch bell jolted me out of my musings. I ran out to the yard and joined the other prisoners. After roll call, we squatted in small circles. In the middle of the yard sat two big pots of vegetables and two pots of meat. The head of our group held a ladle and distributed the food evenly to everyone. As we were about to start, a prison officer appeared. "All rise," the leader of our big group called out grudgingly. The officer, in his twenties, marched into the center, like a straight arrow piercing right through an enemy's heart. Several inmates scurried to put two benches together as a podium. The officer stepped up on the benches and launched into a tirade. I couldn't take my eyes off the meat in my bowl.

"Comrade Deng Xiaoping's call for economic reform is sweeping the nation like a spring wind," the officer lectured us. "We will also introduce reform measures here in prison. We are going to implement a market-oriented competitive mechanism." His speech was littered with the slogans and clichés of the reform agenda. I had no idea what he meant. I was so preoccupied with the fatty pork that I tuned out the rest of the speech.

"Raise your head and straighten your back!"

Startled by the bark of an order, I turned to face the officer who had shouted it. "Let's sing 'Socialism Is Good,'" he yelled. The juxtaposition with the previous mention of "market-oriented mechanism" was absurd, but the officer rolled up his sleeves and waved his fists in the air as he sang.

> Socialism is good. Socialism is good. In socialist countries, the people have high status.
> Reactionaries are overthrown. Imperialism flees with its tail between its legs.
> The entire country is in great unity and is making a new upsurge, a new surge, in the construction of socialism . . .

The officer's arms rose and fell, swinging from side to side, keeping time with the music. We bellowed out the words to the rhythm of his body.

I detested fanatical praise of the totalitarian system; every pore in my body felt like it was bleeding. The officer's arms flung up and down, left and right, like machetes. His eyes shone with excitement and his gaze swept around the yard. If anyone simply mouthed the song, the officer would step down from the podium, sprint toward the inmate, and hack the inmate's neck with his machetelike arm.

We repeated the song three times and the officer was still not satisfied, claiming that we lacked passion. Our food was getting cold, and hunger tore away at my stomach like a tiger. We sang and sang, with spit accumulating at the corners of our mouths. Our blood boiled with hunger-induced furor. "Okay, let's do it one more time!" the officer persisted. "I want you to be more animated and enthusiastic . . . One, two, three . . ."

When the relentless officer finally released us to eat, the yard filled with the cacophony of chewing, slurping, and clicking of chopsticks. I stuffed slices of cold fatty pork, slushy vegetables, and chunks of rice into my dry throat, and washed it all down with big gulps of lukewarm soup.

The food was soon swept away. I wiped the grease from my mouth and tried to engage in some banter with my neighbors. But the convicted robber sitting opposite me was in no mood to chat; he buried his head in the bowl and began licking it. The corners of his mouth, dry from malnourishment, cracked and bled. The blood formed two red grooves on his chin. An inmate on my left side followed suit but did so in a more civilized way. He scraped around the bowl with a finger and then sucked the grease off it — which was more efficient than using the tongue.

The next day, dinner was served an hour ahead of schedule because there was a basketball match. Before long, the playground became alive with sound — some die-hard basketball fans surrounded the court, yelling and screaming, and the rest of us in Section 8 used the opportunity to gossip. Having lived in a cage for two years, I stood there like an idiot, not knowing what to do in this relatively free environment. Suddenly someone patted me on my shoulder. I turned around and saw Jin Hua, my former cellmate.

I was stunned. Grabbing his hands excitedly for several seconds, I didn't know what to say.

"I'm going to finish my sentence soon," he told me excitedly. "Once I'm out, I will try crossing the border again."

Though I was skeptical of the plan, I nodded as he described it. After the basketball match ended, we grudgingly parted ways. Several days later, Jin Hua secretly paid a worker to deliver me a surprise gift — a bag of spicy pig's liver, still warm. It was the tastiest thing I had eaten in ages.

Two years later, after my release in 1994, an unsigned note would land on my door via the post office. From the neat handwriting, I knew immediately that it was from Jin Hua. In the note, he informed me that he had indeed fled overseas and, after moving around for a year, landed in Denmark. "The winter in northern Europe is not as cold as one might think. If you stay in and read by the fire, it feels like you are in Beijing," he wrote.

Unexpected Visitors

ON A SUNNY AFTERNOON in the fall of 1992, after I had been at the penitentiary for nearly two months, the officer in charge summoned me to what he called a "meeting." Thinking it was another interrogation, I followed him past the yard. As I entered the outer section, however, I could discern a small crowd clustered under the castle's tall wall. I was too nearsighted to determine who they were, but when I moved closer, I was shocked to see my friends Zhong and Big Glasses. Standing next to Zhong was A Xia, who was dressed in black and carried our baby in her arms. I quickened my pace but the officer in charge warned me not to cross a thick white line on the ground dividing the yard from the outside.

I reached across the line and patted the baby on the head. According to A Xia, my friend Zhong had arranged the visit through a friend of his who worked at the Chongqing Municipal Justice Bureau. I nodded at Zhong and his friend in gratitude and started shaking hands with everyone across the white line. The sudden appearance of my friends and family was so overwhelming that I could not concentrate on what they said. Acutely aware that I looked like a pathetic criminal, I avoided A Xia's gaze and focused instead on my daughter, who winced, looking scared. A Xia handed her to me, but the toddler began crying and screaming, "No, no!"

My wife calmed her by whispering, "Miao Miao, he is your daddy. He has a big beard. Call him Big Beard Daddy." I grinned and adjusted my countenance, hoping to form a kind fatherly smile, but I couldn't. My facial muscles hurt, and I concluded with rue that I was not made for such feelings.

I clutched my daughter's waist but she hugged her mother's neck tightly and refused to let go. In the end, she submitted to my persistence by closing her eyes, as if she were dreaming of hiding inside her mother's stomach, immersed back in the warm amniotic fluid. As A Xia tearfully cajoled the baby to embrace me, she unwittingly stepped on the borderline on the ground. The guard came over and shoved us apart, but Zhong's friend at the Municipal Justice Bureau came to the rescue. With his intervention, the officer in charge granted an exception and allowed A Xia to come into the yard so we could have a private moment together. The officer found a room on the second floor of an administrative building, and three guards remained in the room to monitor our reunion. Like a widow in mourning, A Xia was in a somber mood and tried to break our awkward silence by pressing our daughter to call me "Big Beard Daddy." I also kept a straight face and all I could say was, "Miao Miao, call Daddy." My daughter ignored both of us.

Time flitted by. In the rustling breeze of fall, my wife and daughter floated away from me like a small boat captured by the current of the Yangtze River. I returned to the dorm, thinking of A Xia and her black outfit. Several years before, while we were still dating, I took a boat from Chengdu to visit A Xia in Fuling. Before the boat arrived, I saw a tiny black spot amid the bobbing heads on the distant shore. It was A Xia; I could feel her presence. She had donned the same black outfit and waited on the pebbled bank for a whole afternoon, her hair tousled by the wind.

In one of Aleksandr Solzhenitsyn's famous books of prison life, the Russian dissident describes a representative day in the life of a prisoner named Ivan Denisovich, but I found it simply beyond my capacity to measure my own incarcerated life in days. Like in a swarm of honeybees, each day swirled in a kind of frenetic repetition, a manic and oppressive sameness. I could not distinguish one day from the next. Some incidents stood out in my memory—like the times I violated the prison code of conduct by fist-fighting or when I met extraordinary people.

However, these were random punctuation marks in a monolithic state of ennui. I once heard of an inmate who had written two hundred letters appealing his murder conviction over a period of twenty years. All the letters had gone unanswered. I had a strong urge to talk with this singular figure but never had the opportunity. Prison rules prohibited inmates from talking to someone outside their group. Many times, someone would point out the stooped figure who pitifully ignored the futility of his appeals and kept assaulting the unresponsive edifice of judicial authority. "It's pointless," my group leader sighed. "No matter how convincing your arguments are, the authorities will never consider you for early release. In the end, the guy will drown in his own petition letters."

One rare, luminous moment was my reunion with Old Xie, the gentle, Bible-reading former government official from the detention center. He was transferred to my prison after getting twelve years for embezzling public funds. His prior status within the government earned him many privileges in jail—one of which was to roam around without any restrictions. One day, he showed up in my section and managed to obtain permission to talk to me in a hallway. After a few minutes of reminiscing, Old Xie revealed his intention to write a book exposing shady practices within the government. Knowing that his book would never be published in China, he vowed to find a secret channel to ship out the manuscript. The revelation astounded me, but I was even more flabbergasted when he shared with me his latest plot to get out of jail by concocting a new, body-ravaging drug.

"Once I get all the ingredients for the formula, I'm going to take it for a month. Guess what will happen? My body will be covered with ulcers. My fingernails and my hair will fall out. Authorities will think I have leprosy. By then, they can't wait to get me out of here and grant me a medical parole."

I could feel my hair stand on end.

"Please keep it confidential," he pleaded.

"You shouldn't have told me this," I complained. "You shouldn't risk your life like this."

"One has to have a goal in life," he said with a tenacity that I had not seen before. "After I recover, I'll find opportunities to seek justice and revenge."

His Christian spirit of forgiveness seemed to have evaporated. I heaved a long sigh and said, "In my dreams, I have also killed many of my enemies."

After that meeting, I never heard from Old Xie again.

On November 6, 1994, barely three months after I arrived at Sichuan No. 2 Provincial Penitentiary, three officials suddenly appeared outside my dormitory, as if they had just landed from outer space. "Liao Yiwu," one thundered. Before I had time to collect myself, two officials scurried around, packing up my suitcase. I would be delivered to a new prison, said one official who ripped the name badge from my coat. He had me strip off the prison uniform and put on my old clothes. A few minutes later, I floated out onto the stone stairs like a wisp of smoke. We flew across the yard and stopped in front of an administrative building, waiting for the final paperwork. It suddenly occurred to me that the prison's party secretary had taken my indictment and verdict papers two weeks before, without stating a reason. Now I wanted them back. The next prison would need them just to let me in. And I would need them again if I were to be released.

"The Party secretary is in a meeting," an officer explained.

"I can wait."

"We received the order to transfer you. You have to leave now," the officer insisted.

"The verdict and indictment documents are a prisoner's admission ticket," I argued. "If I lose my ticket, how am I going to get into jail?"

The officer was bewildered at first and then burst out laughing. "I've never heard it put like that before."

We passed four checkpoints before reaching the main entrance. A military jeep finally lugged me out of Chongqing. Heading north, we zigzagged on small paths as we weaved our way through the deep, dark mountains. On the way, the officer repeatedly promised to retrieve the legal documents for me. "You want to hold on to that stuff in case your verdict is overturned someday, don't you?" he teased me.

I ignored him and closed my eyes, resigning my future to fate. It suddenly struck me that I hadn't written any poems in a long time.

> *The inspiration confiscated during a police pat-down*
> *Has never returned*
> *Even memory*
> *Bears the scars of metal chains.*

The No. 3 Prison

AT ABOUT FOUR O'CLOCK in the afternoon, the police van reached the outskirts of Dazhu County where the Sichuan No. 3 Provincial Penitentiary lay nestled at the foot of Daba Mountain. The township, with its dirty and deserted streets, formed a sharp contrast to the large, crowded city of Chongqing.

At the entrance, the driver waved at the guard, and without any fuss, we zoomed in. The north wind hissed loudly and I could not see a single soul in the outer circle. Even so, I felt certain that I was being monitored by hidden eyes. The van parked in front of what looked like an administrative building. An officer went in, and a quarter of an hour later, a young, bookish-looking man in a green uniform came out with him to receive the new inventory.

I carried my suitcase and followed the young officer. An open drainage ditch welcomed me with its sickening vapors. Apparently all the wastewater from a prison factory was discharged via a sewage pipe into the ditch. On my way, I saw a few soldiers walking on a path that snaked along the ditch; their green outfits added some color to the otherwise drab gray surroundings. At a fork, the young man pointed to the right, which he said would lead to my final destination.

About two hundred yards up the slope, the core of a dilapidated temple with an impregnable facade revealed itself. It was built like the mountainous terrain, with walls as high as forty feet. The fortresslike building reminded me of a bandit camp in old movies. I stood at attention, raised my head toward the watchtower perched high up in the cloud, and shouted, "Sir, may I come in?" It took a few minutes before a gun-toting guard stuck his head out a window and waved me in. The entranceway was narrow; one guard could easily block and beat back anyone trying to escape.

Once inside, I encountered a large stadium with a stage on one end that could hold several thousand people. The stadium was fenced in by barbed wire, and sentry posts dotted the perimeter. On the day that I arrived, a horde of sparrows innocently populated the barbed wire, some frolicking on the stage. I waved a hand and hooted loudly. Within seconds, a storm of birds rose to form a fluttering canopy that covered the sky. "The sparrows and prisoners take turns holding meetings here," the young officer joked. In the fall, he also informed me, the stadium was used to dry out crops and vegetables.

At No. 3 Prison, inmates were grouped into six sections and two special units — a maximum security unit for death row inmates and an educational unit in which a dozen or so prisoners wrote and designed a newsletter and operated the prison library. I was to be in the latter, which, I later learned, had the highest concentration of political prisoners. Each section occupied a two-story building with a front yard about the size of a basketball court. Three buildings linked together to form a block. Prisoners took up the basement and the first level, while the kitchen and the administrative officers were located on the second. Each building had a large balcony, where the guards monitored inmates' every activity in the yard.

Upon arrival, the officer in charge and my section leader grilled me about my crimes and my experiences at previous facilities. They assigned me to Section 2 and called a Red Hair to take me to the dorm.

By now I was becoming an old hand at living in highly public quarters. Connected passageways in my new building allowed the guards to see into every nook. Prisoners at Section 2 shared a dorm near a stairway on the first level. The room reminded me of a stone vault for caskets: two rows of metal-frame bunk beds lined the limestone walls, and a narrow aisle in the middle led to a window secured with iron bars. On the day of my arrival, someone had just been released, leaving a top bunk vacant near the window. Too lazy to move someone with seniority to the choice spot, the section leader assigned it to me. My bed number was eleven, which happened to be my lucky number. I hoped it was an auspicious sign.

The dorm was eerily quiet; everyone else was at work. Exhaling audibly in a long, deep breath, I started to make my bed and lay down with an unfamiliar sense of ease and comfort. The sky hung gray and gloomy outside. Soon it started to drizzle. A tiny lamp above my head caught my attention. I switched it on, touched the warm light bulb, and chuckled like an idiot at the luxury of a lamp. I narrowed my eyes, and through my eyelashes the light dissolved into countless numbers of tiny sparkling gold specks. In my childhood, I had frequently looked at the sky like that, and momentarily I returned to a more stable time.

It didn't take long for the reality of prison life to sink back in, and soon my elation dissipated. I had been resting for only a few minutes in the unusual solitude when I heard someone calling my name. I leaned over the side of my bed and looked down. A bespectacled inmate with a big head stood in front of my bed, waving up at me. His boyish face made him look more like a college student, the yellow-striped prison outfit resembling an ill-fitting school uniform.

"I'm Li Bifeng. You can call me LBF," he said humbly. "I've heard so much about you. I would never have imagined that we would meet here."

I hadn't heard such a heartwarming greeting in what seemed like an age. For a moment, I was speechless.

Seeing my stunned surprise, LBF snatched his hat off and exposed the bald crown of his ample noggin. "I've read your poems 'Dead City' and 'Yellow City.' In fact, I've read them many times. When you went to visit your sister in Mianyang, I almost went to meet you but decided against it."

"Is that true?" I jumped down from my bunk to shake hands with my new acquaintance. "Did you know my sister Fei Fei?"

"A friend of mine was your sister's coworker before his arrest," LBF explained. "He said when your sister died, many women at her collective farm were grief-stricken. They bought wreaths and collected money for your family. She was well loved."

"Yes, yes." I nodded. Listening to a stranger praising my sister, I was so astonished and touched that I found it hard to breathe.

LBF suddenly changed the subject. "Okay, it's almost dinnertime. You can rest up for a few more minutes. We'll catch up later."

With that short farewell, he turned and disappeared; it was as if he had evaporated. I stood there astounded, my shoes untied. "That bastard! He got me all interested and then he ran away," I thought, somewhat annoyed. In later months, I came to realize it was merely LBF's typical manner. The poet and activist was always in a hurry, even in prison, perpetually running against the passage of time.

At dinnertime, LBF hurried over to join me, carrying his bowl of noodles. "I have a jar of pickled vegetables we can share," he said, squatting down next to me. Our section leader, Zhang, greeted LBF warmly. "Mr. Crazy, I heard you are a good fortune-teller. Can you tell mine?"

"I can, but I'm afraid that you might be following Chairman Mao's lesson to 'bait the snake out of its cave to kill it.' Do you see what I mean?" LBF said half jokingly. "What if I tell your fortune and then you go tell the officer in charge that I'm spreading superstition?"

"What do you mean by 'baiting the snake out of its cave'? The snake inside my crotch has been dormant for more than ten years. It can't wait to get out of the cave," the section leader teased.

Other inmates roared with laughter, but somehow LBF didn't get the innuendo. He still wanted to explain what Chairman Mao had meant. "Chairman Mao encouraged everyone to speak their minds but then he clamped down on them . . ."

I interrupted my new friend and dragged him out of the dorm. In the yard, prisoners clustered around with their food. Some were standing and others squatting. A middle-aged officer in a long coat paced up and down the second-floor balcony. "He's watching us," I reminded LBF.

"No need to worry. The hunting dogs are always there, but we are not violating any rules," said LBF. "Our section has gathered several generations of political prisoners. That's why the guards are supervigilant. For example, Old Dai, who is sleeping under you, was a former official. During the Cultural Revolution, the Red Guards went to raid his home. He picked up a knife and fought back, causing serious injury to a Red Guard. He was supposed to be executed, but since he was well connected and very cooperative, the court commuted his death sentence. He's been here for twenty-four years."

"Twenty-four years? How has he managed it?" I shuddered.

Later that night, I lay in bed and rested my head on my hands, staring out into a swarthy sky. The cold stars sparkled over the rooftops like floating lanterns in the netherworld. I blinked my eyes and drifted in and out of dreams. The metal bunk bed seemed to sink, and I was crawling along a dark passageway inside a large grave. From the depths of the earth, ghosts swam out like fish, wagging their fish tails and wading through knee-deep grass on the hills of the tomb. Before they disappeared, they were singing the Communist song "The Sky in the Communist Area Is Brighter."

I joined them and sang along. Suddenly, one of the ghosts from my surreal dream morphed into Hu Feng, the famous poet and literary theorist, and lay on top of me.

"I need someone to seek justice for me," he told me in clear dreamspeak. "I disagreed with Chairman Mao's notion that literature should serve the interests of the proletariat, so he branded me a counterrevolutionary, along with other writers. I was in jail for twenty-four years before they released me and reversed the verdict against me in 1979.

"After I died in 1985, I found myself in a bigger jail. This one is called the universe. Do you know you are sleeping on my spot?"

I woke up and could not get back to sleep. A few minutes later, the sound of the bell pierced the air.

Reform Through Physical Labor

I MADE MY BED AND leapt down like a sleepwalker. All the inmates dashed out of their dorms and rumbled down to the playground for the morning roll call. I looked up at the cold, sparkling stars still pricking the sky. An officer on duty inspected the troops from the second-floor balcony and roared, "It's three forty in the morning. I want you to finish breakfast in twenty minutes. We'll leave at four o'clock sharp."

We squatted in circles. The loud slurping sound of rice porridge being quickly consumed echoed in the empty yard. I scanned around and saw my fellow inmates moving about under the moon like apparitions. I longed to return back to my dream. Before leaving breakfast, I ran some cold water over my head.

Under the close surveillance of six guards, we filed out of the gate in a single line. Once outside, we quickly formed four straight lines and marched down the hill toward the factory in the outer section. On the way, the officer ordered a goose-step march, as if we were part of the National Day parade in Tiananmen Square. "One, two, three, four," we straightened our necks and shouted.

A few minutes later, the army of workers stopped in unison in front of the factory gate where the production manager, nicknamed "Mr.

Owl," gave instructions in his falsetto eunuch voice: "Everyone should have a strong work ethic and pay attention to safety rules."

Like a group of well-trained firemen, everyone put on his boots and safety hat, and the groups disappeared into different high-ceilinged workshops. Prisoners at Section 2 were responsible for iron-casting all types of auto parts. As I was finding my way, a big furnace nearby opened up its bloody mouth and roared. I covered my ears in fear. Seeing quickly that I was too clumsy to work near the furnace, the section leader handed me a six-foot-long broom, entrusting me with the task of sweeping the floor.

In a dark corner, I noticed two inmates dozing off on a bench. I looked around quickly before joining them. Unfortunately, Mr. Owl passed by and caught us red-handed. As a reprimand, he ordered me to collect thirty pounds of scrap metal from other workshops.

Yang Wei, the youngest prisoner at Section 2, promised to help me. He dug out an old bucket and led me around in the name of searching for scrap metal.

As I soon learned, Yang Wei was a native of Dujiangyan. Everyone called him "Big Tongue" because he spoke with a thick accent as if he had a disproportionately big tongue. While in jail, he seldom talked. Beneath that loner's appearance, however, he possessed the agility of a squirrel, smart and alert. He moved swiftly, almost mysteriously.

Big Tongue came from a poor family; both parents worked in the local factory. In 1989, he was in his teens, attending a local vocational school. Like most self-absorbed teenagers, he seldom paid any attention to politics or current affairs. However, the massacre in Beijing outraged him and turned him into an activist. Out of thin air, Big Tongue fabricated an organization called the China Democratic Alliance, and he pretended that CDA was a well-established prodemocracy organization overseas. Inspired, Big Tongue designed and printed a dozen CDA posters urging people in Sichuan to stand up against the brutal regime, avenge the death of the innocent students in Beijing, and overthrow the central government. He pasted the posters prominently in public venues. The sudden appearance of counterrevolutionary posters with such explicit antigovernment messages shocked local officials, who classified the case a top national emergency and requested assistance from both the provincial and central governments. Vaunted experts gathered in Sichuan to share information and conduct joint investigations. More than one hundred policemen were mobilized and ordered to solve the case.

Young and wily, Big Tongue was quick on his feet. Upon hearing that the police were on his trail, he picked up his two big, cherished stamp albums and ran. He remained on the lam in China for half a year, wandering around ten southern cities. "I started collecting stamps as a child," he said. "Each time I arrived in a new city, I would hang out at the stamp market for a couple of hours. The money I got from stamp transactions would last me for a few days."

Big Tongue's case alarmed the central government and gained national notoriety. When he was finally caught, the fatigued police were shocked and disappointed to see the menacing counterrevolutionary that they had pursued for months was merely an innocent-looking teenager. In addition, Big Tongue had none of the overseas connections that the posters had claimed. When asked to cough up the names of the key members of CDA in Sichuan, he admitted: "I, myself, hold the titles of chairman, deputy chairman, publicity manager, and secretary."

Realizing that they had been duped, the humiliated Public Security Bureau and the court staff beat him up savagely and threw him into a detention center. Several days later, indictment papers arrived. He found himself facing a secret trial. "I took lots of mental notes and was prepared to engage in a debate with the judge about the student movement in Tiananmen," Big Tongue recollected. "But they didn't take me to a courtroom. Instead, I was led into a small office, and the verdict had already been prepared. When I walked in, the judge picked up the paper, handed it to me and told me to move my ass out of his way. When I refused to leave, he grabbed a document folder with both hands and began to hit me hard on the head. He yelled, 'Get the hell out of here!'"

The judge charged Big Tongue with inciting counterrevolutionary activities and sentenced him to three years at Sichuan No. 2 Penitentiary.

He was barely twenty years old. Initially, authorities put him in charge of a warehouse. While nobody was looking, he slipped notes into the goatskin gloves that prisoners made for export. On the notes, he informed people that the products were made in prison and urged customers to boycott the manufacturer. As a consequence, the merchandise, valued at about two million yuan, was returned from Hong Kong. The leadership launched an investigation and easily uncovered the culprit. In retaliation, the prison guards hung him upside-down from the ceiling for several days.

When I met Big Tongue, he had just been transferred to No. 3 Prison and assigned to clean the factory workshops. As we sauntered around, he introduced me to Lei Fengyun, a foundry worker, who used to be a graduate student at the Southwest Teacher's University. He organized several student protests, hunger strikes, and petitions in Chongqing. After the government crackdown in Beijing in June 1989, the angry Lei posted a notice near the university entrance, brazenly urging his fellow students to travel to Deng Xiaoping's hometown and dig up Deng's ancestral tomb in retaliation for his decision to send troops to Beijing. Not surprisingly, such a bold, disrespectful act was considered an extraordinary offense in Chinese culture. The notice made Lei famous in Sichuan, and he received a sentence of twelve years for his incitement. When I met him, he was holding a shovel in front of the foundry. His dark protective glasses reflected the rising flames that flared off molten metal ore.

By the time the sun had risen in the east, I had talked with more than a dozen of the '89ers like Lei. "Section 2 used to have nearly thirty '89ers," said Big Tongue. "More than half have been released. Initially, we were locked up in one cell. However, after the 'pigeon incident,' our special group was mixed in with regular criminals at Section 2."

The infamous "pigeon incident," I soon learned, took place in the fall of 1991, while I was still incarcerated at the detention center. The thwarted act of sedition started when an injured pigeon dropped to the ground in the yard and several '89ers picked it up. They nursed it tenderly for two weeks. When it finally recovered, prisoners tied a note around the pigeon's leg. The note said, "We are thirty political prisoners, in jail because of our involvement in the Tiananmen student movement. We aimed to bring democracy to China and we hope people outside don't forget about us."

They each signed their names and set the pigeon free, hoping it would carry the message to the outside world. Little did they know that the pigeon had no intention of leaving and simply circled over the prison and landed on a roof. It kept cooing, as if to thank its rescuers. Inmates hooted but couldn't make it leave. In the end, they found out that the pigeon actually belonged to an officer. The note got all of the '89ers into trouble — several were locked up in dark cells for two weeks. Nobody needed to point out that the pigeon was a great metaphor for their futile efforts at escape.

"What a great story," I laughed.

"It's not funny," Big Tongue castigated me. "Do you know what it's like to be inside a dark cell?"

I held my tongue, but the story lingered in my mind. The urgent shrill of an industrial fan pulled me back to immediate concerns. Our molten metal was ready. Lei blew his whistle, and the lava cascaded down from the great opening of the furnace into a ladle. Several workers held long metal rods and took turns thrusting them forward to stir the hot red magma. Within seconds, a crane lifted the dazzling ladle with its load of dripping iron liquid and glided through the air toward the open spaces where the sand molds awaited insemination. The lava warriors were seasoned inmates in full body armor. Only their eyes were visible behind protective goggles. I watched my fellow inmates scoop the molten metal out of the massive carrier and deposit it in dollops of fire into the molds with mundane strokes, much like peasants spreading fertilizer in vegetable fields. I stood there mesmerized by the magnificent scene until Mr. Owl caught me and shooed me away.

By lunchtime, Big Tongue and I had filled up our bucket with scrap metal. We loitered around as other prisoners shuffled back and forth, their bodies covered with charcoal. Inside the workshop, the dust fogged up the air and people floated around like shadowy ghosts.

"The primitive conditions here remind me of 1958, when the whole country was mobilized to produce iron and steel," I observed. "Look at that furnace. It must be forty or fifty years old."

"Changes of equipment cost money," Big Tongue responded. "They don't need efficiency. We have plenty of laborers to throw around."

"That's a lie," a voice interrupted us. We hadn't realized that Li, a model prisoner, was standing behind us. "The government doesn't exploit labor; it aims to save money on equipment for our sake," he added.

"I'm sure they care a lot about us," Big Tongue smirked. "That's why lung cancer is so common at Section 2."

"You should be assigned a job in the workshop cleaning castings," said Li furiously. "The sulfur water should be powerful enough to cleanse your body and soul."

"You are a model prisoner and a supervisor, not a fucking slave trafficker," Big Tongue retorted.

That remark set Li off. Before he had time to get the officer, I lugged my buddy away. "You fucking counterrevolutionary," I heard him curse behind us.

At three o'clock in the afternoon, I joined a dark throng of workers going to the bathhouse. It was my first hot bath in two years and it felt like heaven. I wanted to linger, of course, but an hour later we all gathered at the place where we had started twelve hours earlier and marched in unison back to the inner section. As we passed the ditch, a fog of sulfur steam rose from the water and assaulted our nostrils. Some began to cough, others teared up. "That's the discharge from the cleaning department," Big Tongue whispered to me.

The well-trained troops marched on in the polluted air undeterred; the sound of our synchronized advance was almost earsplitting. An officer leading the march shouted, "One, two, three, and four!" and we echoed his command in unison, even though the sulfur-induced tears kept rolling down our cheeks.

"Excellent," the officer roared. "Goose-steps, go."

The sound of a tsunami turned into war drums, rumbling on as an army of flesh making robotic thunder. About ten yards down the road, the officer issued another command but received a lukewarm response.

"What's happening?" he asked, looking irritated.

"What's happening?" Prisoners repeated his words mechanically. Soon, all the troops slowed down, their steps sagged, and their heads looked together toward the right at a most unexpected but welcome sight.

A young woman hurried by in the opposite direction. Even though it was early winter, she wore an open-necked sweater and her breasts bounced inside. The group was enthralled by the sight of a woman, not to mention a well-endowed one. Our eyes reached down her shirt and fondled her. Inmates farther ahead turned their heads around just to fix their eyes on her back. The disciplined army fell into total disarray.

The young woman retreated to the side of the road next to the ditch and trod along cautiously like an acrobat balancing on a wire. When she turned her face and took us in with her sweeping glance, prisoners couldn't help cheering.

"Stop it," the officer snarled at us and violently blew his whistle. "Look to the front. Focus and concentrate. What's there to look at? Okay, let's start. One, two, three, and four!"

Titillated and emboldened, the troops followed with a boisterous roar, marching on as an army of erections.

Back in the dorm, several of my cellmates immediately stripped and jumped into bed. I followed their examples, thinking of a delicious predinner nap. My neighbor winked at me: "Do it quickly. We only have one hour before dinner."

"Do what quickly?" Somehow I was befuddled by his mysterious wink.

Old Dai underneath me stuck his gray head out with a reproachful look. "You certainly are slow to pick up on things," he said sarcastically.

"Could you tell me what is going on?" I asked innocently. Everyone laughed and I blushed and took a quick glimpse around. An inmate sleeping in the next row flaunted his steamy penis from inside his mosquito net.

My masturbating neighbor even poked an arm out, gesticulating for me to lie down. "Don't you want to fuck that big-boobed woman we just saw? Screw her while the memory is still fresh."

Old Dai could no longer tolerate the unseemly conduct of his younger cellmates and walked out in a huff. Before he left, he pointed his finger at me. "It is disgusting. Don't follow their examples." His remarks were met with derisive giggling.

As I was dressing hurriedly, several metal bunk beds were already squeaking. I could hear moaning and groaning. Five or six minutes later, the noises abated somewhat. A few inmates opened a crack on their mosquito nets and lay still to relish the pleasure. Two snapping sounds came from a mosquito net across the aisle from me. I saw sparks of fire and thought the inmate was smoking a cigarette, but soon his bed started vibrating. "Is he lighting up a fire to jack off?" I wondered.

Suddenly, the mosquito net caught fire and a big hole appeared. Fortunately, the inmate jumped up and put out the flames before it spread. We soon discovered the cause of the mysterious fire — he had used three meat dishes to barter for a porn-decorated cigarette lighter with a prisoner at a different group. On one side of the cigarette lighter was painted a fully costumed Japanese woman. When the lighter was ignited, the woman's clothes would come off. Masturbating to the image of a naked Japanese woman, my cellmate became too carried away and almost burned down the bed.

I didn't linger inside with my aroused cellmates, but hurried out to join Old Dai in the corridor. To break the ice, I inquired about his long prison term and asked if he knew of any celebrities who had been jailed there.

"Hu Feng was here for more than twenty years before the government rehabilitated him," Old Dai said.

"Have you met Hu Feng in person?" I asked and shared my previous night's dream with Old Dai. "I was crawling inside a big grave and Hu Feng told me that he is now imprisoned in a cell underneath the earth," I said.

"I'm not surprised that you dream of the dead," Old Dai said with a blank expression. "In the old days, Dazhu County was quite tiny. When people died, they buried them here. As time went by, this area turned into a big cemetery. After 1949, the new government leveled the tombs and built a prison on top of them. In the wintertime, I constantly dreamed of homeless ghosts who squeezed in from the window and clutched at my chest and cried . . ."

I could feel the cold air blowing on my back. "Does it mean that Hu Feng's soul has attached itself to my body?"

"He used to sleep on your spot," Old Dai continued.

"On the top bunk?" I said, incredulous.

"In those days, our dorm was in a big one-level room and everyone squeezed in a big bed. Since Hu Feng was a well-known intellectual, the officer assigned him a spot next to the group leader. Ten years ago, they demolished the dorm and constructed this building. If you examine the location, your bunk is right where his spot was."

I was skeptical about Old Dai's story, but later conversations with other inmates who had served time with Hu Feng corroborated his story. "Hu Feng went crazy in his later years and was locked up in a special section," said one person. "Prior to that, he used to be with Section 2, right over in this area. He was tall and constantly hungry. Sometimes he would even steal glue to eat. Some prisoners would chase him around, trying to retrieve the glue can. He would hide in the yard, hunching down like a big prawn lurking in coral and stuffing the glue into his mouth. When he finished, he licked his fingers like a greedy child who has snatched a chocolate bar. It was so sad."

One day, Old Dai even suggested that I might be the reincarnation of Hu Feng since we were both poets and jailed for what we had written. I did not find his comparison amusing. "I haven't done anything offensive. Why are you so mean?" I said to him. My face turned ugly with the insult. For weeks, I couldn't drive the thought out of my mind.

Looking back on the characters I had encountered in the past week, I felt like I was visiting a fossil warehouse where time had stopped. The spirits of the dead, drifting in the sky or swimming underneath the earth, were howling. So much was surreal or baffling. Thinking about the crazy vortex of my dreams and the spirit world that haunted my new reality, I preferred to regard it all as a warp in time or a different dimension, and this made my earlier encounter with Hu Feng less frightening.

At the sound of three piercing whistles, we gathered again for our political study sessions. Each inmate carried a small bench and sat in the aisle between two rows of bunk beds. The production leader stood up to summarize our work during the day. Without mentioning names, he glanced in my direction and reprimanded those who were caught dozing off on the job. I lowered my head. The political study leader took over, encouraging everyone to speak their minds. Inmates stood up eagerly, one by one, reporting eloquently about how physical labor helped transform their thinking. I noticed how they all laced their speeches with political clichés like "I want to start a new chapter in life and contribute to our country, our society, and our group." As I cringed at the performance, Old Dai said in a low voice, "It takes years of practice to reach this stage."

Sha Wanbao, a former bank executive, was an exception. He refused to speak at the political study session. Sha had witnessed the massacre in Beijing on June 4, 1989, when he was on a business trip there. Upon his return, he shared with the public what he saw in a self-published pamphlet and received a four-year sentence. Throughout his time in jail, he never abandoned his interest in banking and spent lots of time reading his accounting books, even during political study sessions. For that, the leader openly criticized Sha, who immediately retorted, "I don't want to blow smoke out my ass. There is no need to score extra points and beg the government to commute my sentence. It doesn't help me anyway because I'm going to be released next month." The bombastic remarks met with strong condemnation from veteran prisoners. Sha remained defiant. He put his book underneath his butt and sat with his legs crossed, as if he were sitting behind his desk in a corner office at the bank.

I also declined the chance to speak, using the excuse that I was still fairly new. Deep down, I worried that my loose lips would get me into unnecessary trouble. At eight o'clock, the much-anticipated bell rang. The study session adjourned. Inmates thronged into the canteen to watch videos. The TV monitor was locked in a cabinet and a group leader controlled the key. Before unlocking the cabinet, he stood up, his eyes scanning the room. People whistled in response. He waited until all was quiet and delivered his opening remarks. "As you all know, we are only allowed to watch TV during the weekend. However, since everyone is actively cooperating with the government and has successfully fulfilled our work quotas today, our officer has granted us a favor by shortening the political study sessions so we can have time for some entertainment. I hope we can all appreciate the kindness and benevolence of the party and our government."

Most of the videos were old kung fu flicks and occasionally soft porn. That night, we watched a somewhat explicit video from Hong Kong. Many inmates reached their hands into their pants. The fake moaning in the movie mixed with inmates' own heavy breathing. I watched it for a few minutes and quietly withdrew.

The '89ers

ON A REGULAR DAY our dinner was served at five o'clock, and afterward inmates could relax and move about inside our compound freely. Those with musical talents used the time to indulge in their hobbies inside the dorm. A middle-aged flautist performed his usual "Soldiers Return from Shooting Practice," a revolutionary tune from the Cultural Revolution. A much older man played the erhu, a two-stringed fiddle, and his favorite tune was "The Water in the River," a legendary piece about a heartbroken woman who mourned the death of her husband in ancient China. The erhu player swayed his head and looked caught up in the music, as if he were performing at a sold-out concert. Two inmates liked to amuse others by singing contemporary love songs, most of which were written for female vocalists. When the sex-starved prisoners belted them out in their hoarse voices, it gave me goose bumps.

During this time, LBF and I would stay away from the chaotic entertainment center and trot around in the yard, where a small group of inmates would stroll or squat in the corners for chats. We soon made the daily trot our compulsory homework. In the early summer evenings, I spent hours in the heat outside, the moon splattering on the walls like pieces of sparkling shards of glass. In one of those leisure moments, I asked about LBF's face, one side of which was slightly mis-shapen, causing his chin to tilt at an odd angle. "Were you born this way?" I said, but he shook his head.

"Those are souvenirs from my various border-crossing adventures," LBF said dismissively.

"During the student protest movement," he continued, "I delivered speeches on the street in Chengdu and distributed many of my anti-government poems. After the crackdown, the local government put me on its most wanted list. So I fled to Yunnan Province with several friends. While seeking shelter in a temple, we became acquainted with a monk who constantly took people across the border to Myanmar. We paid him money and he promised to take us. After hiking through the mountains for several days, we finally stepped out of China. But, after the monk left, we got lost inside a forest in Myanmar. Soon my friends also inexplicably disappeared. I was left alone in the dark woods, and for hours, I couldn't even see the sky. I went around in circles and couldn't find a way out. I was soaked with sweat, and clouds of mosquitoes attacked me like little hand grenades. When the mosquitoes showed up, I knew it was approaching evening and I was sure that I would be eaten alive by wild beasts. Then a voice sounded in the thick leaves. 'Don't move,' it said. I couldn't believe someone was speaking Mandarin to me. I felt my head exploding—I was shaking all over and my poor legs suddenly lost control and buckled. I knelt on the ground. But, don't laugh when I tell you this, I was so scared that I peed my pants. After spending all that money and effort, I ended up getting caught. Suddenly I heard the same voice again: 'Raise your hands above your shoulders. Bow your head. Toss out your weapons.'"

"So you ran around in circles and accidentally stepped back into China?" I asked.

"No, I wasn't that stupid. I was still in Myanmar."

"How come the guard spoke Mandarin?" I asked.

"I ran into the People's Army, a guerrilla group affiliated with the Myanmar Communist Party. It was very active in the 1960s and '70s and attracted many young radical Chinese who were sent down to the rural areas in Yunnan Province. They crossed the border and joined the guerrilla forces, hoping to overthrow the government in Myanmar and spread Communism in the region," LBF explained. "The People's

Army kept close contacts with the Chinese border police. My captors tied me up, blindfolded me, and handed me over to the Chinese border police on the same night. I was detained in an office first, where the mosquitoes continued to feast on my flesh. The next morning, a Chinese soldier used one end of a long rope to tie up both of my hands and connected the other end to the back of a tractor. Just like that, I ran after the tractor on the winding mountain path, like a trafficked slave." LBF held up his wrists as an illustration, and continued. "Sometimes, when I tripped over a bump, the tractor would drag me along for a long period, my body scraping against the muddy surface. I wouldn't be able to get up until the tractor slowed down on an uphill road. One time, I was knocked out by a roadblock. When I woke up again, I was at a detention center, where the border police turned me over to the local police. Four men pulled me to an empty space in the yard and punched me in the face over and over again. That's how my good looks were ruined."

LBF would retell this horrific story often. He was a performance artist and craved public attention.

The No. 3 Prison, is, along with Qincheng on the outskirts of Beijing, a notorious jailhouse for political prisoners. Inmates called the place the largest and most prominent counterrevolutionary camp in Sichuan because it had housed political prisoners from every historical period since 1949. Many long-term residents were reluctant to discuss their past. However, there was one exception, said LBF. "We have a self-proclaimed emperor, who lives in my dorm. He can't wait to share his stories with others. He was a peasant who opposed the one-child policy. So he and his friends declared his village an independent kingdom, free from government rule. The government sent troops and arrested him on subversion charges.

"At his trial, the judge realized that he was uneducated and uninformed, and commuted his death sentence to life imprisonment. His Majesty now spends lots of time reading ancient books on Chinese medicine. Last month, he applied for a correspondence university. Since he had no money for tuition, he wrote to the Chinese president and premier, ordering them to allocate funds from the national treasury to cover his tuition. The authorities intercepted his letter. The prison's party secretary chastised him at a meeting."

"Are you making this up?" I said, marveling at the fellow's boldness.

"I swear it's true. You'll meet him some day. He wrote his letter to the Chinese president with a ballpoint pen and called it his 'holy edict.' He brazenly addressed President Jiang Zemin as his 'loyal minister.' You can imagine how scared the officials are — if this had been during the Cultural Revolution, he would have been dead."

My mouth twisted into a wry smile. LBF went on with stories of other regular criminals, all of which intrigued me at first. But as more stories came my way through other inmates I became numb and started to find them exhausting and repetitive. I felt strangled, as if I had been trapped inside a coal shaft, surrounded by a large group of dark, indistinguishable faces smeared with coal dust. My throat tightened as I listened to the tales, and I wished I could crawl out for some fresh air. The narrative assault was unceasing. The personal histories of the criminals were brutally dissected, admired, disparaged, and gradually erased in the long, dark, and boring hours behind bars.

People like me who had been convicted for involvement in the student protest movement of 1989 served shorter sentences than other criminals and counterrevolutionaries. Most of us were better educated and informed. In addition, the government's brutal crackdown encountered worldwide condemnation. The amount of attention, sympathy, and support that we had garnered from the public and even some police officers was beyond the imagination of counterrevolutionaries in previous political campaigns. "You don't belong here," hissed a hostile inmate who was serving life imprisonment for organizing a revolt in the rural areas. "You are not here to receive punishment. You are here to accumulate political capital. Sooner or later, your verdict will be overturned. You guys have something to look forward to, not like us, who will sit here for the rest of our lives."

The tension between the '89ers and the rest of the prison population ultimately led to a riot. One day, during lunch, an inmate in charge of production accused Jiang, an '89er in our group, of cutting in line. He slapped Jiang hard on the face. "You '89ers are a flock of black sheep, making everyone else's life so miserable," the production leader chided.

Jiang, an honest and mild-mannered scholar, was stunned by the slap. Before he had a chance to fight back, another inmate grabbed

Jiang from behind and wrestled him down to the ground. Helpless, Jiang lay flat on his back. In front of a large crowd, the production leader sat on Jiang and used his fist like a piston to pound his face. Jiang tilted his head instinctively to the side. The fleshy piston flew past Jiang's left ear and hit the ground with a heavy and painful blow. The production leader let out a loud scream.

At that critical moment, several other '89ers converged from all directions, shouting, "Stop fighting!" Before long, they found themselves surrounded by nearly a hundred hostile inmates. Instead of rescuing Jiang, the '89ers were outnumbered by seven to one, and they ended up getting their arms twisted, their heads punched, and their legs kicked. A convicted murderer lifted Big Tongue up in the air and tossed him around like a big bullfrog kicking his legs futilely.

I did not participate in this uneven fight because I knew it would likely go nowhere fast. The duty officer didn't do much, either. He paced around leisurely on the second-floor balcony and calmly lit a cigarette. In the middle of the commotion, he even turned around and disappeared in his office. About ten minutes later, he reemerged as if he weren't aware that there was a fight going on under his nose. He then shouted from above, urging both sides to stop.

News of the riot soon caught the attention of the party secretary, who sent a political commissar to my group to investigate and collect evidence. "I've been here for several decades and this is the first time that something like this has happened," said the commissar at a meeting. "We have to punish the instigator and maintain law and order here."

Since the majority of testimony collected favored the production leader, Jiang and several other badly bruised '89ers were held responsible and confined to the dark cells. Meanwhile, the true instigator became an instant hero and celebrity. With the officer's special approval, the production leader, whose wrist had been severely fractured, was allowed to miss work and stay in the dorm to recuperate.

The unfair treatment prompted all of us '89ers to go on strike. We were determined to regain our collective dignity. Nothing could stop us — not persuasion, threats, or promise of rewards. We gathered in the courtyard, screaming and shouting slogans. The guards dragged us to the office on the second floor and attempted to beat us into submission. Nobody succumbed.

As the situation deteriorated, the party secretary personally intervened to clean up the mess. As a gesture of reconciliation, he released our comrades from the dark cells. It was still not enough to appease us. Invigorated by our common cause, we continued with our strike, requesting a new investigation. Worrying that our defiance could lead to unwanted publicity, the authorities decided to summon individual witnesses who were not affiliated with either side to obtain an objective account of the event. In the end, the person whose testimony helped change the verdict was Old Yang, the nurse for Section 2.

Old Yang was a piece of antiquity at No. 3 Prison. He had been a respected reporter for a large military newspaper under Nationalist rule. After the Communist takeover in 1949, Old Yang was labeled a historical counterrevolutionary and received life imprisonment. In the early 1980s, the court granted him parole and he returned to his home village in northern Sichuan, where he was asked to teach at a village school. In the summer of 1983, during a political campaign to maintain law and order and crack down on criminal activities, village officials targeted Old Yang. They falsely accused him of raping a young student and he was sent back to prison.

By the time I met him, he was approaching seventy and had spent the better part of his life behind bars. His seniority at the prison earned him a cushy assignment as a nurse, whose job it was to dispense over-the-counter drugs and monitor the hygiene of each dorm's inhabitants. In addition, the government let him live in a single room under the stairs. Even though it was damp and cramped, he had the whole space to himself, a rare luxury in prison. Old Yang was known for being eccentric and withdrawn. When I approached him one day to inquire about his past, he simply sighed and walked away. I persisted, especially after I found out that he used to be a journalist. Gradually, he warmed up to me.

When Old Yang was called by the party secretary to give evidence in the prison-riot investigation, he pointed his finger at the production leader. Initially, the party secretary did not believe him because a majority of the witnesses had claimed that Jiang and other '89ers had ambushed the production leader and broken his wrist. But Old Yang stood firm: "I have been in jail for more than forty years and I understand what goes through the minds of prisoners. The '89ers are mostly scholars and receive special treatment. They act arrogantly and look down on regular criminals. Their privileged attitude has made many people angry and jealous. Each time I go around the dorms, I hear complaints against the '89ers. But in this riot, everybody knows that the production leader injured his fist himself."

Old Yang's testimony prompted the party secretary to reverse his earlier decision. According to prison rules, an inmate who provoked a fight had to be locked up in a dark cell for fifteen days. If his victim was seriously injured, the perpetrator would have extra years added onto his sentence. Considering the production leader's record, the authorities took relatively minor disciplinary action against him by deducting some of his points he had earned for good behavior. His accomplices were punished the same way.

In a few years, most of the '89ers gained freedom, but Old Yang is forever buried there. As his memory dims and fades with time, I hope that my writing will serve as a record of this anonymous soul who once sparked a small flame of justice in a totalitarian prison.

The final outcome of the riot investigation rejuvenated all the '89ers, even though several were beaten and had paid a hefty price. To commemorate the occasion, six of us had a group picture taken during a family visit. We wore shabby prison uniforms and our arms were folded behind us.

After my release, I gave a copy of that picture to a friend overseas, and it subsequently appeared in *Newsweek* and *Vanguard,* a magazine based in Hong Kong.

Prison authorities soon learned that the picture had been published. Thinking that it had been leaked by the '89ers still in custody, police raided their dorm. "There were many soldiers that night," LBF told me later. "They searched our beds for pictures and frisked us one by one. They even checked the soles of our shoes. Before the police left, they confiscated all of our writings — letters and journals.

"It's my fault," I said with a pang of guilt. "People must have hated me."

To the contrary, LBF was grateful. "We should thank you for making it possible for people overseas to remember us. No matter how miserable life is, we can take it, but the most unbearable thing for a political prisoner is to fade into oblivion."

LBF's sentiments were shared by Lei, the '89er who called on students to dig up Deng Xiaoping's ancestral tomb. I remember running into him one night after I left the TV room. He pulled me aside and told me about a new plan he was considering. "We want to form an organization for political prisoners here. On the one hand, we hope to advocate for and protect the rights of political prisoners. On the other hand, we want to stay in touch with the outside world, and let them know about our struggles here."

"Why do we need an organization to do that?" I mused.

"For the future. We want to ensure that we have a voice. We have been isolated for many years from the rest of the world. Our city is far away from the political center of Beijing, and it's very easy for people and international human rights organizations to forget us. For journalists, a counterrevolutionary in the periphery of the political center is insignificant. However, when a group of counterrevolutionaries does something, the journalists will notice," said Lei, his melon-shaped face beaming and glowing with idealism behind his thick glasses. "People have to have hope. Suffering without hope is devastating."

"Does your wife visit you often?" I tried to shift gears. "Without you, her life will be very hard. If anything happens to you, what's she going to do?"

He gazed at me and began to say something but stopped.

"I know you are disappointed in me," I blurted out.

"You are not the political prisoner that I had imagined. I'm disappointed that many '89ers are like you. They are not political at all," he said.

I defended my position. "You are not a born politician either. If the student movement hadn't occurred, you would have long completed your graduate studies. Imprisonment is fate and you can't calculate its cost. We can't compare ourselves to the elite who started the movement in Tiananmen Square. They reaped all the political benefits and appeared in the history books because they were at the right place and the right time. To be honest, I knew nothing about politics before my imprisonment. Even now, I don't have a set of mature political views.

I'm an individualist, with many incorrigible habits," I admitted. "I was compelled to protest and put myself on a self-destructive path because the state ideology conflicted violently with the poet's right of free expression. In all honesty, I could not accept a murderous government that carried out a bloodbath and covered it up. I'm in jail now and I have no regrets. As for forming an organization, I lack interest and experience. I doubt you have much experience, either."

"Are you saying that we shouldn't do anything and simply waste our time here?" my fellow inmate asked.

"Without an organization, we are still a collective entity. Everyone should do what he thinks is the right thing," I answered.

Silence fell between us. We both stared into the darkness outside. Since several model prisoners began to saunter around us, trying to eavesdrop on our conversation, we stopped and went back to the dorm.

I personally liked Lei — he was tough and tenacious. His tendency to challenge the status quo and buck authority brought him countless misfortunes. One evening in the winter of 1993, armed guards suddenly rounded us up and ordered us to sit inside the dormitory. Minutes passed, and a precise tromping sound echoed from the corridor. The warden appeared, accompanied by the party secretary and a squad of police. The warden called out the name "Lei" and took him away.

The following afternoon, we were summoned for a public meeting at the playground, where Lei was paraded along with several others accused of violating prison rules. He came in last and was the most eye-catching — unlike other regular prisoners, his hands were not cuffed behind his back and there were no shackles around his ankles. The soldiers showed more restraint when treating a political prisoner; Lei was not kicked or shoved around.

But in the misty rain, Lei looked dejected and miserable as he stood before the podium. The party secretary claimed that Lei had been writing secret letters to a British spy agency. "We have been too benevolent with our enemies, who mistake our kindness as weakness and incompetence, and use every opportunity to sabotage our system. Among the counterrevolutionaries of 1989, there are widespread anti-party and antigovernment sentiments. Lei is a ringleader. Just because he went to school a couple of years more than we did, he thinks he can outsmart us. How dare he send secret messages in English under our noses? This is no ordinary violation of rules. It is an attempt to connect with hostile forces abroad. Lei claims he was writing a greeting card to a professor called Peter. Nonsense! This Peter person must be a British spy, a wolf in sheep's clothing. We are going to look into this. You'll be punished!" shouted the party secretary. Inmates applauded at his remarks.

How could that be? I wondered. Was Lei insane? He had to have known that no letters left the prison unchecked, and even outside there was no respect for privacy; postal inspectors opened all mail sent abroad. We later found out from other inmates that Lei had written a short letter in English to Peter, a foreign professor who used to teach at his college. The letter was no more than a few lines of simple greetings; nothing political. With the prison short on language talent, the party secretary had sent it to the county tourist bureau for translation and, to protect himself, he had Lei locked up in the dark cell while the letter was being translated. That much we understood, but two weeks passed and Lei was still in the hole.

On the seventeenth day, a secret meeting of the '89ers was called during a break and plans were laid for a hunger strike. The protest began on the day we received our only meal with meat for the week, a special day for everyone. My comrades each collected their lunch-time meal — fragrant rice and the saliva-inducing meat — and gathered in the middle of the courtyard, where, one by one, they left their untouched bowls and retreated to their cells.

I did not join the hunger strike. Greedy as a pig, I ate every last grain of rice, chewed every shred of meat, and even licked the bowl.

LBF snatched the book I'd been reading from my hands. He was furious, and so, he said, were all the other political prisoners. I could only apologize. "I suffered acute hunger as a child and at the detention center," I said, by way of explanation, and in memory of my early attempt at a hunger strike while in detention. "Just the thought of a hunger strike gives me headaches and an irregular heartbeat."

LBF was unimpressed and launched into an angry tirade. "If you are in trouble someday, everyone else will do the same . . . solidarity . . ."

I cut him off. "I'll do anything, anything except a hunger strike."

LBF glared at me, but he could see the strength of my resolve and knew better than to waste his energy on my stubbornness. He was clever at finding compromises. "Right, then; you can represent all of us in negotiations with the prison authorities for Lei's release."

I knew that both he and another inmate had gone to talk with the authorities, who kicked them out and threatened to send them to the dark cells. I found myself committed to an impossible task, but I couldn't renege on my promise. I recalled an old saying: "A man honors his credibility more than life." I sat down to consider the problem, and that was when I remembered reading something about prisoners' rights in the *People's Daily*. I tracked down an old copy of the paper and found the story reporting that inmates who were found to have violated prison rules should be subjected to solitary confinement for no more than fifteen days. I counted on my fingers. It had been eighteen days since Lei was taken away. I was sure I could trap the authorities.

"Are you the representative sent by the 1989 counterrevolutionaries?" the party secretary asked as I stood before him. It was a trick question.

"I represent only myself," I said, "and under the law, every prisoner is entitled to question the actions of the prison authorities." I then set out my case, that our very own *People's Daily* supported the argument that Lei had been punished enough and should be released from the hole immediately.

"Let me be clear," the party secretary said. "We will strictly apply the law to anyone who dares to organize opposition and conspires to undermine the rules. How did you manage to become their representative?"

"I represent only myself," I repeated.

"Then I'll just lock you up in a dark cell."

"If you try, I will dash out to the balcony and jump to my death."

With both hands, I held above my head the crumpled copy of the *People's Daily* and shouted melodramatically, aping the revolutionary heroes in old Communist movies, "I'm willing to defend with my blood and my life the purity and dignity of our country's socialist law!"

The party secretary did not like being challenged, but at the same time he couldn't suppress his laughter, clearly seeing the absurdity of my antics. In the end, he relented and Lei was released that night. My comrades proclaimed me a hero.

I must admit I got drunk on my new "hero" status and the exhilaration of my unexpected victory. After welcoming Lei back, I returned to my dorm. It was ten o'clock at night and the officer had conducted roll calls from dorm to dorm before locking the building door. Inmates lay down to rest, but I couldn't sleep. I turned on my bed lamp, pulled out a tiny wooden plaque from underneath my bedding, and spread a piece of paper on it. I sucked on my pen, trying to write, but I didn't know where to start. I had repeated this act for a week now.

"My mind is getting rusty," I thought. Then my sister Fei Fei, who hadn't visited me in my dreams for months, walked out from my memory. "I'll help polish your mind and remove the rust for you," she said, smiling. Her cold index finger poked at my forehead, as if she were trying to pull my brain out and rearrange my ideas. A sense of clarity came to me, and I wrote with fluidity:

> It all started in March 1990, when the Chongqing Municipal Public Security Department uncovered a major "counterrevolutionary plot" in the southwestern city of Chongqing. Seven poets, whose avant-garde works had gained a large underground following, were officially charged.

That was the beginning of my memoir. To prepare for unexpected searches, I put a magazine on top of the paper. I was hunched over and my nose almost touched the paper. Inspired by an unknown force, I continued. My breath accelerated, and the characters, tiny as ants, flew out of my pen. Soon the palm-size paper became warped and I pressed it down hard. I tried to pack as many words as possible in that limited space. It was like pulling a camel through the eye of a needle. Miraculously, for the first time I found my inner freedom.

The Flute Teacher

As MY SECRET WRITING progressed, my work status also improved. A few days later, without any explanation, the authorities promoted me and assigned me to work at the central control office. With the new job, I no longer needed to get up in the predawn hours. My daily routine included visiting each workshop to count the number of people at work. Based on the intensity of their labor, I assigned a grade, which would determine how much food they would get. Next I contacted the cooks, ordering them to prepare and pack food based on the numbers and the grades that I provided them. By noon, with the help of two inmates, I would carry the food to the frontline. Before I even approached the entrance, helpers designated by each group were already waiting to receive food and soup. I checked the list carefully while the other two inmates helped me enforce the rules, no less, no more. When the food tasted right, inmates addressed me endearingly as "our respected controller," but if the soup was not thick enough or the rice half-cooked, their faces lengthened. Some would chase me around, waving their fists and calling me "incompetent" or "scumbag."

My daily duty ended after lunch was delivered. One afternoon, as I came back to the empty building, a gust of cold wind swept the sun away. I shivered with cold. I dashed into the dormitory and climbed up to my warm bed to start my writing.

As I was trying to organize my thoughts, my ears picked up the almost imperceptible sounds of weeping on the breeze that came through the tiny window of my second-floor cell. I rose from the bed — it was not weeping, but a flute playing music unlike anything I had ever heard in concert halls.

I took a half carton of cheap cigarettes from my locker and went down to the courtyard, where I bribed the guard to tell me where the music was coming from. "The clinic," he said gruffly, and he tucked the cigarettes inside his jacket. Through an archway off the courtyard, I followed a long corridor that, after three turns, led me to an open space. To the right was the entrance to the prison clinic. I winced at the smell of pungent antiseptic mixed with the stench of a nearby ditch of excrement.

I found the flautist leaning against a steep wall topped by tendrils of barbed wire and ivy reaching into the sky. His big round bald head sat atop an emaciated body. He seemed oblivious to my presence, and as he blew, his shoulders heaved up and down inside his blue cotton-padded uniform jacket. The tune meandered like a mountain stream, its volume surging in parts, then trickling away to become almost inaudible, drying up to virtually nothing. I could see him playing but I could not hear any sound. What I heard on that day was actually a short tune, but it seemed to linger on and on, unrushed, as if it would take a lifetime to finish.

Time glided by, and soon I felt the dampness from the frozen ground travel up through my body and seep into my bones. My knees began shaking, my teeth chattering. Though the upper half of the prison walls was bathed in sunlight and several sparrows perched quietly on the barbed wire, the space around us was shaded and cold, and a sharp wind blew.

The old man wiped away tears from the cold wind or raw emotion, I could not tell which, and wrapped his flute in a ragged piece of worn cloth. He raised his head and smiled at me, an idiotic young man, shivering but happy. I smiled back. I guess it was karma.

"You want to learn how to play?" he asked. I nodded.

"You need to find a decent flute," he said, then turned and hurried away.

The flautist's name was Sima, a former Buddhist monk, and the prison's oldest inmate. He was eighty-four and had a janitorial job at the clinic. For more than a decade he was seen holding either a broom or a flute with eight holes. His sweeping was precise and measured. During breaks he would sit out in the courtyard and play his flute, as though emptying himself of desolation and loneliness. The sadness that emanated from that hollow bamboo stick seemed out of character for someone who was, or at least had been, a Buddhist monk supposedly detached from worldly suffering. One prisoner, who heard me talk about Monk Sima, mocked him as an illiterate. "That old monk doesn't know how to read, so he thinks if he plays his flute it will make up for not studying scripture."

Monk Sima's past was a mystery to me and to the others, although there was much speculation. One version had the ring of truth: when he was the abbot at a nearby temple, he was accused by the government of belonging to a *huidaomen* — a superstitious sect. The *huidaomen* were declared illegal as subversive cults after the Communists took over China in 1949, but many were rumored to be still active in parts of the countryside. When Monk Sima's case reached police attention in 1982, investigators initially doubted a venerated abbot could be a cultist. But under interrogation Sima refused to speak, so he was deprived of sleep and tortured. After a month, he gave his interrogators just three profound sentences: "I have committed sins. So have you. We are all sinful." The court sentenced him to life imprisonment.

After I met the monk, his bamboo flute danced in my mind. In the following week, I drew it on a piece of paper with some instructions and mailed it with a letter to my mother. Fortunately, it reached her unimpeded, and she said she ran around the city for several days, managing to find five flutes of different designs, which she brought with her on her next visit.

But the fruits of my mother's efforts did not meet muster with the monk. "None of these will work," he said, barely glancing at them. A month later, my mother came back with five more. The monk examined each of them carefully and selected one he said might make a "half-decent" sound. He had me soak the flute in water for seven days, scrape the paint and ornaments from the surface, and bury it in the snow for a couple more days before letting let it dry out in the wind.

On a sunny day following a big winter storm, we began our lessons. I was in my cell and Sima stood outside, near the window. I put my hands in front of my chest, palm to palm, and prayed silently. When I opened my eyes again, I saw my teacher raise his flute to his lips. "Breathe . . ." he instructed. I needed to take the air I inhaled and direct it to my *dantian,* a place beneath my lower abdomen, and then gradually let it out. The process, well-paced and controlled, would transform the air inside my lungs into an energy flow that would circulate through my body and heart. Seduced by music, I put aside my writing.

At the beginning, the bamboo flute was stubborn; no matter how hard I blew into it, no sound came out. When I finally managed to produce some awkward notes, they reminded me of the noise of the bellows that villagers use to fan the flames in the cooking stove. Even so, the noise brought me hope and encouraged me to blow harder. Soon I felt a pain in my chest. My head was about to explode. The monk counseled from outside my window, "Control your breathing." I grew despondent. I was focusing on my flute when my cellmates from the night shift swarmed in. As they disrobed and lay down on their bunk beds to sleep, it was made clear that I should leave. I took my flute and went down to the courtyard where, looking directly at the dazzling sun, I saw seven or eight images of my teacher within the blinding fireball. The cold, unceasing wind battered his face.

That night an inmate I knew as Crazy Wino was jogging around the courtyard, his feet pounding on the snow-covered ground. He ran year-round, always wearing the same cotton-padded hat with ear flaps and a scarf. Everyone compared him to Hua Ziliang, a character in a well-known revolutionary novel.

In the book, Hua was imprisoned by the Kuomintang but refused to betray his comrades. To protect himself he feigned insanity by jogging up and down the courtyard all day long in all weather.

I wondered what Crazy Wino was up to and decided to join him. Carrying my flute, I easily outpaced him and then began lapping him around the courtyard. We soon drew a crowd. "Wow, there is another crazy hero here, an iron man!" They applauded every time I gained a lap on him. I was basking in their attention when Crazy Wino turned around and began running toward me.

Before I knew what was happening, a row of yellow teeth flashed in front of my eyes and sank into my forehead. Crazy Wino was angry as a rabbit gone wild. We fell down in a writhing mass on top of a pile of snow. A roar went up from the crowd as they egged us on. It took several of my fellow '89ers to break up the fight. Crazy Wino wore a mad smile on his face, his protruding teeth showing traces of my blood.

I picked up my flute and walked away, tending to the wound on my forehead, but felt nothing of what should have been searing pain. Of course, the fight got me into trouble with the prison authorities. "A country is governed by law and the prison is managed by rules," the warden told the assembled prisoners soon after the courtyard incident. "Liao is a political prisoner but he should be subjected to the same punishment accorded a common criminal."

Amid thunderous applause, two inmates came forward, shackled my hands and feet, and escorted me from the well-lit common areas of the prison to a section shrouded in darkness. I was pushed tottering along a corridor that reeked of mildew and urine.

At the end of the corridor a door clanked open and in I went. My head hit the low, damp ceiling, sending cold shivers down my spine, and as I reached up to touch it drops of water ran like a slimy snake into my sleeve. I was trembling. "Hello? Anybody in here?"

The door clanged shut and, after the sound of footsteps was gone, there was nothing but silence and emptiness. I felt around me and touched a stone bed. I sat still. I could hear rats squealing and running around, and as I swept the floor with my foot, the shackles around my leg caught a metal toilet container, knocking it over onto the floor. I was immediately returned mentally to my days at the squalid detention center.

Several hours must have passed. The rancid air was stifling. Bugs bit me all over my body and my scratching became incessant. I grew as hungry as the insects.

I was fed twice a day — a small bowl of rotten rice — and the hunger gnawed at my stomach. I wrapped myself in a quilt, assumed the lotus position, and took to meditating. "Breathe," I imagined I heard the monk whisper in my ear. I inhaled, trying to push the air down deep, and then carefully exhaled. Again. Again. Again. Cold sweat trickled down my spine, and the bugs droned around me. I suppressed the urge to gag at the stench as I held my imaginary flute, fingers pressed to the holes, and began to play. The world was reduced again to nothing.

Between my exertions I lay down on the stone bed, at rest like a pool of still water hidden inside a deep, dark cave. Inside this big stomach called the universe, the earth was only a tiny pearl of undigested grain, human beings merely the grain's molecules. Breathe, I ordered myself, and drifted into unconsciousness. I spent two weeks this way, in the dark. Outside, my fellow '89ers staged a hunger strike to protest against my punishment, similar to the one for Lei. When I emerged, like a veteran soldier returning from the battlefield, I was given a warm welcome, with my fellow inmates piling on my bed the food they had saved for me from their daily rations. "We will always act as one," Lei assured me.

Fortunately, I was able to gain back my old job at the central control office. Each day, after I delivered lunches of rice and soup to my fellow inmates, I would return and devote the rest of my time to the flute. Sometimes I directed my attention to the courtyard outside. Everything seemed so familiar: the tall, drab walls, the entangled barbed wire, the stern-looking guards and their patrol dogs. Once, just for a moment, I saw the back of a woman flash by. It had been so long and I was tortured with desire. Slapping myself, I took up my flute to the sound of a weepy tune I heard in the distance. "Teacher," I called out.

It took three months, but I learned to master the flow of air and energy inside my body. If nothing else, my circulation improved and my face glowed with new health. Every few days, Sima would appear outside my window, gesture some brief instructions, and then leave. Not long after, I would hear a tune rising from the place where I first saw him. I would listen, trying to appreciate and absorb the essence of the piece.

One day, when my younger sister, Xiao Fei, came to visit, bringing packages of food, she told me before saying good-bye, "Mum and Dad hope you don't give up your writing."

Yu Tian, a poet friend, also showed up unexpectedly, arguing and begging his way past the guards. He told them I was his cousin. "Your cousin is doing pretty well here," the friend was told. "He plays the flute every day, like a free-spirited deity."

I hadn't seen my friend for many years, and his visit brought back a flood of memories. While he filled me in on the news and gossip he had learned of our former poet friends, I must have looked bored; these memories had long since vanished for me. Yu Tian went on, "Hey, how come you act so indifferently to everything now?"

"All the things you just told me . . . don't seem to have anything to do with me anymore," I stammered. "I feel like I have no past."

"No past?" he snapped. "You are in jail because of your past."

I took in his disheveled hair, his tired bloodshot eyes, not knowing how to respond. He had traveled thousands of miles to see me, a disgraced poet, who used to be like him. How disappointed he must have been to hear me dismiss my past in this way!

In April, green vines crawled over the prison walls. The sky was a clear blue. Quite alarmingly, Sima almost succumbed to an often fatal disease. I was not allowed to look after him, but I made sure he received some of the food my family sent. Returning one afternoon from my usual lunch delivery duties, I snuck into the ward to see him and was surprised to find that he was sitting outside, dozing in the sun, his flute between his knees. He woke at the sound of my approaching footsteps. I bowed, gently shook his hands, and asked about his health.

"I was about to play a tune to let you know that the illness has receded," he said.

He struggled to his feet and raised his flute, but he seemed to lack the strength to begin. After failing several times to draw a sound, he flung the flute against his chair. "You and I have accompanied each other for decades," he yelled at the flute. "You damn fucker. You are taunting me for getting old."

"Teacher, don't be too hard on yourself," I urged.

When he tried again, the flute came to life, the jagged notes conjuring up the image of an aging warrior sharpening his rusty knife by the river. His tune, a melancholy one about autumn, wavered in the air.

The old monk sighed. "I don't care if I live or die. I have to play a couple of tunes a day before I can rest. Oh well." And with that, he returned to his chair, placing the flute horizontally on his lap. Teacher and student sat silently, face-to-face. I could see he had reached the autumn of his life and tried to think how to lift his spirits. "Teacher, the tune you just played was about autumn. Why not perform something for the spring?"

"What are you talking about?" he replied. "There is no season here. For the flute, it is always autumn."

The monk dismissed me with a laugh and I was embarrassed. Sweat beaded on my forehead.

"I play simple folk tunes, popular in the rural areas. They've been passed down from generation to generation; most don't have proper names. Please preserve them and pass them on. I am a monk, but you are a man with a heart and feelings."

"What do you mean by 'a heart and feelings'?" I asked.

"Worldly feelings," he answered.

I thought about what my sister and Yu Tian had said to me. I knew that I should resume my writing, but the flute prevailed. I sensed a conflict within me, a conflict between spiritual yearning and worldly ambition.

With the arrival of summer, my musical technique improved. I practiced afternoon and evening, my repetitions annoying the inmates and guards to the point that a mere note was met with loud protests. I moved my practice sessions to the latrines, where I hoped to cause less of an inconvenience. One evening, someone squatting over the pit called out mockingly for a popular romantic tune to help ease his bowel movement. I took the request seriously and played "My Home Bathed in Moonlight." Midway through the piece the moon broke through the clouds, and those out strolling in the cool air were drawn toward the latrines on hearing my music. I was surprised by their applause.

An inmate at the urinal slapped his stomach and went about his business. A joke quickly spread about how my music "stunk." My sessions in the latrines began to draw crowds. Someone would ask for a favorite tune and, if I knew it, I would comply; if I didn't, I promised to learn it for the next time. It was suggested that I join some of the other musicians among the inmates — players of the guitar, the erhu, and even the suona, a type of oboe. We were the latrine madrigals. When we were asked to rehearse a concerto and present the piece at a holiday celebration to showcase our talents and please the authorities, I abandoned whatever dignity and principles I had left and performed like an obsequious dog. Brandishing my flute, I played lighthearted tunes with vigor, gyrating like a rock musician, eyes closed and head bobbing up and down, soaking up the applause.

Sima, my pure mentor, was clearly not impressed by my new self-regard and swagger. Gently, he asked me to put my flute down. "You have established quite a reputation lately."

It was like a bucket of ice-cold water being poured over my head. "Life in prison is really no different from life outside," he said. "Here, the circle that confines you is merely smaller."

I stared down at the mouth of my flute. A thousand words clogged my throat, but not a single one came out.

"You can go now," my teacher said. I turned and left.

For days after, I felt lost. If the whole world is another prison, a bigger circle of confinement, what's the point of living?

What I had failed to grasp was that Sima had resigned himself to playing the flute. I, on the other hand, in my prime, my blood boiling inside my veins, had a choice. I realized that I could not hope to inherit his techniques and philosophy because we were on different sides of the river of age. We could build bridges to span that river, but there would be no crossing them. I began to approach my music from a different, if not opposite, direction.

"Your music radiates vitality and energy," the old monk said when our paths crossed in the courtyard. "You must be nearly finished serving your sentence."

"Yes, Teacher," I said dutifully.

"What are you planning to do when you leave here?"

"Find something to do so I can make ends meet, I suppose," I said. "Now that I have learned how to play flute from you, what else can I do?"

"You are not telling the truth." He smiled. "Your music conveys a different story, one of more aggressive impulses."

I was taken by surprise. "Please, offer your guidance," I implored.

"I'm not blaming you for your worldly ambitions. You are educated and intelligent. You will preserve and pass down the tradition. With more practice, you'll give meaning to meaningless tunes and vitality to the tired and familiar. You can be on your own now."

I buried my head between my knees. After that, I was too embarrassed to look my teacher in the eye. Our relationship had come to an end.

Sima stopped coming to the courtyard to give instruction; I no longer heard his flute. He shut himself in his room, refusing visitors, and even my attempts to see him ended with disappointment. I practiced alone in the snow, consumed by sadness, until my energy was gone and I lay shivering in bed. As my temperature soared, my fellow inmates exchanged news of my worsening condition. Their concern was tempered by the excitement my illness injected into the tedium of prison life. "Our lunatic iron man is finally wilting," they joked. Old Yang, the nurse, came by and prescribed herbs and antibiotics. He told LBF to give him regular updates.

LBF stood by my side for hours at a time, like a loyal guard of the imperial army, moistening my lips with drops of water and forcing me to swallow herb tonic to make me sweat out the fever. I was covered with a heavy quilt. Several times my temperature climbed precipitously, then plunged. My undergarments were soaked and had to be changed every few hours. Finally I wrapped myself naked in the quilt and threw it off when the heat became unbearable. LBF would climb up to my bunk bed, pin me down like a slab of meat to be butchered, and wrap me up again. Soon I would be too weak to struggle and, panting for breath, would surrender.

In my delirium, I asked for my flute, which hung on the wall near my bed, and hugged it to my chest. I mistook LBF for Sima and went on and on about the song "Su Wu Herding the Sheep" and how Sima played it with dozens of variations of rhythms, making it heart-wrenching yet uplifting. He transformed the famous tune by infusing it with his own life until it was not Su Wu of the ancient legend who tended the sheep while exiled in the remote enemy land, but Sima himself.

"I'm sure it made sense to you at the time," he chuckled later.

My fever broke, but I was very weak. When I was finally able to slide off my bunk and stand before the window, I realized seven days had passed and I had been given new insight into life. I felt transformed, and I was eager to start afresh. I tried my flute but my lungs were weak. I thought I would jog around the courtyard but gasped for air after only two circuits. I heard the familiar flute music, but it sounded empty, devoid of any worldly feeling or attachment. "The monk is only an illusion," I said.

As my lungs recovered, I resumed my practice. Gradually I felt my music rise more and more from my heart. "A tune is like a corpse," I told myself. "Once you blow your essence into it, it comes to life and dances at your will." I tried my hand at the popular revolutionary song "The East Is Red." LBF told me I had turned the Communist anthem into a funeral dirge.

On January 31, 1994, a week before the New Year, I was informed that I was being considered for early release for good behavior. In shock, I emptied my wallet, bought dried sausages and beef, and began planning a big party for my fellow '89ers to mark the holiday. I heard nothing more until, late one evening, the guards fetched me from my cell and took me to a room packed with police. I was puzzled. "What crimes have I committed this time?"

An officer patted me on the shoulder. "No crimes; your family is here. Let's go see them." I feared this was a trick. "Prisoners are not allowed to step out of their cells in the evenings," I said. Everyone laughed, and one of my guards said, "When did you start to understand the rules so well?"

I was escorted outside, through several checkpoints and down a slope to the path that led to the outer buildings of the prison. It was a windy night and I crossed my arms tightly over my chest to hold closed my winter coat. My eyes darted among the shadows cast by the dim lights around us and I drew my head down into my collar, fearful I was being led into a death trap.

When we approached the prison administrative building, I realized that I had stopped breathing. We took the stairs to the third floor. A bright light emerged from an office like a beacon.

My relatives were not in the room. Instead, the party secretary sat behind a big desk, beckoning me forward. I was thirsty and he handed me a glass of water. I gulped it down. A film camera was set up in the corner of the room, aiming its lens at the desk. I stood before the desk. I could feel the heat of the high-powered camera lights scorching my head.

"How are things going with your flute?" He had a big smile splattered across his face. He gave me no time to respond. "Do you want to spend the New Year's holiday with your family?"

"Of course," I said. "But I still have forty-six days to go and, before I leave, I want my diploma."

"Diploma?" The party secretary looked puzzled.

"Yes, a diploma, to show I have served out my sentence. In this life, I didn't have the chance to attend a real university. Instead, I went to prison. I've been here for four years. That's equivalent to an undergraduate degree. I want my diploma."

"You do have a good sense of humor," the party secretary said, but his smile had vanished. He shuffled some papers on his desk. "Okay, let's get down to some serious business. During the past four years, you have abided by the rules and done a good job in reforming yourself. Based on your good performance, the government has decided to grant you an early release. Before we proceed, we need your cooperation on a couple of things."

"I have said before and I will repeat again: I refuse to write a confession."

"No one is asking you to give up your previous views and opinions, but you need to express your willingness to change."

It is easy to say one is willing to change; whether one actually does so is entirely another matter. So, standing at attention, I said smartly, and the party secretary took it as assent, "I am grateful to the government for releasing me ahead of schedule."

"What are you planning to do after you get out of here?"

"Make a living and support myself."

"How would you describe your life in here?"

"Better than life at the detention center."

I don't know how long the "interview" lasted. We were being filmed the whole time, and under the camera lights I felt like I was sitting too close to a fireplace. I glared at the cameraman, downed another glass of water, and stood up. Sweat streaming down my cheeks, I asked permission to leave. The party secretary waved his hands to say yes, and the show was over.

We didn't return to my cell. Instead, two guards escorted me to the prison guesthouse where I was given a single room all to myself. The next morning, I got up and went outside for my routine exercise. The guesthouse stood wedged between two parallel walls that separated the prisoners from the administrators and the outside — a world between worlds.

Two inmates delivered my things and, while the guards weren't watching, one of them slipped me a scrap of paper. "We have moved all your writings to a safe place. Someone will deliver them to you later. Don't worry about us. Your friend, LBF."

I felt at once grateful and guilty. I also felt solidarity with those brought together by the Tiananmen massacre, bound by the same faith. Three days and three nights passed. I played the flute, read, and stared at the sky and at the tall walls that still held me. My mind was a jumble of prison memories so sharp and vivid that my head ached. I wondered about my mother, my wife, and my daughter. In my dreams, Sima came to me, using his flute as a walking stick. I grabbed the front of his shirt, but it changed into a long umbilical cord in a tangle of all my prison memories. Like a clam, heaven and earth sucked my being into their shell.

"Teacher!" I screamed, and I woke as if I had fallen from a great height. It was like nothing I had ever experienced before, nor expected to experience again, no matter how long I lived. The world outside my window resembled a mirror; the moon in a shiny glass bottle. There was frost in the air, whitening the leaves in the yard. I took up my flute, weathered with time, and wetted its mouth. It tasted salty. I sat facing the prison clinic and played a classic flute tune called "Guest." A fat, shiny bug squirmed up an old tree. My heart danced wildly and my eardrums popped. But I heard nothing. I played "Yearning," and sat still for twenty minutes. I wasn't sure at first of the faint sound that reached my ears. It was unmistakable that Sima was playing. The tune floated out and over the mountain-high walls. Tears welled in my eyes.

Go, I told myself. Go until you disappear into oblivion.

Epilogue

On January 31, 1994, I was released from prison forty-three days ahead of schedule. However, freedom did not taste all that sweet.

A police car drove me to Fuling, where A Xia and my daughter lived. Our apartment was locked, and a neighbor informed me that A Xia was in Chengdu, even though the prison authority had notified her of my impending return. Disappointed, I went directly to the home of my in-laws, still wearing my blue prison jacket with a scarf wrapped around my head. A Xia's parents greeted me warmly. They didn't mention my absent wife, but when I inquired after my daughter, my mother-in-law readily brought the fuzzy little toddler out to me.

It was the second time that I had clutched my own flesh to my bosom, and Miao Miao scowled at me in confusion. My mother-in-law urged her to call me Daddy, just like A Xia had during our prison visit. I lowered my head and stared at my offspring. Two large tears rolled down my cheeks and fell onto Miao Miao's face, and she, too, began to cry.

Over the next two days, I stayed by my daughter's side. Quickly becoming closer, we dressed and "fed" her dolls and played hide-and-seek. She sat on top of me to play horsie. Outside, I carried her around in the street and I bought her whatever she fancied. For a while, I thought I was connecting with her. Occasionally she asked for her mother, but other than that, nobody seemed willing to discuss my wife's whereabouts with me.

On the third day, I took Miao Miao with me to a barber's for a quick shave. I thought a trim might make me seem less frightening; with my bald scalp and untrimmed beard, I looked like a man in his fifties, even though I wasn't yet thirty-six. Things started out nicely. Miao Miao waited on the side of the barber's chair, watching excitedly and puckering her lips to sing "A Duck in Our Commune," an old revolutionary song that her mother had taught her. After the barber had finished, Miao Miao gawked at me with her eyes wide open. Turning around, her small frame ran to the door and made a break for it. I caught up with her on the street, where she was almost run over by a taxi, and swooped down to grab her. She scratched my face and screamed in fear, trying to struggle free from my grip. Pedestrians stopped to watch us. Embarrassed by their stares, I carried her and escaped to a hilly side street.

"You have a bald head. You are a bad person!" she yelled. "I don't want you."

"But I'm your daddy," I fumed.

"You are a criminal!" she continued screaming. "I don't want a hairless criminal."

Upon returning home, I dug around and found a hat to cover my baldness. Miao Miao finally calmed down. When the moon rose, the whole family sat on the balcony. The moonlight shimmered on the dark, brooding river flowing past the apartment building. I pointed at the distant moon and said to my daughter, "Miao Miao, does the moon look like Daddy's head?"

She nodded, smiling.

"Daddy is the moon. Don't you want to touch the moon?" I coaxed.

"You are not the moon," she answered unequivocally. "I don't want to touch your stinky head."

My mother-in-law scolded her: "Stop the nonsense. He is your daddy. Call him Daddy, okay?"

Miao Miao shook her head. "He is a bald criminal."

I soon began to wonder if my daughter was merely parroting her mother's words about me. My daughter's rejection was only the beginning of what I was about to encounter. A Xia filed for divorce. Back when I was still at the detention center, she had alluded to her intentions in her letters. "I'm tired of the police harassment. I want our child to live a normal and stable life," she had written. I probably should have addressed her urgent concerns, but at the time I was too caught up in my own desperate situation. Upon my release I soon realized that the damage was irreparable.

A Xia had every reason to leave me, especially after the suffering she had endured. While pregnant, she was put behind bars for forty days, and I only heard all the details later. She put on a brave face to cope with one ferocious interrogation after another, overcoming her daily bouts of sickness and fear. On the day of her release, A Xia trudged slowly under the afternoon sun carrying a small bundle of her belongings with both hands. As she stepped down the stone stairs near a street entrance, someone sprinted out from behind her, snatched the bundle from her bosom, and bolted away. A Xia lost her balance and fell. She was unable to speak, and onlookers did nothing to help. "I struggled to get up for several minutes before I finally pulled myself to my knees," she recalled later. "I was so worried that our unborn daughter would be hurt."

Subsequent police raids of our apartment coupled with the experience of giving birth alone traumatized her. A Xia and I had met through literature, and after my arrest the mere sight of books and manuscripts triggered intense reactions from her.

The last days of our divorce were heartbreaking. She insisted I pay child support for the next ten years in a lump sum so she could sever all ties with me. When I responded that I couldn't afford it, she called me a beast and kicked me out of our apartment. As I was preparing to leave, our daughter, who had been hiding behind the balcony door, spat at me. I shuddered to think that my four-year-old daughter had already learned to hate.

Over the years, A Xia has kept my daughter away from me, even though I started paying child support from the royalties of my books. By the time this book is published, my daughter will have turned twenty-two, but so far, I have spent a total of less than two months with her.

My wife deserted me, and sadly, so did most of my friends. After four years in jail, I was no more than a pile of dog shit to my fellow writers. Some avoided or derided me, while others had completely forgotten me. Except for my family, the only people who still paid steady attention to me were the police officers, who followed me like an invisible tail wherever I went. One officer visited me frequently in the name of checking up on counterrevolutionaries and begged me to play flute for him. Occasionally, the officer would rant about society and his work. In a way, I was grateful to him for keeping me company and listening to me play the flute since no friends bothered to see me.

Reverting to a much younger self, I moved in with my parents. My tireless mother cooked and cleaned for me, so I had lots of time to sit at home and stare at the ceiling. "My era has long since slipped past," I thought. Even the flute, outside prison and away from my mentor, that divine musical instrument had lost its magic and emitted only harsh and menacing sounds. Existence felt as painful as walking on the blades of swords. Life presented only three options for me — dive into the world of business (becoming a clothes vendor, as suggested by a police officer), pick up my pen to write, or commit suicide.

On a cold wintry night in 1994, I consulted my friend Liu Shahe, a poet who had been singled out by Mao Zedong for special condemnation in the 1958 anti-Rightist campaign. Liu, now sixty-three, was curled up on an old couch in his apartment, his ashen complexion accentuated by the redness of his lips. In the dim light he looked like an actor who had just removed his makeup.

As usual, the veteran writer was talkative, his voice sonorous. In three hours I uttered only three sentences, all of which were responses to his questions. "What have you been doing lately?" he asked.

"I'm home writing."

"Are you still writing poetry?" He shot a glance at me, his eyes like two bolts of electricity.

I shook my head and Liu nodded knowingly, as if he had seen through me. "I know you can no longer compose poems that are rich in imagination. For you and I, who have suffered such trauma, the wounds in our heart will never heal." He continued, "Why don't you abandon poetry and be a witness to history? You have a clumsy tongue, but God has bestowed a sharp pen upon you. So many people have suffered injustices, but only a few have crawled out of jail still clearheaded enough to remember and record what they have seen. Sometimes, experiencing despair can be a blessing. You must write honestly. That will be a perfect ending to your story. But remember to tell the truth. False testimony will be condemned by the future generation."

Liu's words warmed my heart, and I remembered the memoir I had begun while in prison. But deep down, I still felt unsure. "Why don't you write?" I asked him.

"I'm too old." He gave a long sigh. "I have stomach ulcers and my eyesight is deteriorating. I wrote a lot before I reached my enlightenment. By the time I achieve it, I'll be too old to do anything."

I stepped out of his building and into the quiet night outside. Ghostly buses and cars sped by. The wind sobbed loudly and lights flickered on the shadowy faces of a few passersby. When my life ended and my soul departed, I wondered, would I have the courage to provide my testimony?

"You need to remain composed and determined," I told myself. "Let go of this face, tear away this veil of depression. Develop a thick skin and turn the wheels of memory to prevent the ravages of rust."

I wrote to my former accomplice Michael Day, asking for money and telling him my plan to finish the memoir I had started in prison. Day sent me four hundred Canadian dollars. "Remember," he wrote, "I admire your efforts to keep your heart true and continue to write. Western governments are busy doing business with China. The media are more interested in reporting stories about criminals and celebrities than human rights issues. Dictators are having an easy time in the post–cold war era."

Day was right. I was encountering a similar situation in China. As the prison's obsession with making medicine packets had signaled, our whole country was suddenly busy making money, which was a corrosive acid that dissolved political dissent. Executioners wiped their blades and swaggered around on the political stage. Political prisoners became outcasts, shunned by the public. The same people who used to march fearlessly in the street for democracy now have become "apolitical" in the current era of rampant materialism — Communist style.

I was disappointed but not shocked when several of my former accomplices and poet friends abandoned their artistic and political aspirations, and joined the rest of the country in the relentless pursuit of money.

A week after the release of Chen Dong, his friend who ran a brand-name men's clothing store gave him a makeover and invited him to an expensive hot-pot restaurant. Over the meal, the intoxicated Chen

Dong toasted his host and said, "I can no longer afford to be a loser and waste time in jail." As expected, Chen Dong entered the business world. So did Hippie Poet. Thus, our different personal choices soured our friendships. In the spring of 1997, Hippie Poet, Chen Dong, and I sat down at a dinner table, drinking. By then, both of them were flush with money but personally bitter and lost. When I told them about my attempt at a prison memoir, Hippie Poet said sarcastically, "Why do you always think you are the only one who is qualified to write about history? Go do something more practical."

Fortunately, I still had the company of a few of my fellow political prisoners who refused to give up their fight.

"Political prisoners are constantly tormented by a fear deeper than the endless confinement and unbearable physical torture," my friend LBF wrote to me. "Whether it is through writing or group protests, we hope people outside the high walls will remember us. We were imprisoned because we fought for our conscience, our dignity, for justice and high principle. I hope your book can serve as a testimony to an important part of Chinese history which has now predictably been distorted and whitewashed by the Chinese government."

LBF was released a few months after me. He married his longtime girlfriend and they had a son. To support his new family, he picked up odd jobs at factories and started an enterprise in the rural area outside Chengdu. A couple of years later, he managed a hotel and fish restaurant near the North Gate Bridge. The place quickly attracted his fellow former '89ers, who ate and slept at his hotel for free. LBF never lost his sense of political conviction. In the spring of 1997, he notified the US-based organization Human Rights in China and the overseas media about a demonstration in his hometown, Mianyang, where several thousand workers at a state-run enterprise blocked the highway to demand pay raises and pensions.

Trouble followed him once again. LBF was soon targeted for arrest and he fled Sichuan. One day, he suffered such homesickness that he went back to Mianyang to see his wife and child. Neighbors alerted the police and half an hour later, two police cars arrived and arrested him. This time, LBF was sentenced to seven years on charges of economic fraud. He served out his sentencing in 2004 but was back in jail in 2012, after I escaped to the West. This third imprisonment was partially linked, heartbreakingly, to me; authorities falsely accused him of assisting in my defection to Germany in the summer of 2011. I have started an international petition to gain his release and try to be in close touch with his family as well as I can be. I know that our story together is not finished. LBF's adventure in life and his brushes with death are enough for a separate book.

In the summer of 1995, my former inmate Lei was released ahead of schedule. He brought his wife and child to Chengdu. I entertained him at a restaurant near my home, and over beers, Lei Fengyun said he needed a job fast. "I will wait for a few weeks until the police relax their control over my daily activities. A friend has promised to find me a teaching job in a rural area where no one knows about my past and local authorities do not need a proper identification card. I can't sit around at home; my wife has suffered for more than a decade and my daughter is growing up. I need to contribute to my family."

I understood his profound frustration. For a year, Lei could not find a job. Even so, he remained true to his political cause. In 1997, he drafted an open letter to the UN Human Rights Commission and Amnesty International, exposing China's egregious human rights abuses. A stranger delivered the seven-page draft to my house. I skimmed through it and decided to take the letter to Beijing the next day and distribute it to the foreign media. Maybe the international community would look beyond the situation of China's elite dissidents and pay attention to the deplorable conditions of ordinary political prisoners.

I planned to leave the next morning. However, at two o'clock that afternoon, three police vans pulled up in front of my mother's house. Police officers dashed out and took me away. After two days of nonstop interrogation, I was put under house arrest for twenty days. Meanwhile, Lei was taken back to the detention center. At one point, he was locked up in a dark cell. We later found out that the person who delivered the letter to me had betrayed us both.

My friend Yang Wei, or Big Tongue, finished serving his sentence in the spring of 1993. He became a laborer, delivering beer by bicycle to small restaurants along the Yangtze River. He soon became restless and wandered the country. One day my phone rang. When I picked it up, it was Big Tongue, who said he was standing right outside my door.

I was startled by his appearance — he looked weary, and his face was covered with dirt. It turned out that he had just gotten off a long ride on a slow train from the coastal city of Shenzhen. "I've gotten gifts for you," he said and handed me two copies of *Beijing Spring,* a popular magazine published by dissident writers in the West. Big Tongue flashed a one hundred Hong Kong dollar bill with Queen Elizabeth's head printed on it. "Have you seen one of these before?"

I shook my head and laughed. "You are very much in tune with the mood of this country — money, money, money," I said. He blushed apple-red.

Later, Big Tongue decided to return to politics and began reading banned books written by dissident writers.

When the activist Wang Youcai and his friends established the China Democratic Party in the summer of 1998, Big Tongue and his friends joined and formed the Sichuan branch. Police soon got wind of their political endeavors. Two leading members were arrested and sentenced to ten years behind bars. Big Tongue also found himself surrounded by plainclothes police who were stationed outside his apartment. He felt like a turtle being cooked in a vat of hot water. Calmly, Yang stepped out of his apartment, pretending to take a bucket of ashes downstairs to the trash. As police closed in on him, he threw the ashes in their faces and ran away.

Like a deer being chased by a wolf, Big Tongue fled north. He tried but failed to cross into Russia through the city of Jiamusi. He had no alternative but to return to Sichuan, where he lived nomadically, staying at different places and playing hide-and-seek with the police. Not long afterward, he forged an identity card and joined a tour group bound for Thailand. Immediately upon arriving in Bangkok, Big Tongue applied for political asylum at the American Embassy. Unfortunately, his request was denied, and he ended up as a homeless person on the streets. Later Big Tongue befriended a monk who helped him get a job as a cleaner at a Buddhist temple. Meanwhile, I contacted friends in the West, seeking assistance for him, and they managed to get him into a refugee camp in Thailand. In 2004, Big Tongue was allowed to enter Canada as a political refugee.

The years had left their scars, however, and the former counterrevolutionary wasn't completely able to escape his old, hot-headed tendencies. In 2012 I learned that Big Tongue had been detained by the Canadian police for getting into a fistfight with a stranger on the street. "He is having a hard time adjusting to his new life in the free world," one friend informed me.

Twenty four years have passed since the Chinese government sent troops to Beijing and suppressed the student protest movement. I have been out of jail for almost twenty. The bloodstains are fading and so are the memories. At present, the official verdict against me and thousands of others remains unchanged. The prospect for political reform in China has never seemed so remote. It's hard not to feel bitter and angry, and sadly, my frustration is often met with derision. Many Chinese people, including members of my family, have long since lost interest in whether my case is reevaluated or not. It seems that all they wanted was for me to get a real job.

In the eyes of my long suffering family, I am more than fifty years old, but I am still immature. I dread the Chinese New Year, when the whole family gathers at my mother's house; invariably, I become a target of criticism. Everyone seems to have the right to tell me how I should live my life and how to see the world. They pretend their advice is born of genuine concern or sympathy, but deep down I suspect that my endless travails have made me self-indulgent and worthless in their eyes.

None of my family members has ever asked to read my writing. When I have insisted on reading passages to them, they barely say anything except to express concern for my safety. If I get upset, they challenge me. "What are you upset about? While you were in jail, the whole family was worried to death about you. You've been out for years, but you are still at home, getting free food and lodging. Nobody has complained. What else do you want?"

It is true. I owe my family a lot. When I was in jail, my friends lobbied for my release, wrote articles to get international attention, raised money to pay my lawyer, and took care of my wife and daughter. Once in my life, I stood up for principles I believed in, but I have accumulated so many debts that I can never pay them back in this lifetime.

Sometimes I wonder, am I still in jail or am I a free person? It really doesn't make any difference in the end because China remains a prison of the mind: prosperity without liberty. Our entire country might as well be gluing medicine packets all day. This is our brave new world.

Years after my sister's death, I went through a period of self-loath-ing, self-indulgence, and destruction. I have learned to grow out of it. I am my own shrink. I am a writer. I am on a mission to be part of something greater, something historical, and not just because it will help me to overcome the trivialities and the craziness of daily life.

When I started this book, I was eager to put my suffering into words and told myself that I was doing it for Fei Fei, who was now residing in a place far away. Yet from the distance she still tickles my blood and whispers to my inner self. She respects men of character and principle, and encourages me to tell an honest story that will speak to universal truths. From my sister's guidance, as from many years of imprison-ment, I have learned that true freedom lies in the heart. These words, which I have shared with you, the reader, form the most sincere and truthful expression of what I have seen and learned. Passing it on has given me a sense of dignity.

Acknowledgments

I want to thank:

Song Yu, who walked into my life soon after my release from prison. Without her companionship and care, I would not have been able to finish this book.

Liu Jinqin, whose courage and support over the past decade has inspired me to continue my career as a writer.

My translator, Wenguang Huang, who discovered my writing ten years ago and brought them to the West and who is not afraid to speak his mind when it comes to keeping me in line.

Writer Kang Zhengguo, who first smuggled the manuscript for The Corpse Walker out of China and who has tirelessly promoted my books.

Michael Day, who has translated the "Massacre" poem from Chinese to English and supported me in my most difficult years.

Writers and critics Hu Ping, Su Xiaokang, Bei Ming, Zheng Yi, Liu Xiaobo, Wang Lixiong, Yu Shicun and Huang Xiang, whose praise and encouragement motivated me.

Li Bifeng, a fellow inmate and an avid reader of my books, who was imprisoned in 2011 for the third time since 1990.

Other '89ers in jail: Pu Yong, who served out a ten-year sentence and died soon after his release; Xu Wanping, who has just been thrown in jail for the third time for his pro-democracy activities: She Wanbao, who was jailed twice for a total of 16 years (he was featured in The Corpse Walker), Lei Fengyun, Hou Duoshu and Tan Lishang.

My mother, my younger sister Xiao Fei, my elder brother Liao Yilong, and my friends inside China — Liu Xia, Zhou Zhonglin, Zhang

Xinqi, Zhou Wei, Wan Chunying, Tang Xiaodu, Yue Jianyi, Mang Ke, Li Yadong, Wang Jianhui, Zhang Xinwu, Tao Wen and Wang Haiwen, Hu Jian, Chen Yong, Jiang Ji, Wang Yi, Ran Yunfei, Yu Jie, my teachers Liu Shahe, Wang Erbei and Zeng Canming — without their warmth and weaknesses, home would be an empty meaningless frame.

My friends in Taiwan, Liao Zhifeng and Liu Wenxiang. Both have generously supported me while they are struggling with their own lives and careers.

Tienchi Martin Liao, who, as my Chinese-language editor and confidante, has helped me tremendously before and during my stay in Germany.

Peter Sillem and Monika Schoeller at S. Fischer Verlag, Uli Schreiber, Festival Direktor, Berlin, Deutschland, Chou Yu-Wen, Zheng Ye and Guo Yeemei.

Katie Salisbury, the editor of this book, Peter and Amy Bernstein, Philip Gourevitch, and Salman Rushdie — without whose help, I wouldn't have been able to walk out of China.

— LIAO YIWU

This book would not have been possible without the expertise and the superior editorial support from three remarkable friends: Ellen Bork at the Foreign Policy Initiative, whose political insights, sharp eye for detail, and meticulous editing skills helped shape the first draft; Patrick Tyler, the former *New York Times* Beijing bureau chief and author of *Fortress Israel,* who reviewed the second draft and greatly enhanced the book with his knowledge of China and his exceptional flair for nonfiction writing; and Carolyn Alessio, the author of the upcoming novel *Mijo,* who adeptly fine-tuned the third draft with the discipline of a tough editor and the cleverness of an astute writer.

As always, I am lucky to have Peter Bernstein as my agent, who, along with my close friend Dr. Amy Bernstein, relentlessly championed this book. The final text also reflects their editorial insights.

As Liao's translator, I want to use this opportunity to thank Esther Allen and Philip Gourevitch, who discovered Liao and tirelessly supported his work.

I am also indebted to Peter Sillem at S. Fischer Verlag, who rescued the German edition from oblivion with his astute sense of the market there; Erroll McDonald at Pantheon for publishing Liao's *The Corpse Walker*; and Mickey Maudlin at HarperOne for *God Is Red*.

I am deeply grateful to PEN America, notably Salman Rushdie, Larry Siems, László Jakab Orsós, Sarah Hoffman, and Elizabeth Weinstein, for their persistent support, especially after Liao was denied a visa to travel abroad, and for organizing Liao's first reading in the United States.

I want to thank Caren Thomas and Eric Swan for their help with the manuscript.

Most important, Liao and I are grateful to our editor, Katie Salisbury, for showing confidence in our work from the beginning and staying closely involved at every stage of the process without interfering in our creative freedom. Katie's insightful suggestions and detailed edits reflect her exceptional understanding of contemporary Chinese politics and culture, and her extraordinary editorial talent.

— WENGUANG HUANG

Massacre

(Translated from the Chinese by Michael Day)

And another sort of massacre takes place at Utopia's core.
The prime minister catches cold, the people must cough; martial law
    declared
again and again.
The toothless machinery of the state rolls towards those who have the
    courage to
resist the sickness.
Unarmed thugs fall by the thousands; iron-clad professional killers
    swim in a sea of
blood, set tires beneath tightly closed windows, wipe their army-
    regulation boots
with the skirts of dead maidens. They're incapable of trembling.
These heartless robots are incapable of trembling!
Their electronic brains possess only one program: an official
    document full of holes.
In the name of the Fatherland, slaughter the constitution!
Replace the constitution, slaughter righteousness!
In the name of mothers, throttle children!
In the name of children, sodomize fathers!
In the name of wives, murder husbands!
In the name of urbanites, blow up cities!
Open fire! Fire!
Upon the elderly!
Upon the children!
Open fire on women!

On students. Workers. Teachers.

Open fire on peddlers!

Open fire! Blast away!

Take aim on those angry faces.

Horrified faces.

Convulsing faces.

Empty all barrels on despairing and peaceful faces!

Fire away to your heart's content!

These faces that come on like a tide and in the next moment are
> *dead are so*

beautiful!

These faces that will be going up to heaven and down to hell are so
> *beautiful!*

Beautiful.

A beauty that turns men into strange beasts!

A beauty that lures men on to ravage, vilify, possess, despoil!

Do away with all beauty!

Do away with all flowers!

Forests. Campuses. Love.

Guitars and pure clean air!

Do away with those ideas that enter into error!

Open fire! Blast away! It feels so good!

Just like smoking a joint.

Going to the toilet.

Back on the base giving the old lady a good fuck!

Open fire! All barrels! Blast away! Feels good! So good!

Smash open a skull!

Fry the skin on his head to a crisp!

Make the brain gush out.

The soul gush out.

Splash on the overpass. Gatehouse. Railings.

Splash on the road!

Splash toward the sky where they become stars!

Escaped stars!

Stars with two human legs!

Sky and earth have reversed positions.

Mankind wears bright, shining hats.

Bright, shining metal helmets.
A troop of soldiers comes charging out of the moon.
Open fire! All barrels! Blast away! It feels so good!
Mankind and stars fall.
Flee together.
Can't make one out from the other.
Chase them up to the clouds!
Chase into the cracks of the earth and into their flesh and waste
    them!
Blow another hole in the soul!
Blow another hole in the stars!
Souls dressed in red shirts!
Souls with white belts!
Souls wearing running shoes doing gymnastics to radio!
Where can you run to?
We will dig you out of the mud.
Tear you out of the flesh.
Scoop you out of the air and water.
Open fire! Blast away! It feels good! So good!
The slaughter takes place in three worlds.
On the wings of birds.
In the stomachs of fish.
Carry it out in the fine dust
In countless living organisms.
Leap! Howl! Fly! Run!
Freedom feels so good!
Snuffing out freedom feels so good!
Power will be triumphant forever.
Will be passed down from generation to generation forever.
Freedom will also come back from the dead.
It will come back to life in generation after generation.
Like that dim light just before the dawn.
No. There's no light.
At Utopia's core there can never be light.
Our hearts are pitch black.
Black and scalding.
Like a corpse incinerator.

A trace of the phantoms of the burned dead.
We will exist.
The government that dominates us will exist.
Daylight comes quickly.
It feels so good.
The butchers are still ranting!
Children. Children, your bodies all cold.
Children, your hands grasping stones.
Let's go home.
Brothers and sisters, your shattered bodies littering the earth.
Let's go home.
We walk noiselessly.
Walk three feet above the ground.
All the time forward, there must be a place to rest.
There must be a place where sounds of gunfire and explosions cannot
    be heard.
We so wish to hide within a stalk of grass.
A leaf.
Uncle. Auntie. Grandpa. Granny. Daddy. Mummy.
How much farther till we're home?
We have no home.
Everyone knows.
Chinese people have no home.
Home is a comforting desire.
Let us die in this desire.
OPEN FIRE, BLAST AWAY, FIRE!
Let us die in freedom.
Righteousness. Equality. Universal love.
Peace, in these vague desires.
Stand on the horizon.
Attract more of the living to death!
It rains.
Don't know if it is rain or transparent ashes.
Run quickly, Mummy!
Run quickly, son!
Run quickly, elder brother!

Run quickly, little brother!
The butchers will not let up.
An even more terrifying day is approaching.

OPEN FIRE! BLAST AWAY! FIRE! IT FEELS GOOD! FEELS SO
    GOOD! . . .
Cry cry cry crycrycrycrycrycrycry
While you still have not been surrounded and annihilated, while you
    still have
strength left to suck milk, crycrycry.
Let your sobs cast you off, fuse into radio, television, radar, give
    repeated testimony of the Massacre
Let your sobs cast you off, fuse into plant life, semivegetable life and
    microorganisms, blossom into flower after flower, year after
    year mourning the dead, mourning yourself.
Let your sobs be distorted, twisted, be annihilated by the tumult of
    sacrosanct battle.
The butchers come from the east of the city, from the west of the city,
    from the south and north of the city.
Metal helmets glint in the light. They're singing . . .
Putrid, sweltering summer, people and ghosts sing . . .
Don't go to the east, don't go to the west, don't go to the south and
    north.

We stand in the midst of brilliance but all people are blind.
We stand on a great road but no one is able to walk.
We stand in the midst of a cacophony but all are mute.
We stand in the midst of heat and thirst but all refuse to drink.

People with no understanding of the times, people in the midst of
    calamity, people who plot to shoot down the sun.
You can only cry, you're still crying, crycrycrycrycrycrycrycrycry!
    CRYCRY! CRY!
You've been smothered to death, baked to death, your whole body is
    on fire!
And yet you are crying.

You get up on the stage and act out a farce, you're paraded before the
    crowds in the
streets, and yet you're crying.
Your eyeballs explode, scald the surrounding crowd, and yet you're
    crying.
You offer a bounty on yourself, find out yourself, you say you were
    mistaken, this accursed epoch is all wrong!
And yet you're crying.
You are stamped into meat pie, you cry.
From meat pie you're trampled into meat, you cry.
A dog licks up the minced meat, you cry inside a dog's belly!
CRY! CRY! CRY!

In this historically unprecedented massacre only the spawn of dogs
    can survive.

Translator's Note

ON THE MORNING OF July 2, 2011, a message from writer Liao Yiwu reached an email inbox I had set up for him when I started translating his books *The Corpse Walker* and *God Is Red*. Our previous messages were mostly craft-related discussions of Liao's books, from fact-checking to finding the proper English equivalent for Chinese slang. However, on that day, Liao's short email with the blank subject line shocked and worried me:

"I have left China. Will fly from Vietnam to Germany tomorrow night. It's important to keep it quiet now."

His trip seemed improbable at best. *Could it be that someone has hacked into Liao's email account and sent out a fake message?* I wondered aloud. Three months before, the local public security bureau denied Liao an exit permit for the sixteenth time to attend literary festivals in Australia, Germany, and the United States on the grounds that his trip could "jeopardize state security." In addition, government officials urged him to annul his publishing contracts abroad because his books allegedly exposed the "dark side of the socialist system." They threatened Liao with jail if he refused to obey. Under such forbidding circumstances, how was he able to leave China?

I read the message carefully and decided it did sound genuine. I surmised that the intrepid poet must have crossed the border into Vietnam via underground channels. Despite the Chinese government's crackdowns, illegal crossings are common in the porous border regions and have been widely reported in the overseas Chinese media.

I immediately replied to Liao, requesting his phone number. Meanwhile, I contacted his friends and his editor in Germany, who verified the authenticity of the message. A few hours later, Liao wrote back with a joking note. "I've been trying to reach you for hours. I'm glad you finally woke up."

Over the next four days, I anxiously followed Liao through his daily phone calls as he traversed from a small border town in Vietnam to the capital city of Hanoi and then boarded a flight to Berlin via Warsaw. The perilous journey, arranged by villagers in the China-Vietnam border, quickly paid off. On July 6, Liao was finally able to walk out on China; he arrived in the free world just in time for the release of the German edition of *For A Song and A Hundred Songs*, which has received much critical acclaim in Germany. In November 2011, the memoir won Liao the Geschwister-Scholl-Preis in Munich and in 2012, he received the prestigious Peace Prize of the German Book Trade.

Liao's escape made it possible for us to meet for the first time at New York's JFK airport in late 2011, when he came to the US to promote *God Is Red*, a book on Christianity in China. At first, I found the meeting surreal—after ten years of communicating through long-distance calls and emails, I couldn't believe I was standing next to him on stage and translating for him while he performed his powerful, incendiary poem "Massacre." Once Liao's U.S. book tour ended, he came to stay with me in Chicago for one month, during which period I consulted with him extensively on the translation of *For a Song and a Hundred Songs*. The original Chinese version is about 200,000 words in length. Liao and I reviewed and shortened it, and made the following adjustments for the English edition:

First, the author has constructed a new preface and epilogue, which contain updates about his life since the initial publication of the book in Chinese in 2002.

Second, the author has amplified Part I by adding more biographical information to shed light on his early literary career and his relationship with his ex-wife, A Xia, a key figure in the book. At the same time, he has also enriched the ending by including stories about his former inmates and the monk Sima, his flute teacher who had a profound impact on him during the last year of his imprisonment.

Third, we have broken up each of the four sections into shorter, reader-friendly chapters with subheadings, and provided background information about certain political events or Communist jargon for Western readers who may not be familiar with Chinese history and politics.

Fourth, we have streamlined the narrative, tightening, deleting, and, in some cases, rearranging the placement of anecdotal stories, first-person dialogues, and political and philosophical observations that were digressive, confusing, or disruptive to the author's story.

Fifth, we have renamed all the key characters in the book. Numerous names, even though written differently in Chinese characters, sound phonetically similar (as in the case of A Xia and Wan Xia). In an attempt to avoid confusion, we opted for catchy but fair nicknames such as "Big Glasses" or "Hippie Poet."

Translating the book has been a transformative experience for me. I finished the work in six months, but the author's powerful stories have lingered in my mind since then. The grisly living conditions and the depth of human suffering shocked and educated me. Like many who grew up in China in the 1970s, I learned about the city of Chongqing through a propaganda movie on Zhazidong, a notorious prison in Chongqing where many Communists were persecuted and tortured by the Nationalists for their political beliefs in the 1940s. Ironically, once the Communists took power they continued to repress dissidents on a much larger scale, and have resorted to more extreme means of maintaining power. Liao's poignant account of prison life sheds light on this dark corner of China.

Since Liao's arrival in the West last year, he has followed the examples of Joseph Brodsky and Aleksandr Solzhenitsyn, two of his literary heroes who had born witness to some of the greatest tragedies in the twentieth century. By taking his stories and music to captivated crowds in cities around the world, Liao helps raise global awareness of China's human rights abuses and petitions for the release of political prisoners in his native country. His memoir is now being translated into Czech, French, Italian, Polish, Portuguese, Spanish, and Swedish.

When asked why he has kept writing, Liao told the journalist Brian Awehali:

Having gone through these sufferings has become part of my capital as a writer, and the experiences I shared with others and what I learned from other people has become my capital as a writer too. I've learned that one can go through very difficult and troubling experiences that could put one into despair, but still be able to survive, and even beyond that, find there is a need, a necessity, to survive.

About the Author

Liao Yiwu is a writer, musician, and poet from Sichuan, China. He is a critic of the Chinese regime, for which he has been imprisoned, and the majority of his writings are banned in China. Liao is the author of *The Corpse Walker* and *God Is Red*. He has received numerous awards for his work, including the prestigious 2012 Peace Prize awarded by the German Book Trade and the Geschwister-Scholl-Preis in 2011 for the publication of his memoir in Germany.

About the Translator

Wenguang Huang, author of *The Little Red Guard* and *A Death in the Lucky Holiday Hotel,* is the English translator of Lio Yiwu's *The Corpse Walker* and *God Is Red,* and Yang Xianhui's *Woman from Shanghai.*